P9-BHU-780

THE

PROVINCES OF THE ROMAN EMPIRE

FROM CAESAR TO DIOCLETIAN

app' Li 227 f, 223   160-

App. Judaea & the Jews   231

~~the~~ writes about 116 —

Jews of E. Mediterran

rose up against imperial

gov't.

ran for his life $\bar{n}$g't. d?ly

made his escape to Pelusion

Trajan annihil. killed ~the

Jews in Alexandria

THE PROVINCES

OF THE

ROMAN EMPIRE

FROM CAESAR TO DIOCLETIAN

BY

THEODOR MOMMSEN

TRANSLATED

WITH THE AUTHOR'S SANCTION AND ADDITIONS

BY

WILLIAM P. DICKSON, D.D., LL.D.

PROFESSOR OF DIVINITY IN THE UNIVERSITY OF GLASGOW

VOL. II

WITH TWO MAPS BY PROFESSOR KIEPERT

MACMILLAN AND CO., LIMITED
ST. MARTIN'S STREET, LONDON
1909

First Edition 1886
Reprinted with corrections 1909

CONTENTS

BOOK EIGHTH

THE PROVINCES AND PEOPLE, FROM CAESAR TO DIOCLETIAN

CHAPTER IX.

THE EUPHRATES FRONTIER AND THE PARTHIANS.

THE only great state with which the Roman empire The empire of Iran. bordered was the empire of Iran,[1] based upon that nationality which was best known in antiquity, as it is in the present day, under the name of the Persians, consolidated politically by the old Persian royal family of the Achaemenids and its first great-king Cyrus, united religiously by the faith of Ahura Mazda and of Mithra. No one of the ancient peoples of culture solved the problem of national union equally early and with equal completeness. The Iranian tribes reached on the south as far as the Indian Ocean, on the north as far as the Caspian Sea; on the north-east the steppes of inland Asia formed the constant battle-ground between the settled Persians and the nomadic tribes of Turan. On the east mighty mountains formed a boundary separating them from the Indians. In western Asia three great nations early encountered one another, each pushing

[1] The conception that the Roman and the Parthian empires were two great states standing side by side, and indeed the only ones in existence, dominated the whole Roman East, particularly the frontier-provinces. It meets us palpably in the Apocalypse of John, in which there is a juxtaposition as well of the rider on the white horse with the bow and of the rider on the red horse with the sword (vi. 2, 3) as of the Megistanes and the Chiliarchs (vi. 15, comp. xviii. 23, xix. 18). The closing catastrophe, too, is conceived as a subduing of the Romans by the Parthians bringing back the emperor Nero (ix. 14, xvi. 12) and Armageddon, whatever may be meant by it, as the rendezvous of the Orientals for the collective attack on the West. Certainly the author, writing in the Roman empire, hints these far from patriotic hopes more than he expresses them.

forward on its own account: the Hellenes, who from Europe grasped at the coast of Asia Minor, the Aramaic peoples, who from Arabia and Syria advanced in a northern and north-eastern direction and substantially filled the valley of the Euphrates, and lastly, the races of Iran, not merely inhabiting the country as far as the Tigris, but even penetrating to Armenia and Cappadocia, while primitive inhabitants of other types in these far-extending regions succumbed under these leading powers and disappeared. In the epoch of the Achaemenids, the culminating point of the glory of Iran, the Iranian rule went far beyond this wide domain proper to the stock on all sides, but especially towards the west. Apart from the times, when Turan gained the upper hand over Iran and the Seljuks and Mongols ruled over the Persians, foreign rule, strictly so called, has only been established over the flower of the Iranian stocks twice, by Alexander the Great and his immediate successors and by the Arabian Abbasids, and on both occasions only for a comparatively short time ; the eastern regions—in the former case the Parthians, in the latter the inhabitants of the ancient Bactria—not merely threw off again the yoke of the foreigner, but dislodged him also from the cognate west.

The rule of the Parthians. When the Romans in the last age of the republic came into immediate contact with Iran as a consequence of the occupation of Syria, they found in existence the Persian empire regenerated by the Parthians. We have formerly had to make mention of this state on several occasions ; this is the place to gather together the little that can be ascertained regarding the peculiar character of the empire, which so often exercised a decisive influence on the destinies of the neighbouring state. Certainly to most questions, which the historical inquirer has here to put, tradition has no answer. The Occidentals give but occasional notices, which may in their isolation easily mislead us, concerning the internal condition of their Parthian neighbours and foes ; and, if the Orientals in general have hardly understood how to fix and to preserve historical tradition, this holds doubly true of the period of the Arsacids, seeing that it was by the later Iranians regarded, together with the preceding foreign rule of the Seleucids, as an unwarranted usurpation between the periods of the old and the new Persian rule —the Achaemenids and the Sassanids ; this period of five hundred years is, so to speak, eliminated by way of correction[1] from the history of Iran, and is as if non-existent.

The standpoint, thus occupied by the court-historio-graphers of the Sassanid dynasty, is more the legitimist-dynastic one of the Persian nobility than that of Iranian nationality.   No doubt the authors of the first imperial epoch describe the language of the Parthians, whose home corresponds nearly to the modern Chorasan, as intermediate between the Median and the Scythian, that is, as an impure Iranian dialect; accordingly they were regarded as immigrants from the land of the Scythians, and in this sense their name is interpreted as " fugitive people," while the founder of the dynasty, Arsaces, is declared by some indeed to have been a Bactrian, but by others a Scythian from the Maeotis.   The fact that their princes did not take up their residence in Seleucia on the Tigris, but pitched their winter quarters in the immediate neighbourhood at Ctesiphon, is traced to their wish not to quarter Scythian troops in the rich mercantile city. Much in the manners and arrangements of the Parthians is alien from Iranian habits, and reminds us of the customs of nomadic life ; they transact business and eat on horseback, and the free man never goes on foot.   It cannot well be doubted that the Parthians, whose name alone of all the tribes of this region is not named in the sacred books of the Persians, stand aloof from Iran proper, in which the Achaemenids and the Magians are at home.   The antagonism of this Iran to the ruling family springing from an uncivilised and half foreign district,

[1] This holds true even in some measure for the chronology.   The official historiography of the Sassanids reduces the space between the last Darius and the first Sassanid from 558 to 266 years (Nöldeke, *Tabari*, p. 1).

and to its immediate followers—this antagonism, which the Roman authors not unwillingly took over from their Persian neighbours—certainly subsisted and fermented throughout the whole rule of the Arsacids, till it at length brought about their fall. But the rule of the Arsacids may not on that account be conceived as a foreign rule. No privileges were conceded to the Parthian stock and to the Parthian province. It is true that the Parthian town Hecatompylos is named as residence of the Arsacids; but they chiefly sojourned in summer at Ecbatana (Hamadan), or else at Rhagae like the Achaemenids, in winter, as already stated, in the camp-town of Ctesiphon, or else in Babylon on the extreme western border of the empire. The hereditary burial-place continued in the Parthian town Nisaea; but subsequently Arbela in Assyria served for that purpose more frequently. The poor and remote native province of the Parthians was in no way suited for the luxurious court-life, and the important relations to the West, especially of the later Arsacids. The chief country continued even now to be Media, just as under the Achaemenids. Although the Arsacids might be of Scythian descent, not so much depended on what they were as on what they desired to be; and they regarded and professed themselves throughout as the successors of Cyrus and of Darius. As the seven Persian family-princes had set aside the false Achaemenid, and had restored the legitimate rule by the elevation of Darius, so needs must other seven have overthrown the Macedonian foreign yoke and placed king Arsaces on the throne. With this patriotic fiction must further be connected the circumstance that a Bactrian nativity instead of a Scythian was assigned to the first Arsaces. The dress and the etiquette at the court of the Arsacids were those of the Persian court; after king Mithradates I. had extended his rule to the Indus and Tigris, the dynasty exchanged the simple title of king for that of king of kings which the Achaemenids had borne, and the pointed Scythian cap for the high tiara adorned with pearls; on the coins the king carries

the bow like Darius. The aristocracy, too, that came
into the land with the Arsacids and doubtless became in
many ways mixed with the old indigenous one, adopted
Persian manners and dress, mostly also Persian names ; of
the Parthian army which fought with Crassus it is said that
the soldiers still wore their hair rough after the Scythian
fashion, but the general appeared after the Median manner
with the hair parted in the middle and with painted face.

The political organisation, as it was established by
the first Mithradates, was accordingly in substance that
of the Achaemenids. The family of the founder of the
dynasty is invested with all the lustre and with all
the consecration of ancestral and divinely-ordained rule ;
his name is transferred *de jure* to each of his successors
and divine honour is assigned to him ; his successors are
therefore called sons of God,[1] and besides brothers of the
sun-god and the moon-goddess, like the Shah of Persia
still at the present day ; to shed the blood of a member
of the royal family even by mere accident is a sacrilege
—all of them regulations, which with few abatements
recur among the Roman Caesars, and are perhaps borrowed
in part from those of the older great-monarchy.

The regal office.

Although the royal dignity was thus firmly attached
to the family, there yet subsisted a certain choice as to
the king. As the new ruler had to belong as well to the
college of the "kinsmen of the royal house" as to the
council of priests, in order to be able to ascend the
throne, an act must have taken place, whereby, it may
be presumed, these same colleges themselves acknowledged
the new ruler.[2] By the "kinsmen" are doubtless to be

Megistanes.

---

[1] The viceroys of Persis are called
in their title constantly " Zag Alohin "
(at least the Aramaean signs correspond to these words, which were
presumably in pronunciation expressed
in the Persian way), son of God
(Mordtmann, *Zeitschrift für Numismatik*, iv. 155 f.), and to this corresponds the title θεοπάτωρ on the
Greek coins of the great-kings. The
designation " God " is also found, as
with the Seleucids and the Sassanids.

—Why a double diadem is attributed
to the Arsacids (Herodian, vi. 2, 1)
is not cleared up.

[2] Τῶν Παρθυαίων συνέδριόν φησιν
(Ποσειδώνιος) εἶναι, says Strabo, xi.
9, 3, p. 515, διττόν, τὸ μὲν συγγενῶν,
τὸ δὲ σόφων καὶ μάγων, ἐξ ὧν ἀμφοῖν
τοὺς βασιλεῖς καθίστασθαι (καθίστησιν
in MSS.) ; Justinus, xvii. 3, 1,
*Mithridates rex Parthorum . . .
propter crudelitatem a senatu Parthico
regno pellitur.*

understood not merely the Arsacids themselves, but the " seven houses " of the Achaemenid organisation, princely families, to which according to that arrangement equality of rank and free access to the great-king belonged, and which must have had similar privileges under the Arsacids.[1] These families were at the same time holders of hereditary crown offices,[2] *e.g.* the Surên—the name is like the name Arsaces, a designation at once of person and of office— the second family after the royal house, as crown-masters, placed on each occasion the tiara on the head of the new Arsaces. But as the Arsacids themselves belonged to the Parthian province, so the Surên were at home in Sacastane (Seistân) and perhaps Sacae, thus Scythians ; the Carên likewise descended from western Media, while the highest aristocracy under the Achaemenids was purely Persian.

Satraps.   The administration lay in the hands of the under- kings or satraps ; according to the Roman geographers of Vespasian's time the state of the Parthians consisted of eighteen " kingdoms." Some of these satrapies were appanages of a second son of the ruling house ; in particular the two north-western provinces, the Atro- patenian Media (Aderbijan) and Armenia, so far as it was in the power of the Parthians, appear to have been entrusted for administration to the prince standing next to the ruler for the time.[3] We may add that prominent

---

[1] In Egypt, whose court ceremonial, as doubtless that of all the states of the Diadochi, is based on that ordained by Alexander, and in so far upon that of the Persian empire, the like title seems to have been conferred also personally (Franz, *C. I. Gr.* iii. 270). That the same occurred with the Arsacids, is possible. Among the Greek-speak- ing subjects of the Arsacid state the appellation μεγιστᾶνες seems in the original stricter use to denote the members of the seven houses ; it is worthy of notice that *megistanes* and *satrapae* are associated (Seneca, *Ep.* 21 ; Josephus, *Arch.* xi. 3, 2 ; xx. 2, 3). The circumstance that in court mourning the Persian king does

not invite the *megistanes* to table (Suetonius, *Gai.* 5) suggests the con- jecture that they had the privilege of taking meals with him. The title τῶν πρώτων φίλων is also found among the Arsacids just as at the Egyptian and Pontic courts (*Bull. de corr. Hell.* vii. p. 349).

[2] A royal cup-bearer, who is at the same time general, is mentioned in Josephus, *Arch.* xiv. 13, 7 = *Bell. Jud.* i. 13, 1. Similar court offices are of frequent occurrence in the states of the Diadochi.

[3] Tacitus, *Ann.* xv. 2, 31. If, according to the preface of Agath- angelos (p. 109, Langlois), at the time of the Arsacids the oldest and

among the satraps were the king of the province of Elymais or of Susa, to whom was conceded a specially powerful and exceptional position, and next to him the king of Persis, the ancestral land of the Achaemenids. The form of administration, if not exclusive, yet preponderant and conditioning the title, was in the Parthian empire—otherwise than in the case of the Caesars—that of vassal - kingdom, so that the satraps entered by hereditary right, but were subject to confirmation by the great-king.[1] To all appearance this continued downwards, so that smaller dynasts and family chiefs stood in the same relation to the under-kings as the latter occupied to the great-king.[2] Thus the office of great-king among the Parthians was limited to the utmost in favour of the high aristocracy by the accompanying subdivision of the hereditary administration of the land. With this it is quite in keeping, that the mass of the population consisted of persons half or wholly non-free,[3] and emancipation was not allowable. In the army which fought against Antonius there are said to have been only 400 free among 50,000. The chief among the vassals of Orodes, who as his general defeated

ablest prince bore rule over the country, and the three standing next to him were kings of the Armenians, of the Indians, and of the Massagetae, there is here perhaps at bottom the same arrangement. That the Partho-Indian empire, if it was combined with the main land, was likewise regarded as an appanage for the second son, is very probable.

[1] These are doubtless meant by Justinus (xli. 2, 2), *proximus maiestati regum praepositorum ordo est ; ex hoc duces in bello, ex hoc in pace rectores habent.* The native name is preserved by the gloss in Hesychius, βίσταξ ὁ βασιλεὺς παρὰ Πέρσαις. If in Ammianus, xxiii. 6, 14, the presidents of the Persian *regiones* are called *vitaxae* (read *vistaxae*), *id est magistri equitum et reges et satrapae*, he has awkwardly referred what is Persian to all Inner Asia (comp. *Hermes*, xvi. 613) ; we may add that the designation "leaders

of horsemen " for these viceroys may relate to the fact that they, like the Roman governors, united in themselves the highest civil and the supreme military power, and the army of the Parthians consisted preponderantly of cavalry.

[2] This we learn from the title σατράπης τῶν σατραπῶν, attributed to one Gotarzes in the inscription of Kermanschahân in Kurdistan (*C. I. Gr.* 4674). It cannot be assigned to the Arsacid king of the same name as such ; but perhaps there may be designated by it, as Olshausen (*Monatsbericht der Berliner Akademie,* 1878, p. 179) conjectures, that position which belonged to him after his renouncing of the great-kingdom (Tacitus, *Ann.* xi. 9).

[3] Still later a troop of horse in the Parthian army is called that "of the free :" Josephus, *Arch.* xiv. 13, 5 = *Bell. Jud.* i. 13, 3.

Crassus, marched to the field with a harem of 200 wives and a baggage train of 1000 sumpter-camels; he himself furnished to the army 10,000 horsemen from his clients and slaves. The Parthians never had a standing army, but at all times the waging of war here was left to depend on the general levy of the vassal-princes and of the vassals subordinate to these, as well as of the great mass of the non-free over whom these bore sway.

The Greek towns of the Parthian empire. Certainly the urban element was not quite wanting in the political organisation of the Parthian empire. It is true that the larger townships, which arose out of the distinctive development of the East, were not urban commonwealths, as indeed even the Parthian royal residence, Ctesiphon, is named in contrast to the neighbouring Greek foundation of Seleucia a village; they had no presidents of their own and no common council, and the administration lay here, as in the country districts, exclusively with the royal officials. But a portion—comparatively small, it is true—of the foundations of the Greek rulers had come under Parthian rule. In the provinces of Mesopotamia and Babylonia by nationality Aramaean the Greek town-system had gained a firm footing under Alexander and his successors. Mesopotamia was covered with Greek commonwealths; and in Babylonia, the successor of the ancient Babylon, the precursor of Bagdad, and for a time the residence of the Greek kings of Asia—Seleucia on the Tigris—had by its favourable commercial position and its manufactures risen to be the first mercantile city beyond the Roman bounds, with more, it is alleged, than half a million of inhabitants. Its free Hellenic organisation, on which beyond doubt its prosperity above all depended, was not touched even by the Parthian rulers in their own interest, and the city preserved not merely its town council of 300 elected members, but also the Greek language and Greek habits amidst the non-Greek East. It is true that the Hellenes in these towns formed only the dominant element; alongside of them lived numerous Syrians, and, as a third constituent, there were associated with these the not much less numerous Jews, so that the population of these Greek towns of the Parthian empire, just like that of Alexandria, was composed of three separate nationalities standing side by side. Between these, just as in Alexandria, conflicts not seldom occurred, as *e.g.* at the time of the reign of Gaius under the eyes of the Parthian government the three nations came to blows, and ultimately the Jews were driven out of the larger towns.

In so far the Parthian empire was the genuine counterpart to the Roman. As in the one the Oriental viceroyship is an exceptional occurrence, so in the other is the Greek city; the general Oriental aristocratic character of the Parthian government is as little injuriously affected by the Greek mercantile towns on the west coast as is the civic organisation of the Roman state by the vassal kingdoms of Cappadocia and Armenia. While in the state of the Caesars the Romano-Greek urban commonwealth spreads more and more, and gradually becomes the general form of administration, the foundation of towns—the true mark of Helleno-Roman civilisation, which embraces the Greek mercantile cities and the military colonies of Rome as well as the grand settlements of Alexander and the Alexandrids—suddenly breaks off with the emergence of the Parthian government in the East, and even the existing Greek cities of the Parthian empire wane in the further course of development. There, as here, the rule more and more prevails over the exceptions.

The religion of Iran with its worship—approximating Religion. to monotheism—of the " highest of the gods, who has made heaven and earth and men and for these everything good," with its absence of images and its spirituality, with its stern morality and truthfulness, with its influence upon practical activity and energetic conduct of life, laid hold of the minds of its confessors in quite another and deeper way than the religions of the West ever could ; and, while neither Zeus nor Jupiter maintained their ground in presence of a developed civilisation, the faith among the

Parsees remained ever young till it succumbed to another gospel—that of the confessors of Mohammed—or at any rate retreated before it to India. It is not our task to set forth how the old Mazda-faith, which the Achaemenids professed, and the origin of which falls in prehistoric time, was related to that which the sacred books of the Persians having their origin probably under the later Achaemenids —the Avestâ—announce as the doctrine of the wise Zarathustra ; for the epoch, when the West is placed in contact with the East, only the later form of religion comes under consideration.   Perhaps the Avestâ took first shape in the east of Iran, in Bactria, but it spread thence to Media and from there it exercised its influence on the West. But the national religion and the national state were bound up with one another in Iran more closely than even among the Celts. It has already been noticed that the legitimate kingship in Iran was at the same time a religious institution, that the supreme ruler of the land was conceived as specially called to the government by the supreme deity of the land, and even in some measure divine.   On the coins of a national type there appears regularly the great fire-altar, and hovering over it the winged god Ahura Mazda, alongside of him in lesser size, and in an attitude of prayer, the king, and overagainst the king the imperial banner.   In keeping with this, the ascendency of the nobility in the Parthian empire goes hand in hand with the privileged position of the clergy.   The priests of this religion, the Magians, appear already in the documents of the Achaemenids and in the narratives of Herodotus, and have, probably with right, always been regarded by the Occidentals as a national Persian institution.   The priesthood was hereditary, and at least in Media, presumably also in other provinces, the collective body of the priests was accounted, somewhat like the Levites in the later Israel, as a separate portion of the people.   Even under the rule of the Greeks the old religion of the state and the national priesthood maintained their place.   When the first Seleucus wished to found the new capital of his empire, the already mentioned Seleucia, he caused the Magians to fix day and hour for it, and it was only after those Persians, not very willingly, had cast the desired horoscope, that the king and his army, in accordance with their indication, accomplished the solemn laying of the foundation-stone of the new Greek city. Thus by his side stood the priests of Ahura Mazda as counsellors, and they, not those of the Hellenic Olympus, were interrogated in public affairs, so far as these concerned divine things. As a matter of course this was all the more the case with the Arsacids. We have already observed that in the election of king, along with the council of the nobility, that of the priests took part. King Tiridates of Armenia, of the house of the Arsacids, came to Rome attended by a train of Magians, and travelled and took food according to their directions, even in company with the emperor Nero, who gladly allowed the foreign wise men to preach their doctrine and to conjure spirits for him. From this certainly it does not follow that the priestly order as such exercised an essentially determining influence on the management of the state ; but the Mazda-faith was by no means re-established only by the Sassanids ; on the contrary, amidst all change of dynasties, and amidst all its own development, the religion of the land of Iran remained in its outline the same.

The language of the land in the Parthian empire was Language. the native language of Iran. There is no trace pointing to any foreign language having ever been in public use under the Arsacids. On the contrary, it is the Iranian land-dialect of Babylonia and the writing peculiar to this— as both were developed before, and in, the Arsacid period under the influence of the language and writing of the Aramaean neighbours—which are covered by the appella- tion Pahlavi, *i.e.* Parthava, and thereby designated as those of the empire of the Parthians. Even Greek did not become an official language there. None of the rulers bear even as a second name a Greek one ; and, had the Arsacids made this language their own, we should not have failed to find Greek inscriptions in their empire.

Certainly their coins show down to the time of Claudius exclusively,[1] and predominantly even later, Greek legends, as they show also no trace of the religion of the land, and in standard attach themselves to the local coinage of the Roman east provinces, while they retain the division of the year as well as the reckoning by years just as these had been regulated under the Seleucids. But this must rather be taken as meaning that the great-kings themselves did not coin at all,[2] and these coins, which in fact served essentially for intercourse with the western neighbours, were struck by the Greek towns of the empire in the name of the sovereign. The designation of the king on these coins as "friend of Greeks" (φιλέλλην), which already meets us early,[3] and is constant from the time of Mithradates I., *i.e.* from the extension of the state as far as the Tigris, has a meaning only, if it is the Parthian Greek city that is speaking on these coins. It may be conjectured that a secondary position was conceded in public use to the Greek language in the Parthian empire alongside of the Persian, similar to that which it possessed in the Roman state by the side of Latin. The gradual disappearance of Hellenism under the Parthian rule may be clearly followed on these urban coins, as well in the emergence of the native language alongside and instead of the Greek, as in the debasement of language which becomes more and more prominent.[4]

Extent of the Parthian empire.

As to extent the kingdom of the Arsacids was far inferior, not merely to the great state of the Achaemenids,

[1] The oldest known coin with Pahlavi writing was struck in Claudius's time under Vologasus I. ; it is bilingual, and gives to the king in Greek his full title, but only the name Arsaces, in Iranian merely the native individual name shortened (*Vol.*).

[2] Usually this is restricted to the large silver money, and the small silver and most of the copper are regarded as of royal coinage. But by this view a singular secondary part in coinage is assigned to the great-king. More correctly perhaps the former coinage is conceived of as

predominantly destined for dealings abroad, the latter as predominantly for internal intercourse ; the diversities subsisting between the two kinds are also explained in this way.

[3] The first ruler that bears it is Phraapates about 188 B.C. (Percy Gardner, *Parthian Coinage*, p. 27).

[4] Thus there stands on the coins of Gotarzes (under Claudius) Γωτέρξης βασιλεὺς βασιλέων υἱὸς κεκαλουμένος Ἀρταβάνου. On the later ones the Greek legend is often quite unintelligible.

but also to that of their immediate predecessors, the state of the Seleucids.   Of its original territory they possessed only the larger eastern half; after the battle with the Parthians, in which king Antiochus Sidetes, a contemporary of the Gracchi, fell, the Syrian kings did not again seriously attempt to assert their rule beyond the Euphrates ; but the country on this side of the Euphrates remained with the Occidentals.

Both coasts of the Persian Gulf, even the Arabian, *Arabia.* were in possession of the Parthians, and the navigation was thus completely in their power ; the rest of the Arabian peninsula did not obey either the Parthians or the Romans ruling over Egypt.

To describe the struggle of the nations for the posses- *The region of the Indus.* sion of the Indus valley, and of the regions bordering on it, to the west and east, so far as the wholly fragmentary tradition allows of a description at all, is not the task of our survey ; but the main lines of this struggle, which constantly goes by the side of that waged for the Euphrates valley, may the less be omitted in this connection, as our tradition does not allow us to follow out in detail the circumstances of Iran to the east in their influence on western relations, and it hence appears necessary at least to realise for ourselves its outlines.   Soon after the death of Alexander the Great, the boundary between Iran and India was drawn by the agreement of his marshal and coheir Seleucus with Chandragupta, or in Greek Sandracottos, the founder of the empire of the Indians.   According to this the latter ruled not merely over the Ganges-valley in all its extent and the whole north-west of India, but in the region of the Indus, at least over a part of the upland valley of what is now Cabul, further over Arachosia or Afghanistan, presumably also over the waste and arid Gedrosia, the modern Beloochistan, as well as over the delta and mouths of the Indus ; the documents hewn in stone, by which Chandragupta's grandson, the orthodox Buddha - worshipper Asoka, inculcated the general moral law on his subjects, have been found, as in all this widely extended domain, so particularly in the region of Peshawur.[1] The Hindoo Koosh, the Parapanisus of the ancients, and its continuation to the east and west, thus separated with their mighty chain—pierced only by few passes—Iran and India. But this agreement did not long subsist.

Bactro-Indian empire.

In the earlier period of the Diadochi the Greek rulers of the kingdom of Bactra, which took a mighty impulse on its breaking off from the Seleucid state, crossed the frontier-mountains, brought a considerable part of the Indus valley into their power, and perhaps established themselves still farther inland in Hindostan, so that the centre of gravity of this empire was shifted from western Iran to eastern India, and Hellenism gave way to an Indian type. The kings of this empire were called Indian, and bore subsequently non-Greek names ; on the coins the native Indian language and writing appear by the side, and instead, of the Greek, just as in the Partho-Persian coinage the Pahlavi comes up alongside of the Greek.

Indo-Scythians.

Then one nation more entered into the arena ; the Scythians, or, as they were called in Iran and India, the Sacae, broke off from their ancestral settlements on the Jaxartes and crossed the mountains southward. The Bactrian province came at least in great part into their power, and at some time in the last century of the Roman republic they must have established themselves in the

---

[1] While the kingdom of Darius, according to his inscriptions, includes in it the Gādara (the Gandhāra of the Indians, Γανδαρῖτις of the Greeks on the Cabul river) and the Hîdu (the dwellers by the Indus), the former are in one of the inscriptions of Asoka adduced among his subjects, and a copy of his great edict has been found in Kapurdi Giri, or rather in Shahbaz Garhi (Yusufzai-district), nearly 27 miles north-west of the point where the Cabul river falls into the Indus at Attock. The seat of the government of these north-west provinces of Asoka's kingdom was (according to the inscription *C. I. Indicar.* i. p. 91) Takkhasilâ, Τάξιλα of the Greeks, some 40 miles E.S.E. of Attock, the seat of government for the south-western provinces was Ujjênî ('Οζήνη). The eastern part of the Cabul valley thus belonged at any rate to Asoka's empire. It is not quite impossible that the Khyber pass formed the boundary ; but probably the whole Cabul valley belonged to India, and the boundary to the south of Cabul was formed by the sharp line of the Suleiman range, and farther to the south-west by the Bolan pass. Of the later Indo-Scythian king Huvishka (Ooerke of the coins), who seems to have resided on the Yamunâ in Mathurâ, an inscription has been found at Wardak not far northward from Cabul (according to information from Oldenberg).

modern Afghanistan and Beloochistan. On that account in the early imperial period the coast on both sides of the mouth of the Indus about Minnagara is called Scythian, and in the interior the district of the Drangae lying to the west of Candahar bears subsequently the name "land of the Sacae," Sacastane, the modern Seistân. This immigration of the Scythians into the provinces of the Bactro-Indian empire doubtless restricted and injured it, somewhat as the Roman empire was affected by the first migrations of the Germans, but did not destroy it ; under Vespasian there still subsisted a probably independent Bactrian state.[1]

Under the Julian and Claudian emperors the Parthians seem to have been the leading power at the mouth of the Indus. A trustworthy reporter from the Augustan age specifies that same Sacastane among the Parthian provinces, and calls the king of the Saco-Scythians an under-king of the Arsacids ; as the last Parthian province towards the east he designates Arachosia with the capital Alexandropolis, probably Candahar. Soon afterwards, indeed, in Vespasian's time, Parthian princes rule in Minnagara. This, however, was for the empire on the river Indus more a change of dynasty than an annexation proper to the state of Ctesiphon. The Parthian prince Gondopharus, whom the Christian legend connects with St. Thomas, the apostle of the Parthians and Indians,[2] certainly ruled from Minnagara as far up as Peshawur and Cabul ; but these rulers use, like their superiors in the Indian empire, the Indian language alongside of the Greek, and name themselves great-kings like those of Ctesiphon ; they appear to have been not the less rivals to the Arsacids, on account of their belonging to the same princely house.[3]

Partho-Indian empire.

---

[1] The Egyptian merchant named in note 3 makes mention, c. 47, of "the warlike people of the Bactrians, who have their own king." At that time, therefore, Bactria was separated from the Indus-empire that was under Parthian princes. Strabo, too (xi. 11, 1, p. 516) treats the Bactro-Indian empire as belonging to the past.

[2] Probably he is the Kaspar—in older tradition Gathaspar—who appears among the holy three kings from the East (Gutschmid, *Rhein. Mus.* xix. 162).

[3] The most definite testimony to the Parthian rule in these regions is found in the description of the coasts of the Red Sea drawn up by an

Empire of
the Sacae
on the
Indus.

This Parthian dynasty was then followed in the Indian empire after a short interval by what is designated in Indian tradition as that of the Sacae or that of king Kanerku or Kanishka, which begins with 78 A.D. and subsisted at least down to the third century.[1] They

Egyptian merchant under Vespasian, c. 38: "Behind the mouth of the Indus in the interior lies the capital of Scythia Minnagara; but this is ruled by the Parthians, who constantly chase away one another" (ὑπὸ Πάρθων συνεχῶς ἀλλήλους ἐνδιωκόν-των). The same is repeated in a somewhat confused way, c. 41; it might here appear as if Minnagara lay in India itself above Barygaza, and Ptolemy has already been led astray by this; but certainly the writer, who speaks as to the interior only from hearsay, has only wished to say that a large town Minnagara lay inland not far from Barygaza, and much cotton was brought thence to Barygaza. The numerous traces also of Alexander, which occur according to the same authority in Minnagara, can be found only on the Indus, not in Gujerat. The position of Minnagara on the lower Indus not far from Hyderabad, and the existence of a Parthian rule there under Vespasian, appear hereby assured. — With this we may be allowed to combine the coins of king Gondopharus or Hyndopherres, who in a very old Christian legend is converted to Christianity by St. Thomas, the apostle of the Parthians and Indians, and in fact appears to belong to the first period of the Roman empire (Sallet, *Num. Zeitschr.* vi. 355; Gutschmid, *Rhein. Mus.* xix. 162); of his brother's son Abdagases (Sallet, *ib.* p. 365), who may be identical with the Parthian prince of this name in Tacitus, *Ann.* vi. 36, at any rate bears a Parthian name; and lastly of king Sanabarus, who must have reigned shortly after Hyndopherres, perhaps was his successor. Here belongs also a number of other coins marked with Parthian names, Arsaces, Pacorus, Vonones. This coinage attaches itself decidedly to that of

the Arsacids (Sallet, *ib.* p. 277); the silver pieces of Gondopharus and of Sanabarus—of the others the coins are almost solely copper—correspond exactly to the Arsacid drachmae. To all appearance these belong to the Parthian princes of Minnagara; the appearance here of Indian legend alongside of the Greek, as of Pahlavi writing among the late Arsacids, suits this view. These, however, are not coins of satraps, but, as the Egyptian indicates, of great-kings rivalling those of Ctesiphon; Hyndopherres names himself in very corrupt Greek βασιλεὺς βασιλέων μέγας αὐτοκράτωρ, and in good Indian "Maharajah Rajadi Rajah." If, as is not improbable, under the Mambaros or Akabaros, whom the Periplus, c. 41, 52, designates as ruler of the coast of Barygaza, there lurks the Sanabarus of the coins, the latter belongs to the time of Nero or Vespasian, and ruled not merely at the mouths of the Indus, but also over Gujerat. Moreover, if an inscription found not far from Peshawur is rightly referred to king Gondopharus, his rule must have extended up thither, probably as far as Cabul.—The fact that Corbulo in the year 60 sent the embassy of the Hyrcanians who had revolted from the Parthians—in order that they might not be intercepted by the latter—to the coast of the Red Sea, whence they might reach their home without setting foot on Parthian territory (Tacitus, *Ann.* xv. 25), tells in favour of the view that the Indus valley at that time was not subject to the ruler of Ctesiphon.

[1] That the great kingdom of the Arsacids of Minnagara did not subsist much beyond the time of Nero, is probable from the coins. It is questionable what rulers followed them. The Bactro-Indian rulers of Greek

influence on the wars of succession of the Arsacids as well
as on their disputes with Rome.

We have set forth in its due place how the attitude
of the Parthians to the Romans came to be shaped and
the boundaries of the two great powers to be established.
While the Armenians had been rivals of the Parthians,
and the kingdom on the Araxes set itself to play the
part of great-king in anterior Asia, the Parthians had in
general maintained friendly relations with the Romans
as the foes of their foes.   But, after the overthrow of
Mithradates and Tigranes, the Romans had, particularly
through the arrangements made by Pompeius, taken up
a position which was hardly compatible with serious and
lasting peace between the two states.   In the south
Syria was now under direct Roman rule, and the Roman
legions kept guard on the margin of the great desert
which separates the lands of the coast from the valley of
the Euphrates.   In the north Cappadocia and Armenia
were vassal-principalities of Rome.   The tribes bordering
on Armenia to the northward, the Colchians, Iberians,
Albanians, were thereby necessarily withdrawn from
Parthian influence, and were, at least according to the
Roman way of apprehending the matter, likewise Roman
dependencies.   The lesser Media or Atropatene (Aderbijân), adjoining Armenia to the south-east, and separated
from it by the Araxes, had maintained, despite the
Seleucidae, its ancient native dynasty reaching back
to the time of the Achaemenids, and had even asserted
its independence ; under the Arsacids the king of this
region appears, according to circumstances, as a vassal
of the Parthians or as independent of these by leaning
on the Romans.   The determining influence of Rome
consequently reached as far as the Caucasus and the
western shore of the Caspian Sea.   This involved an
overlapping of the limits indicated by the national
relations.   The Hellenic nationality had doubtless so
far gained a footing on the south coast of the Black
Sea and in the interior of Cappadocia and Commagene,
that here the Roman ascendency found in it a base of

The Ro-
mano-Par-
thian fron-
tier-regions.

support ; but Armenia, even under the long years of
Roman rule, remained always a non-Greek land, knit
to the Parthian state with indestructible ties, by community
of language and of faith, the numerous intermarriages of
people of rank, and similarity of dress and of armour.[1]   The
Roman levy and the Roman taxation were never extended
to Armenia ; at most the land defrayed the raising and
the maintenance of its own troops, and the provisioning
of the Roman troops stationed there.   The Armenian
merchants formed the channel for the exchange of goods
over the Caucasus with Scythia, over the Caspian Sea
with east Asia and China, down the Tigris with Babylonia
and India, towards the west with Cappadocia ; nothing
would have been more natural than to include the
politically dependent land in the domain of Roman
tribute and customs ; yet this step was never taken.

The incongruity between the national and the political
connections of Armenia forms an essential element in the
conflict—prolonged through the whole imperial period—
with its eastern neighbour.   It was discerned doubtless
on the Roman side that annexation beyond the Euphrates
was an encroachment on the family-domain of Oriental
nationality, and was not any increase proper of power
for Rome.   But the ground or, if the phrase be preferred,
the excuse for the continuance of such encroachment
lay in the fact that the subsistence side by side of great
states with equal rights was incompatible with the system
of Roman policy, we may even say with the policy of
antiquity in general.   The Roman empire knew as limit,
in the strict sense, only the sea or a land-district un-
armed.   To the weaker but yet warlike commonwealth
of the Parthians the Romans always grudged a position
of power, and took away from it what these in their turn

---

[1] Arrian, who, as governor of
Cappadocia, had himself wielded
command over the Armenians (*contra
Al.* 29), always in the *Tactica* names
the Armenians and Parthians together
(4, 3, 44, 1, as respects the heavy
cavalry, the mailed κοντοφόροι and
the light cavalry, the ἀκροβολισταί
or ἱπποτοξόται ; 34, 7 as respects the
wide hose) ; and, where he speaks of
Hadrian's introduction of barbaric
cavalry into the Roman army, he
traces the mounted archers back to
the model of " the Parthians or
Armenians " (44, 1).

could not forego ; and therefore the relation between Rome and Iran through the whole imperial period was one of perpetual feud, interrupted only by armistices, concerning the left bank of the Euphrates.

In the treaties concluded with the Parthians by Lucullus (iv. 71) and Pompeius (iv. 127) the Euphrates was recognised as the boundary, and so Mesopotamia was ceded to them. But this did not prevent the Romans from receiving the rulers of Edessa among their clients, and from laying claim to a great part of northern Mesopotamia at least for their indirect rule, apparently by extending the limits of Armenia towards the south (iv. 146). On that account, after some delay, the Parthian government began the war against the Romans, in the form of declaring it against the Armenians. The answer to this was the campaign of Crassus, and, after the defeat at Carrhae (iv. 351 f.), the bringing back of Armenia under Parthian power ; we may add, the resumption of their claims on the western half of the Seleucid state, the carrying out of which, it is true, proved at that time unsuccessful (iv. 356). During the whole twenty years of civil war, in which the Roman republic perished and ultimately the principate was established, the state of war between the Romans and Parthians continued, and not seldom the two struggles became intermixed. Pompeius had, before the decisive battle, attempted to gain king Orodes as ally ; but, when the latter demanded the cession of Syria, Pompeius could not prevail on himself to deliver up the province which he had personally made Roman. After the catastrophe he had nevertheless resolved to do so ; but accidents directed his flight not to Syria, but to Egypt, where he met his end (iv. 446). The Parthians appeared on the point of once more breaking into Syria ; and the later leaders of the republicans did not disdain the aid of the public foe. Even in Caesar's lifetime Caecilius Bassus, when he raised the banner of revolt in Syria, had at once called in the Parthians. They had followed this call ; Pacorus, the son of Orodes, had defeated Caesar's lieuten-

The Parthians during the civil wars.
iv. 67, 122.

iv. 140.

iv. 335 f.

iv. 339.

iv. 424.

ant and liberated the troops of Bassus besieged by him in
44. Apamea (709). For this reason, as well as in order to
take revenge for Carrhae, Caesar had resolved to go in
the next spring personally to Syria and to cross the
Euphrates; but his death prevented the execution of
this plan. When Cassius thereupon took arms in Syria,
he entered into relations with the Parthian king; and in
42. the decisive battle at Philippi (712) Parthian mounted
archers joined in fighting for the freedom of Rome.
When the republicans succumbed, the great-king, in the
first instance, maintained a quiet attitude; and Antonius,
while designing probably to execute the plans of the
dictator, had at first enough to do with the settlement
of the East. The collision could not fail to take place;
the assailant this time was the Parthian king.

41.
The Par-
thians in
Syria and
Asia Minor.

In 713 when Caesar the son fought in Italy with the
generals and the wife of Antonius, and the latter tarried
inactive in Egypt beside queen Cleopatra, Orodes responded to the pressure of a Roman living with him
in exile, Quintus Labienus, and sent the latter, a son of
the dictator's embittered opponent Titus Labienus, and
41. formerly an officer in the army of Brutus, as well as (713)
his son Pacorus with a strong army over the frontier.
The governor of Syria, Decidius Saxa, succumbed to
the unexpected attack; the Roman garrisons, formed in
great part of old soldiers of the republican army, placed
themselves under the command of their former officer;
Apamea and Antioch, and generally all the towns of
Syria, except the island-town of Tyre which could not
be subdued without a fleet, submitted; on the flight to
Cilicia Saxa, in order not to be taken prisoner, put
himself to death. After the occupation of Syria Pacorus
turned against Palestine, Labienus towards the province
of Asia; here too the cities far and wide submitted or
were forcibly vanquished, with the exception of the
Carian Stratonicea. Antonius, whose attention was
claimed by the Italian complications, sent no succour
to his governors, and for almost two years (from the end
41, 39. of 713 to the spring of 715) Syria and a great part of

Asia Minor were commanded by the Parthian generals
and by the republican imperator Labienus—*Parthicus*,
as he called himself with shameless irony, not the Roman
who vanquished the Parthians, but the Roman who with
Parthian aid vanquished his countrymen.

Only after the threatened rupture between the two
holders of power was averted, Antonius sent a new army
under the conduct of Publius Ventidius Bassus, to whom
he entrusted the command in the provinces of Asia and
Syria. The able general encountered in Asia Labienus
alone with his Roman troops, and rapidly drove him out
of the province. At the boundary between Asia and
Cilicia, in the passes of the Taurus, a division of Parthians
wished to rally their fugitive allies ; but they too were
beaten before they could unite with Labienus, and
thereupon the latter was caught on his flight in Cilicia
and put to death. With like good fortune Ventidius
gained by fighting the passes of the Amanus on the
border of Cilicia and Syria ; here Pharnapates, the best
of the Parthian generals, fell (715). Thus was Syria
delivered from the enemy. Certainly in the following
year Pacorus once more crossed the Euphrates ; but only
to meet destruction with the greatest part of his army in
a decisive engagement at Gindarus, north-east of Antioch
(9th June 716). It was a victory which counterbalanced
in some measure the day of Carrhae, and one of permanent
effect ; for long the Parthians did not again show their
troops on the Roman bank of the Euphrates.

If it was in the interest of Rome to extend her
conquests towards the East, and to enter on the inheritance of Alexander the Great there in all its extent, the
circumstances were never more favourable for doing so
than in the year 716. The relations of the two rulers
to each other had become re-established seasonably for
that purpose, and even Caesar at that time had probably
a sincere wish for an earnest and successful conduct of
the war by his co-ruler and brother-in-law. The disaster
of Gindarus had called forth a severe dynastic crisis
among the Parthians. King Orodes, deeply agitated by

Marginal notes:
Driven out by Ventidius Bassus.

39.

38.

Position of Antonius.

38.

the death of his eldest and ablest son, resigned the government in favour of his second son Phraates. The latter, in order the better to secure for himself the throne, exercised a reign of terror, to which his numerous brothers and his old father himself, as well as a number of the high nobles of the kingdom, fell victims ; others of them left the country and sought protection with the Romans, among them the powerful and respected Monaeses. Never had Rome in the East an army of equal numbers and excellence as at this time : Antonius was able to lead over the Euphrates no fewer than 16 legions, about 70,000 Roman infantry, about 40,000 auxiliaries, 10,000 Spanish and Gallic, and 6000 Armenian horsemen ; at least half of them were veteran troops brought up from the West, all ready to follow anywhere their beloved and honoured leader, the victor of Philippi, and to crown the brilliant victories, which had been already achieved not by but for him over the Parthians, with still greater successes under his own leadership.

His aims.   In reality Antonius had in view the erection of an Asiatic great-kingdom after the model of that of Alexander. As Crassus before his invasion had announced that he would extend the Roman rule as far as Bactria and India, so Antonius named the first son, whom the Egyptian queen bore to him, by the name of Alexander. He appears to have directly intended, on the one hand, to bring—excluding the completely Hellenised provinces of Bithynia and Asia—the whole imperial territory in the East, so far as it was not already under dependent petty princes, into this form ; and on the other hand, to make all the regions of the East once occupied by Occidentals subject to himself in the form of satrapies. Of eastern Asia Minor the largest portion and the military primacy were assigned to the most warlike of the princes there, the Galatian Amyntas (I. 335). Alongside of the Galatian prince stood the princes of Paphlagonia, the descendants of Deiotarus, dispossessed from Galatia ; Polemon, the new prince in Pontus, and the husband of Pythodoris the granddaughter of Antonius ;

and moreover, as hitherto, the kings of Cappadocia and Commagene. Antonius united a great part of Cilicia and Syria, as well as of Cyprus and Cyrene, with the Egyptian state, to which he thus almost restored its limits as they had been under the Ptolemies ; and as he had made queen Cleopatra, Caesar's mistress, his own or rather his wife, so her illegitimate child by Caesar, Caesarion, already earlier recognised as joint ruler of Egypt,[1] obtained the reversion of the old kingdom of the Ptolemies, and her illegitimate son by Antonius, Ptolemaeus Philadelphus, obtained that of Syria. To another son, whom she had borne to Antonius, the already mentioned Alexander, Armenia was for the present assigned as a payment to account for the rule of the East conceived as in reserve for him. With this great-kingdom organised after the Oriental fashion [2] he thought to combine the principate over the West. He himself did not assume the name of king, on the contrary bore in presence of his countrymen and the soldiers only those titles which also belonged to Caesar. But on imperial coins with a Latin legend Cleopatra is called queen of kings, her sons by Antonius at least kings ; the coins show the head of his eldest son along with that of his father, as if the hereditary character were a matter of course ; the marriage and the succession of the legitimate and the illegitimate children are treated by him, as was the usage with the great-kings of the

---

[1] Caesar's illegitimate son Πτολε-μαῖος ὁ καὶ Καῖσαρ θεὸς φιλοπάτωρ φιλομήτωρ, as his royal designation runs (*C. I. Gr.* 4717), entered on the joint rule of Egypt in the Egyptian year 29 Aug. 711/2, as the era shows (Wescher, *Bullett. dell' Inst.* 1866, p. 199 ; Krall, *Wiener Studien,* v. 313). As he came in place of Ptolemaeus the younger, the husband and brother of his mother, the setting aside of the latter by Cleopatra, of which the particulars are not known, must have taken place just then, and have furnished the occasion to proclaim him as king of Egypt. Dio also, xlvii. 31, places his nomination in the summer of 712 before the

battle of Philippi. It was thus not the work of Antonius, but sanctioned by the two rulers in concert at a time when it could not but be their object to meet the wishes of the queen of Egypt, who certainly had from the outset ranged herself on their side.

[2] This is what Augustus means when he says that he had brought again to the empire the provinces of the East in great part distributed among kings *(Mon. Ancyr.* 5, 41 : *provincias omnis, quae trans Hadrianum mare vergunt ad orientem, Cyrenasque, iam ex parte magna regibus eas possidentibus . . . reciperavi).*

42.

East, or, as he himself said, with the divine freedom of his ancestor Herakles :[1] the said Alexander and his twin sister were named by him, the former Helios, the latter Selene, after the model of those same great-kings, and, as once upon a time the Persian king bestowed on the refugee Themistocles a number of Asiatic cities, so he bestowed on the Parthian Monaeses, who went over to him, three cities of Syria. In Alexander too the king of the Macedonians and the king of kings of the East went in some measure side by side, and to him too the bridal bed in Susa was the reward for the camp-tent of Gaugamela ; but the Roman copy shows in its exactness a strong element of caricature.

Prepara-
tions for the
Parthian
war.

Whether Antonius apprehended his position in this way, immediately on his taking up the government in the East, cannot be decided ; it may be conjectured that the creation of a new Oriental great-kingdom in connection with the Occidental principate ripened in his mind gradually, and that the idea was only thought out completely, after, in the year 717, on his return from Italy to Asia, he had once more entered into relations with the last

37.

---

[1] The decorum, which was as characteristic of Augustus as its opposite was of his colleague, did not fail him here. Not merely in the case of Caesarion was the paternity, which the dictator himself had virtually acknowledged, afterwards officially denied ; the children also of Antonius by Cleopatra, where indeed nothing was to be denied, were regarded doubtless as members of the imperial house, but were never formally acknowledged as children of Antonius. On the contrary the son of the daughter of Antonius by Cleopatra, the subsequent king of Mauretania Ptolemaeus, is called in the Athenian inscription, *C. I. A.* iii. 555, grandson of Ptolemaeus ; for Πτολεμαίου ἔκγονος cannot well in this connection be taken otherwise. This maternal grandfather was invented in Rome, that they might be able officially to conceal the real one. Any one who prefers — as O. Hirschfeld proposes — to take ἔκγονος as great-grandson, and to refer it to the maternal great-grandfather, comes to the same result ; for then the grandfather is passed over, because the mother was in the legal sense fatherless. — Whether the fiction, which is in my view more probable, went so far as to indicate a definite Ptolemaeus, possibly to prolong the life of the last Lagid who died in 712, or whether they were content with inventing a father without entering into particulars, cannot be decided. But the fiction was adhered to in this respect, that the son of Antonius's daughter obtained the name of the fictitious grandfather. The circumstance that in this case preference was given to the descent from the Lagids over that from Massinissa may probably have been occasioned more by regard to the imperial house, which treated the illegitimate child as belonging to it, than by the Hellenic inclination of the father.

42.

queen of the Lagid house not to be again broken off. But his temperament was not equal to such an enterprise. One of those men of military capacity, who knew how, in presence of the enemy, and especially in a position of difficulty, to strike prudently and boldly, he lacked the will of the statesman, the sure grasp and resolute pursuit of a political aim. Had the dictator Caesar assigned to him the problem of subduing the East, he would probably have solved it : the marshal was not fitted to be the ruler. After the expulsion of the Parthians from Syria, almost two years (summer of 716 to summer of 718) elapsed with- 38, 36. out any step being taken towards the object aimed at. Antonius himself, inferior also in this respect that he grudged to his generals important successes, had removed the conqueror of Labienus and of Pacorus, the able Ventidius, immediately after this last success, and taken the chief command in person in order to pursue and to miss the pitiful honour of occupying Samosata, the capital of the small Syrian dependent state, Commagene ; annoyed at this, he left the East, in order to negotiate in Italy with his father-in-law as to the future arrangements, or to enjoy life with his young spouse Octavia. His governors in the East were not inactive. Publius Canidius Crassus advanced from Armenia towards the Caucasus, and there subdued Pharnabazus king of the Iberians, and Zober king of the Albanians. Gaius Sossius took in Syria the last town still adhering to the Parthians, Aradus ; he further re-established in Judaea the rule of Herodes, and caused the pretender to the throne installed by the Parthians, the Hasmonean Antigonus, to be put to death. The consequences of the victory on Roman territory were thus duly drawn, and the recognition of Roman rule was enforced as far as the Caspian Sea and the Syrian desert. But Antonius had reserved for himself the beginning of the warfare against the Parthians, and he came not.

When at length, in 718, he escaped from the arms, 36. not of Octavia, but of Cleopatra, and set the columns of the army in motion, a good part of the appropriate season

Parthian war of Antonius

of the year had already elapsed.   Still more surprising
than this delay was the direction which Antonius chose.
All aggressive wars of the Romans against the Parthians,
earlier and later, took the route for Ctesiphon, the capital
of the kingdom and at the same time situated on its
western frontier, and so the natural and immediate aim
of operations for armies marching downward on the
Euphrates or on the Tigris.   Antonius too might, after
he had reached the Tigris through northern Mesopotamia,
nearly along the route which Alexander had traversed,
have advanced down the river upon Ctesiphon and
Seleucia.   But instead of this he preferred to go in a
northerly direction at first towards Armenia, and from that
point, where he united his whole military resources and
reinforced himself in particular by the Armenian cavalry,
to the table-land of Media Atropatene (Aderbijân).   The
allied king of Armenia may possibly have recommended this
plan of campaign, seeing that the Armenian rulers at all
times aspired to the possession of this neighbouring land,
and King Artavazdes of Armenia might hope now to
subdue the satrap of Atropatene of the same name, and
to add the latter's territory to his own.   But Antonius
himself cannot possibly have been influenced by such considerations.   He may have rather thought that he should
be able to push forward from Atropatene into the heart
of the enemy's country, and might regard the old Persian
court-residences of Ecbatana and Rhagae as the goal of his
march.   But, if this was his plan, he acted without
knowledge of the difficult ground, and altogether
underrated his opponents' power of resistance, besides
which the short time available for operations in this
mountainous country and the late beginning of the campaign weighed heavily in the scale.   As a skilled and
experienced officer, such as Antonius was, could hardly
deceive himself on such points, it is probable that special
political considerations influenced the matter.   The rule
of Phraates was tottering, as we have said ; Monaeses,
of whose fidelity Antonius held himself assured, and whom
he hoped perhaps to put into Phraates's place, had returned

in accordance with the wish of the Parthian king to his native country ;[1] Antonius appears to have reckoned on a rising on his part against Phraates, and in expectation of this civil war to have led his army into the interior of the Parthian provinces. It would doubtless have been possible to await the result of this design in the friendly Armenia, and, if operations thereafter were requisite, to have at least the full summer-time at his disposal in the following year ; but this waiting was not agreeable to the hasty general. In Atropatene he encountered the obstinate resistance of the powerful and half independent under-king, who resolutely sustained a siege in his capital Praaspa or Phraarta (southward from the lake of Urumia, presumably on the lower course of the Jaghatu) ; and not only so, but the hostile attack brought, as it would seem, to the Parthians internal peace. Phraates led on a large army to the relief of the assailed city. Antonius had brought with him a great siege-train, but impatiently hastening forward, he had left this behind in the custody of two legions under the legate Oppius Statianus. Thus he on his part made no progress with the siege ; but king Phraates sent his masses of cavalry under that same Monaeses to the rear of the enemy, against the corps of Statianus laboriously pursuing its march. The Parthians cut down the covering force, including the general himself, took the rest prisoners, and destroyed the whole train of 300 waggons. Thereby the campaign was lost.

The Armenian, despairing of the success of the campaign, collected his men and went home. Antonius did not immediately abandon the siege, and even defeated the royal army in the open field, but the alert horsemen escaped without substantial loss, and it was a victory without effect. An attempt to obtain from the king at

Progress of the struggle.

---

[1] It is in itself credible that Antonius concealed the impending invasion from Phraates as long as possible, and therefore, when sending back Monaeses, declared himself ready to conclude peace on the basis of the restitution of the lost standards (Plutarch, 37 ; Dio, xlix. 24 ; Florus, ii. 20 [iv. 10]). But he knew presumably that this offer would not be accepted, and in no case can he have been in earnest with those proposals ; beyond doubt he wished for the war and the overthrow of Phraates.

least the restitution of the old and the newly lost eagles, and thus to conclude peace, if not with advantage, at least with honour, failed ; the Parthian did not give away his sure success so cheaply.   He only assured the envoys of Antonius that, if the Romans would give up the siege, he would not molest them on their return home.   This neither honourable nor trustworthy promise of the enemy would hardly have induced Antonius to break up.   It was natural to take up quarters for the winter in the enemy's country, seeing that the Parthian troops were not acquainted with continuous military service, and presumably most of their forces would have gone home at the commencement of winter.   But a strong basis was lacking, and supplies in the exhausted land were not secured ; above all Antonius himself was not capable of such a tenacious conduct of the war.   Consequently he abandoned the machines, which the besieged immediately burnt; and entered on the difficult retreat, either too early or too late.   Fifteen days' march (300 Roman miles) through a hostile country separated the army from the Araxes, the border river of Armenia, whither in spite of the ambiguous attitude of the ruler the retreat could alone be directed.   A hostile army of 40,000 horsemen, in spite of the given promise, accompanied the returning force, and, with the marching off of the Armenians, the Romans had lost the best part of their cavalry.   Provisions and draught animals were scarce, and the season of the year far advanced.   But in the perilous position Antonius recovered his energy and his martial skill, and in some measure also his good fortune in war ; he had made his choice, and the general as well as the troops solved the task in a commendable way.   Had they not had with them a former soldier of Crassus, who, having become a Parthian, knew most accurately every step of the way, and, instead of conducting them back through the plain by which they had come, guided them by mountain paths, which were less exposed to cavalry attacks—apparently over the mountains about Tabreez—the army would hardly have reached its goal ; and had not Mon-

aeses, paying off in his way his debt of thanks to
Antonius, informed him in right time of the false assurances and the cunning designs of his countrymen, the
Romans would doubtless have fallen into one of the
ambushes which on several occasions were laid for them.

The soldierly nature of Antonius was often brilliantly
conspicuous during these troublesome days, in his dexterous
use of any favourable moment, in his sternness towards the
cowardly, in his power over the minds of the soldiers, in his
faithful care for the wounded and the sick.   Yet the
rescue was almost a miracle ; already had Antonius instructed a faithful attendant in case of extremity not to
let him fall alive into the hands of the enemy.   Amidst
constant attacks of the artful enemy, in weather of wintry
cold, without adequate food and often without water,
they reached the protecting frontier in twenty-seven days,
where the enemy desisted from following them.   The loss
was enormous ; there were reckoned up in those twenty-
seven days eighteen larger engagements, and in a single
one of them the Romans counted 3000 dead and 5000
wounded.   It was the very best and bravest that those
constant assaults on the vanguard and on the flanks swept
away.   The whole baggage, a third of the camp-followers,
a fourth of the army, 20,000 foot soldiers, and 4000
horsemen had perished in this Median campaign, in great
part not through the sword, but through famine and
disease.   Even on the Araxes the sufferings of the unhappy troops were not yet at an end.   Artavazdes received them as a friend, and had no other choice ; it
would doubtless have been possible to pass the winter
there.   But the impatience of Antonius did not tolerate
this ; the march went on, and from the ever increasing
inclemency of the season and the state of health of the
soldiers, this last section of the expedition from the Araxes
to Antioch cost, although no enemy hampered it, other
8000 men.   No doubt this campaign was a last flash of
what was brave and capable in the character of Antonius;
but it was politically his overthrow all the more, as at the
same time Caesar by the successful termination of the

Difficulties
of the
retreat.

Sicilian war gained the dominion in the West and the confidence of Italy for the present and all the future.

The responsibility for the miscarriage, which Antonius in vain attempted to deny, was thrown by him on the dependent kings of Cappadocia and Armenia, and on the latter so far with justice, as his premature marching off from Praaspa had materially increased the dangers and the losses of the retreat. For the plan of the campaign, however, it was not he who was responsible, but Antonius ;[1] and the failure of the hopes placed on Monaeses, the disaster of Statianus, the breaking down of the siege of Praaspa, were not brought about by the Armenian. Antonius did not abandon the subjugation of the East, but set out next year (719) once more from Egypt. The circumstances were still even now comparatively favourable. A friendly alliance was formed with the Median king Artavazdes ; he had not merely fallen into variance with his Parthian suzerain, but was indignant above all at his Armenian neighbour, and, considering the well-known exasperation of Antonius against the latter, he might reckon on finding a support in the enemy of his enemy. Everything depended on the firm accord of the two possessors of power—the victory-crowned master of the West and the defeated ruler in the East ; and, on the news that Antonius proposed to continue the war, his legitimate wife, the sister of Caesar, resorted from Italy to the East to bring up to him new forces, and to strengthen anew his relations to her and to her brother. If Octavia was magnanimous enough to offer the hand of reconciliation to her husband in spite of his relations to the Egyptian queen, Caesar must—as was further confirmed by the commencement, which just then took place, of the war on the north-east frontier of Italy—have been still ready at that time to maintain the subsisting relation.

35.

---

[1] The account of the matter given by Strabo, xi. 13, 4, p. 524, evidently after the description of this war compiled by Antonius's comrade in arms Dellius, and, it may be conjectured, at his bidding (comp. *ib.* xi. 13, 3 ; Dio, xlix. 39), is a very sorry attempt to justify the beaten general. If Antonius did not take the nearest route to Ctesiphon, king Artavazdes cannot be brought in for the blame of it as a false guide ; it was a military, and doubtless still more a political, miscalculation of the general in chief.

The brother and sister subordinated their personal interests
magnanimously to those of the commonwealth.   But
loudly as interest and honour called for the acceptance
of the offered hand, Antonius could not prevail on himself
to break off the relation with the Egyptian queen ; he
sent back his wife, and this was at the same time a rupture with her brother, and, as we may add, an abandonment of the idea of continuing the war against the
Parthians.   Now, ere that could be thought of, the
question of mastery between Antonius and Caesar had to
be settled.   Antonius accordingly returned at once from
Syria to Egypt, and in the following year undertook
nothing further towards the execution of his plans of
Oriental conquest ; only he punished those to whom he
assigned the blame of the miscarriage.   He caused
Ariarathes the king of Cappadocia to be executed,[1] and
gave the kingdom to an illegitimate kinsman of his,
Archelaus.   The like fate was intended for the Armenian.
If Antonius in 720 appeared in Armenia, as he said, 34
for the continuance of the war, this had simply the object
of getting into his power the person of the king, who had
refused to go to Egypt.   This act of revenge was ignobly
executed by way of surprise, and was not less ignobly
celebrated by a caricature of the Capitoline triumph exhibited in Alexandria.   At that time the son of Antonius,
destined for lord of the East, as was already stated, was
installed as king of Armenia, and married to the daughter
of the new ally, the king of Media ; while the eldest son
of the captive king of Armenia executed some time afterwards by order of queen Cleopatra, Artaxes, whom the
Armenians had proclaimed king instead of his father,
took refuge with the Parthians.   Armenia and Media
Atropatene were thus in the power of Antonius or allied
with him ; the continuance of the Parthian war was
announced doubtless, but remained postponed till after
the overcoming of the western rival.   Phraates on his

---

[1] The fact of the deposition and
execution, and the time, are attested
by Dio, xlix. 32, and Valerius

Maximus, ix. 15, ext. 2 ; the cause or
the pretext must have been connected
with the Armenian war.

part advanced against Media, at first without success, as
the Roman troops stationed in Armenia afforded help to
the Medians ; but when Antonius, in the course of his
armaments against Caesar, recalled his forces from that
quarter, the Parthians gained the upper hand, vanquished
the Medians, and installed in Media, as well as also in
Armenia, the king Artaxes, who, in requital for the execution of his father, caused all the Romans scattered in the
land to be seized and put to death.   That Phraates did
not turn to fuller account the great feud between Antonius
and Caesar, while it was in preparation and was being
fought out, was probably due to his being once more
hampered by the troubles breaking out in his own land.
These ended in his expulsion, and in his going to the
Scythians of the East.   Tiridates was proclaimed as
great-king in his stead.   When the decisive naval battle
was fought on the coast of Epirus, and thereupon the
overthrow of Antonius was completed in Egypt, this new
great-king sat on his tottering throne in Ctesiphon, and
at the opposite frontier of the empire the hordes of Turan
were making arrangements to reinstate the earlier ruler,
in which they soon afterwards succeeded.

First
arrange-
ments of
Augustus
in the East.

The sagacious and clear-seeing man, to whom it fell to
liquidate the undertakings of Antonius and to settle the
relations of the two portions of the empire, needed moderation quite as much as energy.   It would have been the
gravest of errors to enter into the ideas of Antonius as to
conquering the East, or even merely making further conquests there.   Augustus perceived this ; his military
arrangements show clearly that, while he viewed the possession of the Syrian coast as well as that of Egypt as an
indispensable complement to the empire of the Mediterranean, he attached no value to inland possessions there.
Armenia, however, had now been for a generation Roman,
and could, in the nature of the circumstances, only be
Roman or Parthian ; the country was by its position, in a
military point of view, a sally-port for each of the great
powers into the territory of the other.   Augustus had no
thought of abandoning Armenia and leaving it to the

Parthians ; and, as things stood, he could hardly think of
doing so.   But, if Armenia was retained, the matter could
not end there ; the local relations compelled the Romans
further to bring under their controlling influence the basin
of the river Cyrus, the territories of the Iberians on its
upper, and of the Albanians on its lower course—that
is, the inhabitants of the modern Georgia and Shirvan,
skilled in combat on horseback and on foot—and not to
allow the domain of the Parthian power to extend to the
north of the Araxes beyond Atropatene.   The expedition
of Pompeius had already shown that the settlement in
Armenia necessarily led the Romans on the one hand as
far as the Caucasus, on the other as far as the western
shore of the Caspian Sea.   The initial steps were everywhere taken.   The legates of Antonius had fought with
the Iberians and Albanians ; Polemon, confirmed in his
position by Augustus, ruled not merely over the coast
from Pharnacea to Trapezus, but also over the territory
of the Colchians at the mouth of the Phasis.   To this
general state of matters fell to be added the special circumstances of the moment, which most urgently suggested
to the new monarch of Rome not merely to show his sword
in presence of the Orientals, but also to draw it.   That
king Artaxes, like Mithradates formerly, had given orders
to put to death all the Romans within his bounds, could
not be allowed to remain unrequited.   The exiled king of
Media also had now sought help from Augustus, as he
would otherwise have sought it from Antonius.   Not
merely did the civil war and the conflict of pretenders in
the Parthian empire facilitate the attack, but the expelled
ruler Tiridates likewise sought protection with Augustus,
and declared himself ready as a Roman vassal to accept
his kingdom in fief from the latter.   The restitution of
the Romans who had fallen into the power of the Parthians at the defeats of Crassus and of the Antonians, and
of the lost eagles, might not in themselves seem to the
ruler worth the waging of war ; the restorer of the Roman
state could not allow this question of military and political
honour to drop.

Policy open
to him.

The Roman statesman had to reckon with these facts ; considering the position, which Antonius took in the East, the policy of action was imperative generally, and doubly so from the preceding miscarriages. Beyond doubt it was desirable soon to undertake the organisation of matters in Rome, but for the undisputed monarch there subsisted no stringent compulsion to do this at once. He found himself after the decisive blows of Actium and Alexandria on the spot and at the head of a strong and victorious army ; what had to be done some day was best done at once. A ruler of the stamp of Caesar would hardly have returned to Rome without having restored the protectorate in Armenia, having obtained recognition for the Roman supremacy as far as the Caucasus and the Caspian Sea, and having settled accounts with the Parthians. A ruler of caution and energy would have now at once organised the defence of the frontier in the East, as the circumstances required ; it was from the outset clear that the four Syrian legions, together about 40,000 men, were not sufficient to guard the interests of Rome simultaneously on the Euphrates, on the Araxes, and on the Cyrus, and that the militia of the dependent kingdoms only concealed, and did not cover, the want of imperial troops. Armenia by political and national sympathy held more to the Parthians than to the Romans ; the kings of Commagene, Cappadocia, Galatia, Pontus, were inclined doubtless on the other hand more to the Roman side, but they were untrustworthy and weak. Even a policy keeping within bounds needed for its foundation an energetic stroke of the sword, and for its maintenance the near arm of a superior Roman military power.

Inadequate
measures.

Augustus neither struck nor protected ; certainly not because he deceived himself as to the state of the case, but because it was his nature to execute tardily and feebly what he perceived to be necessary, and to let considerations of internal policy exercise a more than due influence on the relations abroad. The inadequacy of the protection of the frontier by the client states of Asia Minor he well perceived ; and in connection therewith, already in the

year 729, after the death of king Amyntas who ruled all   25.
the interior of Asia Minor, he gave to him no successor,
but placed the land under an imperial legate. Presumably
the neighbouring more important client-states, and particularly Cappadocia, were intended to be in like manner
converted after the decease of the holders for the time
into imperial governorships.   This was a step in advance,
in so far as thereby the militia of these countries was incorporated with the imperial army and placed under
Roman officers ; these troops could not exercise a serious
pressure on the insecure border-lands or even on the neighbouring great-state, although they now counted among
those of the empire.   But all these considerations were
outweighed by regard to the reduction of the numbers of
the standing army and of the expenditure for the military
system to the lowest possible measure.

Equally insufficient, in presence of the relations of the
moment, were the measures adopted by Augustus on his
return home from Alexandria. He gave to the dispossessed king of the Medes the rule of the Lesser Armenia,
and to the Parthian pretender Tiridates an asylum in
Syria, in order through the former to keep in check the
king Artaxes who persevered in open hostility against
Rome, by the latter to press upon king Phraates.   The
negotiations instituted with the latter regarding the restitution of the Parthian trophies of victory were prolonged
without result, although Phraates in the year 731 had   23.
promised their return in order to obtain the release of a
son who had accidentally fallen into the power of the
Romans.

It was only when Augustus went in person to Syria   Augustus
in the year 734, and showed himself in earnest, that the   20.] in
Orientals submitted.   In Armenia, where a powerful   Syria.
party had risen against king Artaxes, the insurgents
threw themselves into the arms of the Romans and
sought imperial investiture for Artaxes's younger brother
Tigranes, brought up at the imperial court and living in
Rome.   When the emperor's stepson Tiberius Claudius
Nero, then a youth of twenty-two years, advanced with

a military force into Armenia, king Artaxes was put to death by his own relatives, and Tigranes received the imperial tiara from the hand of the emperor's representative, as fifty years earlier his grandfather of the same name had received it from Pompeius (iv. 127). Atropatene was again separated from Armenia and passed under the sway of a ruler likewise brought up in Rome, Ariobarzanes, son of the already-mentioned Artavazdes ; yet the latter appears to have obtained the land not as a Roman but as a Parthian dependency. Concerning the organisation of matters in the principalities on the Caucasus we learn nothing ; but as they are subsequently reckoned among the Roman client-states, probably at that time the Roman influence prevailed here also. Even king Phraates, now put to the choice of redeeming his word or fighting, resolved with a heavy heart on the surrender—keenly as it did violence to the national feelings of his people—of the few Roman prisoners of war still living and the standards won.

Boundless joy saluted this bloodless victory achieved by this prince of peace. After it there subsisted for a considerable time a friendly relation with the king of the Parthians, as indeed the immediate interests of the two great states came little into contact. In Armenia, on the other hand, the Roman vassal-rule, which rested only on its own basis, had a difficulty in confronting the national opposition. After the early death of king Tigranes his children, or the leaders of the state governing under their name, joined this opposition. Against them another ruler Artavazdes was set up by the friends of the Romans ; but he was unable to prevail against the stronger opposing party. These Armenian troubles disturbed also the relation to the Parthians ; it was natural that the Armenians antagonistic to Rome should seek to lean on these, and the Arsacids could not forget that Armenia had been formerly a Parthian appanage for the second son. Bloodless victories are often feeble and dangerous. Matters went so far that the Roman government, in the year 748, commissioned the same Tiberius,

who, fourteen years before had installed Tigranes as vassal-
king of Armenia, to enter it once more with a military
force and to regulate the state of matters in case of need
by arms.   But the quarrels in the imperial family, which
had interrupted the subjugation of the Germans (I. 35),
interfered also here and had the same bad effect.   Tiberius
declined his stepfather's commission, and in the absence
of a suitable princely general the Roman government for
some years looked on, inactive for good or evil, at the
doings of the anti-Roman party in Armenia under Parthian protection.   At length, in the year 753, not merely **1.**
was the same commission given to the elder adopted son
of the emperor, Gaius Caesar, at the age of twenty, but the
subjugation of Armenia was to be, as the father hoped,
the beginning of greater things; the Oriental campaign of
the crown-prince of twenty was, we might almost say, to
continue the expedition of Alexander.   Literati commissioned by the emperor or in close relations to the
court, the geographer Isidorus, himself at home at the
mouth of the Euphrates, and king Juba of Mauretania,
the representative of Greek learning among the princely
personages of the Augustan circle, dedicated—the former
his information personally acquired in the East, the latter
his literary collections on Arabia—to the young prince, who
appeared to burn with the desire of achieving the conquest of that land—over which Alexander had met his
death—as a brilliant compensation for a miscarriage of
the Augustan government which a considerable time ago
had there occurred.   In the first instance for Armenia
this mission was just as successful as that of Tiberius.
The Roman crown-prince and the Parthian great-king
Phraataces met personally on an island of the Euphrates ; the Parthians once more gave up Armenia, the
imminent danger of a Parthian war was averted, and the
understanding, which had been disturbed, was at least outwardly re-established.   Gaius appointed Ariobarzanes, a
prince of the Median princely house, as king over the
Armenians, and the suzerainty of Rome was once more
confirmed.   The Armenians, however, opposed to Rome

did not submit without resistance ; matters came not merely to the marching in of the legions, but even to fighting. Before the walls of the Armenian stronghold Artageira the young crown-prince received from a Parthian officer through treachery the wound (2 A.D.) of which he died after months of sickness. The intermixture of imperial and dynastic policy punished itself anew. The death of a young man changed the course of great policy ; the Arabian expedition so confidently announced to the public fell into abeyance, after its success could no longer smooth the way of the emperor's son to the succession. Further undertakings on the Euphrates were no longer thought of ; the immediate object—the occupation of Armenia and the re-establishment of the relations with the Parthians—was attained, however sad the shadows that fell on this success through the death of the crown-prince.

Mission of Germani-cus to [20. the East.

The success had no more endurance than that of the more brilliant expedition of 734. The rulers of Armenia installed by Rome were soon hard pressed by those of the counter-party with the secret or open participation of the Parthians, and supplanted. When the Parthian prince Vonones, reared in Rome, was called to the vacant Parthian throne, the Romans hoped to find in him a support ; but on that very account he had soon to vacate it, and in his stead came king Artabanus of Media, an energetic man, sprung on the mother's side from the Arsacids, but belonging to the Scythian people of the Daci, and brought up in native habits (about 10 A.D.) Vonones was then received by the Armenians as ruler, and thereby these were kept under Roman influence. But the less could Artabanus tolerate his dispossessed rival as a neighbour prince ; the Roman government must, in order to sustain a man in every respect unfitted for his position, have applied armed force against the Parthians as against his own subjects. Tiberius, who meanwhile had come to reign, did not order an immediate invasion, and for the moment the anti-Roman party in Armenia was victorious ; but it was not his intention to abandon the important border-land. On the contrary,

the annexation, probably long resolved on, of the kingdom of Cappadocia was carried out in the year 17 ; the
old Archelaus, who had occupied the throne there from
the year 718, was summoned to Rome and was there in- 36.
formed that he had ceased to reign. Likewise the petty,
but on account of the fords of the Euphrates important,
kingdom of Commagene came at that time under immediate imperial administration. Thereby the direct frontier
of the empire was pushed forward as far as the middle
Euphrates. At the same time the crown-prince Germanicus, who had just commanded with great distinction
on the Rhine, went with extended full powers to the
East, in order to organise the new province of Cappadocia
and to restore the sunken repute of the imperial authority.

This mission also attained its end soon and easily. And its
Germanicus, although not supported by the governor of results.
Syria, Gnaeus Piso, with such a force of troops as he was
entitled to ask and had asked, went nevertheless to
Armenia, and by the mere weight of his person and of
his position brought back the land to allegiance. He
allowed the incapable Vonones to fall, and, in accordance
with the wishes of the chief men favourable to Rome,
appointed as ruler of the Armenians a son of that
Polemon whom Antonius had made king in Pontus,
Zeno, or, as he was called as king of Armenia, Artaxias ;
the latter was, on the one hand, connected with the
imperial house through his mother queen Pythodoris, a
granddaughter of the triumvir Antonius, on the other
hand, reared after the manner of the country, a vigorous
huntsman and a brave carouser at the festal board. The
great-king Artabanus also met the Roman prince in a
friendly way, and asked only for the removal of his
predecessor Vonones from Syria, in order to check the
intrigues concocted between him and the discontented
Parthians. As Germanicus responded to this request
and sent the inconvenient refugee to Cilicia, where he
soon afterwards perished in an attempt to escape, the
best relations were established between the two great
states. Artabanus wished even to meet personally with

Germanicus at the Euphrates, as Phraataces and Gaius had done ; but this Germanicus declined, doubtless with reference to the easily excited suspicion of Tiberius. In truth the same shadow of gloom fell on this Oriental expedition as on the last preceding one ; from this too the crown-prince of the Roman empire came not home alive.

Artabanus and Tiberius.

For a time the arrangements made did their work. So long as Tiberius bore sway with a firm hand, and so long as king Artaxias of Armenia lived, tranquillity continued in the East ; but in the last years of the old emperor, when he from his solitary island allowed things to take their course and shrank back from all interference, and especially after the death of Artaxias (about 34), the old game once more began. King Artabanus, exalted by his long and prosperous government and by many successes achieved against the border peoples of Iran, and convinced that the old emperor would have no inclination to begin a heavy war in the East, induced the Armenians to proclaim his own eldest son, Arsaces, as ruler ; that is, to exchange the Roman suzerainty for the Parthian. Indeed he seemed directly to aim at war with Rome ; he demanded the estate left by his predecessor and rival Vonones, who had died in Cilicia, from the Roman government, and his letters to it as undisguisedly expressed the view that the East belonged to the Orientals, as they called by the right name the abominations at the imperial court, of which people in Rome ventured only to whisper in their most intimate circles. He is said even to have made an attempt to possess himself of Cappadocia. But he had miscalculated on the old lion. Tiberius was even at Capreae formidable not merely to his courtiers, and was not the man to let himself, and in himself Rome, be mocked with impunity. He sent Lucius Vitellius, the father of the subsequent emperor, a resolute officer and skilful diplomatist, to the East with plenary power similar to that which Gaius Caesar and Germanicus had formerly had, and with the commission in case of need to lead the Syrian legions over the

Mission of Vitellius.

Euphrates. At the same time he applied the often tried
means for giving trouble to the rulers of the East by
insurrections and pretenders in their own land. To the
Parthian prince, whom the Armenian nationalists had
proclaimed as ruler, he opposed a prince of the royal
house of the Iberians, Mithradates, brother of the Armenian
king Pharasmanes, and directed the latter, as well as the
prince of the Albanians, to support the Roman pretender
to Armenia with military force. Large bands of the
Transcaucasian Sarmatae, warlike and easy of access to
every wooer, were hired with Roman money for the
inroads into Armenia. The Roman pretender succeeded
in poisoning his rival through bribed courtiers, and in
possessing himself of the country and of the capital
Artaxata. Artabanus sent in place of the murdered
prince another son Orodes to Armenia, and attempted
also on his part to procure Transcaucasian auxiliaries ;
but only few made good their way to Armenia, and the
bands of Parthian horsemen were not a match for the
good infantry of the Caucasian peoples and the dreaded
Sarmatian mounted archers. Orodes was vanquished in
a hard pitched battle, and himself severely wounded in
single combat with his rival. Then Artabanus in person
set out for Armenia. But now Vitellius also put in
motion the Syrian legions, in order to cross the Euphrates
and to invade Mesopotamia, and this brought the long
fermenting insurrection in the Parthian kingdom to an
outbreak. The energetic and, with successes, more and
more rude demeanour of the Scythian ruler, had offended
many persons and interests, and had especially estranged
from him the Mesopotamian Greeks and the powerful
urban community of Seleucia, from which he had taken
away its municipal constitution, democratic after a Greek
type. Roman gold fostered the movement which was
in preparation. Discontented nobles had already put
themselves in communication with the Roman government, and besought from it a genuine Arsacid. Tiberius
had sent the only surviving son of Phraates, of the same
name with his father, and—after the old man, accustomed

to Roman habits, had succumbed to his exertions while still in Syria—in his stead a grandson of Phraates, likewise living in Rome, by name Tiridates. The Parthian prince Sinnaces, the leader of these plots, now renounced allegiance to the Scythian and set up the banner of the Arsacids. Vitellius with his legions crossed the Euphrates, and in his train the new great-king by grace of Rome. The Parthian governor of Mesopotamia, Ornospades, who had once as an exile shared under Tiberius in the Pannonian wars, placed himself and his troops at once at the disposal of the new ruler ; Abdagaeses, the father of Sinnaces, delivered over the imperial treasure ; very speedily Artabanus found himself abandoned by the whole country, and compelled to take flight to his Scythian home, where he wandered about in the forests without settled abode, and kept himself alive with his bow, while the tiara was solemnly placed on the head of Tiridates in Ctesiphon by the princes who were, according to the Parthian constitution, called to crown the ruler.

Tiridates superseded.   But the rule of the new great-king sent by the national foe did not last long. The government, conducted less by himself, young, inexperienced, and incapable, than by those who had made him king, and chiefly by Abdagaeses, soon provoked opposition. Some of the chief satraps had remained absent even from the coronation festival, and again brought forth the dispossessed ruler from his banishment ; with their assistance and the forces supplied by his Scythian countrymen Artabanus returned, and already in the following year (36) the whole kingdom, with the exception of Seleucia, was again in his power, Tiridates was a fugitive, and was compelled to demand from his Roman protectors the shelter which could not be refused to him. Vitellius once more led the legions to the Euphrates ; but, as the great-king appeared in person and declared himself ready for all that was asked, provided that the Roman government would stand aloof from Tiridates, peace was soon concluded. Artabanus not merely recognised Mithradates as king of Armenia, but presented also to the effigy of the Roman emperor the homage which was wont to be required of vassals, and furnished his son Darius as a hostage to the Romans. Thereupon the old emperor died ; but he had lived long enough to see this victory, as bloodless as complete, of his policy over the revolt of the East.

What the sagacity of the old man had attained was undone at once by the indiscretion of his successor. Apart from the fact that he cancelled judicious arrange- ments of Tiberius, re-establishing, *e.g.* the annexed kingdom of Commagene, his foolish envy grudged the dead emperor the success which he had gained ; he summoned the able governor of Syria as well as the new king of Armenia to Rome to answer for themselves, deposed the latter, and, after keeping him for a time a prisoner, sent him into exile. As a matter of course the Parthian government took action for itself, and once more seized possession of Armenia which was without a master.[1] Claudius, on coming to reign in the year 41, had to begin afresh the work that had been done. He dealt with it after the example of Tiberius. Mithradates, recalled from exile, was reinstated, and directed with the help of his brother to possess himself of Armenia. The fraternal war then waged among the three sons of king Artabanus III. in the Parthian kingdom smoothed the way for the Romans. After the murder of the eldest son, Gotarzes and Vardanes contended over the throne for years ; Seleucia, which had already renounced allegiance to the father, defied him and subsequently his sons throughout seven years ; the peoples of Turan also interfered, as they always did, in this quarrel of princes of Iran. Mithradates was able, with the help of the troops of his brother and

The East under Gaius.

---

[1] The account of the seizure of Armenia is wanting, but the fact is clearly apparent from Tacitus, *Ann.* xi. 9. To this connection probably belongs what Josephus, *Arch.* xx. 3, 3, tells of the design of the successor of Artabanus to wage war against the Romans, from which Izates the satrap of Adiabene vainly dissuades him. Josephus names this successor, pro- bably in error, Bardanes. The im- mediate successor of Artabanus III. was, according to Tacitus, *Ann.* xi. 8, his son of the same name, whom along with his son thereupon Gotarzes put out of the way ; and this Arta- banus IV. must be here meant.

of the garrisons of the neighbouring Roman provinces, to
overpower the Parthian partisans in Armenia and to make
himself again master there ;[1] the land obtained a Roman
garrison.   After Vardanes had come to terms with his
brother and had at length reoccupied Seleucia, he seemed
as though he would march into Armenia ; but the
threatening attitude of the Roman legate of Syria withheld him, and very soon the brother broke the agreement
and the civil war began afresh. Not even the assassination
of the brave and, in combat with the peoples of Turan,
victorious Vardanes put an end to it ; the opposition
party now turned to Rome and besought from the
government there the son of Vonones, the prince Meherdates then living in Rome, who thereupon was placed
by the emperor Claudius before the assembled senate at
the disposal of his countrymen and sent away to Syria
with the exhortation to administer his new kingdom well
and justly, and to remain mindful of the friendly
protectorate of Rome (49).   He did not reach the
position in which these exhortations might be applied.
The Roman legions, which escorted him as far as the
Euphrates, there delivered him over to those who had
called him—the head of the powerful princely family
of the Carên and the kings Abgarus of Edessa and
Izates of Adiabene. The inexperienced and unwarlike
youth was as little equal to the task as all the other
Parthian rulers set up by the Romans ; a number of his
most noted adherents left him so soon as they learned
to know him, and went to Gotarzes ; in the decisive
battle the fall of the brave Carên turned the scale.
Meherdates was taken prisoner and not even executed,

---

[1] The statement of Petrus Patricius
(*fr.* 3 Müll.) that king Mithradates
of Iberia had planned revolt from
Rome, but in order to preserve the
semblance of fidelity, had sent his
brother Cotys to Claudius, and then,
when the latter had given information
to the emperor of those intrigues,
had been deposed and replaced by
his brother, is not compatible with
the assured fact that in Iberia, at
least from the year 35 (Tacitus, *Ann.*
vi. 32) till the year 60 (Tacitus, *Ann.*
xiv. 26), Pharasmanes, and in the
year 75 his son Mithradates (*C. I. L.*
iii. 6052) bore rule.   Beyond doubt
Petrus has confused Mithradates of
Iberia and the king of the Bosporus
of the same name (I. 316, note 1),
and here at the bottom lies the
narrative, which Tacitus, *Ann.* xii.
18, presupposes.

but only, after the Oriental fashion, rendered incapable of
government by mutilation of the ears.

Nothwithstanding this defeat of Roman policy in the
Parthian kingdom, Armenia remained with the Romans,
so long as the weak Gotarzes ruled over the Parthians.
But so soon as a more vigorous hand grasped the reins
of sovereignty, and the internal conflicts ceased, the
struggle for that land was resumed.   King Vologasus,
who after the death of Gotarzes and the short reign of
Vonones II. succeeded this his father in the year 51,[1]
ascended the throne, exceptionally, in full agreement with
his two brothers Pacorus and Tiridates.   He was an
able and prudent ruler—we find him even as a founder
of towns, and exerting himself with success to divert the
trade of Palmyra towards his new town Vologasias on
the lower Euphrates—averse to quick and extreme
resolutions, and endeavouring, if possible, to keep peace
with his powerful neighbour.   But the recovery of
Armenia was the leading political idea of the dynasty,
and he too was ready to make use of any opportunity
for realising it.

Armenia occupied by the Parthians.

This opportunity seemed now to present itself.   The
Armenian court had become the scene of one of the
most revolting family tragedies which history records.
The old king of the Iberians, Pharasmanes, undertook
to eject his brother Mithradates, the king of Armenia,
from the throne and to put his own son Rhadamistus in
his place.   Under the pretext of a quarrel with his
father Rhadamistus appeared at the court of his uncle
and father-in-law, and entered into negotiations with
Armenians of repute in that sense.   After he had secured
a body of adherents, Pharasmanes, in the year 52, under
frivolous pretexts involved his brother in war, and
brought the country into his own or rather his son's

Rhada-mistus.

---

[1] If the coins, which it is true,
for the most part admit of being
distinguished only by resemblance of
effigy, are correctly attributed, those
of Gotarzes reach to Sel. 362 Daesius
= A.D. 51 June, and those of Vologasus (we know none of Vonones
II.) begin with Sel. 362 Gorpiaeus
= A.D. 51 Sept. (Percy Gardner,
Parthian Coinage, pp. 50, 51), which
agrees with Tacitus, *Ann.* xii. 14,
44.

power.   Mithradates placed himself under the protection of the Roman garrison of the fortress of Gorneae.[1] Rhadamistus did not venture to attack this ; but the commandant, Caelius Pollio, was well known as worthless and venal.   The centurion holding command under him resorted to Pharasmanes to induce him to recall his troops, which the latter promised, but did not keep his word.   During the absence of the second in command Pollio compelled the king—who doubtless guessed what was before him—by the threat of leaving him in the lurch, to deliver himself into the hands of Rhadamistus. By the latter he was put to death, and with him his wife, the sister of Rhadamistus, and their children, because they broke out in cries of lamentation at the sight of the dead bodies of their parents.   In this way Rhadamistus attained to sovereignty over Armenia.   The Roman government ought neither to have looked on at such horrors, of which its officers shared the guilt, nor to have tolerated that one of its vassals should make war on another.   Nevertheless the governor of Cappadocia, Julius Paelignus, acknowledged the new king of Armenia.   Even in the council of the governor of Syria, Ummidius Quadratus, the opinion preponderated that it might be matter of indifference to the Romans whether the uncle or the nephew ruled Armenia ; the legate, sent to Armenia with a legion, received only instructions to maintain the *status quo* till further orders.   Then the Parthian king, on the assumption that the Roman government would not be zealous to take part for king Rhadamistus, deemed the moment a fit one for resuming his old claims upon Armenia.   He invested his brother Tiridates with Armenia, and the Parthian troops marching in possessed themselves, almost without striking a blow, of the two capitals, Tigranocerta and Artaxata, and of the whole land.   When Rhadamistus made an attempt to retain the price of his deeds of blood, the Armenians themselves drove him out of the land.   The Roman garrison appears

---

[1] Gorneae, called by the Armenians *Garhni,* as the ruins (nearly east of   Erivân) are still at present named. (Kiepert.)

to have left Armenia after the giving over of Gorneae ; the governor recalled the legion put upon the march from Syria, in order not to fall into conflict with the Parthians.

When this news came to Rome (at the end of 54) the emperor Claudius had just died, and the ministers Burrus and Seneca practically governed for his young successor, seventeen years old. The procedure of Vologasus could only be answered by a declaration of war. In fact the Roman government sent to Cappadocia, which otherwise was a governorship of the second rank and was not furnished with legions, by way of exception the consular legate Gnaeus Domitius Corbulo. He had come rapidly into prominence as brother-in-law of the emperor Gaius, had then under Claudius been legate of lower Germany in the year 47 (I. 125), and was thenceforth regarded as one of the able commanders, not at that time numerous, who energetically maintained the stringency of discipline—in person a Herculean figure, equal to any fatigue, and of unshrinking courage in presence not of the enemy merely but also of his own soldiers. It appeared to be a sign of things becoming better that the government of Nero gave to him the first important command which it had to fill. The incapable Syrian legate of Syria, Quadratus, was not recalled, but was directed to put two of his four legions at the disposal of the governor of the neighbouring province. All the legions were brought up to the Euphrates, and orders were given for the immediate throwing of bridges over the stream. The two regions bordering immediately on Armenia to the westward, Lesser Armenia and Sophene, were assigned to two trustworthy Syrian princes, Aristobulus, of a lateral branch of the Herodian house, and Sohaemus, of the ruling family of Hemesa, and both were placed under Corbulo's command. Agrippa, the king of the remnant of the Jewish state still left at that time, and Antiochus, king of Commagene, likewise received orders to march.

At first, however, no fighting took place. The reason

lay partly in the state of the Syrian legions ; it was a
bad testimonial of poverty for the previous administration,
that Corbulo was compelled to describe the troops assigned
to him as quite unserviceable.   The legions levied and
doing garrison duty in the Greek provinces had always
been inferior to the Occidentals ; now the enervating
power of the East with the long state of peace and the
laxity of discipline completely demoralised them.   The
soldiers abode more in the towns than in the camps ; not
a few of them were unaccustomed to carry arms, and
knew nothing of pitching camps and of service on the
watch ; the regiments were far from having their full
complement and contained numerous old and useless
men ; Corbulo had, in the first instance, to dismiss a
great number of soldiers, and to levy and train recruits
in still larger numbers.   The exchange of the comfortable
winter quarters on the Orontes for those in the rugged
mountains of Armenia, and the sudden introduction of
inexorably stern discipline in the camp, brought about
various ailments and occasioned numerous desertions.
In spite of all this the general found himself, when
matters became serious, compelled to ask that one of the
better legions of the West might be sent to him.   Under
these circumstances he was in no haste to bring his
soldiers to face the enemy ; nevertheless it was political
considerations that preponderantly influenced him in this
course.

If it had been the design of the Roman government
to drive out the Parthian ruler at once from Armenia,
and to put in his place not indeed Rhadamistus, with
whose blood-guiltiness the Romans had no occasion to
stain themselves, but some other prince of their choice,
the military resources of Corbulo would probably have at
once sufficed, since king Vologasus, once more recalled
by internal troubles, had led away his troops from
Armenia.   But this was not embraced in the plan of
the Romans ; they wished, on the contrary, rather to
acquiesce in the government of Tiridates there, and only
to induce and, in case of need, compel him to an acknow-

ledgment of the Roman supremacy ; only for this object
were the legions, in case of extremity, to march.   This in
reality came very near to the cession of Armenia to the
Parthians.   What told in favour of this course, and what
prevented it, has formerly been set forth (p. 34 f.).   If Armenia were now arranged as a Parthian appanage for
a second son, the recognition of the Roman suzerainty
was little more than a formality, strictly taken, nothing
but a screen for military and political honour.   Thus the
government of the earlier period of Nero, which, as is well
known, was equalled by few in insight and energy, intended to get rid of Armenia in a decorous way ; and
that need not surprise us.   In fact they were in this case
pouring water into a sieve.   The possession of Armenia
had doubtless been asserted and brought to recognition
within the land itself, as among the Parthians, through
Tiberius in the year 20 B.C., then by Gaius in the year 2,
by Germanicus in the year 18, and by Vitellius in the
year 36.   But it was just these extraordinary expeditions
regularly repeated and regularly crowned with success,
and yet never attaining to permanent effect, that justified
the Parthians, when in the negotiations with Nero they
maintained that the Roman suzerainty over Armenia was
an empty name—that the land was, and could be, none
other than Parthian.   For the vindication of the Roman
supreme authority there was always needed, if not the
waging of war, at least the threat of it ; and the constant
irritation thereby produced made a lasting state of peace
between the two neighbouring great powers impossible.
The Romans had, if they were to act consistently, only
the choice between either bringing Armenia and the left
bank of the Euphrates in general effectively under their
power by setting aside the mere mediate government, or
leaving the matter to the Parthians, so far as was compatible with the supreme principle of the Roman government to acknowledge no frontier-power with equal rights.
Augustus and the rulers after him had so far decidedly
declined the former alternative, and they ought therefore
to have taken the second course.   But this too they had

at least attempted to decline, and had wished to exclude the Parthian royal house from the rule over Armenia, without being able to do so. This the leading statesmen of the earlier Neronian period must have regarded as an error, since they left Armenia to the Arsacids, and restricted themselves to the smallest conceivable measure of rights thereto. When the dangers and the disadvantages, which the retention of this region only externally attached to the empire brought to the state, were weighed against those which the Parthian rule over Armenia involved for the Romans, the decision might, especially in view of the small offensive power of the Parthian kingdom, well be found in the latter sense. But under all the circumstances this policy was consistent, and sought to attain in a clearer and more rational way the aim pursued by Augustus.

Negotiations with Vologasus.

From this standpoint we understand why Corbulo and Quadratus, instead of crossing the Euphrates, entered into negotiations with Vologasus ; and not less why the latter, informed doubtless of the real designs of the Romans, agreed to submit to the Romans in a similar way with his predecessor, and to deliver to them as a pledge of peace a number of hostages closely connected with the royal house. The return tacitly agreed on for this was that the rule of Tiridates over Armenia should be tolerated, and that a Roman pretender should not be set up. So some years passed in a *de facto* state of peace. But when Vologasus and Tiridates did not agree to apply to the Roman government for the investing of the latter with Armenia,[1] Corbulo took the offensive against Tiridates in the year 58. The very policy of withdrawal and concession, if it was not to appear to friend and foe as weakness, needed a foil, and so either a formal and solemn recognition of the Roman supremacy or, better still, a victory won by arms.

---

[1] Even after the attack Tiridates complained *cur datis nuper obsidibus redintegrataque amicitia . . . vetere Armeniae possessione depelleretur,* and Corbulo presented to him, in case of his turning as a suppliant to the emperor, the prospect of a *regnum stabile* (Tacitus, *Ann.* xii. 37). Elsewhere too the refusal of the oath of fealty is indicated as the proper ground of war (Tacitus, *Ann.* xii. 34).

In the summer of the year 58 Corbulo led an army, Corbulo in Armenia.
tolerably fit for fighting, of at least 30,000 men, over the
Euphrates.   The reoganisation and the hardening of the
troops were completed by the campaign itself, and the
first winter-quarters were taken up on Armenian soil.   In
the spring of 59[1] he began the advance in the direction
of Artaxata.   At the same time Armenia was invaded
from the north by the Iberians, whose king Pharasmanes,
to cover his own crimes, had caused his son Rhadamistus
to be executed, and now further endeavoured by good
services to make his guilt be forgotten ; and not less by
their neighbours to the north-west, the brave Moschi, and
on the south by Antiochus, king of Commagene.   King
Vologasus was detained by the revolt of the Hyrcanians
on the opposite side of the kingdom, and could or would
not interfere directly in the struggle.   Tiridates offered
a courageous resistance, but he could do nothing against
the crushing superiority of force.   In vain he sought to
throw himself on the lines of communication of the
Romans, who obtained their necessary supplies by way
of the Black Sea and the port of Trapezus.   The strongholds of Armenia fell under the attacks of the Roman
assailants, and the garrisons were cut down to the last
man.   Defeated in a pitched battle under the walls of
Artaxata, Tiridates gave up the unequal struggle, and
went to the Parthians.   Artaxata surrendered, and here,
in the heart of Armenia, the Roman army passed the

---

[1] The report in Tacitus, *Ann.* xiii.
34-41, embraces beyond doubt the
campaigns of 58 and 59, since Tacitus under the year 59 is silent as to
the Armenian campaign, while under
the year 60, *Ann.* xiv. 23 joins on
immediately to xiii. 41, and evidently
describes merely a single campaign ;
generally, where he condenses in this
way, he as a rule anticipates.   That
the war cannot have begun only in 59,
is further confirmed by the fact that
Corbulo observed the solar eclipse of
30th April 59 on Armenian soil (Plin.
H. N. ii. 70, 180); had he not entered the country till 59, he could
hardly have crossed the enemy's frontier so early in the year.   The narrative of Tacitus, *Ann.* xiii. 34-41, does
not in itself show an intercalation of a
year, but with his mode of narrating it
admits the possibility that the first
year was spent in the crossing of the
Euphrates and the settling in Armenia, and so the winter mentioned
in *c.* 35 is that of the year 58-9, especially as in view of the character of
the army such a beginning to the war
would be quite in place, and in view
of the short Armenian summer it was
militarily convenient thus to separate
the marching into the country and
the conduct proper of the war.

winter. In the spring of 60 Corbulo broke up from thence, after having burnt down the town, and marched right across the country to its second capital Tigranocerta, above Nisibis, in the basin of the Tigris. The terrors of the destruction of Artaxata preceded him ; serious resistance was nowhere offered ; even Tigranocerta voluntarily opened its gates to the victor, who here in a well-calculated way allowed mercy to prevail. Tiridates still made an attempt to return and to resume the struggle, but was repulsed without special exertion. At the close of the summer of 60 all Armenia was subdued, and stood at the disposal of the Roman government.

Tigranes, king of Armenia.

It is intelligible that people in Rome now put Tiridates out of account. The prince Tigranes, a great-grandson on the father's side of Herod the Great, on the mother's of king Archelaus of Cappadocia, related also to the old Marenian royal house on the female side, and a nephew of one of the ephemeral rulers of Armenia in the last years of Augustus, brought up in Rome, and entirely a tool of the Roman government, was now (60) invested by Nero with the kingdom of Armenia, and at the emperor's command installed by Corbulo in its rule. In the country there was left a Roman garrison, 1000 legionaries, and from 3000 to 4000 cavalry and infantry of auxiliaries. A portion of the border land was separated from Armenia and distributed among the neighbouring kings, Polemon of Pontus and Trapezus, Aristobulus of Lesser Armenia, Pharasmanes of Iberia and Antiochus of Commagene. On the other hand the new master of Armenia advanced, of course with consent of the Romans, into the adjacent Parthian province of Adiabene, defeated Monobazus the governor there, and appeared desirous of wresting this region also from the Parthian state.

Negotiations with the Parthians.

This turn of affairs compelled the Parthian government to emerge from its passiveness ; the question now concerned no longer the recovery of Armenia, but the integrity of the Parthian empire. The long-threatened collision between the two great states seemed inevitable. Vologasus in an assembly of the grandees of the empire

confirmed Tiridates afresh as king of Armenia, and sent
with him the general Monaeses against the Roman usurper
of the land, who was besieged by the Parthians in Tigranocerta, which the Roman troops kept in their possession.   Vologasus in person collected the Parthian main
force in Mesopotamia, and threatened (at the beginning
of 61) Syria.   Corbulo, who, after Quadratus's death, held
the command for a time in Cappadocia as in Syria, but
had besought from the government the nomination of
another governor for Cappadocia and Armenia, sent provisionally two legions to Armenia to lend help to Tigranes,
while he in person moved to the Euphrates in order to
receive the Parthian king.   Again, however, they came
not to blows, but to an agreement.   Vologasus, well
knowing how dangerous was the game which he was
beginning, declared himself now ready to enter into the
terms vainly offered by the Romans before the outbreak
of the Armenian war, and to allow the investiture of his
brother by the Roman emperor.   Corbulo entered into the
proposal.   He let Tigranes drop, withdrew the Roman
troops from Armenia, and acquiesced in Tiridates establish-
ing himself there, while the Parthian auxiliary troops likewise withdrew ; on the other hand, Vologasus sent an
embassy to the Roman government, and declared the
readiness of his brother to take the land in fee from
Rome.

These measures of Corbulo were of a hazardous kind,[1] The Par-
and led to a bad complication.   The Roman general may thian war
possibly have been, still more thoroughly than the states- under Nero.
men in Rome, impressed by the uselessness of retaining
Armenia ; but, after the Roman government had installed
Tigranes as king of Armenia, he could not of his own
accord fall back upon the conditions earlier laid down,
least of all abandon his own acquisitions and withdraw the
Roman troops from Armenia.   He was the less entitled
to do so, as he administered Cappadocia and Armenia

---

[1] From the representation of Taci-   does not venture to express the sur-
tus, *Ann.* xv. 6, the partiality and   render of Armenia to Tiridates, and
the perplexity are clearly seen.   He   only leaves the reader to infer it.

merely *ad interim*, and had himself declared to the government that he was not in a position to exercise the command at once there and in Syria ; whereupon the consular Lucius Caesennius Paetus was nominated as governor of Cappadocia and was already on the way thither. The suspicion can hardly be avoided that Corbulo grudged the latter the honour of the final subjugation of Armenia, and wished before his arrival to establish a definitive solution by the actual conclusion of peace with the Parthians. The Roman government accordingly declined the proposals of Vologasus and insisted on the retention of Armenia, which, as the new governor who arrived in Cappadocia in the course of the summer of 61 declared, was even to be taken under direct Roman administration. Whether the Roman government had really resolved to go so far cannot be ascertained ; but this was at all events implied in the consistent following out of their policy. The installing of a king dependent on Rome was only a prolongation of the previous untenable state of things ; whoever did not wish the cession of Armenia to the Parthians had to contemplate the conversion of the kingdom into a Roman province. The war therefore took its course ; and on that account one of the Moesian legions was sent to the Cappadocian army.

Measures of Paetus. When Paetus arrived, the two legions assigned to him by Corbulo were encamped on this side of the Euphrates in Cappadocia ; Armenia was evacuated, and had to be reconquered. Paetus set at once to work, crossed the Euphrates at Melitene (Malatia), advanced into Armenia, and reduced the nearest strongholds on the border. The advanced season of the year, however, compelled him soon to suspend operations and to abandon for this year the intended reoccupation of Tigranocerta ; nevertheless, in order to resume his march at once next spring, he, after Corbulo's example, took up his winter-quarters in the enemy's country at Rhandeia, on a tributary of the Euphrates, the Arsanias, not far from the modern Charput, while the baggage and the women and children had quarters not far from it in the strong fortress of Arsamosata. But he had

underrated the difficulty of the undertaking. One, and
that the best of his legions, the Moesian, was still on the
march, and spent the winter on this side of the Euphrates
in the territory of Pontus ; the two others were not those
whom Corbulo had taught to fight and conquer, but the
former Syrian legions of Quadratus, not having their full
complement, and hardly capable of use without thorough
reorganisation. He had withal to confront not, like Corbulo, the Armenians alone, but the main body of the
Parthians ; Vologasus had, when the war became in earnest, led the flower of his troops from Mesopotamia to
Armenia, and judiciously availed himself of the strategical
advantage that he commanded the inner and shorter lines.
Corbulo might, especially as he had bridged over the
Euphrates and constructed *tetes de pont* on the other bank,
have at least hampered, or at any rate requited this marching off by a seasonable incursion into Mesopotamia ; but
he did not stir from his positions and he left it to Paetus
to defend himself, as best he could, against the whole
force of his foes. The latter was neither himself military
nor ready to accept and follow military advice, not even
a man of resolute character; arrogant and boastful in onset,
despairing and pusillanimous in presence of misfortune.

Thus there came what could not but come. In the
spring of 62 it was not Paetus who assumed the aggressive, but Vologasus ; the advanced troops who were to
bar the way of the Parthians were crushed by the superior
force ; the attack was soon converted into a siege of the
Roman positions pitched far apart in the winter camp and
the fortress. The legions could neither advance nor
retreat ; the soldiers deserted in masses ; the only hope
rested on Corbulo's legions lying inactive far off in northern Syria, beyond doubt at Zeugma. Both generals
shared in the blame of the disaster: Corbulo on account of
the lateness of his starting to render help,[1] although, when

Capitulation of Rhandeia.

---

[1] This is said by Tacitus himself,
Ann. xv. 10: *nec a Corbulone pro-
peratum, quo gliscentibus periculis
etiam subsidii laus augeretur,* in naive
unconcern at the severe censure which
this praise involves. How partial is
the tone of the whole account resting
on Corbulo's despatches, is shown
among other things by the circumstance that Paetus is reproached in

he did recognise the whole extent of the danger, he hastened his march as much as possible ; Paetus, because he could not take the bold resolution to perish rather than to surrender, and thereby lost the chance of rescue that was near—in three days longer the 5000 men whom Corbulo was leading up would have brought the longed-for help. The conditions of the capitulation were free retreat for the Romans and evacuation of Armenia, with the delivering up of all fortresses occupied by them, and of all the stores that were in their hands, of which the Parthians were urgently in need. On the other hand Vologasus declared himself ready, in spite of this military success, to ask Armenia as a Roman fief for his brother from the imperial government, and on that account to send envoys to Nero.[1] The moderation of the victor may have rested on the fact that he had better information of Corbulo's approach than the enclosed army ; but more probably the sagacious man was not concerned to renew the disaster of Crassus and bring Roman eagles again to Ctesiphon. The defeat of a Roman army—he knew— was not the overpowering of Rome ; and the real concession, which was involved in the recognition of Tiridates, was not too dearly purchased by the compliance as to form.

Conclusion of peace.

The Roman government once more declined the offer of the Parthian king and ordered the continuance of the war. It could not well do otherwise ; if the recognition of Tiridates was hazardous before the recommencement of war, and hardly capable of being accepted after the Parthian declaration of war, it now, as a consequence of the capitulation of Rhandeia, appeared directly as its

---

one breath with the inadequate provisioning of the camp (xv. 8) and with the surrender of it in spite of copious supplies (xv. 16), and the latter fact is inferred from this, that the retiring Romans preferred to destroy the stores which, according to the capitulation, were to be delivered to the Parthians. As the exasperation against Tiberius found its expression in the painting of Germanicus in fine colours, so did the exas-

peration against Nero in the picture of Corbulo.

[1] The statement of Corbulo that Paetus bound himself on oath in presence of his soldiers and of the Parthian deputies to send no troops to Armenia till the arrival of Nero's answer, is declared by Tacitus, *Ann.* xv. 16, unworthy of credit ; it is in keeping with the state of the case, and nothing was done to the contrary.

ratification.   From Rome the resumption of the struggle against the Parthians was energetically promoted.   Paetus was recalled ; Corbulo, in whom public opinion, aroused by the disgraceful capitulation, saw only the conqueror of Armenia, and whom even those who knew exactly and judged sharply the state of the matter could not avoid characterising as the ablest general and one uniquely fitted for this war, took up again the governorship of Cappadocia, and at the same time the command over all the troops available for this campaign, who were further reinforced by a seventh legion brought up from Pannonia ; accordingly all the governors and princes of the East were directed to comply in military matters with his orders, so that his official authority was nearly equivalent to that which had been assigned to the crown-princes Gaius and Germanicus for their missions to the East. If these measures were intended to bring about a serious reparation of the honour of the Roman arms they missed their aim.   How Corbulo looked at the state of affairs, is shown by the very agreement which he made with the Parthian king not long after the disaster of Rhandeia ; the latter withdrew the Parthian garrisons from Armenia, the Romans evacuated the fortresses constructed on Mesopotamian territory for the protection of the bridges. For the Roman offensive the Parthian garrisons in Armenia were just as indifferent as the bridges of the Euphrates were important ; whereas, if Tiridates was to be recognised as a Roman vassal-king in Armenia, the latter certainly were superfluous and Parthian garrisons in Armenia impossible.   In the next spring (63) Corbulo certainly entered upon the offensive enjoined upon him, and led the four best of his legions at Melitene over the Euphrates against the Partho-Armenian main force stationed in the region of Arsamosata.   But not much came of the fighting ; only some castles of Armenian nobles opposed to Rome were destroyed.   On the other hand, this encounter led also to agreement.   Corbulo took up the Parthian proposals formerly rejected by his government, and that, as the further course of things

showed, in the sense that Armenia became once for all
a Parthian appanage for the second son, and the Roman
government, at least according to the spirit of the
agreement, consented to bestow this crown in future
only on an Arsacid. It was only added that Tiridates
should oblige himself to take from his head the royal
diadem publicly before the eyes of the two armies in
Rhandeia, just where the capitulation had been concluded,
and to deposit it before the effigy of the emperor, promising
not to put it on again until he should have received it
from his hand, and that in Rome itself. This was done
(63). By this humiliation there was no change in the
fact that the Roman general, instead of waging the war
intrusted to him, concluded peace on the terms rejected
by his government.[1] But the statesmen who formerly
took the lead had meanwhile died or retired, the personal
government of the emperor was installed in their stead,
and the solemn act in Rhandeia and the spectacle in
prospect of the investiture of the Parthian prince with
the crown of Armenia in the capital of the empire failed
not to produce their effect on the public, and above all

Tiridates in Rome. on the emperor in person. The peace was ratified and
fulfilled. In the year 66 the Parthian prince appeared
according to promise in Rome, escorted by 3000 Parthian
horsemen, bringing as hostages the children of his three
brothers as well as those of Monobazus of Adiabene.
Falling on his knees he saluted his liege lord seated on
the imperial throne in the market-place of the capital,
and here the latter in presence of all the people bound
the royal chaplet round his brow.

The East under the Flavians. The conduct on both sides, cautious, and we might

[1] As, according to Tacitus, *Ann.*
xv. 25 (comp. Dio, lxii. 22), Nero
dismissed graciously the envoys of
Vologasus, and allowed them to see
the possibility of an understanding if
Tiridates appeared in person, Corbulo
may in this case have acted according to his instructions; but this was
rather perhaps one of the turns added
in the interest of Corbulo. That
these events were brought under discussion in the trial to which he was
subjected some years after, is probable
from the statement that one of the
officers of the Armenian campaign
became his accuser. The identity
of the cohort-prefect, Arrius Varus,
in Tacitus, *Ann.* xiii. 9, and of the
primipilus, *Hist.* iii. 6, has been
without reason disputed; comp. on
C. I. L. v. 867.

almost say peaceful, of the last nominally ten years' war, and its corresponding conclusion by the actual transfer of Armenia to the Parthians, while the susceptibilities of the mightier western empire were spared, bore good fruit. Armenia, under the national dynasty recognised by the Romans, was more dependent on them than formerly under the rulers forced upon the country. A Roman garrison was left at least in the district of Sophene, which most closely bordered on the Euphrates.[1] For the re-establishment of Artaxata the permission of the emperor was sought and granted, and the building was helped on by the emperor Nero with money and workmen. Between the two mighty states separated from each other by the Euphrates at no time has an equally good relation subsisted as after the conclusion of the treaty of Rhandeia in the last years of Nero and onward under the three rulers of the Flavian house. Other circumstances contributed to this. The masses of Transcaucasian peoples, perhaps allured by their participation in the last wars, during which they had found their way to Armenia as mercenaries, partly of the Iberians, partly of the Parthians, began then to threaten especially the western Parthian provinces, but at the same time the eastern provinces of the Roman empire. Probably in order to check them, immediately after the Armenian war in the year 63, the annexation was ordained of the so-called kingdom of Pontus, *i.e.* the south-east corner of the coast of the Black Sea, with the town of Trapezus and the region of the Phasis. The great Oriental expedition, which this emperor was just on the point of beginning when the catastrophe overtook him (68), and for which he already had put the flower of the troops of the West on the march, partly to Egypt, partly along the Danube, was meant no doubt to push forward the imperial frontier in other directions ;[2] but its proper aim was the passes of the

---

1 In Ziata (Charput) there have been found two inscriptions of a fort, which one of the legions led by Corbulo over the Euphrates, the 3d Gallica, constructed there by Cor-

bulo's orders in the year 64 (*Eph. epigr.* v. p. 25).

2 Nero intended *inter reliqua bella*, an Ethiopian one (Plin. vi. 29, comp. 184). To this the sending

Caucasus above Tiflis, and the Scythian tribes settled on the northern slope, in the first instance the Alani.[1] These were just assailing Armenia on the one side and Media on the other. So little was that expedition of Nero directed against the Parthians that it might rather be conceived of as undertaken to help them ; overagainst the wild hordes of the north a common defensive action was at any rate indicated for the two civilised states of the West and East. Vologasus indeed declined with equal friendliness the amicable summons of his Roman colleague to visit him, just as his brother had done, at Rome, since he had no liking on his part to appear in the Roman forum as a vassal of the Roman ruler ; but he declared himself ready to present himself before the emperor when he should arrive in the East, and the Orientals doubtless, though not the Romans, sincerely mourned for Nero. King Vologasus addressed to the senate officially an entreaty to hold Nero's memory in honour, and, when a pseudo-Nero subsequently emerged, he met with sympathy above all in the Parthian state.

Arrangements of Vespasian.

Nevertheless the Parthian was not so much concerned about the friendship of Nero as about that of the Roman

of troops to Alexandria (Tacitus, *Hist.* i. 31, 70) had reference.

[1] As the aim of the expedition both Tacitus, *Hist.* i. 6, and Suetonius, *Ner.* 19, indicate the Caspian gates, *i.e.* the pass of the Caucasus between Tiflis and Vladi-Kavkas at Darial, which, according to the legend, Alexander closed with iron gates (Plin. *H. N.* vi. 11, 30; Josephus, *Bell. Jud.* vii. 7, 4 ; Procopius, *Pers.* i. 10). Both from this locality and from the whole scheme of the expedition it cannot possibly have been directed against the Albani on the western shore of the Caspian Sea ; here, as well as at another passage (*Ann.* ii. 68, *ad Armenios, inde Albanos Heniochosque*), only the Alani can be meant, who in Josephus, *l. c.* and elsewhere appear just at this spot and are frequently confounded with the Caucasian Albani. No doubt the account of Josephus is also confused. If here the Albani, with consent of the king of the Hyrcanians, invade Media and then Armenia through the Caspian gates, the writer has been thinking of the other Caspian gate eastward from Rhagae ; but this must be his mistake, since the latter pass, situated in the heart of the Parthian kingdom, cannot possibly have been the aim of the Neronian expedition, and the Alani had their seats not on the eastern shore of the Caspian but to the north of the Caucasus. On account of this expedition the best of the Roman legions, the 14th, was recalled from Britain, although it went only as far as Pannonia (Tacitus, *Hist.* ii. 11, comp. 27, 66), and a new legion, the 1st Italic, was formed by Nero (Suetonius, *Ner.* 19). One sees from this what was the scale on which the project was conceived.

state. Not merely did he refrain from any encroachment during the crises of the four-emperor-year,[1] but correctly estimating the probable result of the pending decisive struggle, he offered to Vespasian, when still in Alexandria, 40,000 mounted archers for the conflict with Vitellius, which, of course, was gratefully declined. But above all he submitted without more ado to the arrangements which the new government made for the protection of the east frontier. Vespasian had himself as governor of Judaea become acquainted with the inadequacy of the military resources statedly employed there ; and, when he exchanged this governorship for the imperial power, not only was Commagene again converted, after the precedent of Tiberius, from a kingdom into a province, but the number of the standing legions in Roman Asia was raised from four to seven, to which number they had been temporarily brought up for the Parthian and again for the Jewish war. While, further, there had been hitherto in Asia only a single larger military command, that of the governor of Syria, three such posts of high command were now instituted there. Syria, to which Commagene was added, retained as hitherto four legions ; the two provinces hitherto occupied only by troops of the second order, Palestine and Cappadocia, were furnished, the first with one the second with two legions.[2] Armenia remained a Roman dependent principality in possession

---

[1] In what connection he refused to Vespasian the title of emperor (Dio, lxvi. 11) is not clear ; possibly immediately after his insurrection, before he had perceived that the Flavians were the stronger. His intercession for the princes of Commagene (Josephus, *Bell. Jud.* vii. 7, 3) was attended with success, and so was purely personal, by no means a protest against the conversion of the kingdom into a province.

[2] The four Syrian legions were the 3d *Gallica*, the 6th *ferrata* (both hitherto in Syria), the 4th *Scythica* (hitherto in Moesia, but having already taken part in the Parthian as in the Jewish war), and the 16th *Flavia* (new). The one legion of Palestine was the 10th *fretensis* (hitherto in Syria). The two of Cappadocia were the 12th *fulminata* (hitherto in Syria, moved by Titus to Melitene, Josephus, *Bell. Jud.* vii. 1, 3), and the 15th *Apollinaris* (hitherto in Pannonia, but having taken part, like the 4th *Scythica*, in the Parthian as in the Jewish war). The garrisons were thus changed as little as possible, only two of the legions already called earlier to Syria received fixed stations there, and one newly instituted was moved thither. —After the Jewish war under Hadrian the 6th *ferrata* was despatched from Syria to Palestine.

of the Arsacids, but under Vespasian a Roman garrison was stationed beyond the Armenian frontier in the Iberian fortress Harmozika near Tiflis,[1] and accordingly at this time Armenia also must have been militarily in the Roman power.   All these measures, however little they contained even a threat of war, were pointed against the eastern neighbour.   Nevertheless Vologasus was after the fall of Jerusalem the first to offer to the Roman crown-prince his congratulations on the strengthening of the Roman rule in Syria, and he accepted without remonstrance the encampment of the legions in Commagene, Cappadocia, and Lesser Armenia.   Nay, he even once more incited Vespasian to that Transcaucasian expedition, and besought the sending of a Roman army against the Alani under the leadership of one of the imperial princes ; although Vespasian did not enter into this far-seeing plan, that Roman force can hardly have been sent into the region of Tiflis for any other object than for closing the pass of the Caucasus, and in so far it represented there also the interests of the Parthians.   In spite of the strengthening of the military position of Rome on the Euphrates, or even perhaps in consequence of it—for to instil respect into a neighbour is a means of preserving the peace—the state of peace remained essentially undisturbed during the whole rule of the Flavians.   If— as cannot be surprising, especially when we consider the constant change of the Parthian dynasts—collisions now and then occurred, and war-clouds even made their appearance, they disappeared again as quickly.[2]   The emergence of a pseudo-Nero in the last years of Vespasian—he it was who gave the impulse to the Revelation

---

[1] At this time (comp. *C. I. L.* v. 6988), probably falls also the Cappadocian governorship of C. Rutilius Gallicus, of which it is said (Statius, i. 4, 78) : *hunc . . . timuit . . . Armenia et patiens Latii iam pontis Araxes*, with reference presumably to a bridge-structure executed by this Roman garrison.   That Gallicus served under Corbulo, is

from the silence of Tacitus not probable.

[2] That war threatened to break out under Vespasian in the year 75 on the Euphrates, while M. Ulpius Trajanus, the father of the emperor, was governor of Syria, is stated by Pliny in his panegyric on the son, c. 14, probably with strong exaggeration ; the cause is unknown.

of John—might almost have led to such a collision. The pretender, in reality a certain Terentius Maximus from Asia Minor, but strikingly resembling the poet-emperor in face, voice, and address, found not merely a conflux of adherents in the Roman region of the Euphrates, but also support among the Parthians. Among these at that time, as so often, several rulers seem to have been in conflict with each other, and one of them, Artabanus, because the emperor Titus declared against him, seems to have adopted the cause of the Roman pretender. This, however, had no consequences ; on the contrary, soon afterwards the Parthian government delivered up the pretender to the emperor Domitian.[1] The commercial intercourse, advantageous for both parties between Syria and the lower Euphrates, where just then king Vologasus called into existence the new emporium Vologasias or Vologasocerta, not far from Ctesiphon, must have contributed its part towards promoting the state of peace.

Things came to a conflict under Trajan. In the earlier years of his government he had made no essential change in eastern affairs, apart from the conversion of the two client-states hitherto subsisting on the border of the Syrian desert—the Nabataean of Petra and the Jewish of Caesarea Paneas—into administrative districts directly Roman (A.D. 106). The relations with the ruler of the Parthian kingdom at that time, king Pacorus, were not the most friendly,[2] but it was only under his brother

The Parthian war of Trajan.

---

[1] There are coins dated, and provided with the individual names of the kings, of (V)ologasus from the years 389 and 390 = 77 - 78 ; of Pacorus from the years 389 - 394 = 77 - 82 (and again 404 - 407 = 92-95) ; of Artabanus from the year 392 = 80-1. The corresponding historical dates are lost, with the exception of the notice connecting Titus and Artabanus in Zonaras, xi. 18 (comp. Suetonius, *Ner.* 57 ; Tacitus, *Hist.* i. 2), but the coins point to an epoch of rapid changes on the throne, and, apparently, of simultaneous coinage by rival pretenders.

[2] This is proved by the detached notice from Arrian in Suidas (*s. v.* ἐπίκλημα) : ὁ δὲ Πάκορος ὁ Παρθυαίων βασιλεὺς καὶ ἄλλα τινὰ ἐπικλήματα ἐπέφερε Τραιανῷ τῷ βασιλεῖ, and by the attention which is devoted in Pliny's report to the emperor, written about the year 112 (*ad Trai.* 74), to the relations between Pacorus and the Dacian king Decebalus. The time of the reign of this Parthian king cannot be sufficiently fixed. There are no Parthian coins with the king's name from the whole period of Trajan ; the coining of silver seems to have been in abeyance during that period.

and successor Chosroes that a rupture took place, and that again concerning Armenia. The Parthians were to blame for it. When Trajan bestowed the vacated throne of the Armenian king on Axidares the son of Pacorus, he kept within the limits of his right ; but king Chosroes described this personage as incapable of governing, and arbitrarily installed in his stead another son of Pacorus, Parthomasiris, as king.[1] The answer to this was the Roman declaration of war. Trajan left the capital towards the end of the year 114,[2] to put himself at the head of the Roman troops of the East, which were certainly once more found in the deepest degeneracy, but were reorganised in all haste by the emperor, and reinforced besides by better legions brought up from Pannonia.[3]

[1] That Axidares (or Exedares) was a son of Pacorus and king of Armenia before Parthomasiris, but had been deposed by Chosroes, is shown by the remnants of Dio's account, lxviii. 17 ; and to this point also the two fragments of Arrian (16 Müller), the first, probably from an address of a supporter of the interests of Axidares to Trajan : Ἀξιδάρην δὲ ὅτι ἄρχειν χρὴ Ἀρμενίας, οὔ μοι δοκεῖ εἶναί σε ἀμφίλογον, whereupon doubtless the complaints brought against Parthomasiris followed ; and the answer, evidently of the emperor, that it is not the business of Axidares, but his, to judge as to Parthomasiris, because he—apparently Axidares—had first broken the treaty and suffered for it. What fault the emperor imputes to Axidares is not clear ; but in Dio also Chosroes says that he has not satisfied either the Romans or the Parthians.

[2] The remnants of Dio's account in Xiphilinus and Zonaras show clearly that the Parthian expedition falls into two campaigns, the first (Dio, lvi. 17, 1, 18, 2, 23 - 25), which is fixed at 115 A.D. by the consulate of Pedo (the date also of Malalas, p. 275, for the earthquake of Antioch, 13 Dec. 164 of the Antiochene era = 115 A.D. agrees therewith), and the second (Dio, c. 26-

32, 3), which is fixed at 116 A.D. by the conferring of the title *Parthicus* (c. 28, 2), took place between April and August of that year (see my notice in Droysen, *Hellenismus*, iii. 2, 361). That at c. 23 the titles *Optimus* (conferred in the course of 114 A.D.) and *Parthicus* are mentioned out of the order of time, is shown as well by their juxtaposition as by the later recurrence of the second honour. Of the fragments most belong to the first campaign ; c. 22, 3 and probably also 22, 1, 2 to the second. — The acclamations of *imperator* do not stand in the way. Trajan was demonstrably in the year 113 imp. VI. (*C. I. L.* vi. 960) ; in the year 114 imp. VII. (*C. I. L.* ix. 1558 *et al.*) ; in the year 115 imp. IX. (*C. I. L.* ix. 5894 *et al.*), and imp. XI. (Fabretti, 398, 289 *et al.*) ; in the year 116 imp. XII. (*C. I. L.* viii. 621, x. 1634), and XIII. (*C. I. L.* iii. D. xxvii.). Dio attests an acclamation from the year 115 (lxviii. 19), and one from the year 116 (lxviii. 28) ; there is ample room for both, and there is no reason to refer imp. VII. precisely, as has been attempted, to the subjugation of Armenia.

[3] The pungent description of the Syrian army of Trajan in Fronto (p. 206 f. Naber) agrees almost

Envoys of the Parthian king met him at Athens; but they had nothing to offer except the information that Parthomasiris was ready to accept Armenia as a Roman fief, and were dismissed. The war began. In the first conflicts on the Euphrates the Romans fared worst;[1] but when the old emperor, ready to fight and accustomed to victory, placed himself at the head of the troops in the spring of 115, the Orientals submitted to him almost without resistance. Moreover, among the Parthians civil war once more prevailed, and a pretender, Manisarus, had appeared against Chosroes. From Antioch the emperor marched to the Euphrates and farther northward as far as the most northerly legion-camp Satala in Lesser Armenia, whence he advanced into Armenia and took the direction of Artaxata. On the way Parthomasiris appeared in Elegeia and took the diadem from his head, in the hope of procuring investiture through this humiliation, as Tiridates had once done. But Trajan was resolved to make this vassal-state a province, and to shift the eastern frontier of the empire generally. This he declared to the Parthian prince before the assembled army, and directed him with his suite to quit at once the camp and the kingdom; thereupon a tumult took place, in which the pretender lost

---

literally with that of the army of Corbulo in Tacitus, *Ann.* xiii. 35. "The Roman troops generally had sadly degenerated (*ad ignaviam redactus*) through being long disused to military service; but the most wretched of the soldiers were the Syrian, insubordinate, refractory, unpunctual at the call to arms, not to be found at their post, drunk from midday onward; unaccustomed even to carry arms and incapable of fatigue, ridding themselves of one piece of armour after another, half naked like the light troops and the archers. Besides they were so demoralised by the defeats they had suffered that they turned their backs at the first sight of the Parthians, and the trumpets were regarded by them, as it were, as giving the signal to run away." In the contrasting description of Trajan it is said among other things: "He did not pass through the tents without closely concerning himself as to the soldiers, but showed his contempt for the Syrian luxury, and looked closely into the rough doings of the Pannonians (*sed contemnere*—so we must read—*Syrorum munditias, introspicere Pannoniorum inscitias*); so he judged of the serviceableness (*ingenium*) of the man according to his bearing (*cultus*)." In the Oriental army of Severus also the "European" and the Syrian soldiers are distinguished (Dio, lxxv. 12).

[1] This is shown by the *mala proelia* in the passage of Fronto quoted, and by Dio's statement, lxviii. 19, that Trajan took Samosata without a struggle; thus the 16th legion stationed there had lost it.

his life. Armenia yielded to its fate, and became a Roman governorship. The princes also of the Caucasian tribes, the Albani, the Iberi, farther on toward the Black Sea the Apsilae, the Colchi, the Heniochi, the Lazi, and various others, even those of the trans-Caucasian Sarmatae were confirmed in the relation of vassalage, or now subjected to it. Trajan thereupon advanced into the territory of the Parthians and occupied Mesopotamia. Here, too, all submitted without a blow ; Batnae, Nisibis, Singara came into the power of the Romans ; in Edessa the emperor received not merely the subjection of Abgarus, the ruler of the land, but also that of the other dynasts, and, like Armenia, Mesopotamia became a Roman province. Trajan took up once more his winter quarters in Antioch, where a violent earthquake demanded more victims than the campaign of the summer. In the next spring (116) Trajan, the "victor of the Parthians," as the senate now saluted him, advanced from Nisibis over the Tigris, and occupied, not without encountering resistance at the crossing and subsequently, the district of Adiabene ; this became the third new Roman province, named Assyria. The march went onward down the Tigris to Babylonia ; Seleucia and Ctesiphon fell into the hands of the Romans, and with them the golden throne of the king and his daughter ; Trajan reached even the Persian satrapy of Mesene, and the great mercantile town at the mouth of the Tigris, Charax Spasinu. This region also seems to have been incorporated with the empire in such a way that the new province Mesopotamia embraced the whole region enclosed by the two rivers.

Revolt of
Seleucia,
and its
siege.

Full of longing, Trajan is said now to have wished for himself the youth of Alexander, in order to carry from the margin of the Persian Sea his arms into the Indian land of marvels. But he soon learned that he needed them for nearer opponents. The great Parthian empire had hitherto scarcely confronted in earnest his attack, and ofttimes sued in vain for peace. But now on the way back at Babylon news reached the emperor of the revolt of Babylonia and Mesopotamia ; while he tarried at the mouth of the Tigris the whole population of these new provinces had risen against him ;[1] the citizens of Seleucia on the Tigris, of Nisibis, indeed of Edessa itself, put the Roman garrisons to death or chased them away and closed their gates. The emperor saw himself compelled to divide his troops, and to send separate corps against the different seats of the insurrection ; one of these legions under Maximus was, with its general, surrounded and cut to pieces in Mesopotamia. Yet the emperor mastered the insurgents, particularly through his general Lusius Quietus, already experienced in the Dacian war, a native sheikh of the Moors. Seleucia and Edessa were besieged and burnt down. Trajan went so far as to declare Parthia a Roman vassal-state, and invested with it at Ctesiphon a partisan of Rome, the Parthian Parthamaspates, although the Roman soldiers had not set foot on more than the western border of the great-kingdom.

Then he began his return to Syria by the route along which he had come, detained on the way by a vain attack on the Arabs in Hatra, the residence of the king of the brave tribes of the Mesopotamian desert, whose mighty works of fortification and magnificent buildings are still at the present day imposing in their ruins. He intended to continue the war next year, and so to make the subjection of the Parthians a reality. But the combat in the desert of Hatra, in which the sixty-year-old emperor had bravely fought with the Arab horsemen, was to be his last. He sickened and died on the journey home (8th Aug. 117), without being able to complete his victory and to hold

Death of Trajan.

---

[1] It may be that at the same time Armenia also revolted. But when Gutschmid (quoted by Dierauer in Büdinger's *Untersuchungen*, i. 179), makes Meherdotes and Sanatrukios, whom Malalas adduces as kings of Persia in the Trajanic war, into kings of Armenia again in revolt, this result is attained by a series of daring conjectures, which shift the names of persons and peoples as much as they transform the causal nexus of events. There are certainly found in the con-fused coil of legends of Malalas some historical facts, *e.g.* the installation of Parthamaspates (who is here son of king Chosroes of Armenia) as king of Parthia by Trajan ; and so, too, the dates of Trajan's departure from Rome in October (114), of his landing in Seleucia in December, and of his entrance into Antioch on the 7th Jan. (115) may be correct. But, as this report stands, the historian can only decline to accept it ; he cannot rectify it.

the celebration of it in Rome ; it was in keeping with his spirit that even after death the honour of a triumph was accorded to him, and hence he is the only one of the deified Roman emperors who even as god still bears the title of victory.

Trajan's Oriental policy.

Trajan had not sought war with the Parthians, but it had been forced upon him ; not he, but Chosroes had broken the agreement as to Armenia, which during the last forty years had been the basis of the state of peace in the region of the Euphrates. If it is intelligible that the Parthians did not acquiesce in it, since the continuing suzerainty of the Romans over Armenia carried in itself the stimulus to revolt, we must on the other hand acknowledge that in the way hitherto followed further steps could not be taken than were taken by Corbulo ; the unconditional renunciation of Armenia, and—which was the necessary consequence of it — the recognition of the Parthian state on a footing of full equality, lay indeed beyond the horizon of Roman policy as much as the abolition of slavery and similar ideas that could not be thought of at that time. But if permanent peace could not be attained by this alternative, there was left in the great dilemma of Roman Oriental policy only the other course—the extension of direct Roman rule to the left bank of the Euphrates. Therefore Armenia now became a Roman province, and no less Mesopotamia. This was only in keeping with the nature of the case. The conversion of Armenia from a Roman vassal-state with a Roman garrison into a Roman governorship made not much change externally ; the Parthians could only be effectively ejected from Armenia when they lost possession of the neighbouring region ; and above all, the Roman rule as well as the Roman provincial constitution found a far more favourable soil in the half-Greek Mesopotamia than in the thoroughly Oriental Armenia. Other considerations fell to be added. The Roman customs-frontier in Syria was badly constituted, and to get the international traffic from the great commercial marts of Syria towards the Euphrates and the Tigris entirely into its power was an essential gain to the Roman state, as indeed Trajan immediately set to work to institute the new customs-dues at the Euphrates and Tigris.[1] Even in a military point of view the boundary of the Tigris was easier of defence than the previous frontier-line which ran along the Syrian desert and thence along the Euphrates. The conversion of the region of Adiabene beyond the Tigris into a Roman province, whereby Armenia became an inland one, and the transformation of the Parthian empire itself into a Roman vassal-state were corollaries of the same idea. It is not meant to be denied that in a policy of conquest consistency is a dangerous praise, and that Trajan after his fashion yielded in these enterprises more than was reasonable to the effort after external success, and went beyond the rational goal;[2] but wrong is done to him when his demeanour in the East is referred to blind lust of conquest. He did what Caesar would have done had he lived. His policy is but the other side of that of Nero's statesmen, and the two are as opposite, as they are equally consistent and equally warranted. Posterity has justified more the policy of conquest than that of concession.

For the moment no doubt it was otherwise. The Oriental conquests of Trajan lit up the gloomy evening of the Roman empire like flashes of lightning in the darkness of the night ; but, like these, they brought no new morning. His successor found himself compelled to choose between completing the unfinished work of subduing the Parthians or allowing it to drop. The extension of the frontier could not be carried out at all without a considerable increase of the army and of the budget ; and the shifting of the centre of gravity to the East, thereby rendered inevitable, was a dubious strengthening of the empire. Hadrian and Pius therefore returned entirely

Reaction under Hadrian and Pius.

[1] Fronto, *Princ. hist.* p. 209 Naber : *cum praesens Traianus Euphratis et Tigridis portoria equorum et camelorum trib[utaque ordinaret, Ma]cer* (?) *caesus est.* This applies to the moment when Babylonia and Mesopotamia revolted, while Trajan was tarrying at the mouth of the Tigris.

[2] Nearly with equal warrant, Julian (*Caes.* p. 328) makes the emperor say that he had not taken up arms against the Parthians before they had violated right, and Dio (lxviii. 17) reproaches him with having waged the war from ambition.

into the paths of the earlier imperial period. Hadrian allowed the Roman vassal-king of Parthia, Parthamaspates, to drop, and portioned him off in another way. He evacuated Assyria and Mesopotamia, and voluntarily gave back these provinces to their earlier ruler. He sent to him as well his captive daughter ; the permanent token of the victory won, the golden throne of Ctesiphon, even the pacific Pius refused to deliver up again to the Parthians. Hadrian as well as Pius earnestly endeavoured to live in peace and friendship with their neighbour, and at no time do the commercial relations between the Roman entrepôts on the Syrian east frontier and the mercantile towns on the Euphrates seem to have been more lively than at this epoch.

Armenia a vassal-state. Armenia ceased likewise to be a Roman province, and returned to its former position as a Roman vassal-state and a Parthian appanage of the second son.[1] The princes of the Albani, and the Iberians on the Caucasus, and the numerous small dynasts in the south-eastern corner of the Black Sea likewise remained dependent.[2]

[1] Hadrian cannot possibly have released Armenia from the position of a Roman dependency. The notice of his biographer, c. 21 : *Armeniis regem habere permisit, cum sub Traiano legatum habuissent* points rather to the contrary, and we find at the end of Hadrian's reign a contingent of Armenians in the army of the governor of Cappadocia (Arrian. *c. Alan.* 29). Pius did not merely induce the Parthians by his representations to desist from the intended invasion of Armenia (*vita*, 9), but also in fact invested them with Armenia (coins from the years 140-144, Eckhel, vii. p. 15). The fact also that Iberia certainly stood in the relation of dependence under Pius, because otherwise the Parthians could not have brought complaints as to its king in Rome (Dio, lxix. 15), presupposes a like dependent relation for Armenia. The names of the Armenian kings of this period are not known. If the *proximae gentes*, with the rule of

which Hadrian compensated the Parthian prince nominated as Parthian king by Trajan (*vita*, c. 5), were in fact Armenians, which is not improbable, there lies in it a confirmation as well of the lasting dependence of Armenia on Rome as of the continuous rule of the Arsacids there. Even the Ἀυρήλιος Πάκορος βασιλεὺς μεγάλης Ἀρμενίας, who erected a monument in Rome to his brother Aurelius Merithates who died there (*C. I. Gr.* 6559), belongs from his name to the house of the Arsacids. But he was hardly the king of Armenia installed by Vologasus IV. and deposed by the Romans (p. 74) ; if the latter had come to Rome as a captive, we should know it, and even he would hardly have been allowed to call himself king of Great Armenia in a Roman inscription.

[2] As vassals holding from Trajan or Hadrian, Arrian (*Peripl.* c. 15) adduces the Heniochi and Machelones (comp. Dio, lxviii. 18 ; lxxi. 14) ; the Lazi (comp. Suidas, *s. v.* Δομετιανός),

Roman garrisons were stationed not merely on the coast in Apsarus[1] and on the Phasis, but, as can be shown, under Commodus in Armenia itself, not far from Artaxata ; in a military point of view all these states belonged to the district of the commandant of Cappadocia.[2] This supremacy, however, very indefinite in its nature, seems to have been dealt with generally, and in particular by Hadrian,[3] in such a way that it appeared more as a right of protection than as subjection proper, and at least the more powerful of these princes did, and left undone, in the main what pleased them. The common interest—which we have formerly brought out—in warding off the wild trans-Caucasian tribes became still more definitely prominent in this epoch, and evidently served as a bond in particular between Romans and Parthians. Towards the end of the reign of Hadrian the Alani, in agreement apparently with the king of Iberia, at that time Pharasmanes II., on whom it primarily devolved to bar the pass of the Caucasus against them, invaded the southern regions, and pillaged not only the territory of the Albanians and Armenians, but also the Parthian province of Media and the Roman province of Cappadocia, though matters did not come to a waging of war in common, but the gold of the ruler then reigning in Parthia, Vologasus III., and the mobilising of the Cappadocian army on the part of the Romans,[4]

over whom also Pius put a king (*vita*, 9) ; the Apsilae ; the Abasgi ; the Sanigae, these all within the imperial frontier reaching as far as Dioscurias = Sebastopolis ; beyond it, in the region of the Bosporan vassal-state, the Zichi or Zinchi (*ib.* c. 27).

[1] This is confirmed not only by Arrian, *Peripl.* c. 7, but by the officer of Hadrian's time *praepositus numerorum tendentium in Ponto Absaro* (*C. I. L.* x. 1202).

[2] Comp. p. 75 note 2. The detachment probably of 1000 men (because under a tribune) doing garrison duty in the year 185 in Valarshapat (Etshmiazin) not far from Artaxata, belonged to one of the Cappadocian legions (*C. I. L.* iii. 6052).

[3] Hadrian's efforts after the friendship of the Oriental vassal-princes are often brought into prominence, not without a hint that he was more than fairly indulgent to them (*vita*, c. 13, 17, 21). Pharasmanes of Iberia did not come to Rome on his invitation, but complied with that of Pius (*vita Hadr.* 13, 21 ; *vita Pii*, 9 ; Dio, lxix. 15, 2, which excerpt belongs to Pius).

[4] We still possess the remarkable report of the governor of Cappadocia under Hadrian, Flavius Arrianus, upon the mobilising of the Cappadocian army against the "Scythians" among his minor writings ; he was himself at the Caucasus and visited the passes there (Lydus, *de Mag.* iii. 53).

induced the barbarians to return, yet their interests coincided, and the complaint which the Parthians lodged in Rome as to Pharasmanes of Iberia, shows the concert of the two great powers.[1]

Parthian
war under
Marcus and
Verus.

The disturbances of the *status quo* came again from the Parthian side. The suzerainty of the Romans over Armenia played a part in history similar to that of the German empire over Italy ; unsubstantial as it was, it was yet constantly felt as an encroachment, and carried within it the danger of war. Already under Hadrian the conflict was imminent ; the emperor succeeded in keeping the peace by a personal interview with the Parthian prince. Under Pius the Parthian invasion of Armenia seemed once more impending; his earnest dissuasive was in the first instance successful. But even this most pacific of all emperors, who had it more at heart to save the life of a burgess than to kill a thousand foes, was obliged in the last period of his reign to prepare himself for the attack and to reinforce the armies of the East. Hardly had he closed his eyes (161), when the long-threatening thunder-cloud discharged itself. By command of Vologasus IV. the Persian general Chosroes[2] advanced into Armenia, and placed the Arsacid prince Pacorus on the throne. The governor of Cappadocia Severianus did what was his duty, and led on his part the Roman troops over the Euphrates. At Elegeia, just where a generation before the king Parthomasiris, likewise placed by the Parthians on the Armenian throne, had humbled himself in vain before Trajan, the armies encountered each other ; the Roman was not merely beaten but annihilated in a three days' conflict ; the unfortunate general put himself to death, as Varus had formerly done. The victorious Orientals were not content with the occupation of Armenia, but crossed

---

[1] This we learn from the fragments of Dio's account in Xiphilinus, Zonaras, and in the Excerpts ; Zonaras has preserved the correct reading 'Αλανοί instead of 'Αλβανοί ; that the Alani pillaged also the territory of the Albani, is shown by the setting of the exc. Ursin. lxxii.

[2] So he is named in Lucian, *Hist. conscr.* 21 ; if the same calls him (*Alex.* 27) Othryades, he is drawing here from a historian of the stamp of those whom he ridicules in that treatise, and of whom another Hellenised the same man as Oxyroes (*Hist. conscr.* c. 18).

the Euphrates and invaded Syria ; the army stationed there was also defeated, and there were fears as to the fidelity of the Syrians. The Roman government had no choice. As the troops of the East showed on this occasion their small capacity for fighting, and were besides weakened and demoralised by the defeat which they had suffered, further legions were despatched to the East from the West, even from the Rhine, and levies were ordered in Italy itself. Lucius Verus, one of the two emperors who shortly before had come to govern, went in person to the East (162) to take up the chief command, and if he, neither warlike nor yet even faithful to his duty, showed himself unequal to the task, and of his deeds in the East hardly anything else is to be told than that he married his niece there and was ridiculed for his theatrical enthusiasm even by the Antiochenes, the governors of Cappadocia and Syria—in the former case first Statius Priscus, then Martius Verus, in the latter Avidius Cassius,[1] the best generals of this epoch—managed the cause of Rome better than the wearer of the crown. Once more, before the armies met, the Romans offered peace ; willingly would Marcus have avoided the severe war. But Vologasus abruptly rejected the reasonable proposals ; and this time the pacific neighbour was also the stronger. Armenia was immediately recovered ; already, in the year 163, Priscus took the capital Artaxata, and destroyed it. Not far from it the new capital of the country, Kainepolis, in Armenia Nor-Khalakh or Valarshapat (Etshmiazin) was built by the Romans and provided with a strong garrison.[2] In the succeeding year instead of Pacorus

---

[1] Syria was administered when the war broke out by L. Attidius Cornelianus (*C. I. Gr.* 4661 of the year 160 ; *vita Marci*, 8 ; *C. I. L.* iii. 129 of the year 162), after him by Julius Verus (*C. I. L.* iii. 199, probably of the year 163) and then by Avidius Cassius presumably from the year 164. The statement that the other provinces of the East were assigned to Cassius's command (Philostratus, *vit. Soph.* i. 13 ; Dio, lxxi.

3), similarly to what was done to Corbulo as legate of Cappadocia, can only relate to the time after the departure of the emperor Verus ; so long as the latter held the nominal chief command there was no room for it.

[2] A fragment probably of Dio (in Suidas *s. v.* Μάρτιος), tells that Priscus in Armenia laid out the Καινὴ πόλις and furnished it with a Roman garrison, his successor Martius Verus

Sohaemus, by descent also an Arsacid, but a Roman subject and Roman senator, was nominated as king of Great Armenia.[1] In a legal point of view nothing was changed in Armenia ; yet the bonds which joined it to Rome were drawn tighter.

Conflicts in Syria and Mesopotamia.

The conflicts in Syria and Mesopotamia were more serious. The line of the Euphrates was obstinately defended by the Parthians ; after a keen combat on the right bank at Sura the fortress of Nicephorium (Ragga) on the left was stormed by the Romans. Still more vehemently was the passage at Zeugma contested; but here too victory remained with the Romans in the decisive battle at Europus (Djerabis to the south of Biredjik). They now advanced on their part into Mesopotamia. Edessa was besieged, Dausara not far from it stormed ; the Romans appeared before Nisibis ; the Parthian general saved himself by swimming over the Tigris. The Romans might from Mesopotamia undertake the march to Babylon. The satraps forsook in part the banners of the defeated

---

silenced the national movement that had arisen there, and declared this city the first of Armenia. This was Valarshapat (Οὐαλαρσαπάτ or Οὐαλερ-οκτίστη in Agathangelos) thenceforth the capital of Armenia. Καινή πόλις was, as Kiepert informs me, already recognised by Stilting as translation of the Armenian Nôr-Khalakh, which second name Valarshapat constantly bears in Armenian authors of the fifth century alongside of the usual one. Moses of Chorene, following Barde-sanes, makes the town originate from a Jewish colony brought thither under king Tigranes VI., who according to him reigned 150-188 ; he refers the enclosing of it with walls and the naming of it to his son Valarsch II. 188-208. That the town had a strong Roman garrison in 185 is shown by the inscription C. I. L. iii. 6052.

[1] That Sohaemus was Achaemenid and Arsacid (or professed to be) and king's son and king, as well as Roman senator and consul, before he became

king of Great Armenia, is stated by his contemporary Jamblichus (c. 10 of the extract in Photius). Probably he belonged to the dynastic family of Hemesa (Josephus, Arch. xx. 8, 4, et al.) If Jamblichus the Babylonian wrote " under him," this can doubt-less only be understood to the effect that he composed his romance in Artaxata. That Sohaemus ruled over Armenia before Pacorus is nowhere stated, and is not probable, since neither Fronto's words (p. 127 Naber), quod Sohaemo potius quam Vologaeso regnum Armeniae dedisset aut quod Pacorum regno privasset, or those of the fragment from Dio (?) lxxi. 1 : Μάρτιος Οὐῆρος τὸν Θουκυδίδην ἐκ-πέμπει καταγαγεῖν Σόαιμον ἐς Ἀρμενίαν point to reinstatement, and the coins with rex Armeniis datus (Eckhel, vii. 91, comp. vita Veri, 7, 8) in fact exclude it. We do not know the predecessor of Pacorus, and are not even aware whether the throne which he took possession of was vacant or occupied.

great-king ; Seleucia, the great capital of the Hellenes
on the Euphrates, voluntarily opened its gates to the
Romans, but was afterwards burnt down by them, because
the burgesses were rightly or wrongly accused of an
understanding with the enemy.   The Parthian capital,
Ctesiphon, was also taken and destroyed ; with good
reason at the beginning of the year 165 the senate could
salute the two rulers as the Parthian grand-victors.   In
the campaign of this year Cassius even penetrated into
Media ; but the outbreak of a pestilence, more especially
in these regions, decimated the troops and compelled
them to return, accelerating perhaps even the conclusion
of peace.   The result of the war was the cession of the
western district of Mesopotamia ; the princes of Edessa
and of Osrhoene became vassals of Rome, and the town
of Carrhae, which had for long Greek leanings, became
a free town under Roman protection.[1]   As regards extent,
especially in presence of the complete success of the war,
the increase of territory was moderate, but yet of importance, inasmuch as thereby the Romans gained a footing
on the left bank of the Euphrates.   We may add that
the territories occupied were given back to the Parthians
and the *status quo* was restored.   On the whole, therefore,
the policy of reserve adopted by Hadrian was now
abandoned once more, and there was a return to the
course of Trajan.   This is the more remarkable, as the
government of Marcus certainly cannot be reproached
with ambition and longing after aggrandisement ; what
it did it did under compulsion and in modest limits.

The emperor Severus pursued the same course further
and more decidedly.   The year of the three emperors,
193, had led to the war between the legions of the West
and those of the East, and with Pescennius Niger the
latter had succumbed.   The Roman vassal-princes of the
East, and as well the ruler of the Parthians, Vologasus V.,
son of Sanatrucius, had, as was natural, recognised Niger,
and even put their troops at his disposal ; the latter

Parthian wars under Severus.

---

[1] This is shown by the Mesopotamian royal and urban coins. There
are no accounts in our tradition as to
the conditions of peace.

had at first gratefully declined, and then, when his cause took a turn to the worse, invoked their aid. The other Roman vassals, above all the prince of Armenia, cautiously kept back ; only Abgarus, the prince of Edessa, sent the desired contingent. The Parthians promised aid, and it came at least from the nearest districts, from the prince Barsemias of Hatra in the Mesopotamian desert, and from the satrap of the Adiabeni beyond the Tigris. Even after Niger's death (194) these strangers not merely remained in the Roman Mesopotamia, but even demanded the withdrawal of the Roman garrisons stationed there and the giving back of this territory.[1]

Province of Meso-potamia.

Thereupon Severus advanced into Mesopotamia and took possession of the whole extensive and important region. From Nisibis an expedition was conducted against the Arab prince of Hatra, which, however, did not succeed in taking the fortified town ; even beyond the Tigris against the satrap of Adiabene the generals of Severus accomplished nothing of importance.[2] But Mesopotamia,

---

[1] The beginning of the Ursinian excerpt of Dio, lxxv. 1, 2, is confused. Οἱ Ὀρροηνοί, it is said, καὶ οἱ Ἀδιαβηνοὶ ἀποστάντες καὶ Νίσιβιν πολιορκοῦντες καὶ ἡττηθέντες ὑπὸ Σεουήρου ἐπρεσβεύσαντο πρὸς αὐτὸν μετὰ τὸν τοῦ Νίγρου θάνατον. Osrhoene was then Roman, Adiabene Parthian ; from whom did the two districts revolt ? and whose side did the Nisibenes take ? That their opponents were defeated by Severus before the sending of the embassy is inconsistent with the course of the narrative ; for the latter makes war upon them because their envoys make unsatisfactory offers to him. Probably the supporting of Niger by subjects of the Parthians and their concert with Niger's Roman partisan are now strictly apprehended as a revolt from Severus ; the circumstance that the people afterwards maintain that they had intended rather to support Severus, is clearly indicated as a makeshift. The Nisibenes may have refused to co-operate, and therefore have been attacked by the adherents of Niger. Thus is explained what is clear from the extract given by Xiphilinus from Dio, lxxv. 2, that the left bank of the Euphrates was for Severus an enemy's land, but not Nisibis ; therefore the town need not have been Roman at that time ; on the contrary, according to all indications, it was only made Roman by Severus.

[2] As the wars against the Arabians and the Adiabenians were in fact directed against the Parthians, it was natural that the titles *Parthicus*, *Arabicus*, and *Parthicus Adiabenicus*, should on that account be conferred on the emperor ; they are also so found, but usually Parthicus is omitted, evidently because, as the biographer of Severus says (c. 9), *excusavit Parthicum nomen, ne Parthos lacesseret*. With this agrees the notice certainly belonging to the year 195 in Dio, lxxv. 9, 6, as to the peaceful agreement with the Parthians and the cession of a portion of Armenia to them.

i.e. the whole region between the Euphrates and Tigris as far as the Chaboras, became a Roman province, and was occupied with two legions newly created on account of this extension of territory. The principality of Edessa continued to subsist as a Roman fief, but was now no longer border-territory but surrounded by land directly imperial. The considerable and strong city of Nisibis, thenceforth called after the name of the emperor and organised as a Roman colony, became the capital of the new province and seat of the governor. After an important portion of territory had thus been torn from the Parthian kingdom, and armed force had been used against two satraps dependent on it, the great-king made ready with his troops to oppose the Romans. Severus offered peace, and ceded for Mesopotamia a portion of Armenia. But the decision of arms was thereby only postponed. As soon as Severus had started for the West, whither the complication with his co-ruler in Gaul recalled him, the Parthians broke the peace[1] and advanced into Mesopotamia ; the prince of Osrhoene was driven out, the land was occupied, and the governor, Laetus, one of the most excellent warriors of the time, was besieged in Nisibis. He was in great danger, when Severus once more arrived in the East in the year 198, after Albinus had succumbed. Thereupon the fortune of war turned. The Parthians retreated, and now Severus took the offensive. He advanced into Babylonia, and won Seleucia and Ctesiphon ; the Parthian king saved himself with a few horsemen by flight, the crown-treasure became the spoil of the victors, the Parthian capital was abandoned to the pillage of the Roman soldiers, and more than 100,000 captives were brought to the Roman slave market. The Arabians indeed in Hatra defended themselves better than the Parthian state itself ; in vain Severus endeavoured in two severe sieges to reduce the desert-stronghold. But in the main the success of the two campaigns of 198 and 199 was complete. By the

[1] That Armenia also fell into their power is indicated by Herodian, v. 9, 2 ; no doubt his representation is warped and defective.

erection of the province of Mesopotamia and of the
great command there, Armenia lost the intermediate
position which it hitherto had; it might remain in its
previous relations and apart from formal incorporation.
The land retained thus its own troops, and the imperial
government even paid for these subsequently a contribution
from the imperial chest.[1]

The change of government in the West and in the East.   The further development of these relations as neighbours was essentially influenced by the changes which
internal order underwent in the two empires.   If under
the dynasty of Nerva, and not less under Severus, the
Parthian state, often torn asunder by civil war and
contention for the crown, had been confronted by the
relatively stable Roman monarchy as superior, this order
of things broke down after Severus's death, and almost
for a century there followed in the western empire mostly
wretched and thoroughly ephemeral regents, who in
presence of other countries were constantly hesitating
between arrogance and weakness.   While the scale of the
West thus sank that of the East rose.   A few years
after the death of Severus (211) a revolution took place
in Iran, which not merely, like so many earlier crises,
overthrew the ruling regent, nor even merely called to
the government another dynasty instead of the decayed
Arsacids, but, unchaining the national and religious
elements for a mightier upward flight, substituted for
the bastard civilisation—pervaded by Hellenism—of the
Parthian state the state-organisation, faith, manners, and
princes of that province which had created the old
Persian empire, and, since its transition to the Parthian

---

[1] When at the peace in 218 the old
relation between Rome and Armenia
was renewed, the king of Armenia
gave himself the prospect of a renewal
of the Roman annual moneys (Dio,
lxxviii. 27 : τοῦ Τιριδάτου τὸ ἀργύριον
ὃ κατ᾽ ἔτος παρὰ τῶν Ῥωμαίων
εὑρίσκετο ἐλπίσαντος λήψεσθαι). Payment of tribute proper by the Romans
to the Armenians is excluded for the
period of Severus and the time before
Severus, and by no means agrees

with the words of Dio ; the connection must be what we have indicated.
In the fourth and fifth centuries the
fortress of Biriparach in the Caucasus,
which barred the Dariel pass, was
maintained by the Persians, who
played the part of masters here after
the peace of 364, with a Roman
contribution, and this was likewise
conceived as payment of tribute
(Lydus, de Mag. iii. 52, 53 ; Priscus,
fr. 31, Müll.).

dynasty, preserved within it as well the tombs of Darius and Xerxes as the germs of the regeneration of the people. The re-establishment of the great-kingdom of the Persians overthrown by Alexander ensued through the emergence of the dynasty of the Sassanids. Let us cast a glance at this new shape of things before we pursue further the course of Romano-Parthian relations in the East.

It has already been stated that the Parthian dynasty, although it had wrested Iran from Hellenism, was yet regarded by the nation as, so to speak, illegitimate. Artahshatr, or in new Persian Ardashir—so the official biography of the Sassanids reports—came forward to revenge the blood of Dara murdered by Alexander, and to bring back the rule to the legitimate family and re-establish it, such as it had been at the time of his forefathers before the divisional kings. Under this legend lies a good deal of reality. The dynasty which bears the name of Sasan, the grandfather of Ardashir, was no other than the royal dynasty of the Persian province ; Ardashir's father, Papak or Pabek,[1] and a long list of his ancestors had, under the supremacy of the Arsacids, swayed the sceptre in this ancestral land of the Iranian nation,[2] had resided in Istachr, not far from the old Persepolis, and marked their coins with Iranian language and Iranian writing, and with the sacred emblems of the Persian national faith, while the great-kings had their abode in the half-Greek border-land, and had their coins stamped in the Greek language and after the Greek style. The fundamental organisation of the Iranian state-system—the great-kingdom holding

The Sassanids.

---

[1] Artaxares names his father Papacus in the inscription, quoted at p. 83, note 1, king ; how it is to be reconciled with this, that not merely does the native legend (in Agathias ii. 27) make Pabek a shoemaker, but also the contemporary Dio (if in reality Zonaras, xii. 15, has borrowed these words from him) names Artaxares ἐξ ἀφανῶν καὶ ἀδόξων, we do not know. Naturally the Roman authors take the side of the weak legitimate Arsacid against the dangerous usurper.

[2] Strabo (under Tiberius) xv. 3, 24 : νῦν δ'ἤδη καθ' αὐτοὺς συνεστῶτες οἱ Πέρσαι βασιλέας ἔχουσιν ὑπηκόους ἑτέροις βασιλεῦσι, πρότερον μὲν Μακεδόσι, νῦν δὲ Παρθυαίοις.

superiority over the divisional kings—was under the
two dynasties as little different as that of the empire
of the German nation under the Saxon and the Suabian
emperors. Only for this reason in that official version
the time of the Arsacids is designated as that of the
divisional-kings, and Ardashir as the first common head
of all Iran after the last Darius, because in the old Persian
empire the Persian province stood related alike to the
other provinces and to the Parthians, as in the Roman
state Italy stood related to the provinces, and the Persian
disputed with the Parthian the legitimate title to the
great-kingdom connected *de jure* with his province.[1]

Extent of the Sassanid kingdom.

What was the relation of the Sassanid kingdom to
that of the Arsacids in point of extent, is a question to
which tradition gives no sufficient answer. The provinces
of the west collectively remained subject to the new
dynasty after it sat firm in the saddle, and the claims
which it set up against the Romans went, as we shall see,
far beyond the pretensions of the Arsacids. But how
far the rule of the Sassanids reached towards the West,
and when it advanced to the Oxus which was subsequently
regarded as the legitimate boundary between Iran and
Turan, are matters withdrawn from our field of vision.[2]

[1] When Nöldeke says (*Tabari*, p.
449), "The subjection of the chief
lands of the monarchy directly to the
crown formed the chief distinction
of the Sassanid kingdom from the
Arsacid, which had real kings in its
various provinces," the power of the
great-kingdom beyond doubt is
thoroughly dependent on the personality of the possessor, and under
the first Sassanids must have been
much stronger than under the last
decayed Arsacids. But a contrast in
principle is not discoverable. From
Mithradates I., the proper founder
of the dynasty, onward the Arsacid
ruler names himself "king of kings,"
just as did subsequently the Sassanid,
while Alexander the Great and the
Seleucids never bore this title. Even
under them individual vassal-kings
ruled, *e.g.* in Persis (p. 81, note 2);

but the vassal-kingdom was not then
the regular form of imperial administration, and the Greek rulers did not
name themselves according to it, any
more than the Caesars assumed the
title of great-king on account of
Cappadocia or Numidia. The satraps
of the Arsacid state were essentially
the Marzbans of the Sassanids. Perhaps rather the great imperial offices,
which in the Sassanid polity correspond to the supreme administrative
posts of the Diocletiano-Constantinian
constitution, and probably were the
model for the latter, were wanting to
the Arsacid state ; then certainly the
two would be related to each other
much as the imperial organisation of
Augustus to that of Constantine. But
we know too little of the Arsacid organisation to affirm this with certainty.

[2] According to the Persian records

The state-system of Iran did not undergo quite a fundamental transformation in consequence of the coming in of the new dynasty. The official title of the first Sassanid ruler, as it is given uniformly in three languages under the rock-relief of Nakshi-Rustam, "The Mazda-servant God Artaxares, king of kings of the Arians, of divine descent,"[1] is substantially that of the Arsacids, except that the Iranian nation, as already in the old native regal title, and the indigenous god are now expressly named. That a dynasty having its home in Persis came in lieu of one originally alien in race and only nationalised, was a work and a victory of national reaction; but the force of circumstances placed various insurmountable barriers in the way of the consequences thence resulting. Persepolis, or, as it is now called, Istachr, becomes again nominally the capital of the empire, and there on the same rock-wall, alongside of the similar monuments of Darius, the remarkable statues and still more remarkable inscriptions just mentioned proclaim the fame of Ardashir and Shapur; but the administration could not well be conducted from this remote locality, and Ctesiphon continued still to be its centre. The new Persian government did

The state of the Sassanids.

---

of the last Sassanid period preserved in the Arabic chronicle of Tabari Ardashir, after he has cut off with his own hand the head of Ardawan and has assumed the title Shahan-shah, king of kings, conquers first Hamadhan (Ecbatana) in Great Media, then Aderbijan (Atropatene), Armenia, Mosul (Adiabene); and further Suristan or Sawad (Babylonia). Thence he returns to Istachr unto his Persian home, and then starting afresh conquers Sagistan, Gurgan (Hyrcania), Abrashahr (Nisapur in the Parthian land), Merv (Margiane), Balkh (Bactra), and Charizm (Khiva) up to the extreme limits of Chorasan. "After he had killed many people and had sent their heads to the fire-temple of Anahedh (in Istachr), he returned from Merv to Pars and settled in Gor" (Feruzabad). How much of this is legend, we do not

know (comp. Nöldeke, *Tabari*, p. 17, 116).

[1] The title runs in Greek (*C. I. Gr.* 4675), Μάσδασνος (Mazda - servant, treated as a proper name) θεὸς Ἀρταξάρης βασιλεὺς βασιλέων Ἀριανῶν ἐκ γένους θεῶν; with which closely agrees the title of his son Sapor I. (*ib.* 4676), only that after Ἀριανῶν there is inserted καὶ Ἀναριανῶν, and so the extension of the rule to foreign lands is brought into prominence. In the title of the Arsacids, so far as it is clear from the Greek and Persian legends of coins, θεὸς, βασιλεὺς βασιλέων, θεοπάτωρ (= ἐκ γένους θεῶν) recur, whereas there is no prominence given to the Arians and, significantly, to the "Mazda-servant"; by their side appear numerous other titles borrowed from the Syrian kings, such as ἐπιφάνης, δίκαιος, νικάτωρ, also the Roman αὐτοκράτωρ.

not resume the *de jure* prerogative of the Persians, as it had
subsisted under the Achaemenids ; while Darius named
himself " a Persian son of a Persian, an Arian from Arian
stock," Ardashir named himself, as we saw, simply king of
the Arians.   We do not know whether Persian elements
were introduced afresh into the great houses apart from
the royal ; in any case several of them remained, like the
Surên and the Carên ; only under the Achaemenids, not
under the Sassanids these were exclusively Persian.

Church and
priesthood
under the
Sassanids.

Even in a religious point of view no change, strictly
so called, set in ; but the faith and the priests gained
under the Persian great-kings an influence and a power
such as they had never possessed under the Parthian.   It
may well be that the twofold diffusion of foreign worships
in the direction of Iran—of Buddhism from the East and
of the Jewish-Christian faith from the West—brought by
their very hostility a regeneration to the old religion of
Mazda.   The founder of the new dynasty, Ardashir, was,
as is credibly reported, a zealous fire-worshipper, and himself took priestly orders ; therefore, it is further said, from
that time the order of the Magi became influential and
arrogant, while it had hitherto by no means had such
honour and such freedom, but on the contrary had not
been held in much account by the rulers.   " Thenceforth
all the Persians honour and revere the priests ; public
affairs are arranged according to their counsels and
oracles ; each treaty and each law-dispute undergoes
their inspection and their judgment, and nothing appears
to the Persian right and legal which has not been confirmed by a priest."   Accordingly we encounter an arrangement of spiritual administration which reminds us
of the position of the Pope and the bishops alongside of
the Emperor and the princes.   Each circle is placed under
a chief-Magian (Magupat, lord of Magians, in new Persian
Mobedh), and these all in turn under the chiefest of the
chief Magians (Mobedhan-Mobedh), the counterpart of
" the king of kings," and now it is he who crowns the
king.   The consequences of this priestly dominion did
not fail to appear : the rigid ritual, the restrictive precepts

as to guilt and expiation, science resolving itself into a wild system of oracles and of magic, while belonging from the first to Parsism, in all probability only attained to their full development at this epoch.

Traces of the national reaction appear also in the use of the native language and the native customs. The largest Greek city of the Parthian empire, the ancient Seleucia, continued to subsist, but it was thenceforth called not after the name of the Greek marshal, but after that of its new master, Beh, or better, Ardashir. The Greek language hitherto at any rate always in use, although debased and no longer ruling alone, disappears on the emergence of the new dynasty at once from the coins, and only on the inscriptions of the first Sassanids is it still to be met with by the side of, and behind, the language proper of the land. The "Parthian writing," the Pahlavî, maintains its ground, but alongside of it comes a second little 'different and indeed, as the coins show, as properly official, probably that used hitherto in the Persian province, so that the oldest monuments of the Sassanids, like those of the Achaemenids, are trilingual, somewhat as in the German middle ages Latin, Saxon, and Franconian were employed side by side. After king Sapor I. († 272) the bilingual usage disappears, and the second mode of writing alone retains its place, inheriting the name Pahlavî. The year of the Seleucids, and the names of the months belonging to it, disappear with the change of dynasty ; in their stead come, according to old Persian custom, the years of the rulers and the native Persian names of months.[1] Even the old Persian legend is transferred to the new Persia. The still extant " history of Ardashir, son of Papak," which makes this son of a Persian shepherd arrive at the Median court, perform menial offices there, and then become the deliverer of his people, is nothing but the old tale of Cyrus changed to

The languages of the country under the Sassanids.

---

[1] Frawardin, Ardhbehesht, etc. (Ideler, *Chronologie*, ii. 515). It is remarkable that essentially the same names of the months have maintained themselves in the provincial calendar of the Roman province Cappadocia (Ideler, i. 443) ; they must proceed from the time when it was a Persian satrapy.

the new names. Another fable-book of the Indian
Parsees is able to tell how king Iskander Rumi, *i.e.* " Alexander the Roman," had caused the holy books of Zarathustra to be burnt, and how they were then restored by
the pious Ardaviraf when king Ardashir had mounted
the throne. Here the Romano-Hellene confronts the
Persian ; the legend has, as might be expected, forgotten
the illegitimate Arsacid.

Govern-
ment of the
Sassanids.

In other respects the state of things remained essentially the same. In a military point of view in particular,
the armies of the Sassanids were certainly not regular
and trained troops, but the levy of men capable of arms,
into which with the national movement a new spirit may
doubtless have passed, but which afterwards, as before,
was based in the main on the cavalry-service of the
nobility. The administration too remained as it was ;
the able ruler took steps with inexorable sternness against
the highway-robber as against the exacting official, and,
compared at least with the later Arabic and the Turkish
rule, the subjects of the Sassanid empire found themselves
prosperous and the state-chest full.

The new
Persians
and the
Romans.

But the alteration in the position of the new kingdom
with reference to the Roman is significant. The Arsacids
never felt themselves quite on a level with the Caesars.
Often as the two states encountered each other in war
and peace as powers equal in weight, and decidedly
as the view of two great-powers dominated the Roman
East (p. 1), there remained with the Roman power a
precedence similar to that which the holy Roman empire
of the German nation possessed throughout centuries, very
much to its hurt. Acts of subjection, such as the Parthian kings took upon themselves in presence of Tiberius
(p. 44) and of Nero (52), without being compelled to
them by extreme necessity, cannot be at all conceived
of on the Roman side. It cannot be accident that a gold
coin was never struck under the government of the Arsacids, and the very first Sassanid ruler practised coining in
gold ; this is the most palpable sign of sovereignty un-
restricted by any duties of a vassal. To the claim of the

empire of the Caesars alone to the power of coining money for universal circulation the Arsacids without exception yielded, at least in so far that they themselves refrained generally from coining, and left coinage in silver and copper to the towns or the satraps ; the Sassanids again struck gold pieces, as did king Darius. The great-kingdom of the East at length demanded its full right ; the world no longer belonged to the Romans alone. The submissiveness of the Orientals and the supremacy of the Occidentals were of the past. Accordingly, in place of the relations between Romans and Parthians, as hitherto, always reverting afresh to peace, there now came for generations embittered hostility.

After having set forth the new state organisation, with which the sinking Rome was soon to contend, we resume the thread of our narrative. Antoninus, son and successor of Severus, not a warrior and statesman like his father, but a dissolute caricature of both, must have had the design—so far as in the case of such personages we can speak of design at all—to bring the East entirely into the Roman power. It was not difficult to place the princes of Osrhoene and of Armenia, after they had been summoned to the imperial court, under arrest, and to declare their fiefs forfeited. But on the arrival of the news a revolt broke out in Armenia. The Arsacid prince Tiridates was proclaimed king, and invoked the protection of the Parthians. Thereupon Antoninus put himself at the head of a large military force, and appeared in the East in the year 216, to put down the Armenians, and in case of need also the Parthians. Tiridates himself at once gave up the cause as lost, although the division sent to Armenia subsequently encountered vehement resistance there ; and he fled to the Parthians. The Romans demanded his surrender. The Parthians were not inclined on his account to enter into a war, the more especially as just then the two sons of king Vologasus V., Vologasus VI. and Artabanus, were in bitter feud over the succession to the throne. The former yielded when the Roman demand was imperiously repeated, and delivered up Tiridates.

Parthian war of Severus Antoninus.

Thereupon the emperor desired from Artabanus, who had meanwhile obtained recognition, the hand of his daughter for the express object of thus obtaining the kingdom by marriage, and of bringing East and West under one rule.   The rejection of this wild proposal[1] was the signal for war ; the Romans declared it, and crossed the Tigris. The Parthians were unprepared ; without encountering resistance the Romans burnt down the towns and villages in Adiabene, and ruthlessly destroyed even the old royal tombs at Arbela.[2]   But Artabanus made the utmost exertions for the next campaign, and put into the field a powerful force in the spring of 217.   Antoninus, who had spent the winter in Edessa, was assassinated by his officers just as he was setting out for this second campaign.   His successor Macrinus, unconfirmed in the government and held in little repute, at the head, moreover, of an army defective in discipline and tone and shaken by the murder of the emperor, would gladly have rid himself of a war wantonly instigated and assuming very serious proportions.   He sent the prisoners back to the Parthian king, and threw the blame of the outrages committed on his predecessor.   But Artabanus was not content with this ; he demanded compensation for all the devastation committed, and the evacuation of Mesopotamia. Thus matters came to a battle at Nisibis, in which the Romans had the worst.   Nevertheless the Parthians, partly because their levy seemed as though it would break up, perhaps also under the influence of Roman money, granted peace (218) on comparatively favourable terms.   Rome paid a considerable war compensation (50,000,000 denarii), but retained Mesopotamia.   Armenia remained with Tiridates, but the latter took it as in dependency on the Romans.   In Osrhoene also the old princely house was reinstated.

---

[1] Such is the account of the trustworthy Dio, lxxviii. 1 ; the version of Herodian, iv. 11, that Artabanus promised his daughter, and at the celebration of the betrothal allowed Antoninus to cut down the Parthians present, is unauthenticated

[2] If there is any truth in the mention of the Cadusians in the biography, c. 6, the Romans induced this wild tribe, not subject to the government in the south-west of the Caspian Sea, to fall at the same time upon the Parthians.

This was the last treaty of peace which the Arsacid King Ardashir. dynasty concluded with Rome. Almost immediately afterwards, and perhaps partly in consequence of this bargain, which certainly, as things stood, might be looked upon by the Orientals as an abandonment by their own government of the victories achieved, the insurrection began, which converted the state of the Parthians into a state of the Persians. Its leader, king Ardashir or Artaxares (A.D. 224-241) strove for several years with the adherents of the old dynasty before he attained full success ;[1] after three great battles, in the last of which king Artabanus fell, he was master in the Parthian empire proper, and could march into the Mesopotamian desert to subdue the Arabs of Hatra and thence to advance against the Roman Mesopotamia. But the brave and independent Arabs defended themselves now against the Persians as formerly against the Roman invasion, in their huge walls with good success ; and Artaxares found himself led to operate in the first instance against Media and Armenia, where the Arsacids still maintained themselves, and the sons of Artabanus had found a refuge. It was not till about the year 230 that he turned against the Romans, and not merely declared war against them, but demanded back all the provinces which had formerly belonged to the kingdom of his predecessors, Darius and Xerxes—in other words, the cession of all Asia. To emphasise his threatening words, he led a mighty army over the Euphrates ; Mesopotamia was occupied and Nisibis besieged ; the enemy's cavalry appeared in Cappadocia and in Syria.

The Roman throne was then occupied by Severus Severus Alexander. Alexander, a ruler in whom nothing was warlike but the

---

[1] The subsequently received chronology puts the beginning of the Sassanid dynasty in the Seleucid year 538 = 1st Oct. 226-7 A.D., or the fourth (full) year of Severus Alexander, reigning since spring 222 (Agathias, iv. 24). According to other data king Ardashir numbered the year from the autumn 223-4 A.D. as his first, and so doubtless assumed in this the title of great-king (Nöldeke, *Tabari*, p. 410). The last dated coin as yet known of the older system is of the year 539. When Dio wrote between 230 and 234, Artabanus was dead and his adherents were overpowered, and the advance of Artaxares into Armenia and Mesopotamia was expected.

name, and for whom in reality his mother Mamaea conducted the government. Urgent, almost humble proposals of peace on the part of the Roman government remained without effect; nothing was left but the employment of arms. The masses of the Roman army gathered together from all the empire were divided; the left wing took the direction of Armenia and Media, the right that of Mesene at the mouth of the Euphrates and Tigris, perhaps in the calculation that they might in the former as in the latter quarter have the support of the adherents of the Arsacids; the main army went to Mesopotamia. The troops were numerous enough, but without discipline and tone; a Roman officer of high position at this time himself testifies that they were pampered and insubordinate, refused to fight, killed their officers, and deserted in crowds. The main force did not get beyond the Euphrates,[1] for his mother represented to the emperor that it was not his business to fight for his subjects, but theirs to fight for him. The right wing, assailed in the level country by the Persian main force and abandoned by the emperor, was cut up. Thereupon, when the emperor issued orders to the wing which had pushed forward towards Media to draw back, the latter also suffered severely in the winter retreat through Armenia. If the matter went no further than this sorry return of the great Oriental army to Antioch, if no complete disaster occurred, and even Mesopotamia remained in Roman power, this appears due, not to the merit of the Roman troops or their leaders but to the fact that the Persian levy was weary of the conflict and went home.[2] But they went not for long, the more especially

---

[1] The emperor remained probably in Palmyra; at least a Palmyrene inscription, *C. I. Gr.* 4483, mentions the ἐπιδημία θεοῦ ᾿Αλεξάνδρου.

[2] The incomparably wretched accounts of this war (relatively the best is that drawn from a common source in Herodian, Zonaras, and Syncellus, p. 674) do not even decide the question who remained victor in these conflicts. While Herodian speaks of an unexampled defeat of the Romans, the Latin authorities, the Biography as well as Victor, Eutropius, and Rufius Festus, celebrate Alexander as the conqueror of Artaxerxes or Xerxes, and according to these latter the further course of things was favourable. Herodian vi. 6, 5, offers the means of adjustment. According to the Armenian accounts (Gutschmid, *Zeitschr. der deutschen morgenländ. Gesellschaft*, xxxi. 47) the Arsacids with the support of the

as soon after, upon the murder of the last offshoot of the dynasty of Severus, the several army-commanders and the government in Rome began to fight about the occupation of the Roman throne, and consequently were at one in their concern for the affairs of external foes. Under Maximinus (235-238) the Roman Mesopotamia fell into the power of Ardashir, and the Persians once more prepared to cross the Euphrates.[1]

After the internal troubles were in some measure pacified, and Gordian III., almost still a boy, under the protection of the commandant of Rome and soon of his father-in-law Furius Timesitheus, bore undisputed sway in the whole empire, war was solemnly declared against the Persians, and in the year 242 a great Roman army advanced under the personal conduct of the emperor, or rather of his father-in-law, into Mesopotamia. It had complete success ; Carrhae was recovered, at Resaina between Carrhae and Nisibis the army of the Persian king Shahpuhr or Sapor (reigning 241-272), who shortly before had followed his father Ardashir, was routed, and in consequence of this victory Nisibis was occupied. All Mesopotamia was reconquered ; it was resolved to march back to the Euphrates, and thence down the stream against the enemy's capital Ctesiphon. Unhappily Timesitheus died, and his successor, Marcus Julius Philippus, a native of Arabia from the Trachonitis, used the opportunity to set aside the young ruler. When the army had accomplished the difficult march through the valley of the Chaboras towards the Euphrates, the soldiers in Circesium, at the confluence of the Chaboras with the Euphrates, did not find—in consequence, it is alleged, of arrangements made by Philippus—the provisions and stores which they had expected, and laid the blame of this on the emperor.

The Persian war of Gordian.

tribes of the Caucasus held their ground in Armenia down to the year 237 against Ardashir ; this diversion may be correct and may have tended to the advantage of the Romans.

[1] The best account is furnished by Syncellus, p. 683 and Zonaras, xii. 18, drawing from the same source. With this accord the individual statements of Ammianus, xxiii. 5, 7, 17, and nearly so the forged letter of Gordian to the Senate in the Biography, c. 27, from which the narrative, c. 26, is ignorantly prepared ; Antioch was in danger, but not in the hands of the Persians.

Nevertheless the march in the direction of Ctesiphon was begun, but at the very first station, near Zaitha (somewhat below Mejadîn), a number of insurgent guards killed the emperor (in the spring or summer of 244), and proclaimed their commandant, Philippus, as Augustus in his stead. The new ruler did what the soldiers or at least the guardsmen desired, and not merely gave up the intended expedition against Ctesiphon, but led the troops at once back to Italy. He purchased the permission to do so from the conquered enemy by the cession of Mesopotamia and Armenia, and so of the Euphrates frontier. But this conclusion of peace excited such indignation that the emperor did not venture to put it in execution, and allowed the garrisons to remain in the ceded provinces.[1] The fact that the Persians, at least provisionally, acquiesced in this, gives the measure of what they were then able to do. It was not the Orientals, but the Goths, the pestilence that raged for fifteen years, and the dissensions of the corps-leaders quarrelling with one another for the crown, that broke the last strength of the empire.

Palmyra.   At this point, when the Roman East in its struggle with the Persian is left to its own resources, it will be appropriate to make mention of a remarkable state, which, created by and for the desert-traffic, now for a short time takes up a leading part in political history. The oasis of Palmyra, in the native language Tadmor, lies half-way between Damascus and the Euphrates. It is of importance solely as intermediate station between the Euphrates and the Mediterranean ; this significance it was late in acquiring, and early lost again, so that the flourishing time of Palmyra coincides nearly with the period which we are here describing. As to the rise of the town there is an utter absence of tradition.[2] It is mentioned first on

[1] So Zonaras, xii. 19, represents the course of affairs ; with this Zosimus, iii. 33, agrees, and the later course of things shows that Armenia was not quite in Persian possession. If, according to Euagrius, v. 7, at that time merely Lesser Armenia remained Roman, this may not be incorrect, in so far as the dependence of the vassal-king of Great Armenia after the peace was doubtless merely nominal.

[2] The Biblical account (1 Kings ix. 18) as to the building of the town Thamar in Idumaea by king Solomon has only been transferred to Tadmor by a misunderstanding doubtless old;

occasion of the abode of Antonius in Syria in the year
713, when he made a vain attempt to possess himself of 41.
its riches ; the documents found there—the oldest dated
Palmyrene inscription is of the year 745—hardly reach 9.
much further back.   It is not improbable that its flourishing was connected with the establishment of the Romans
in the Syrian coast-region.   So long as the Nabataeans
and the towns of Osrhoene were not directly Roman, the
Romans had an interest in providing another direct communication with the Euphrates, and this thereupon led
necessarily by way of Palmyra.   Palmyra was not a
Roman foundation ; Antonius took as the occasion for
that predatory expedition the neutrality of the merchants
who were the medium of traffic between the two great
states, and the Roman horsemen turned back, without having performed their work, before the chain of archers which
the Palmyrenes opposed to the attack.   But already in
the first imperial period the city must have been reckoned
as belonging to the empire, because the tax-ordinances of
Germanicus and of Corbulo issued for Syria applied also
for Palmyra ; in an inscription of the year 80 we meet
with a Claudian *phyle* there ; from Hadrian's time the city
calls itself Hadriana Palmyra, and in the third century it
even designates itself a colony.

    The subjection of the Palmyrenes to the empire was, Military in-
however, of a different nature to the ordinary one, and depend-
similar in some measure to the client-relation of the ence of
dependent kingdoms.   Even in Vespasian's time Palmyra Palmyra.
is called an intermediate region between the two great
powers, and in every collision between the Romans and
Parthians the question was asked, what policy the Palmyrenes would pursue.   We must seek the key to its
distinctive position in the relations of the frontier and
the arrangements made for frontier-protection.   The
Syrian troops, so far as they were stationed on the
Euphrates itself, had their chief position at Zeugma,

at all events the erroneous reference the oldest testimony for its existence
of it to this town among the later   (Hitzig, *Zeitschr. der deutschen mor-*
Jews (2 Chron. viii. 4, and the Greek *genl. Gesellschaft,* viii. 222).
translation of 1 Kings, ix. 18) form

opposite to Biredjik, at the great passage of the Euphrates. Further down the stream, between the immediately Roman and the Parthian territory was interposed that of Palmyra, which reached to the Euphrates and included the next important place of crossing at Sura opposite to the Mesopotamian town Nicephorium (later Callinicon, now er-Ragga). It is more than probable that the guarding of this important border-fortress as well as the securing of the desert-road between the Euphrates and Palmyra, and also perhaps of a portion of the road from Palmyra to Damascus, was committed to the community of Palmyra, and that it was thus entitled and bound to make the military arrangements necessary for this far from slight task.[1] Subse-

[1] This is nowhere expressly stated; but all the circumstances tell in favour of it. That the Romano-Parthian frontier, before the Romans established themselves on the left bank of the Euphrates, was on the right a little below Sura, is most distinctly said by Pliny (*H. N.* v. 26, 89: *a Sura proxime est Philiscum*—comp. p. 95, note 1—*oppidum Parthorum ad Euphratem; ab eo Seleuciam dierum decem navigatio*), and there it remained till the erection of the province of Mesopotamia under Severus. The Palmyrene of Ptolemy (v. 15, 24, 25) is a district of Coele-Syria, which seems to embrace a good part of the territory to the south of Palmyra, but certainly reaches as far as the Euphrates and includes Sura; other urban centres besides Palmyra seem not to be mentioned, and there is nothing to stand in the way of our taking this large district as civic territory. So long in particular as Mesopotamia was Parthian, but subsequently also with reference to the adjoining desert, a permanent protection of the frontier could not here be dispensed with; as indeed in the fourth century, according to the tenor of the Notitia, Palmyrene was strongly occupied, the northern portion by the troops of the Dux of Syria, Palmyra itself and the southern half by those of the Dux of Phoenice. That in the earlier imperial period no Roman troops were stationed here, is vouched for by the silence of authors and the absence of inscriptions, which in Palmyra itself are numerous. If in the Tabula Peutingeriana it is remarked under Sura: *fines exercitus Syriatici et commercium barbarorum*, that is, "here end the Roman garrisons and here is the place of exchange for the traffic of the barbarians," this is only saying, what at a later time is repeated by Ammianus (xxiii. 3, 7: *Callinicum munimentum robustum et commercandi opimitate gratissimum*) and further by the emperor Honorius (*Cod. Just.* iv. 63, 4), that Callinicon was one of the few entrepots devoted to the Romano-barbarian frontier-traffic; but it does not at all follow from this as regards the time when the Tabula originated, that these imperial troops were stationed there, since in fact the Palmyrenes in general belonged to the Syrian army and might be thought of in using the expression *exercitus Syriaticus*. The city must have furnished a force of its own in a way similar to that of the princes of Numidia and of Panticapaeum. By this means alone we come to understand as well the rejection of the troops of Antonius as the attitude of the Palmyrenes in the troubles of the third century, and not less the emergence of the *numeri Pal-*

quently doubtless the imperial troops were brought up closer to Palmyra, and one of the Syrian legions was moved to Danava between Palmyra and Damascus, and the Arabian legion to Bostra ; after Severus united Mesopotamia with the empire, even here both banks of the Euphrates were in the Roman power, and the Roman territory on the Euphrates ended no longer at Sura but at Circesium, at the confluence of the Chaboras with the Euphrates above Mejadin. Then Mesopotamia also was strongly occupied with imperial troops. But the Mesopotamian legions lay on the great road in the north near Resaina and Nisibis, and even the Syrian and Arabian troops did not supersede the need for the co-operation of the Palmyrenes. Even the protection of Circesium and of this part of the bank of the Euphrates may have been entrusted to the Palmyrenes. It was not till after the decline of Palmyra, and perhaps in compensation for it, that Circesium[1] was made by Diocletian a strong fortress, which thenceforth was here the basis of frontier-defence.

The traces of this distinctive position of Palmyra are demonstrable also in its institutions. The absence of the emperor's name on the Palmyrene coins is probably to be explained not from it, but from the fact that the community issued almost nothing but small money. But the treatment of the language speaks clearly. From the rule elsewhere followed almost without exception by the Romans—of allowing in their immediate territory only the use of the two imperial languages—Palmyra was excepted. Here that language, which in the rest of Syria and not less after the exile in Judaea was the usual medium of private intercourse, but was restricted to the latter, maintained its ground in public use, so long as the city existed at all. Essential differences cannot be shown between the Palmyrene Syriac and that of the other

Administrative independence of Palmyra.

myrenorum among the military novelties of this epoch.

[1] Ammianus, xxiii. 5, 2 : *Cercusium . . . Diocletianus exiguum ante hoc et suspectum muris turribusque circumdedit celsis, . . . ne vagarentur per Syriam Persae ita ut paucis*

ante annis cum magnis provinciarum contigerat damnis. Comp. Procopius de aed. ii. 6. Perhaps this place is not different from the Φάλγα or Φάλγα of Isidorus of Charax (mans. Parth. 1 ; Stephanus Byz. s. v.) and the *Philiscum* of Pliny (p. 94, note).

regions just named ; the proper names, having not
seldom an Arabic or Jewish, or even Persian form, show
the striking mixture of peoples, and numerous words borrowed from Greek or Latin show the influence of the
Occidentals. It becomes subsequently a rule to append
to the Syrian text a Greek one, which in a decree of the
Palmyrene common-council of the year 137 is placed
after the Palmyrene, but afterwards usually precedes it ;
but mere Greek inscriptions of native Palmyrenes are rare
exceptions. Even in votive inscriptions which Palmyrenes
set up to their native gods in Rome,[1] and in tombs of
Palmyrene soldiers that died in Africa or Britain, the Palmyrene rendering is added. So too in Palmyra—while the
Roman year was made the basis of dating as in the rest
of the empire—the names of the months were not the
Macedonian officially received in Roman Syria, but those
which were current in it in common intercourse at least
among the Jews, and were in use, moreover, among the
Aramaean tribes living under Assyrian and subsequently
Persian rule.[2]

Palmyrene magis-trates.

The municipal organisation was moulded in the main
after the pattern of the Greek municipality of the Roman
empire ; the designations for magistrates and council[3] and
even those of the colony are in the Palmyrene texts re-

---

[1] Of the seven dedications, hitherto
found outside of Palmyra, to the
Palmyrene Malach Belos the three
brought to light in Rome (C. I. L.
vi. 51, 710; C. I. Gr. 6015) have
along with a Greek or Latin also a
Palmyrene text, two African (C. I. L.
viii. 2497, 8795 add.) and two Dacian
(Arch. epig. Mitth. aus Oesterreich,
vi. 109, 111) merely Latin. One of
the latter was set up by P. Aelius
Theimes a duoviralis of Sarmizegetusa,
evidently a native of Palmyra, diis
patriis Malagbel et Bebellahamon et
Benefal et Manavat.

[2] Whence these names of the
months come, is not clear ; they first
appear in the Assyrian cuneiform
writing, but are not of Assyrian origin.
In consequence of the Assyrian rule

they then remained in use within the
sphere of the Syrian language. Varia-
tions are found ; the second month,
the Dios of the Greek-speaking Syrians, our November, is called among
the Jews Markeshvan, among the
Palmyrenes Kanun (Waddington, n.
2574b). We may add that these
names of the months, so far as they
came to be applied within the Roman
empire, are adapted, like the Macedonian, to the Julian calendar, so that
only the designation of the month
differs, the year-beginning (1 Oct.) of
the Syro-Roman year finds uniformly
application to the Greek as to the
Aramaean appellations.

[3] E.g. Archon, Grammateus, Proe-
dros, Syndikos, Dekaprotoi.

tained for the most part from the imperial languages. But in administration the district retained a greater independence than is elsewhere assigned to urban communities. Alongside of the civic officials we find, at least in the third century, the city of Palmyra with its territory under a separate " headman " of senatorial rank and Roman appointment, but chosen from the family of most repute in the place ; Septimius Hairanes, son of Odaenathus, is substantially a prince of the Palmyrenes,[1] who was doubtless not otherwise dependent on the legate of Syria than were the client-princes on the neighbouring imperial governors generally. A few years later we meet with his son,[2] Septimius Odaenathus, in the like position—indeed even raised in rank — of hereditary prince.[3] Similarly, Palmyra formed a customs-district apart, in which the customs were leased on account, not of the state, but of the community.[4]

[1] This is shown by the inscription of Palmyra (*C. I. Gr.* 4491, 4492 = Waddington 2600 = Vogué, *Insc. sém. Palm.* 22) set up to this Hairanes in the year 251 by a soldier of the legion stationed in Arabia. His title is in Greek ὁ λαμπρότατος συνκλητικός, ἔξα[ρχος (=*princeps*) Παλμυ]ρηνῶν, in Palmyrene " illustrious senator, head of Tadmor." The epitaph (*C. I. Gr.* 4507 = Waddington 2621 = Vogué,21) of the father of Hairanes, Septimios Odaenathos, son of Hairanes, grandson of Vaballathos, great-grandson of Nassoros, gives to him also senatorial rank.

[2] Certainly the father of this Odaenathus is nowhere named ; but it is as good as certain that he was the son of the Hairanes just named, and bore the name of his grandfather. Zosimus, too, i. 39, terms him a Palmyrene distinguished from the days of his forefathers by the government (ἄνδρα Παλμυρηνὸν καὶ ἐκ προγόνων τῆς παρὰ τῶν βασιλέων ἀξιωθέντα τίμης).

[3] In the inscription Waddington 2603 = Vogué 23, which the guild of gold and silver workers of Palmyra set up in the year 257 to Odaenathus

he is called ὁ λαμπρότατος ὑπατικός, and so *vir consularis*, and in Greek δεσπότης, in Syriac *mâran.* The former designation is not a title of office, but a statement of the class in which he ranked ; so *vir consularis* stands not unfrequently after the name quite like *vir clarissimus* (*C. I. L.* x. p. 1117 and elsewhere), and ὁ λαμπρότατος ὑπατικός is found alongside of and before official titles of various kinds, *e.g.* that of the proconsul of Africa (*C. I. Gr.* 2979, where λαμπρότατος is absent), of the imperial legate of Pontus and Bithynia (*C.I.Gr.* 3747, 3748, 3771) and of Palestine (*C. I. Gr.* 4151), of the governor of Lycia and Pamphylia (*C. I. Gr.* 4272) ; it is only in the age after Constantine that it is in combination with the name of the province employed as an official title (*e.g. C.I. Gr.* 2596, 4266*e*). From this, therefore, no inference is to be drawn as to the legal position of Odaenathus. Likewise, in the Syriac designation of " lord," we may not find exactly the ruler ; it is also given to a procurator (Waddington 2606 = Vogué 25).

[4] Syria in the imperial period formed an imperial customs-district of

Commercial position of Palmyra.

The importance of Palmyra depended on the caravan-traffic. The heads of the caravans (συνοδιάρχαι), which went from Palmyra to the great entrepots on the Euphrates, to Vologasias, the already mentioned Parthian foundation not far from the site of the ancient Babylon, and to Forath or Charax Spasinu, twin towns at its mouth, close on the Persian Gulf, appear in the inscriptions as the most respected city-burgesses,[1] and fill not merely

its own, and the imperial dues were levied not merely on the coast but also at the Euphrates-frontier, in particular at Zeugma. Hence it necessarily follows that farther to the south, where the Euphrates was no longer in the Roman power, similar dues were established on the Roman eastern frontier. Now a decree of the council of Palmyra of the year 137 informs us that the city and its territory formed a special customs-district, and the dues were levied for the benefit of the town upon all goods imported or exported. That this territory lay beyond the imperial dues, is probable—first, because, if there had existed an imperial customs-line enclosing the Palmyrene territory, the mention of it could not well be omitted in that detailed enactment ; secondly, because a community of the empire enclosed by the imperial customs-lines would hardly have had the right of levying dues at the boundary of its territory to this extent. We shall thus have to discern in the levying of dues by the community of Palmyra the same distinctive position which must be attributed to it in a military point of view. Perhaps, on the other hand, there was an impost laid on it for the benefit of the imperial exchequer, possibly the delivering up of a quota of the produce of the dues or a heightened tribute. Arrangements similar to those for Palmyra may have existed also for Petra and Bostra ; for goods were certainly not admitted here free of dues, and according to Pliny, *H. N.* xii. 14, 65, imperial dues from the Arabic frankincense exported by way of Gaza seem only to have been levied at Gaza on

the coast. The indolence of Roman administration was stronger than its fiscal zeal ; it may frequently have devolved the inconvenient tolls of the land-frontier away from itself on the communities.

[1] These caravans (συνοδίαι) appear on the Palmyrene inscriptions as fixed companies, which undertake the same journeys beyond doubt at definite intervals under their foreman (συνοδιάρχης, Waddington, 2589, 2590, 2596) ; thus a statue is erected to such a one by " the merchants who went down with him to Vologasias " (οἱ σὺν αὐτῷ κατελθόντες εἰς Ὀλογεσιάδα ἔνποροι, Waddington 2599 of the year 247), or " up from Forath (comp. Pliny, *H. N.* vi. 28, 145) and Vologasias " (οἱ συναναβάντες μετ' αὐτοῦ ἔμποροι ἀπὸ Φοράθου κὲ Ὀλογασιάδος, Waddington, 2589 of the year 142), or " up from Spasinu Charax " (οἱ σὺν αὐτῷ ἀναβάντες ἀπὸ Σπασίνου Χάρακος, Waddington, 2596 of the year 193 ; similarly 2590 of the year 155). All these conductors are men of standing furnished with lists of ancestors ; their honorary monuments stand in the great colonnade beside those of queen Zenobia and her family. Specially remarkable is one of them, Septimius Vorodes, of whom there exists a series of honorary monuments of the years 262-267 (Waddington, 2606-2610) ; he, too, was a caravan-head (ἀνακομίσαντα τὰς συνοδίας ἐκ τῶν ἰδίων καὶ μαρτυρηθέντα ὑπὸ τῶν ἀρχεμπόρων, Waddington, n. 2606 *a* ; consequently he defrayed the costs of the journey back for the whole company, and was on account of this liberality publicly praised by the wholesale traders). But

the magistracies of their home, but in part also imperial
offices ; the great traders (ἀρχέμπopoι) and the guild of
workers in gold and silver testify to the importance of the
city for trade and manufactures, and not less is its prosperity attested by the still standing temples of the city and
the long colonnades of the city halls, as well as the massy and
richly decorated tombs.   The climate is little favourable to
agriculture—the place lies near to the northern limit of
the date palm, and does not derive its Greek name from
it—but there are found in the environs the remains of
great subterranean aqueducts and huge water-reservoirs
artificially constructed of square blocks, with the help of
which the ground, now destitute of all vegetation, must
once upon a time have artificially developed a rich culture.
This riches, this national idiosyncrasy not quite set aside
even under Roman rule, and this administrative independence, explain in some measure the part of Palmyra about
the middle of the third century in the great crisis, to the
presentation of which we now return.

After the emperor Decius had fallen in the year 251   Capture of
when fighting against the Goths in Europe, the government the emperor
of the empire, if at that time there was still an empire Valerian.
and a government at all, left the East entirely to its fate.
While the pirates from the Black Sea ravaged the coasts
far and wide and even the interior, the Persian king Sapor
again assumed the aggressive. While his father had been
content with calling himself lord of Iran, he first designated himself—as did the succeeding rulers after his example—the great-king of Iran and non-Iran (p. 83, note),
and thereby laid down, as it were, the programme of his
policy of conquest.   In the year 252 or 253 he occupied
Armenia, or it submitted to him voluntarily, beyond doubt
carried likewise away by that resuscitation of the old Persian faith and Persian habits ; the legitimate king Tiridates
sought shelter with the Romans, the other members of the
royal house placed themselves under the banners of the

he filled not merely the civic offices of   (*ducenarius*) and *argapetes* (p. 104,
strategos and *agoranomos*, he was even   note 1).
imperial procurator of the second class

Persian.[1] After Armenia thus had become Persian, the
hosts of the Orientals overran Mesopotamia, Syria, and
Cappadocia ; they laid waste the level country far and
wide, but the inhabitants of the larger towns, first of all
the brave Edessenes, repelled the attack of enemies little
equipped for besieging.   In the West, meanwhile at least,
a recognised government had been set up.   The emperor
Publius Licinius Valerianus, an honest and well-disposed
ruler, but not resolute in character or equal to dealing
with difficulties, appeared at length in the East and resorted to Antioch.   Thence he went to Cappadocia, which
the Persian roving hordes evacuated.   But the plague
decimated his army, and he delayed long to take up the
decisive struggle in Mesopotamia.   At length he resolved
to bring help to the sorely pressed Edessa, and crossed
the Euphrates with his forces.   There, not far from Edessa,
occurred the disaster which had nearly the same significance for the Roman East as the victory of the Goths at
the mouth of the Danube and the fall of Decius—the
capture of the emperor Valerianus by the Persians (end
of 259 or beginning of 260).[2]   As to the more precise circumstances the accounts are conflicting.   According to one
version, when he was attempting with a weak band to reach
Edessa, he was surrounded and captured by the far superior
Persians.   According to another, he, although defeated,
reached the beleaguered town, but, as he brought no sufficient help and the provisions came to an end only the
more rapidly, he dreaded the outbreak of a military insurrection, and therefore delivered himself voluntarily into the
hands of the enemy.   According to a third, he, reduced
to extremities, entered into negotiations with Sapor ; when

---

[1] According to the Greek account
(Zonaras, xii. 21) king Tiridates takes
refuge with the Romans, but his sons
take the side of the Persians ; according to the Armenian, king Chosro
is murdered by his brethren, and
Chosro's son, Tiridates, fled to the
Romans (Gutschmid, *Zeitschrift der
deutschen morgenl. Gesellsch.* xxxi. 48).
Perhaps the latter is to be preferred.

[2] The only fixed chronological

basis is furnished by the Alexandrian
coins, according to which Valerian
was captured between 29th August 259
and 28th August 260.   That after his
capture he was no longer regarded as
emperor, is easily explained, seeing
that the Persians compelled him in
their interest to issue orders to his
former subjects (continuation of Dio,
fr. 3).

the Persian king declined to treat with envoys, he appeared personally in the enemy's camp, and was perfidiously
made a prisoner.

Whichever of these narratives may come nearest to
the truth, the emperor died in the captivity of the enemy,[1]
and the consequence of this disaster was the forfeiture
of the East to the Persians. Above all Antioch, the
largest and richest city of the East, fell for the first time
since it was Roman into the power of the public foe,
and in good part through the fault of its own citizens.
Mareades, an Antiochene of rank, whom the council had
expelled for the embezzlement of public monies, brought
the Persian army to his native town ; whether it be a
fable that the citizens were surprised in the theatre itself
by the advancing foes, there is no doubt that they not
merely offered no resistance, but that a great part of the
lower population, partly in consideration of Mareades, partly
in the hope of anarchy and pillage, saw with pleasure
the entrance of the Persians.   Thus the city with all its
treasures became the prey of the enemy, and fearful
ravages were committed in it ; Mareades indeed also was
—we know not why—condemned by king Sapor to
perish by fire.[2]   Besides numerous smaller places, the
capitals of Cilicia and Cappadocia—Tarsus and Caesarea,
the latter, it is stated, a town of 400,000 inhabitants—
suffered the same fate.   Endless trains of captives, who
were led like cattle once a day to the watering, covered
the desert-routes of the East.   On the return home the
Persians, it is alleged, in order the more rapidly to cross
a ravine, filled it up with the bodies of the captives

*The East
without an
emperor.*

---

[1] The better accounts simply know
the fact that Valerian died in Persian
captivity. That Sapor used him as
a footstool in mounting his horse
(Lactantius, *de Mort. persec.* 5 ;
Orosius, vii. 22, 4 ; Victor, *Ep.* 33),
and finally caused him to be flayed
(Lactantius, *l. c.* ; Agathias, iv. 23 ;
Cedrenus, p. 454) is a Christian
invention — a requital for the persecution of the Christians ordered by
Valerian.

[2] The tradition according to which
Mareades (so Ammianus, xxiii. 5, 3 ;
Mariades in Malalas, 12, p. 295 ;
Mariadnes in contin. of Dio, *fr.* 1),
or, as he is here called, Cyriades,
had himself proclaimed as Augustus
(*Vit. trig. tyr.* 1) is weakly attested ; otherwise there might doubtless be found in it the occasion
why Sapor caused him to be put to
death.

whom they brought with them. It is more credible that the great "imperial dam" (Bend-i-Kaiser) at Sostra (Shuster) in Susiana, by which still at the present day the water of the Pasitigris is conveyed to the higher-lying regions, was built by these captives; as indeed the emperor Nero's architects had helped to build the capital of Armenia, and generally in this domain the Occidentals always maintained their superiority. The Persians nowhere encountered resistance from the empire; but Edessa still held out, and Caesarea had bravely defended itself, and had only fallen by treachery. The local resistance gradually passed beyond a mere defensive behind the walls of towns, and the breaking up of the Persian hosts, brought about by the wide extent of the conquered territory, was favourable to the bold partisan. A self-appointed Roman leader, Callistus,[1] succeeded in a happy *coup de main;* with the vessels which he had brought together in the ports of Cilicia he sailed for Pompeiopolis—which the Persians were just besieging, while they at the same time laid waste Lycaonia,—killed several thousand men, and possessed himself of the royal harem. This induced the king, under pretext of celebrating a festival that might not be put off, to go home at once in such haste that, in order not to be detained, he purchased from the Edessenes free passage through their territory in return for all the Roman gold money which he had captured as booty. Odaenathus, prince of Palmyra, inflicted considerable losses on the bands returning home from Antioch before they crossed the Euphrates. But hardly was the most urgent danger from the Persians obviated, when two of the most noted among the army leaders of the East, left to themselves, Fulvius Macrianus, the officer who administered the chest and the depot of the army in Samosata,[2] and the

---

[1] He is called Callistus in the one tradition, doubtless traceable to Dexippus, in Syncellus, p. 716, and Zonaras, xii. 23, on the other hand, Ballista in the biographies of the emperors and in Zonaras, xii. 24.

[2] He was, according to the most trustworthy account, *procurator summarum* (ἐπὶ τῶν καθόλου λόγων βασιλέως: Dionysius in Eusebius, *H. E.* vii. 10, 5), and so finance-minister with equestrian rank; the continu-

Callistus just mentioned, renounced allegiance to the son and co-regent and now sole ruler Gallienus—for whom, it is true, the East and the Persians were non-existent—and, themselves refusing to accept the purple, proclaimed the two sons of the former, Fulvius Macrianus and Fulvius Quietus, emperors (261). This step taken by the two distinguished generals had the effect of obtaining recognition for the two young emperors in Egypt and in all the East, with the exception of Palmyra, the prince of which took the side of Gallienus. One of them, Macrianus, went off with his father to the West, in order to install this new government also there. But soon fortune turned ; in Illyricum Macrianus lost a battle and his life, not against Gallienus, but against another pretender. Odaenathus turned against the brother who remained behind in Syria ; at Hemesa, where the armies met, the soldiers of Quietus replied to the summons to surrender that they would rather submit to anything than deliver themselves into the hands of a barbarian. Nevertheless Callistus, the general of Quietus, betrayed his master to the Palmyrene,[1] and thus ended also his short government.

Therewith Palmyra stepped into the first place in the East. Gallienus, more than sufficiently occupied by the barbarians of the West and the military insurrections everywhere breaking out there, gave to the prince of Palmyra, who alone had preserved fidelity to him in the crisis just mentioned, an exceptional position without a parallel, but under the prevailing circumstances readily intelligible ; he, as hereditary prince, or, as he was now called, king of Palmyra, became, not indeed joint ruler, but independent lieutenant of the emperor for the East.[2]

Government of Odaenathus in the East.

ator of Dio (*fr.* 3 Müll.) expresses this in the language of the later age by κόμης τῶν θησαυρῶν καὶ ἐφεστὼς τῇ ἀγορᾷ τοῦ σίτου.

[1] At least according to the report, which forms the basis of the imperial biographies (*vita Gallieni*, 3, and elsewhere). According to Zonaras, xii. 24, the only author who mentions besides the end of Callistus, Odae-nathus caused him to be put to death.

[2] That Odaenathus, as well as after him his son Vaballathus (apart, of course, from the time after the rupture with Aurelian), were by no means Augusti (as the *vit. Gallieni*, 12, erroneously states), is shown both by the absence of the name of Augustus

The local administration of Palmyra was conducted under him by another Palmyrene, at the same time as imperial procurator and as his deputy.[1] Therewith the whole imperial power, so far as it still subsisted at all in the East, lay in the hand of the "barbarian," and the latter with his Palmyrenes, who were strengthened by the remains of the Roman army corps and the levy of the land, re-established the sway of Rome alike rapidly and brilliantly. Asia and Syria were already evacuated by the enemy. Odaenathus crossed the Euphrates, relieved at length the brave Edessenes, and retook from the Persians the conquered towns Nisibis and Carrhae (264). Probably Armenia also was at that time brought back under

on the coins and by the title possible only for a subject, *v*(*ir*) *c*(*onsularis*) = ὑ(πατικός), which, like the father (p. 97, note 3), the son still bears. The position of governor is designated on the coins of the son by *im*(*perator*) *d*(*ux*) *R*(*omanorum*) = αὐτ(οκράτωρ) σ(τρατηγός) ; in agreement therewith Zonaras (xii. 23, and again xii. 24) and Syncellus (p. 716) state that Gallienus appointed Odaenathus, on account of his victory over the Persians and Ballista, as στρατηγὸς τῆς ἑῴας, or πάσης ἀνατολῆς ; and the biographer of Gallienus, 10, that he *obtinuit totius Orientis imperium*. By this is meant all the Asiatic provinces and Egypt ; the added *imperator* = αὐτο- κράτωρ (comp. *Trig. tyr.* 15, 6, *post reditum de Perside*—Herodes son of Odaenathus—*cum patre imperator est appellatus*) is intended beyond doubt to express the freer handling of power, different from the usual authority of the governor.—To this was added further the now formally assumed title of a king of Palmyra (*Trig. tyr.* 15, 2 : *adsumpto nomine regali*), which also the son bears, not on the Egyptian, but on the Syrian coins. The circumstance that Odaenathus is probably called *melekh malkê*, "king of kings," on an inscription set up in August 271, and so after his death and during the war of his adherents with Aurelian (Vogué, n. 28), belongs

to the revolutionary demonstrations of this period and forms no proof for the earlier time.

[1] The numerous inscriptions of Septimius Vorodes, set up in the years 262 to 267 (Waddington, 2606-2610), and so in the lifetime of Odaenathus, all designate him as imperial procurator of the second class (*ducenarius*), but at the same time partly by the title ἀργαπέτης, which Persian word, current also among the Jews, signifies "lord of a castle," "viceroy" (Levy, *Zeitsch. der deutschen morgenl. Gesellschaft*, xviii. 90 ; Nöldeke, *ib.* xxiv. 107), partly as δικαιοδότης τῆς μητρο- κολωνίας, which, beyond doubt, is in substance at any rate, if not in language, the same office. Presumably we must understand by it that office on account of which the father of Odaenathus is called the "head of Tadmor" (p. 97, note 2); the one chief of Palmyra competent for martial law and for the administration of justice ; only that, since extended powers were given to the position of Odaenathus, this post as a subordinate office is filled by a man of equestrian rank. The conjecture of Sachau (*Zeitschr. der d. morgenl. Gesellsch.* xxxv. 738) that this Vorodes is the "Wurud" of a copper coin of the Berlin cabinet, and that both are identical with the elder son of Odaenathus, Herodes,

Roman allegiance.[1] Then he took—for the first time since Gordianus—the offensive against the Persians, and marched on Ctesiphon.   In two different campaigns the capital of the Persian kingdom was invested by him, and the neighbouring region laid waste, and there was a successful battle with the Persians under its walls.[2]   Even the Goths, whose predatory raids extended into the interior, retired when he set out for Cappadocia. A development of power of this sort was a blessing for the hard-pressed empire, and at the same time a serious danger.   Odaenathus no doubt observed all due formalities towards his Roman lord-paramount, and sent the captured officers of the enemy and the articles of booty to Rome for the emperor, who did not disdain to triumph over them ; but in fact the East under Odaenathus was not much less independent than the West under Postumus, and we can easily understand how the officers favourably disposed towards Rome made opposition to the Palmyrene vice-emperor,[3] and on the one hand there was talk of attempts

who was killed at the same time with his father, is liable to serious difficulties.   Herodes and Orodes are different names (in the Palmyrene inscription, Waddington, 2610, the two stand side by side) ; the son of a senator cannot well fill an equestrian office ; a procurator coining money with his image is not conceivable even for this exceptional state of things.   Probably the coin is not Palmyrene at all.   "It is," von Sallet writes to me, "probably older than Odaenathus, and belongs perhaps to an Arsacid of the second century A.D. ; it shows a head with a headdress similar to the Sassanid ; the reverse, S C in a chaplet of laurel, appears imitated from the coins of Antioch."—If subsequently, after the breach with Rome in 271, on an inscription of Palmyra (Waddington, 2611) two generals of the Palmyrenes are distinguished, ὁ μέγας στρατηλάτης, the historically known Zabdas, and ὁ ἐνθάδε στρατηλάτης, Zabbaeos, the latter is, it may be presumed, just the Argapetes.

[1] The state of the case speaks in favour of this ; evidence is wanting. In the imperial biographies of this epoch the Armenians are wont to be adduced among the border peoples independent of Rome (*Valer.* 6 ; *Trig. tyr.* 30, 7, 18 ; *Aurel.* 11, 27, 28, 41) ; but this is one of their quite untrustworthy elements of embellishment.

[2] This more modest account (Eutropius, ix. 10 ; *vita Gallieni*, 10 ; *Trig. tyr.* 15, 4 ; Zos. i. 39, who alone attests the two expeditions) must be preferred to that which mentions the capture of the city (Syncellus, p. 716).

[3] This is shown by the accounts as to Carinus (cont. of Dio, p. 8) and as to Rufinus (p. 106, note 2). That after the death of Odaenathus Heraclianus, a general acting on Gallienus's orders against the Persians, was attacked and conquered by Zenobia (*vita Gallieni*, 13, 5), is in itself not impossible, seeing that the princes of Palmyra possessed *de iure* the chief command in all the East, and such an action,

of Odaenathus to attach himself to the Persians, which were alleged to have broken down only through Sapor's arrogance,[1] while on the other hand the assassination of Odaenathus at Hemesa in 266-7 was referred to instigation of the Roman government.[2]   The real murderer was a brother's son of Odaenathus, and there are no proofs of the participation of the government.   At any rate the crime made no change in the position of affairs.

Govern-
ment of
Zenobia. The wife of the deceased, the queen Bat Zabbai, or in Greek, Zenobia, a beautiful and sagacious woman of masculine energy,[3] in virtue of the hereditary right to the principate claimed for the son of herself and Odaenathus, still in boyhood, Vaballathus or Athenodorus[4]—the elder, Herodes, had perished with his father—the position of the deceased, and in fact carried her point as well in Rome as in the East : the regnal years of the son are reckoned from the death of the father.   For the son, not capable of government, the mother took part in counsel and action,[5] and she did not restrict herself to preserving the

even if it were suggested by Gallienus, might be treated as offending against this right, and this would clearly indicate the strained relation ; but the authority vouching it is so bad that little stress can be laid on it.

[1] This we learn from the characteristic narrative of Petrus, *fr.* 10, which is to be placed before *fr.* 11.

[2] The account of the continuator of Dio, *fr.* 7, that the old Odaenathus was put to death, as suspected of treason, by one (not elsewhere mentioned) Rufinus, and that the younger, when he had impeached this person at the bar of the emperor Gallienus, was dismissed on the declaration of Rufinus that the accuser deserved the same fate, cannot be correct as it stands.   But Waddington's proposal to substitute Gallus for Gallienus, and to recognise in the accuser the husband of Zenobia, is not admissible, since the father of this Odaenathus was Hairanes, in whose case there existed no ground at all for such an execution, and the excerpt in its whole character undoubtedly applies

to Gallienus.   Rather must the old Odaenathus have been the husband of Zenobia, and the author have erroneously assigned to Vaballathus, in whose name the charge was brought, his father's name.

[3] All the details which are current in our accounts of Zenobia originate from the imperial biographies ; and they will only be repeated by such as do not know this source.

The name Vaballathus is given, in addition to the coins and inscriptions, by Polemius Silvius, p. 243 of my edition, and the biographer of Aurelian, c. 38, while he describes as incorrect the statement that Odaenathus had left two sons, Timolaus and Herennianus.   In reality these two persons emerging simply in the imperial biographies appear along with all that is connected with them as invented by the writer, to whom the thorough falsification of these biographies is to be referred.   Zosimus too, i. 59, knows only of one son, who went into captivity with his mother.

[5] Whether Zenobia claimed for her-

state of possession, but on the contrary her courage or her arrogance aspired to mastery over the whole imperial domain of the Greek tongue.   In the command over the East, which was committed to Odaenathus and inherited from him by his son, the supreme authority over Asia Minor and Egypt may doubtless have been included ; but *de facto* Odaenathus had in his power only Syria and Arabia, and possibly Armenia, Cilicia, and Cappadocia. Now an influential Egyptian, Timagenes, summoned the queen to occupy Egypt ; accordingly she despatched her chief general Zabdas with an army of, it is alleged, 70,000 men to the Nile.   The land resisted with energy ; but the Palmyrenes defeated the Egyptian levy and possessed themselves of Egypt.   A Roman admiral Probus attempted to dislodge them again, and even vanquished them, so that they set out for Syria ; but, when he attempted to bar their way at the Egyptian Babylon not far from Memphis, he was defeated by the better local knowledge of the Palmyrene general Timagenes, and he put himself to death.[1]   When about the beginning of the year 270, after the death of the emperor Claudius Aurelian came in his stead, the Palmyrenes bore sway over Alexandria. In Asia Minor too they made preparations to establish themselves ; their garrisons were pushed forward as far as Ancyra in Galatia, and even in Chalcedon opposite Byzan-

self formal joint-rule, cannot be certainly determined.   In Palmyra she names herself still after the rupture with Rome merely βασίλισση (Waddington, 2611, 2628), in the rest of the empire she may have laid claim to the title *Augusta*, Σεβαστή ; for, though there are no coins of Zenobia from the period prior to the breach with Rome, yet on the one hand the Alexandrian inscription with βασίλισσης καὶ βασιλέως προσταξάντων (*Eph. epigr.* iv. p. 25, p. 33) cannot lay any claim to official redaction, and on the other hand the inscription of Byblos, *C. I. Gr.* 4503 b=Waddington, n. 2611, gives in fact to Zenobia the title Σεβαστή alongside of Claudius or Aurelian, while it refuses it

to Vaballathus.   This is so far intelligible, as Augusta was an honorary designation, Augustus an official one, and thus that might well be conceded to the woman which was refused to the man.

[1] So Zosimus, i. 44, narrates the course of events with which Zonaras, xii. 27 and Syncellus, p. 721, in the main agree.   The report in the life of Claudius, c. 11, is more displaced than properly contradictory ; the first half is only indicated by the naming of Saba ; the narrative begins with the successful attempt of Timagenes to ward off the attack of Probus (here Probatus).   The view taken of this by me in Sallet (*Palmyra*, p. 44) is not tenable.

tium they had attempted to assert the rule of their queen. All this happened without the Palmyrenes renouncing the Roman government, nay probably on the footing that the control of the East committed by the Roman government to the prince of Palmyra was realised in this way, and they taxed the Roman officers, who resisted the extension of the Palmyrene rule, with rebellion against the imperial orders ; the coins struck in Alexandria name Aurelianus and Vaballathus side by side, and give the title of Augustus only to the former. In substance, no doubt, the East here detached itself from the empire, and the latter was divided into two in the execution of an ordinance wrung from the wretched Gallienus by necessity.

Aurelian against the Palmyrenes.

The vigorous and prudent emperor, to whom the dominion now had fallen, broke at once with the Palmyrene co-ordinate government, which then could not but have and had as its consequence, that Vaballathus himself was proclaimed by his people as emperor. Egypt was already, at the close of the year 270, brought back to the empire after hard struggles by the brave general Probus, afterwards the successor of Aurelian.[1] It is true that the second city of the empire, Alexandria, paid for this victory almost with its existence, as will be set forth in the following section. More difficult was the reduction of the remote Syrian oasis. All other Oriental wars of the imperial period had chiefly been waged by imperial troops having their home in the East ; here, where the West had once more to subdue the revolted East, there fought once more, as in the time of the free republic,

---

[1] The determination of the date depends on the fact that the usurpation-coins of Vaballathus cease already in the fifth year of his Egyptian reign, *i.e.* 29th August 270-71 ; the fact that they are very rare speaks for the beginning of the year. With this essentially agrees the circumstance that the storming of the Prucheion (which, we may add, was no part of the city, but a locality close by the city on the side of the great oasis ; Hieronymus, *vit. Hilarionis*, c. 33, 34, vol. ii. p. 32 Vall.) is put by Eusebius in his Chronicle in the first year of Claudius, by Ammianus, xxii. 16, 15, under Aurelian ; the most exact report in Eusebius, *H. Eccl.* vii. 32, is not dated. The reconquest of Egypt by Probus stands only in his biography, c. 9 ; it may have happened as it is told, but it is possible also that in this thoroughly falsified source the history of Timagenes has been *mutatis mutandis* transferred to the emperor.

Occidentals against Orientals,[1] the soldiers of the Rhine and of the Danube with those of the Syrian desert.   The mighty expedition began, apparently towards the close of the year 271 ; without encountering resistance the Roman army arrived at the frontier of Cappadocia ; here the town of Tyana, which barred the Cilician passes, gave serious opposition.   After it had fallen, and Aurelian, by gentle treatment of the inhabitants, had smoothed his way to further successes, he crossed the Taurus, and, passing through Cilicia, arrived in Syria.   If Zenobia, as is not to be doubted, had reckoned on active support from the side of the Persian king, she found herself deceived.   The aged king Shapur did not interfere in this war, and the mistress of the Roman East continued to be left to her own military resources, of which perhaps even a portion took the side of the legitimate Augustus.   At Antioch the Palmyrene chief force under the general Zabdas stopped the emperor's way ; Zenobia herself was present.   A successful combat against the superior Palmyrene cavalry on the Orontes delivered into the hands of Aurelian the town, which not less than Tyana received full pardon—he justly recognised that the subjects of the empire were hardly to be blamed, when they had submitted to the Palmyrene prince appointed as commander in chief by the Roman government itself.   The Palmyrenes, after having engaged in a conflict on their retreat at Daphne, the suburb of Antioch, marched off, and struck into the great route which leads from the capital of Syria to Hemesa and thence through the desert to Palmyra.

Aurelian summoned the queen to submit, pointing to the notable losses endured in the conflicts on the Orontes. These were Romans only, answered the queen ; the Orientals did not yet admit that they were conquered.

Battle at Hemesa.

[1] This is perhaps what the report on the battle of Hemesa, extracted by Zosimus, i. 52, wished to bring out, when it enumerates among the troops of Aurelian the Dalmatians, Moesians, Pannonians, Noricans, Raetians, Mauretanians, and the guard.   When he associates with these the troops of Tyana and some divisions from Mesopotamia, Syria, Phoenice, Palestine, this applies beyond doubt to the Cappadocian gar-

At Hemesa[1] she took her stand for the decisive battle. It was long and bloody ; the Roman cavalry gave way and broke up in flight ; but the legions decided, and victory remained with the Romans. The march was more difficult than the conflict. The distance from Hemesa to Palmyra amounts in a direct line to seventy miles, and, although at that epoch of highly developed Syrian civilisation the region was not waste in the same degree as at present, the march of Aurelian still remains a considerable feat, especially as the light horsemen of the enemy swarmed round the Roman army on all sides. Aurelian, however, reached his goal, and began the siege of the strong and well-provisioned city ; more difficult than the siege itself was the bringing up of provisions for the besieging army. At length the courage of the princess sank, and she escaped from the city to seek aid from the Persians. Fortune still further helped the emperor. The pursuing Roman cavalry took her captive with her son, just when she had arrived at the Euphrates and was about to embark in the rescuing boat; and the town, discouraged by her flight, capitulated (272). Aurelian granted here too, as in all this campaign, full pardon to the subdued burgesses. But a stern punishment was decreed over the queen and her functionaries and officers. Zenobia, after she had for years borne rule with masculine energy, did not now disdain to invoke a woman's privileges, and to throw the responsibility on her advisers, of whom not a few, including the celebrated scholar, Cassius Longinus, perished under the axe of the executioner. She herself might not be wanting from the triumphal procession of the emperor, and she did not

---

risons, which had joined after the capture of Tyana, and to some divisions of the armies of the East favourably disposed to Rome, who went over to Aurelian upon his marching into Syria.

[1] By mistake Eutropius, ix. 13, places the decisive battle *haud longe ab Antiochia :* the mistake is heightened in Rufius, c. 24 (on whom Hieronymus, *chron. a. Abr.* 2289 depends), and in Syncellus, p. 721, by the addition *apud Immas,* ἐν Ἴμμαυς, which place, lying 33 Roman miles from Antioch on the road to Chalcis, is far away from Hemesa. The two chief accounts, in Zosimus and the biographer of Aurelian, agree in all essentials.

take the course of Cleopatra, but marched in golden
chains, as a spectacle to the Roman multitude, before the
chariot of the victor to the Roman capitol.   But before
Aurelian could celebrate his victory he had to repeat it.

A few months after the surrender the Palmyrenes once
more rose, killed the small Roman garrison serving there,
and proclaimed one Antiochus[1] as ruler, while they at
the same time attempted to induce the governor of Mesopotamia, Marcellinus, to revolt.   The news reached the
emperor when he had just crossed the Hellespont.   He
returned at once, and stood, earlier than friend or foe had
anticipated, once more before the walls of the insurgent
city.   The rebels had not been prepared for this ; there
was this time no resistance, but also no mercy.   Palmyra
was destroyed, the commonwealth dissolved, the walls
razed, the ornaments of the glorious temple of the sun
transferred to the temple which, in memory of this victory,
the emperor built to the sun-god of the East in Rome ;
only the forsaken halls and walls remained, as they still
stand in part at the present day.   This occurred in the
year 273.[2]   The flourishing of Palmyra was artificial,
produced by the routes assigned to traffic and the great
public buildings dependent on it.   Now the government
withdrew its hand from the unhappy city.   Traffic sought
and found other paths ; as Mesopotamia was then viewed
as a Roman province and soon came again to the empire,

Destruction
of Palmyra.

---

[1] This is the name given by Zosimus, i. 60, and Polemius Silvius,
p. 243 ; the Achilleus of the biographer of Aurelian, c. 31, seems a confusion with the usurper of the time of
Diocletian.—That at the same time in
Egypt a partisan of Zenobia and at
the same time robber-chief, by name
Firmus, rose against the government,
is doubtless possible, but the statement
rests only on the imperial biographies,
and the details added sound very
suspiciously.

[2] The chronology of these events
is not quite settled.   The rarity of
the Syrian coins of Vaballathus as
Augustus shows that the rupture with
Aurelian (end of 270) was soon followed

by the conquest.   According to the
dated inscriptions of Odaenathus and
Zenobia of August 271 (Waddington,
2611), the rule of the queen was at
that time still intact.   As an expedition of this sort, from the conditions of the climate, could not well
take place otherwise than in spring,
the first capture of Palmyra must
have ensued in the spring of 272.
The most recent (merely Palmyrene)
inscription which we know from that
quarter (Vogué, n. 116) is of August
272. The insurrection probably falls at
this time ; the second capture and the
destruction somewhere in the spring of
the year 273 (in accordance with which,
I. 166, note 1, is to be corrected).

and the territory of the Nabataeans as far as the port of
Aelana was in Roman hands, this intermediate station
might be dispensed with, and the traffic may have betaken
itself instead to Bostra or Beroea (Aleppo). The short
meteor-like splendour of Palmyra and its princes was
immediately followed by the desolation and silence which,
from that time down to the present day, enwrap the
miserable desert-village and the ruins of its colonnades.

Persian war
of Carus.

The ephemeral kingdom of Palmyra was in its origin
as in its fall closely bound up with the relations of the
Romans to the non-Roman East, but not less a part of
the general history of the empire. For, like the western
empire of Postumus, the eastern empire of Zenobia was
one of those masses into which the mighty whole seemed
then about to resolve itself. If during its subsistence its
leaders endeavoured earnestly to set limits to the onset
of the Persians, and indeed the development of its power
was dependent on that very fact, not merely did it in its
collapse seek deliverance from those same Persians, but
probably in consequence of the revolt of Zenobia
Armenia and Mesopotamia were lost to the Romans,
and after the subjugation of Palmyra the Euphrates
again for a time formed the frontier. The queen, when
she arrived at it, hoped to find a reception among the
Persians ; and Aurelian omitted to lead the legions over
it, seeing that Gaul, along with Spain and Britain, still at
that time refused to recognise the government. He and
his successor Probus were not able to take up this struggle.
But when in the year 282, after the premature end of the
latter, the troops proclaimed the commander next in rank,
Marcus Aurelius Carus, as emperor, it was the first saying
of the new ruler that the Persians should remember this
choice, and he kept it. Immediately he advanced with
the army into Armenia and re-established the earlier
order there. At the frontier of the land he was met by
Persian envoys, who declared themselves ready to grant
all that was reasonable ;[1] but they were hardly listened

---

[1] It throws no light on the position
of the Armenians, that in descriptions otherwise thoroughly apocryphal
(*vita Valer.* 6 ; *vita Aurel.* 27, 28)

to, and the march went on incessantly. Mesopotamia too became once more Roman, and the Parthian residential cities Seleucia and Ctesiphon were again occupied by the Romans without encountering lengthened resistance— to which the war between brothers then raging in the Persian empire contributed its part.[1] The emperor had just crossed the Tigris, and was on the point of penetrating into the heart of the enemy's country, when he met his death by violence, presumably by the hand of an assassin, and thereby the campaign also met its end. But his successor obtained in peace the cession of Armenia and Mesopotamia ;[2] although Carus wore the purple little more than a year, he re-established the imperial frontier of Severus.

Some years afterwards (293) a new ruler, Narseh, son of king Shapur, ascended the throne of Ctesiphon, and declared war on the Romans in the year 296 for the

Persian war under Diocletian.

the Armenians after the catastrophe of Valerian keep to the Persians, and appear in the last crisis of the Palmyrenes as allies of Zenobia by the side of the Persians ; both are obvious consequences from the general position of things. That Aurelian did not subdue Armenia any more than Mesopotamia, is supported in this case partly by the silence of the authorities, partly by the account of Synesius (*de regno*, p. 17) that the emperor Carinus (rather Carus) had in Armenia, close to the frontier of the Persian territory, summarily dismissed a Persian embassy, and that the young Persian king, alarmed by its report, had declared himself ready for any concession. I do not see how this narrative can be referred to Probus, as von Gutschmid thinks (*Zeitschr. d. deutsch. morgenl. Gesell.* xxxi. 50) ; on the other hand it suits very well the Persian expedition of Carus.

[1] The reconquest of Mesopotamia is reported only by the biographer, c. 8 ; but at the outbreak of the Persian war under Diocletian it is Roman. There is mention at the same place of internal troubles in the

Persian empire ; also in a discourse held in the year 289 (*Paneg.* iii. c. 17) there is mention of the war, which is waged against the king of Persia—this was Bahram II.—by his own brother Ormies or rather Hormizd *adscitis Sacis et Ruffis* (?) *et Gellis* (comp. Nöldeke, *Tabari*, p. 479). We have altogether only some detached notices as to this important campaign.

[2] This is stated clearly by Mamertinus (*Paneg.* ii. 7, comp. ii. 10, iii. 6) in the oration held in 289 : *Syriam velut amplexu suo tegebat Euphrates antequam Diocletiano sponte* (that is, without Diocletian needing to have recourse to arms, as is then further set forth) *se dederent regna Persarum ;* and further by another panegyrist of the year 296 (*Paneg.* v. 3) : *Partho ultra Tigrim reducto.* Turns like that in Victor, *Caes.* xxxix. 33, that Galerius *relictis finibus* had marched to Mesopotamia, or that Narseh, according to Rufius Festus, c. 25, ceded Mesopotamia in peace, cannot on the other hand be urged ; and as little, that Oriental authorities place the Roman occupation of Nisibis in 609 Sel. = 297/8 A.D. (Nöldeke, *Tabari*,

possession of Mesopotamia and Armenia.[1] Diocletian, who then had the supreme conduct of the empire generally, and of the East in particular, entrusted the management of the war to his imperial colleague Galerius Maximianus, a rough but brave general. The beginning was unfavourable. The Persians invaded Mesopotamia and reached as far as Carrhae ; the Caesar led against them the Syrian legions over the Euphrates at Nicephorium ; between these two positions the armies encountered each other, and the far weaker Roman force gave way. It was a hard blow, and the young general had to submit to severe reproaches, but he did not despair. For the next campaign reinforcements were brought up from the whole empire, and both rulers personally took the field ; Diocletian took his position in Mesopotamia with the chief force, while Galerius, reinforced by the flower of the Illyrian troops that had in the meantime come up, met, with a force of 25,000 men, the enemy in Armenia, and inflicted on him a decisive defeat. The camp and the treasure, nay, even the harem, of the great-king fell into the hands of the warriors, and with difficulty Narseh himself escaped from capture. In order to recover the women and the children the king declared himself ready to conclude peace on any terms ; his envoy Apharban conjured the Romans to spare the Persians, saying that the two empires, the Roman and the Parthian, were, as it were, the two eyes of the world, and neither could dispense with the other. It would have lain in the power of the Romans to add one more to their Oriental provinces ; the prudent ruler contented himself with regulating the state of possession in the north-east. Mesopotamia remained, as a matter of course, in the Roman possession ; the important commercial intercourse with the neigh-

p. 50). If this were correct, the exact account as to the negotiations for peace of 297 in Petrus Patricius, *fr.* 14, could not possibly be silent as to the cession of Mesopotamia and merely make mention of the regulation of the frontier-traffic.

[1] That Narseh broke into Armenia at that time Roman, is stated by Ammianus, xxiii. 5, 11 ; for Mesopotamia the same follows from Eutropius, ix. 24. On the 1st March 296 peace was still subsisting, or at any rate the declaration of war was not yet known in the west (*Paneg.* v. 10).

bouring foreign land was placed under strict state-control and essentially directed to the strong city of Nisibis, the basis of the Roman frontier-guard in eastern Mesopotamia. The Tigris was recognised as boundary of the direct Roman rule, to such an extent, however, that the whole of southern Armenia as far as the lake Thospitis (lake of Van) and the Euphrates, and so the whole upper valley of the Tigris, should belong to the Roman empire. This region lying in front of Mesopotamia did not become a province proper, but was administered after the previous fashion as the Roman satrapy of Sophene. Some decades later the strong fortress of Amida (Diarbekir) was constructed here, thenceforth the chief stronghold of the Romans in the region of the upper Tigris. At the same time the frontier between Armenia and Media was regulated afresh, and the supremacy of Rome over that land, as over Iberia, was once more confirmed. The peace did not impose important cessions of territory on the conquered, but it established a frontier favourable to the Romans, which for a considerable time served in these much contested regions as a demarcation of the two empires.[1] The policy of Trajan thereby obtained its complete accomplishment ; at all events the centre of gravity of the Roman rule shifted itself just at this time from the West to the East.

---

[1] The differences in the exceptionally good accounts, particularly of Petrus Patricius, *fr.* 14, and Ammianus, xxv. 7, 9, are probably only of a formal kind. The fact that the Tigris was to be the proper boundary of the empire, as Priscus says, does not exclude, especially considering the peculiar character of its upper course, the possibility of the boundary there partially going beyond it ; on the contrary, the five districts previously named in Petrus appear to be adduced just as beyond the Tigris, and to be excepted from the following general definition. The districts adduced by Priscus here and, expressly as beyond the Tigris, by Ammianus—these are in both Arzanene, Carduene, and Zabdicene, in Priscus Sophene and Intilene ("rather Ingilene, in Armenia Angel, now Egil" ; Kiepert), in Ammianus Moxoene and Rehimene (?)—cannot possibly all have been looked on by the Romans as Persian before the peace, when at any rate Armenia was already *Romano iuri obnoxia* (Ammianus, xxiii. 5, 11); beyond doubt the more westerly of them already then formed a part of Roman Armenia, and stand here only in so far as they were, in consequence of the peace, incorporated with the empire as the satrapy of Sophene. That the question here concerned not the boundary of the cession, but that of the territory directly imperial, is shown by the conclusion, which settles the boundary between Armenia and Media.

CHAPTER X.

SYRIA AND THE LAND OF THE NABATAEANS.

Conquest
of Syria.

IT was very gradually that the Romans, after acquiring the western half of the coasts of the Mediterranean, resolved on possessing themselves also of the eastern half. Not the resistance, which they here encountered in comparatively slight measure, but a well-founded fear of the denationalising consequences of such acquisitions, led to as prolonged an effort as possible on their part merely to preserve decisive political influence in those regions, and to the incorporation proper at least of Syria and Egypt taking place only when the state was already almost a monarchy. Doubtless the Roman empire became thereby geographically compact ; the Mediterranean Sea, the proper basis of Rome after it was a great power, became on all sides a Roman inland lake ; the navigation and commerce on its waters and shores formed politically an unity to the advantage of all that dwelt around. But by the side of geographical compactness went national bipartition. Through Greece and Macedonia the Roman state would never have become binational, any more than the Greek cities of Neapolis and Massalia had Hellenised Campania and Provence. But, while in Europe and Africa the Greek domain vanishes in presence of the compact mass of the Latin, so much of the third continent as was drawn, with the Nile-valley rightfully pertaining to it, into this cycle of culture belonged exclusively to the Greeks, and Antioch and Alexandria in particular were the true pillars of the Hellenic development that attained its culmination in

Alexander—centres of Hellenic life and Hellenic culture, and great cities, as was Rome. After having set forth in the preceding chapter the conflict between the East and West in and around Armenia and Mesopotamia, that filled the whole period of the empire, we turn to describe the relations of the Syrian regions, as they took shape at the same time. What we mean is the territory which is separated by the mountain-chain of Pisidia, Isauria, and Western Cilicia from Asia Minor; by the eastern continuation of these mountains and the Euphrates from Armenia and Mesopotamia, by the Arabian desert from the Parthian empire and from Egypt ; only it seemed fitting to deal with the peculiar fortunes of Judaea in a special section. In accordance with the diversity of political development under the imperial government, we shall speak in the first instance of Syria proper, the northern portion of this territory, and of the Phoenician coast that stretches along under the Libanus, and then of the country lying behind Palestine—the territory of the Nabataeans. What was to be said about Palmyra has already found its place in the preceding chapter.

After the partition of the provinces between the emperor and the senate, Syria was under imperial administration, and was in the East, like Gaul in the West, the central seat of civil and military control. This governorship was from the beginning the most esteemed of all, and only became in course of time all the more thought of. Its holder, like the governor of the two Germanies, wielded the command over four legions, and while the administration of the inland Gallic districts was taken away from the commanders of the Rhine-army and a certain restriction was involved in the very fact of their coordination, the governor of Syria retained the civil administration of the whole large province undiminished, and held for long alone in all Asia a command of the first rank. Under Vespasian, indeed, he obtained in the governors of Palestine and Cappadocia two colleagues likewise commanding legions ; but, on the other hand, through the annexation of the kingdom of Commagene,

Provincial government.

and soon afterwards of the principalities in the Libanus, the field of his administration was increased.   It was only in the course of the second century that a diminution of his prerogatives occurred, when Hadrian took one of the four legions from the governor of Syria and handed it over to the governor of Palestine.   It was Severus who at length withdrew the first place in the Roman military hierarchy from the Syrian governor.   After having subdued the province—which had wished at that time to make Niger emperor, as it had formerly done with its governor Vespasian—amidst resistance from the capital Antioch in particular, he ordained its partition into a northern and a southern half, and gave to the governor of the former, which was called Coele-Syria, two legions, to the governor of the latter, the province of Syro-Phoenicia, one.

Syrian troops.

Syria may also be compared with Gaul, in so far as this district of imperial administration was divided more sharply than most into pacified regions and border-districts needing protection.   While the extensive coast of Syria and the western regions generally were not exposed to hostile attacks, and the protection on the desert frontier against the roving Bedouins devolved on the Arabian and Jewish princes, and subsequently on the troops of the province of Arabia as also on the Palmyrenes, more than on the Syrian legions, the Euphrates-frontier required, particularly before Mesopotamia became Roman, a watch against the Parthians similar to that on the Rhine against the Germans.   But if the Syrian legions came to be employed on the frontier, they could not be dispensed with in western Syria as well.[1]   The troops of the Rhine were

---

[1] We cannot exactly determine the standing quarters of the Syrian legions ; yet what is here said is substantially assured. Under Nero the 10th legion lay at Raphaneae, north-west from Hamath (Josephus, *Bell. Jud.* vii. 1, 3) ; and at that same place, or at any rate nearly in this region under Tiberius the 6th (Tacitus, *Ann.* ii. 79) ; probably in or near Antioch the 12th under Nero (Josephus, *Bell. Jud.* ii. 18, 19).   At least one legion lay on the Euphrates ; for the time before the annexation of Commagene Josephus attests this (*Bell. Jud.* vii. 1, 3), and subsequently one of the Syrian legions had its headquarters in Samosata (Ptolemaeus, v. 15, 11 ; inscription from the time of Severus, *C. I. L.* vi. 1409 ; *Itin. Antonini*, p. 186). Probably the staffs of most of the Syrian legions had their seat in the western districts, and the ever-recurring complaint that encamping in the

certainly there also on account of the Gauls; yet the Romans might say with justifiable pride that for the great capital of Gaul and the three Gallic provinces a direct garrison of 1200 men sufficed. But for the Syrian population, and especially for the capital of Roman Asia, it was not enough to station legions on the Euphrates. Not merely on the edge of the desert, but also in the retreats of the mountains there lodged daring bands of robbers, who roamed in the neighbourhood of the rich fields and large towns—not to the same extent as now, but constantly even then—and, often disguised as merchants or soldiers, pillaged the country houses and the villages. But even the towns themselves, above all Antioch, required like Alexandria garrisons of their own. Beyond doubt this was the reason why a division into civil and military districts, like that enacted for Gaul by Augustus, was never even so much as attempted in Syria, and why the large self-subsistent camp-settlements, out of which *e.g.* originated Mentz on the Rhine, Leon in Spain, Chester in England, were altogether wanting in the Roman East. But beyond doubt this was also the reason why the Syrian army was so much inferior in discipline and spirit to that of the Western provinces; why the stern discipline, which was exercised in the military standing camps of the West, never could take root in the urban cantonments of the East. When stationary troops have, in addition to their more immediate destination, the task of police assigned to them, this of itself has a demoralising effect; and only too often, where they are expected to keep in check turbulent civic masses, their own discipline in fact is thereby undermined. The Syrian wars formerly described furnish the far from pleasant commentary on this; none of them found an army capable of warfare in existence, and regu-

---

towns disorganised the Syrian army, applies chiefly to this arrangement. It is doubtful whether in the better times there existed headquarters proper of the legions on the edge of the desert; at the frontier-posts there detachments of the legions were employed, and in particular the specially disturbed district between Damascus and Bostra was strongly furnished with legionaries provided on the one hand by the command of Syria, on the other by that of Arabia after its institution by Trajan.

larly there was need to bring up Occidental troops in order to give the turn to the struggle.

Hellenising of Syria.   Syria in the narrower sense and its adjoining lands, the Plain Cilicia and Phoenicia, never had under the Roman emperors a history properly so called. The inhabitants of these regions belonged to the same stock as the inhabitants of Judaea and Arabia, and the ancestors of the Syrians and the Phoenicians were settled in a remote age at one spot with those of the Jews and the Arabs, and spoke one language. But while the latter clung to their peculiar character and to their language, the Syrians and the Phoenicians became Hellenised even before they came under Roman rule. This Hellenising took effect throughout in the formation of Hellenic polities. The foundation for this had indeed been laid by the native development, particularly by the old and great mercantile cities on the Phoenician coast. But above all the formation of states by Alexander and the Alexandrids, just like that of the Roman republic, had as its basis not the tribe, but the urban community ; it was not the old Macedonian hereditary principality, but the Greek polity that Alexander carried into the East ; and it was not from tribes, but from towns that he designed, and the Romans designed, to constitute their empire. The idea of the autonomous burgess-body is an elastic one, and the autonomy of Athens and Thebes was a different thing from that of the Macedonian and Syrian city, just as in the Roman circle the autonomy of free Capua had another import than that of the Latin colonies of the republic or even of the urban communities of the empire ; but the fundamental idea is everywhere that of self-administering citizenship sovereign within its own ring-wall. After the fall of the Persian empire, Syria, along with the neighbouring Mesopotamia, was, as the military bridge of connection between the West and the East, covered more than any other land with Macedonian settlements. The Macedonian names of places transferred thither to the greatest extent, and nowhere else recurring in the whole empire of Alexander, show that here the flower of the Hellenic conquerors of the East

was settled, and that Syria was to become for this state
the New-Macedonia ; as indeed, so long as the empire of
Alexander retained a central government, this had there its
seat.   Then the troubles of the last Seleucid period had
helped the Syrian imperial towns to greater independence.

These arrangements the Romans found existing.   Of
non-urban districts administered directly by the empire
there were probably none at all in Syria according to the
organisation planned by Pompeius, and, if the dependent
principalities in the first epoch of the Roman rule embraced
a great portion of the southern interior of the province,
these were withal mostly mountainous and poorly inhabited
districts of subordinate importance.   Taken as a whole,
for the Romans in Syria not much was left to be done as
to the increase of urban development—less than in Asia
Minor.   Hence there is hardly anything to be told from
the imperial period of the founding of towns in the strict
sense as regards Syria.   The few colonies which were laid
out here, such as Berytus under Augustus and probably
also Heliopolis, had no other object than those conducted
to Macedonia, namely, the settlement of veterans.

How the Greeks and the older population in Syria
stood to one another, may be clearly traced by the very
local names.   The majority of districts and towns here
bear Greek names, in great part, as we have observed,
derived from the Macedonian home, such as Pieria, An-
themusias, Arethusa, Beroea, Chalcis, Edessa, Europus,
Cyrrhus, Larisa, Pella, others named after Alexander or
the members of the Seleucid house, such as Alexandria,
Antioch, Seleucis and Seleucia, Apamea, Laodicea,
Epiphaneia.   The old native names maintain themselves
doubtless side by side, as Beroea, previously in Aramaean
Chalep, is also called Chalybon, Edessa or Hierapolis, previously Mabog, is called also Bambyce, Epiphaneia, previously Hamat, is also called Amathe.   But for the most
part the older appellations give way before the foreign
ones, and only a few districts and larger places, such as
Commagene, Samosata, Hemesa, Damascus, are without
newly-formed Greek names.   Eastern Cilicia has few

Continu-
ance of the
native
language
and habits
under Hel-
lenism.

Macedonian foundations to show ; but the capital Tarsus became early and completely Hellenised, and was long before the Roman time one of the centres of Hellenic culture.   It was somewhat otherwise in Phoenicia ; the mercantile towns of old renown, Aradus, Byblus, Berytus, Sidon, Tyrus, did not properly lay aside the native names; but how here too the Greek gained the upper hand, is shown by the Hellenising transformation of these same names, and still more clearly by the fact that New-Aradus is known to us only under the Greek name Antaradus, and likewise the new town founded by the Tyrians, the Sidonians, and the Aradians in common on this coast only under the name Tripolis, and both have developed their modern designations Tartus and Tarabulus from the Greek.   Already in the Seleucid period the coins in Syria proper bear exclusively, and those of the Phoenician towns most predominantly, Greek legends ; and from the beginning of the imperial period the sole rule of Greek is here an established fact.[1]   The oasis of Palmyra alone, not merely separated by wide stretches of desert, but also preserving a certain political independence, formed, as we saw (p. 95), an exception in this respect.   But in intercourse the native idioms were retained.   In the mountains of the Libanus and the Anti-Libanus, where in Hemesa (Homs), Chalcis, Abila (both between Berytus and Damascus) small princely houses of native origin ruled till towards the end of the first century after Christ, the native language had probably the sole sway in the imperial period, as indeed in the mountains of the Druses so difficult of access the language of Aram has only in recent times yielded to Arabic.   But two thousand years ago it was in fact the language of the people in all Syria.[2] That in the case of the double-named towns the Syrian designation predominated in common life just as did the

---

[1] There is a coin of Byblus from the time of Augustus with Greek and Phoenician legend (Imhoof-Blumer, *Monnaies grecques*, 1883, p. 443).

[2] Johannes Chrysostomus of Antioch († 407) points on several occa-sions (*de sanctis martyr*. Opp. ed. Paris, 1718, vol. ii. p. 651; *Homil.* xix. *ibid*. p. 188) to the ἑτεροφωνία, the βάρβαρος φωνή of the λαός in contrast to the language of the cultured.

Greek in literature, appears from the fact that at the present day Beroea-Chalybon is named Haleb (Aleppo), Epiphaneia-Amathe Hamat, Hierapolis-Bambyce-Mabog Membid, Tyre by its Aramaean name Sur; that the Syrian town known to us from documents and authors only as Heliopolis still bears at the present day its primitive native name Baalbec, and, in general, the modern names of places have come, not from the Greek, but from the Aramaean.

In like manner the worship shows the continued life Worship. of Syrian nationality. The Syrians of Beroea bring their votive gifts with Greek legend to Zeus Malbachos, those of Apamea to Zeus Belos, those of Berytus as Roman citizens to Jupiter Balmarcodes—all deities, in which neither Zeus nor Jupiter had real part. This Zeus Belos is no other than the Malach Belos adored at Palmyra in the Syriac language (p. 96, note 1). How vivid was, and continued to be, the hold of the native worship of the gods in Syria, is most clearly attested by the fact that the lady of Hemesa, who by her marriage-relationship with the house of Severus obtained for her grandson the imperial dignity at the beginning of the third century, not content with the boy's being called supreme Pontifex of the Roman people, urged him also to entitle himself before all Romans the chief priest of the native sun-god Elagabalus. The Romans might conquer the Syrians; but the Roman gods had in their own home yielded the field to those of Syria.

No less are the numerous Syrian proper names that have come to us mainly non-Greek, and double names are not rare; the Messiah is termed also Christus, the apostle Thomas also Didymus, the woman of Joppa raised up by Peter "the gazelle," Tabitha or Dorcas. But for literature, and presumably also for business-intercourse and the intercourse of the cultured, the Syrian idiom was as little in existence as the Celtic in the West; in these Jam-
blichus. circles Greek exclusively prevailed, apart from the Latin required also in the East for the soldiers. A man of letters of the second half of the second century, whom

Sohaemus the king of Armenia formerly mentioned (p. 76) brought to his court, has inserted in a romance, which has its scene in Babylon, some points of the history of his own life that illustrate this relation. He is, he says, a Syrian, not, however, one of the immigrant Greeks, but of native lineage on the father's and mother's side, Syrian by language and habits, acquainted also with the Babylonian language and with Persian magic. But this same man, who in a certain sense declines the Hellenic character, adds that he had appropriated Hellenic culture ; and he became an esteemed teacher of youth in Syria, and a notable romance-writer of the later Greek literature.[1]

Later Syriac literature.

If subsequently the Syrian idiom again became a written language and developed a literature of its own, this is to be traced not to an invigoration of national feeling, but to the immediate needs of the propagation of Christianity. That Syriac literature, which began with the translation of the writings of the Christian faith into Syriac, remained confined to the sphere of the specific culture of the Christian clergy, and hence took up only the small fragments of general Hellenic culture which the theologians of that time found conducive to, or compatible with, their ends ;[2] this authorship did not attain, and doubtless did not strive after, any higher aim than the transference of the library of the Greek monastery to the Maronite cloisters. It hardly reaches further back than to the second century of our era, and had its centre,

---

[1] The extract of Photius from the romance of Jamblichus, c. 17, which erroneously makes the author a Babylonian, is essentially corrected and supplemented by the *scholion* upon it. The private secretary of the great-king, who comes among Trajan's captives to Syria, becomes there tutor of Jamblichus, and instructs him in the "barbarian wisdom," is naturally a figure of the romance running its course in Babylon, which Jamblichus professes to have heard from this his instructor ; but characteristic of the time is the Armenian court-man-of-letters and princes' tutor (for it was doubtless as " good rhetor " that he was called by Sohaemus to Valarshapat) himself, who in virtue of his magical art not merely understands the charming of flies and the conjuring of spirits, but also predicts to Verus the victory over Vologasus, and at the same time narrates in Greek to the Greeks stories such as might stand in the *Thousand and One Nights*.

[2] Syriac literature consists almost exclusively of translations of Greek works. Among profane writings treatises of Aristotle and Plutarch stand in the first rank, then practical writings of a juristic or agronomic

not in Syria, but in Mesopotamia, particularly in Edessa,[1] where the native language had not become so entirely a dialect as in the older Roman territory.

Among the manifold bastard forms which Hellenism assumed in the course of its diffusion at once civilising and degenerating, the Syro-Hellenic is doubtless that in which the two elements are most equally balanced, but perhaps at the same time that which has most decisively influenced the collective development of the empire.   The Syrians received, no doubt, the Greek urban organisation and appropriated Hellenic language and habits ; nevertheless they did not cease to feel themselves as Orientals, or rather as organs of a double civilisation.   Nowhere is this perhaps more sharply expressed than in the colossal tomb-temple, which at the commencement of the imperial period Antiochus king of Commagene erected for himself on a solitary mountain-summit not far from the Euphrates. He names himself in the copious epitaph a Persian ; the priest of the sanctuary is to present to him the memorial-offering in the Persian dress, as the custom of his family demands; but he calls the Hellenes also, like the Persians, the blessed roots of his race, and entreats the blessing of all the gods of Persis as of Macetis, that is of the Persian as well as of the Macedonian land, to rest upon his descendants. For he is the son of a native king of the family of the Achaemenids and of a Greek prince's daughter of the house of Seleucus ; and, in keeping with this, the images on the one hand of his paternal ancestors back to the first Darius, on the other hand of his maternal back to Alexander's marshal, embellished the tomb in a long double row.   But the gods, whom he honours, are at the same time Persian and Greek, Zeus Oromasdes, Apollon Mithras Helios Hermes, Artagnes Herakles Ares, and the effigy of this latter, for example, bears the club of the Greek hero and at the same time the Persian tiara.   This Persian

Syro-Hellenic mixed culture

Tomb of Antiochus of Commagene.

character, and books of popular entertainment, such as the romance of Alexander, the fables of Aesop, the sentences of Menander.

[1] The Syriac translation of the New Testament, the oldest text of the Syriac language known to us, probably originated in Edessa ; the στρατιῶται of the Acts of the Apostles are here called " Romans."

prince, who calls himself at the same time a friend of the
Hellenes, and as loyal subject of the emperor a friend of
the Romans, as not less that Achaemenid called by Marcus
and Lucius to the throne of Armenia, Sohaemus, are true
representatives of the native aristocracy of imperial Syria,
which bears in mind alike Persian memories and the
Romano-Hellenic present.   From such circles the Persian
worship of Mithra reached the West.   But the population, which was placed at the same time under this great
nobility Persian or calling itself Persian, and under the
government of Macedonian and later of Italian masters,
was in Syria, as in Mesopotamia and Babylonia, Aramaean ;
it reminds us in various respects of the modern Roumans
in presence of the upper ranks of Saxons and Magyars.
Certainly it was the most corrupt and most corrupting
element in the conglomerate of the Romano-Hellenic
peoples.   Of the so-called Caracalla, who was born at
Lyons as son of an African father and a Syrian mother, it
was said that he united in himself the vices of three races,
Gallic frivolity, African savageness, and Syrian knavery.

Christi-
anity and
Neopla-
tonism. This interpenetration of the East and Hellenism,
which has nowhere been carried out so completely as in
Syria, meets us predominantly in the form of the good
and noble becoming ruined in the mixture.   This, however, is not everywhere the case ; the later developments
of religion and of speculation, Christianity and Neoplaton-
ism, have proceeded from the same conjunction ; if with
the former the East penetrates into the West, the latter is
the transformation of the Occidental philosophy in the
sense and spirit of the East—a creation in the first instance
of the Egyptian Plotinus (204-270) and of his most considerable disciple the Syrian Malchus or Porphyrius (233
till after 300), and thereafter pre-eminently cultivated in
the towns of Syria.   For a discussion of these two
phenomena, so significant in the history of the world,
this is not the place ; but they may not be forgotten in
estimating the position of matters in Syria.

Antioch. The Syrian character finds its eminent expression in
the capital of the country and, before Constantinople was

founded, of the Roman East generally—inferior as respects population only to Rome and Alexandria, and possibly also to the Babylonian Seleucia—Antioch, on which it appears requisite to dwell for a moment.   The town, one of the youngest in Syria and now of small importance, did not become a great city by the natural circumstances of commerce, but was a creation of monarchic policy.   The Macedonian conquerors called it into life, primarily from military considerations, as a fitting central place for a rule which embraced at once Asia Minor, the region of the Euphrates, and Egypt, and sought also to be near to the Mediterranean.[1]   The like aim and the different methods of the Seleucids and the Lagids find their true expression in the similarity and the contrast of Antioch and Alexandria; as the latter was the centre for the naval power and the maritime policy of the Egyptian rulers, so Antioch was the centre for the continental Eastern monarchy of the rulers of Asia.   The later Seleucids at different times undertook large new foundations here, so that the city, when it became Roman, consisted of four independent and walled-in districts, all of which again were enclosed by a common wall.   Nor were immigrants from a distance wanting.   When Greece proper fell under the rule of the Romans, and Antiochus the Great had vainly attempted to dislodge them thence, he granted at least to the emigrant Euboeans and Aetolians an asylum in his capital. In the capital of Syria, as in that of Egypt, a commonwealth in some measure independent and a privileged position were conceded to the Jews, and the position of the towns as centres of the Jewish Diaspora was not the weakest element in their development.   Once made a residency and the seat of the supreme administration of a great empire, Antioch remained even in Roman times the

---

[1] This is said by Diodorus, xx. 47, of the forerunner of Antioch, the town of Antigonea, situated about five miles farther up the river.   Antioch was for the Syria of antiquity nearly what Aleppo is for the Syria of the present day, the rendezvous of inland traffic ; only that, in the case of that foundation, as the contemporary construction of the port of Seleucia shows, the immediate connection with the Mediterranean was designed, and hence the town was laid out farther to the west.

capital of the Asiatic provinces of Rome. Here resided the emperors, when they sojourned in the East, and regularly the governor of Syria ; here was struck the imperial money for the East, and here especially, as well as in Damascus and Edessa, were found the imperial manufactories of arms. It is true that the town had lost its military importance for the Roman empire; and under the changed circumstances the bad communication with the sea was felt as a great evil, not so much on account of the distance, as because the port—the town of Seleucia, planned at the same time with Antioch—was little fitted for large traffic. The Roman emperors from the Flavians down to Constantius expended enormous sums to hew out of the masses of rocks surrounding this locality the requisite docks with their tributary canals, and to provide sufficient piers ; but the art of the engineers, which at the mouth of the Nile had succeeded in throwing up the highest mounds, contended vainly in Syria with the insurmountable difficulties of the ground. As a matter of course the largest town of Syria took an active part in the manufactures and the commerce of this province, of which we shall have to speak further on ; nevertheless it was a seat of consumers more than of producers.

Daphne.　　In no city of antiquity was the enjoyment of life so much the main thing, and its duties so incidental, as in " Antioch upon Daphne," as the city was significantly called, somewhat as if we should say " Vienna upon the Prater." For Daphne [1] was a pleasure-garden, about five miles from the city, ten miles in circumference, famous for its laurel-trees, after which it was named, for its old cypresses which even the Christian emperors ordered to be spared, for its flowing and gushing waters, for its shining temple of Apollo, and its magnificent much-frequented festival of the 10th August. The whole environs of the

[1] The space between Antioch and Daphne was filled with country-houses and villas (Libanius, *pro rhetor.* ii. p. 213 Reiske), and there was also here a suburb Heraclea or else Daphne (O. Müller, *Antiq. Antioch*, p. 44 ; comp. *vita Veri*, 7); but when Tacitus, *Ann.* ii. 83, names this suburb Epidaphne, this is one of his most singular blunders. Plinius, *H. N.* v. 27, 79, says correctly : *Antiochia Epidaphnes cognominata.*

city, which lies between two wooded mountain-chains in the valley of the Orontes abounding in water, fourteen miles upward from its mouth, are even at the present day, in spite of all neglect, a blooming garden and one of the most charming spots on earth.   No city in all the empire excelled it in the splendour and magnificence of its public structures.   The chief street, which to the length of thirty-six stadia, nearly four and a half miles, with a covered colonnade on both sides, and a broad carriage-way in the middle, traversed the city in a straight direction along the river, was imitated in many ancient towns, but had not its match even in imperial Rome.   As the water ran into every good house in Antioch,[1] so the people walked in those colonnades through the whole city at all seasons protected from rain as from the heat of the sun, and during the evening also in lighted streets, of which we have no record as to any other city of antiquity.[2]

[1] " That wherein we especially beat all," says the Antiochene Libanius, in the Panegyric on his home delivered under Constantius (i. 354 R.), after having described the springs of Daphne and the aqueducts thence to the city, "is the water-supply of our city ; if in other respects any one may compete with us, all give way so soon as we come to speak of the water, its abundance and its excellence. In the public baths every stream has the proportions of a river, in the private several have the like, and the rest not much less. He who has the means of laying out a new bath does so without concern about a sufficient flow of water, and has no need to fear that, when ready, it will remain dry. Therefore every district of the city (there were eighteen of these) carefully provides for the special elegance of its bathing-establishment ; these district-bathing-establishments are so much finer than the general ones, as they are smaller than these are, and the inhabitants of the district strive to surpass one another. One measures the abundance of running water by the number of the (good) dwelling-houses ; for as many as are the dwelling-houses, so many are also the running waters, nay there are even in individual houses often several ; and the majority of the workshops have also the same advantage. Therefore we have no fighting at the public wells as to who shall come first to draw—an evil, under which so many considerable towns suffer, when there is a violent crowding round the wells and outcry over the broken jars. With us the public fountains flow for ornament, since every one has water within his doors.   And this water is so clear that the pail appears empty, and so pleasant that it invites us to drink."
[2] " Other lights," says the same orator, p. 363, " take the place of the sun's light, lamps which leave the Egyptian festival of illumination far behind ; and with us night is distinguished from day only by the difference of the lighting ; diligent hands find no difference and forge on, and he who will sings and dances, so that Hephaestos and Aphrodite here share the night between them."   In the street-sport which the prince Gallus indulged in, the lamps of Antioch were very inconvenient to him (Ammianus, xiv. 1, 9).

But amidst all this luxury the Muses did not find themselves at home ; science in earnest and not less earnest
art were never truly cultivated in Syria and more especially
in Antioch. However complete was the analogy in other
respects between Egypt and Syria as to their development,
their contrast in a literary point of view was sharp ; the
Lagids alone entered on this portion of the inheritance
of Alexander the Great. While they fostered Hellenic
literature and promoted scientific research in an Aristotelian sense and spirit, the better Seleucids doubtless by
their political position opened up the East to the Greeks—
the mission of Megasthenes to king Chandragupta in
India on the part of Seleucus I., and the exploring of the
Caspian Sea by his contemporary the admiral Patrocles,
were epoch-making in this respect—but of immediate
interposition in literary interests on the part of the
Seleucids the history of Greek literature has nothing more
to tell than that Antiochus the Great, as he was called,
made the poet Euphorion his librarian. Perhaps the
history of Latin literature may make a claim to serious
scientific work on the part of Berytus, the Latin island in
the sea of Oriental Hellenism. It is perhaps no accident
that the reaction against the modernising tendency in
literature of the Julio-Claudian epoch, and the reintroduc-
tion of the language and writings of the republican time
into the school as into literature, originated with a Bery-
tian belonging to the middle class, Marcus Valerius
Probus, who in the schools that were left in his remote
home moulded himself still on the old classics, and then,
in energetic activity more as a critical author than as
strictly a teacher, laid the foundation for the classicism of
the later imperial period. The same Berytus became
later, and remained through the whole period of the empire,
for all the East, the seat of the study of jurisprudence requisite towards an official career. As to Hellenic literature no doubt the poetry of the epigram and the wit of
the *feuilleton* were at home in Syria ; several of the most
noted Greek minor poets, like Meleager, Philodemus of
Gadara, and Antipater of Sidon, were Syrians and unsur-

passed in sensuous charm as in refined versification ; and the father of the *feuilleton* literature was Menippus of Gadara.   But these performances lie for the most part before, and some of them considerably before, the imperial period.

In the Greek literature of this epoch no province is so poorly represented as Syria; and this is hardly an accident, although, considering the universal position of Hellenism under the empire, not much stress can be laid on the home of the individual writers.   On the other hand the subordinate authorship which prevailed in this epoch —such as stories of love, robbers, pirates, procurers, soothsayers, and dreams, destitute of thought or form, and fabulous travels—had probably its chief seat here. Among the colleagues of the already-mentioned Jamblichus, author of the Babylonian history, his countrymen must have been numerous ; the contact of this Greek literature with the Oriental literature of a similar kind doubtless took place through the medium of Syrians.   The Greeks indeed had no need to learn lying from the Orientals ; yet the no longer plastic but fanciful story-telling of their later period has sprung from Scheherazade's horn of plenty not from the pleasantry of the Graces.   It is perhaps not accidentally that the satire of this period, when it views Homer as the father of lying travels, makes him a Babylonian with the proper name of Tigranes.   Apart from this entertaining reading, of which even those were somewhat ashamed who spent their time in writing or reading it, there is hardly any other prominent name to be mentioned from these regions than the contemporary of that Jamblichus, Lucian of Commagene.   He, too, wrote nothing except, in imitation of Menippus, essays and fugitive pieces after a genuinely Syrian type, witty and sprightly in personal banter, but where this is at an end, incapable of saying amid his laughter the earnest truth or of even handling the plastic power of comedy.

This people valued only the day.   No Greek region has so few memorial-stones to show as Syria ; the great Antioch, the third city in the empire, has—to say nothing

Minor literature.

Daily life and amusements.

of the land of hieroglyphics and obelisks—left behind fewer
inscriptions than many a small African or Arabian village.
With the exception of the rhetorician Libanius from the
time of Julian, who is more well-known than important,
this town has not given to literature a single author's
name. The Tyanitic Messiah of heathenism, or his
apostle speaking for him, was not wrong in terming the
Antiochenes an uncultivated and half-barbarous people,
and in thinking that Apollo would do well to transform
them as well as their Daphne ; for " in Antioch, while the
cypresses knew how to whisper, men knew not how to
speak." In the artistic sphere Antioch had a leading
position only as respected the theatre and sports generally.
The exhibitions which captivated the public of Antioch
were, according to the fashion of this time, less strictly
dramatic than noisy musical performances, ballets, animal
hunts, and gladiatorial games. The applauding or hissing
of this public decided the reputation of the dancer throughout the empire. The jockeys and other heroes of the
circus and theatre came pre-eminently from Syria.[1] The
ballet-dancers and the musicians, as well as the jugglers
and buffoons, whom Lucius Verus brought back from his
Oriental campaign—performed, so far as his part went,
in Antioch—to Rome, formed an epoch in the history of
Italian theatricals. The passion with which the public in
Antioch gave itself up to this pleasure is characteristically
shown by the fact, that according to tradition the gravest
disaster which befell Antioch in this period, its capture
by the Persians in 260 (p. 101), surprised the burgesses
of the city in the theatre, and from the top of the mount,
on the slope of which it was constructed, the arrows flew

---

[1] The remarkable description of the
empire from the time of Constantius
(Müller, *Geog. Min.* ii. p. 213 ff.), the
only writing of the kind in which the
state of industry meets with a certain
consideration, says of Syria in this
respect : "Antioch has everything
that one desires in abundance, but
especially its races. Laodicea, Berytus, Tyre, Caesarea (in Palestine) have
races also. Laodicea sends abroad
jockeys, Tyre and Berytus actors,
Caesarea dancers (*pantomimi*), Heliopolis on Lebanon flute-players (*chor-
aulae*), Gaza musicians (*auditores*, by
which ἀκροάματα is incorrectly rendered), Ascalon wrestlers (*athletae*),
Castabala (strictly speaking in Cilicia)
boxers."

into the ranks of the spectators. In Gaza, the most south-
erly town of Syria, where heathenism possessed a stronghold in the famous temple of Marnas, at the end of the
fourth century the horses of a zealous heathen and of a
zealous Christian ran at the races, and, when on that occasion " Christ beat Marnas," St. Jerome tells us, numerous
heathens had themselves baptised.

All the great cities of the Roman empire doubtless
vied with each other in dissoluteness of morals ; but in
this the palm probably belongs to Antioch.   The decorous
Roman, whom the severe moral-portrait-painter of Trajan's
time depicts, as he turns his back on his native place, because it had become a city of Greeks, adds that the Achae-
ans formed the least part of the filth ; that the Syrian
Orontes had long discharged itself into the river Tiber,
and flooded Rome with its language and its habits, its
street-musicians, female harp-players and triangle-beaters,
and the troops of its courtesans.   The Romans of
Augustus spoke of the Syrian female flute-player, the *am-
bubaia*,[1] as we speak of the Parisian *cocotte*.   In the Syrian
cities, it is stated even in the last age of the republic by
Posidonius, an author of importance, who was himself
a native of the Syrian Apamea, the citizens have become
disused to hard labour ; the people there think only of
feasting and carousing, and all clubs and private parties
serve for this purpose ; at the royal table a garland is put
on every guest, and the latter is then sprinkled with Babylonian perfume ; flute-playing and harp-playing sound
through the streets ; the gymnastic institutes are converted
into hot baths—by the latter is meant the institution of
the so-called Thermae, which probably first emerged in
Syria and subsequently became general ; they were in
substance a combination of the gymnasium and the hot-
bath.   Four hundred years later matters went on after
quite a similar fashion in Antioch.   The quarrel between
Julian and these townsmen arose not so much about the
emperor's beard, as because in this city of taverns, which,
as he expresses himself, has nothing in view but dancing

_Immor-
ality._

[1] From the Syrian word *abbubo*, fife.

and drinking, he regulated the prices for the hosts. The religious system of the Syrian land was also, and especially, pervaded by these dissolute and sensuous doings. The cultus of the Syrian gods was often an appanage of the Syrian brothel.[1]

It would be unjust to make the Roman government responsible for this state of affairs in Syria ; it had been the same under the government of the Diadochi, and was merely transmitted to the Romans. But in the history of this age the Syro-Hellenic element was an essential factor, and, although its indirect influence was of far more weight, it still in many ways made itself perceptible directly in politics. Of political partisanship proper there can be still less talk in the case of the Antiochenes of this and every age, than in the case of the burgesses of the other great cities of the empire ; but in mocking and disputation they apparently excelled all others, even the Alexandrians that vied with them in this respect. They never made a revolution, but readily and earnestly supported every pretender whom the Syrian army set up, Vespasian against Vitellius, Cassius against Marcus, Niger against Severus, always ready, where they thought that they had support in reserve, to renounce allegiance to the existing government. The only talent which indisputably belonged to them—their mastery of ridicule—they exercised not merely against the actors of their stage, but no less against the rulers sojourning in the capital of the East, and the ridicule was quite the same against the actor as against the emperor ; it applied to personal appearance and to individual peculiarities, just as if their sovereign appeared only to amuse them with his part. Thus there existed between the public of Antioch and their rulers—particularly those who spent a considerable time there, Hadrian, Verus, Marcus, Severus,

[1] The little treatise, ascribed to Lucian, as to the Syrian goddess at Hierapolis adored by all the East, furnishes a specimen of the wild and voluptuous fable-telling which was characteristic of the Syrian cultus. In this narrative—the source of Wieland's Kombabus—self-mutilation is at once celebrated and satirised in turn as an act of high morality and of pious faith.

Julian—so to speak, a perpetual warfare of sarcasm, one document of which, the reply of the last named emperor to the "beard-mockers" of Antioch, is still preserved. While this imperial man of letters met their sarcastic sayings with satirical writings, the Antiochenes at other times had to pay more severely for their evil speaking and their other sins. Thus Hadrian withdrew from them the right of coining silver ; Marcus withdrew the right of assembly, and closed for some time the theatre. Severus took even from the town the primacy of Syria, and transferred it to Laodicea, which was in constant neighbourly warfare with the capital ; and, if these two ordinances were soon again withdrawn, the partition of the province, which Hadrian had already threatened, was carried into execution, as we have already said (p. 118), under Severus, and not least because the government wished to humble the turbulent great city. This city even made a mockery of its final overthrow. When in the year 540 the Persian king Chosroes Nushirvan appeared before the walls of Antioch he was received from its battlements not merely with showers of arrows but with the usual obscene sarcasms ; and, provoked by this, the king not merely took the town by storm, but carried also its inhabitants away to his New-Antioch in the province of Susa.

The brilliant aspect of the condition of Syria was the economic one ; in manufactures and trade Syria takes, alongside of Egypt, the first place among the provinces of the Roman empire, and even claims in a certain respect precedence over Egypt. Agriculture throve under the permanent state of peace, and under a sagacious administration which directed its efforts particularly to the advancement of irrigation, to an extent which puts to shame modern civilisation. No doubt various parts of Syria are still at the present day of the utmost luxuriance ; the valley of the lower Orontes, the rich garden round Tripolis with its groups of palms, groves of oranges copses of pomegranates and jasmine, the fertile coast-plain north and south of Gaza, neither the Bedouins nor the Pashas have hitherto been able to make desolate. But

Culture of the soil.

their work is nevertheless not to be estimated lightly.
Apamea in the middle of the Orontes valley, now a rocky
wilderness without fields and trees, where the poor flocks
on the scanty pasturages are decimated by the robbers of
the mountains, is strewed far and wide with ruins, and
there is documentary attestation that under Quirinius the
governor of Syria, the same who is named in the Gospels,
this town with its territory included numbered 117,000
free inhabitants. Beyond question the whole valley of
the Orontes abounding in water—already at Hemesa it
is from 30 to 40 mètres broad and one and a half to
three mètres deep—was once a great seat of cultivation.
But even of the districts, which are now mere deserts, and
where it seems to the traveller of the present day impossible for man to live and thrive, a considerable portion
was formerly a field of labour for active hands. To
the east of Hemesa, where there is now not a green leaf
nor a drop of water, the heavy basalt-slabs of former oil-
presses are found in quantities. While at the present day
olives scantily grow only in the valleys of the Lebanon
abounding in springs, the olive woods must formerly have
stretched far beyond the valley of the Orontes. The
traveller now from Hemesa to Palmyra carries water with
him on the back of camels, and all this part of the route
is covered with the remains of former villas and hamlets.[1]
The march of Aurelian along this route (p. 110) no army
could now undertake. Of what is at present called desert
a good portion is rather the laying waste of the blessed
labour of better times. "All Syria," says a description
of the earth from the middle of the fourth century, "over-

---

[1] The Austrian engineer, Joseph Tschernik (Petermann's *Geogr. Mittheil.* 1875, *Ergänzungsheft,* xliv. p. 3, 9) found basalt-slabs of oil-presses not merely on the desert plateau at Kala'at el-Hossn between Hemesa and the sea, but also to the number of more than twenty eastward from Hemesa at el-Ferklûs, where the basalt itself does not occur, as well as numerous walled terraces and mounds of ruins at the same place; with terracings on the whole stretch of seventy miles between Hemesa and Palmyra. Sachau (*Reise in Syrien und Mesopotamien,* 1883, p. 23, 55) found remains of aqueducts at different places of the route from Damascus to Palmyra. The cisterns of Aradus cut in the rock, already mentioned by Strabo (xvi. 2, 13, p. 753), still perform their service at the present day (Renan, *Phénicie,* p. 40).

flows with corn, wine, and oil." But Syria was not even in antiquity an exporting land, in a strict sense, for the fruits of the earth, like Egypt and Africa, although the noble wines were sent away, *e.g.* that of Damascus to Persia, those of Laodicea, Ascalon, Gaza, to Egypt and from thence as far as Ethiopia and India, and even the Romans knew how to value the wine of Byblus, of Tyre, and of Gaza.

Of far more importance for the general position of the province were the Syrian manufactures. A series of industries, which came into account for export, were here at home, especially of linen, purple, silk, glass. The weaving of flax, practised from of old in Babylonia, was early transplanted thence to Syria ; as that description of the earth says : " Scytopolis (in Palestine), Laodicea, Byblus, Tyrus, Berytus, send out their linen into all the world," and in the tariff-law of Diocletian accordingly there are adduced as fine linen goods those of the three first-named towns alongside of those of the neighbouring Tarsus and of Egypt, and the Syrian have precedence over all. That the purple of Tyre, however many competitors with it arose, always retained the first place, is well known ; and besides the Tyrian there were in Syria numerous purple dyeworks likewise famous on the coast above and below Tyre at Sarepta, Dora, Caesarea, even in the interior, in the Palestinian Neapolis and in Lydda. The raw silk came at this epoch from China and especially by way of the Caspian Sea, and so to Syria ; it was worked up chiefly in the looms of Berytus and of Tyre, in which latter place especially was prepared the purple silk that was much in use and brought a high price. The glass manufactures of Sidon maintained their primitive fame in the imperial age, and numerous glass-vases of our museums bear the stamp of a Sidonian manufacturer.

Manufactures.

To the sale of these wares, which from their nature belonged to the market of the world, fell to be added the whole mass of goods which came from the East by the Euphrates-routes to the West. It is true that the Arabian

Commerce.

and Indian imports at this time turned away from this road, and took chiefly the route by way of Egypt ; but not merely did the Mesopotamian traffic remain necessarily with the Syrians ; the emporia also at the mouth of the Euphrates stood in regular caravan-intercourse with Palmyra (p. 98), and thus made use of the Syrian harbours.

How considerable this intercourse was with the eastern neighbours is shown by nothing so clearly as by the similarity of the silver coinage in the Roman East and in the Parthian Babylonia ; in the provinces of Syria and Cappadocia the Roman government coined silver, varying from the imperial currency, after the sorts and the standards of the neighbouring empire. The Syrian manufactures themselves, *e.g.* of linen and silk, were stimulated by the very import of the similar Babylonian articles of commerce, and, like these, the leather and skin goods, the ointments, the spices, the slaves of the East, came during the imperial period to a very considerable extent by way of Syria to Italy and the West in general. But this always remained characteristic of these primitive seats of commercial intercourse, that the men of Sidon and their countrymen, in this matter very different from the Egyptians, not merely sold their goods to those of other lands, but themselves conveyed them thither, and, as the ship-captains in Syria formed a prominent and respected class,[1] so Syrian merchants and Syrian factories in the imperial period were to be found nearly as much everywhere as in the remote times of which Homer tells. The Tyrians had such factories in the two great import-harbours of Italy, Ostia and Puteoli, and, as these themselves in their documents describe their establishments as the greatest and most spacious of their kind, so in the description of the earth which we have often quoted, Tyre is named the first place of the East for commerce and traffic[2] ; in like manner

---

[1] In Aradus, a town very populous in Strabo's time (xvi. 2, 13, p. 753), there appears under Augustus a πρόβουλος τῶν ναυαρχησάντων (*C. I. Gr.* 4736 *h*, better in Renan, *Mission de Phénicie*, p. 31).

[2] *Totius orbis descriptio*, c. 24 : *nulla forte civitas Orientis est eius spissior in negotio.* The documents of the *statio* (*C. I. Gr.* 5853 ; *C. I. L.* x. 1601) give a lively picture of these factories. They serve in the

Strabo brings forward as a specialty at Tyre and at Aradus the unusually high houses, consisting of many stories. Berytus and Damascus, and certainly many other Syrian and Phoenician commercial towns, had similar factories in the Italian ports.[1] Accordingly we find, particularly in the later period of the empire, Syrian merchants, chiefly Apamean, settled not merely in all Italy but likewise in all the larger emporia of the West, at Salonae in Dalmatia, Apulum in Dacia, Malaca in Spain, but above all in Gaul and Germany, *e.g.* at Bordeaux, Lyons, Paris, Orleans, Treves, so that these Syrian Christians also, like the Jews, live according to their own customs and make use of their Greek in their meetings.[2]

first instance for religious ends, that is, for the worship of the Tyrian gods at a foreign place ; for this object a tax is levied at the larger station of Ostia from the Tyrian mariners and merchants, and from its produce there is granted to the lesser a yearly contribution of 1000 sesterces, which is employed for the rent of the place of meeting ; the other expenses are raised by the Tyrians in Puteoli, doubtless by voluntary contributions.

[1] For Berytus this is shown by the Puteolan inscription *C. I. L.* x. 1634 ; for Damascus it is at least suggested by that which is there set up (x. 1576) to the *Iupiter optimus maximus Damascenus.*—We may add that it is here apparent with how good reason Puteoli is called Little Delos. At Delos in the last age of its prosperity, that is, nearly in the century before the Mithradatic war, we meet with Syrian factories and Syrian worships in quite a like fashion and in still greater abundance ; we find there the guild of the Herakleistae of Tyre (τὸ κοινὸν τῶν Τυρίων 'Ηρακλεϊστῶν καὶ ναυκλήρων, *C. I. Gr.* 2271) of the Poseidoniastae of Berytus (τὸ κοινὸν Βηρυτίων Ποσειδωνιαστῶν ἐμπόρων καὶ ναυκλήρων καὶ ἐγδοχέων, *Bull. de corr. Hell.* vii., p. 468), of the woshippers of Adad and Atargatis of Heliopolis (*ib.* vi. 495 f.), apart from the numerous memorial-stones of Syrian mer-

chants. Comp. Homolle *ib.* viii. p. 110 f.

[2] When Salvianus (towards 450) remonstrates with the Christians of Gaul that they are in nothing better than the heathens, he points (*de gub. Dei,* iv. 14, 69) to the worthless *negotiatorum et Syricorum omnium turbae, quae maiorem ferme civitatum universarum partem occupaverunt.* Gregory of Tours relates that king Guntchram was met at Orleans by the whole body of citizens and extolled, as in Latin, so also in Hebrew and in Syriac (viii. 1 : *hinc lingua Syrorum, hinc Latinorum, hinc . . . Judaeorum in diversis laudibus varie concrepabat*), and that after a vacancy in the episcopal see of Paris a Syrian merchant knew how to procure it for himself, and gave away to his countrymen the places belonging to it (x. 26 : *omnem scholam decessoris sui abiciens Syros de genere suo ecclesiasticae domui ministros esse statuit*). Sidonius (about 450) describes the perverse world of Ravenna (Ep. 1, 8) with the words : *fenerantur clerici, Syri psallunt ; negotiatores militant, monachi negotiantur.* *Usque hodie,* says Hieronymus (in Ezech. 27, vol. v. p. 513 Vall.) *permanet in Syris ingenitus negotiationis ardor, qui per totum mundum lucri cupiditate discurrunt et tantam mercandi habent vesaniam, ut occupato nunc orbe*

The state of things formerly described among the
Antiochenes and the Syrian cities generally becomes intelligible only on this basis. The world of rank there consisted
of rich manufacturers and merchants, the bulk of the population of the labourers and the mariners ;[1] and, as later the
riches acquired in the East flowed to Genoa and Venice,
so then the commercial gains of the West flowed back
to Tyre and Apamea. With the extensive field of traffic
that lay open to these traders on a great scale, and with
the on the whole moderate frontier and inland tolls, the
Syrian export trade, embracing a great part of the most
lucrative and most transportable articles, already brought
enormous capital sums into their hands; and their business
was not confined to native goods.[2] What comfort of life
once prevailed here we learn, not from the scanty remains
of the great cities that have perished, but from the more
forsaken than desolated region on the right bank of the
Orontes, from Apamea on to the point where the river

Romano (written towards the end
of the fourth century) *inter gladios et
miserorum neces quaerant divitias et
paupertatem periculis fugiant.* Other
proofs are given by Friedländer, *Sitten-
geschichte,* ii.[5] p. 67. Without doubt we
may be allowed to add the numerous
inscriptions of the West which proceed from Syrians, even if those do
not designate themselves expressly as
merchants. Instructive as to this
point is the Coemeterium of the small
north-Italian country-town Concordia
of the fifth century ; the foreigners
buried in it are all Syrians, mostly
of Apamea (*C. I.* iii. p. 1060) ;
likewise all the Greek inscriptions
found in Treves belong to Syrians
(*C. I. Gr.* 9891, 9892, 9893). These
inscriptions are not merely dated in
the Syrian fashion, but show also
peculiarities of the dialectic Greek
there (*Hermes,* xix. 423).—That this
Syro-Christian Diaspora, standing in
relation to the contrast between the
Oriental and Occidental clergy, may
not be confounded with the Jewish
Diaspora, is clearly shown by the
account in Gregorius ; it evidently

stood much higher, and belonged
throughout to the better classes.

[1] This is partly so even at the
present day. The number of silk-
workers in Höms is estimated at
3000 (Tschernik, *l.c.*)

[2] One of the oldest (*i.e.* after
Severus and before Diocletian) epitaphs of this sort is the Latin-Greek
one found not far from Lyons (Wil-
manns, 2498 ; comp. Lebas-Waddington, n. 2329) of a Θαῖμος ὁ καὶ
Ἰουλιανὸς Σαάδου (in Latin *Thaemus
Iulianus Sati fil.*), a native of Atheila
(*de vico Athelani*), not far from Canatha in Syria (still called ' Atîl, not
far from Kanawât in the Hauran),
and *decurio* in Canatha, settled in
Lyons (πάτραν λείπων ἧκε τῷδ' ἐπὶ
χώρῳ), and a wholesale trader there
for Aquitanian wares ([ἐs πρ]ᾶσιν ἔχων
ἐνπόρ[ιο]ν ἀγορασμῶν [με]στὸν ἐκ Ἀκου-
ιτανίης ὧδ' ἐπὶ Λουγουδούνοιο—*nego-
tiatori Luguduni et prov. Aquitanica*).
Accordingly these Syrian merchants
must not only have dealt in Syrian
goods, but have, with their capital
and their knowledge of business, practised wholesale trading generally.

turns towards the sea. In this district of about a hundred miles in length there still stand the ruins of nearly a hundred townships, with whole streets still recognisable, the buildings with the exception of the roofs executed in massive stone-work, the dwelling-houses surrounded by colonnades, embellished with galleries and balconies, windows and portals richly and often tastefully decorated with stone arabesques, with gardens and baths laid out, with farm-offices in the ground-story, stables, wine and oil presses hewn in the rocks,[1] as also large burial chambers likewise hewn in the rock, filled with sarcophagi, and with the entrances adorned with pillars. Traces of public life are nowhere met with ; it is the country-dwellings of the merchants and of the manufacturers of Apamea and Antioch, whose assured prosperity and solid enjoyment of life are attested by these ruins. These settlements, of quite a uniform character, belong throughout to the late times of the empire, the oldest to the beginning of the fourth century, the latest to the middle of the sixth, immediately before the onslaught of Islam, under which this prosperous and flourishing life succumbed. Christian symbols and Biblical language are everywhere met with, and likewise stately churches and ecclesiastical structures. The development of culture, however, did not begin merely under Constantine, but simply grew and became consolidated in those centuries. Certainly those stone-buildings were preceded by similar villa and garden structures of a less enduring kind. The regeneration of the imperial government after the confused troubles of the third century has its expression in the upward impulse which the Syrian mercantile world then received ; but up to a certain degree this picture of it left to us may be referred also to the earlier imperial period.

The relations of the Jews in the time of the Roman empire were so peculiar and, one might say, so little

Jewish traffic.

---

[1] Characteristic is the Latin epigram on a press-house, *C. I. L.* iii. 188, in this home of the "Apamean grape" (*vita Elagabali*, c. 21).

dependent on the province which was named in the earlier
period after them, in the later rather by the revived name
of the Philistaeans or Palaestinenses, that, as we have
already said, it appeared more suitable to treat of them in a
separate section.   The little which is to be remarked as
to the land of Palestine, especially the not unimportant
share of its maritime and partly also of its inland towns
in Syrian industry and Syrian trade, has already been
mentioned in the exposition given above of these matters.
The Jewish Diaspora had already, before the destruction
of the temple, extended in such a way that Jerusalem,
even while it still stood, was more a symbol than a home,
very much as the city of Rome was for the so-called
Roman burgesses of later times.   The Jews of Antioch
and Alexandria, and the numerous similar societies of
lesser rights and minor repute took part, as a matter of
course, in the commerce and intercourse of the places
where they dwelt.   Their Judaism comes into account in
the case only perhaps so far as the feelings of mutual
hatred and mutual contempt, which had become developed
or rather increased since the destruction of the temple,
and the repeated national-religious wars between Jews and
non-Jews must have exercised their effect also in these
circles.   As the Syrian merchants resident abroad met
together in the first instance for the worship of their
native deities, the Syrian Jew in Puteoli cannot well have
belonged to the Syrian merchant-guilds there ; and, if the
worship of the Syrian gods found more and more an echo
abroad, that which benefited the other Syrians drew one
barrier the more between the Syrians believing in Moses
and the Italians.   If those Jews who had found a home
outside of Palestine, attached themselves beyond it not to
those who shared their dwelling-place but to those who
shared their religion, as they could not but do, they
thereby renounced the esteem and the toleration which
the Alexandrians and the Antiochenes and the like met
with abroad, and were taken for what they professed to
be—Jews.   The Palestinian Jews of the West, however,
had for the most part not originated from mercantile emigra-

tion, but were captives of war or descendants of such, and in every respect homeless ; the Pariah position which the children of Abraham occupied, especially in the Roman capital—that of the mendicant Jew, whose household furniture consisted in his bundle of hay and his usurer's basket, and for whom no service was too poor and too menial—linked itself with the slave-market. Under these circumstances we can understand why the Jews during the imperial period played in the West a subordinate part alongside of the Syrians. The religious fellowship of the mercantile and proletarian immigrants told heavily on the collective body of the Jews, along with the general disparagement connected with their position. But that Diaspora, as well as this, had little to do with Palestine.

There remains still a frontier territory to be looked at, which is not often mentioned, and which yet well deserves consideration ; it is the Roman province of Arabia. It bears its name wrongly ; the emperor who erected it, Trajan, was a man of big deeds but still bigger words. The Arabian peninsula, which separates the region of the Euphrates from the valley of the Nile, lacking in rain, without rivers, on all sides surrounded by a rocky coast poor in harbours, was little fitted for agriculture or for commerce, and in old times by far the greater part of it remained the undisputed heritage of the unsettled inhabitants of the desert. In particular the Romans, who understood how to restrict their possession in Asia as in Egypt better than any other of the changing powers in the ascendant, never even attempted to subdue the Arabian peninsula. Their few enterprises against its south-eastern portion, the most rich in products, and from its relation to India the most important also for commerce, will be set forth when we discuss the business-relations of Egypt. Roman Arabia, even as a Roman client-state and especially as a Roman province, embraced only a moderate portion of the north of the peninsula, but, in addition, the land to

Province of Arabia.

the south and east of Palestine between this and the great desert till beyond Bostra. At the same time with this let us take into account the country belonging to Syria between Bostra and Damascus, which is now usually named after the Haurân mountains, according to its old designation Trachonitis and Batanaea.

These extensive regions were only to be gained for civilisation under special conditions. The steppe-country proper (Hamâd) to the eastward from the region with which we are now occupied as far as the Euphrates, was never taken possession of by the Romans, and was incapable of cultivation ; only the roving tribes of the desert, such as at the present day the Haneze, traverse it, to pasture their horses and camels in winter along the Euphrates, in summer on the mountains south of Bostra, and often to change the pasture-ground several times in the year. The pastoral tribes settled westward of the steppe, who pursue in particular the breeding of sheep to a great extent, stand already at a higher degree of culture. But there is manifold room for agriculture also in these districts. The red earth of the Haurân, decomposed lava, yields in its primitive state much wild rye, wild barley, and wild oats, and furnishes the finest wheat. Individual deep valleys in the midst of the stone-deserts, such as the " seed-field," the Ruhbe in the Trachonitis, are the most fertile tracts in all Syria ; without ploughing, to say nothing of manuring, wheat yields on the average eighty and barley a hundredfold, and twenty-six stalks from one grain of wheat are not uncommon. Nevertheless no fixed dwelling-place was formed here, because in the summer months the great heat and the want of water and pasture compel the inhabitants to migrate to the mountain pastures of the Haurân. But there was not wanting opportunity even for fixed settlement. The garden-quarter around the town of Damascus, watered by the river Baradâ in its many arms, and the fertile even now populous districts which enclose it on the east, north, and south, were in ancient as in modern times the pearl of Syria. The plain round Bostra, particularly the so-called Nukra to the west of it, is at the present day the granary for Syria, although from the want of rain on an average every fourth harvest is lost, and the locusts often invading it from the neighbouring desert remain a scourge of the land which cannot be exterminated. Wherever the water-courses of the mountains are led into the plain, fresh life flourishes amidst them. " The fertility of this region," says one who knows it well, " is inexhaustible ; and even at the present day, where the Nomads have left neither tree nor shrub, the land, so far as the eye reaches, is like a garden." Even on the lavasurfaces of the mountainous districts the lava-streams have left not a few places (termed Kâ' in the Haurân), free for cultivation.

This natural condition has, as a rule, handed over the country to shepherds and robbers. The necessarily nomadic character of a great part of the population leads to endless feuds, particularly about places of pasture, and to constant seizures of those regions which are suited for fixed settlement ; here, still more than elsewhere, there is need for the formation of such political powers as are in a position to procure quiet and peace on a wider scale, and for these there is no right basis in the population. There is hardly a region in the wide world in which, so much as in this case, civilisation has not grown up spontaneously, but could only be called into existence by the ascendency of conquest from without. When military stations hem in the roving tribes of the desert and force those within the limit of cultivation to a peaceful pastoral life, when colonists are conducted to the regions capable of culture, and the waters of the mountains are led by human hands into the plains, then, but only then, a cheerful and plentiful life thrives in this region.

The pre-Roman period had not brought such blessings to these lands. The inhabitants of the whole territory as far as Damascus belong to the Arabian branch of the great Semitic stock ; the names of persons at least are throughout Arabic. In it, as in northern Syria, Oriental and Occidental civilisation met ; yet up to the time of the empire the two had made but little progress. The lan-

Greek influence in eastern Syria.

guage and the writing, which the Nabataeans used, were those of Syria and of the Euphrates-lands, and could only have come from thence to the natives. On the other hand the Greek settlement in Syria extended itself, in part at least, also to these regions. The great commercial town of Damascus had become Greek with the rest of Syria. The Seleucids had carried the founding of Greek towns even into the region beyond the Jordan, especially into the northern Decapolis ; further to the south at least the old Rabbath Ammon had been converted by the Lagids into the city of Philadelphia. But further away and in the eastern districts bordering on the desert the Nabataean kings were not much more than nominally obedient to the Syrian or Egyptian Alexandrids, and coins or inscriptions and buildings, which might be attributed to pre-Roman Hellenism, have nowhere come to light.

Arrangements of Pompeius.

64-63.

When Syria became Roman, Pompeius exerted himself to strengthen the Hellenic urban system, which he found in existence ; as indeed the towns of the Decapolis subsequently reckoned their years from the year 690-91, in which Palestine had been added to the empire.[1] But in this region the government as well as the civilisation continued to be left to the two vassal-states, the Jewish and the Arabian.

The territory of Herod beyond the Jordan.

Of the king of the Jews, Herod and his house, we shall have to speak elsewhere ; here we have to mention his activity in the extending of civilisation toward the east. His field of dominion stretched over both banks of the Jordan in all its extent, northwards as far at least as

---

[1] That the Decapolis and the reorganisation of Pompeius reached at last as far as Kanata (Kerak), north-west of Bostra, is established by the testimonies of authors and by the coins dated from the Pompeian era (Waddington on 2412, *d*). To the same town probably belong the coins with the name Γαβ(ε)ίν(ια) Κάναθα, with the name and dates of the same era (Reichardt, *Num. Zeitschrift*, 1880, p. 53); this place would accordingly belong to the numerous ones restored by Gabinius (Josephus, *Arch.* xiv. 5, 3). Waddington no doubt (on no. 2329) assigns these coins, so far as he knew them, to the second place of this name, the modern Kanawât, the proper capital of the Haurân, to the northward of Bostra ; but it is far from probable that the organisation of Pompeius and Gabinius extended so far eastward. Presumably this second city was younger and named after the first, the most easterly town of the Decapolis.

Chelbon north-west from Damascus, southward as far as
the Dead Sea, while the region farther to the east between
his kingdom and the desert was assigned to the king of
the Arabians. He and his descendants, who still bore
sway here after the annexation of the lordship of Jerusalem down to Trajan, and subsequently resided in Caesarea Paneas in the southern Lebanon, had endeavoured
energetically to tame the natives. The oldest evidences
of a certain culture in these regions are doubtless the
cave-towns, of which there is mention in the Book of
Judges, large subterranean collective hiding-places made
habitable by air-shafts, with streets and wells, fitted to
shelter men and flocks, difficult to be found and, even
when found, difficult to be reduced. Their mere existence
shows the oppression of the peaceful inhabitants by the
unsettled sons of the steppe. " These districts," says
Josephus, when he describes the state of things in the
Haurân under Augustus, " were inhabited by wild tribes,
without towns and without fixed fields, who harboured with
their flocks under the earth in caves with narrow entrance
and wide intricate paths, but copiously supplied with water
and provisions were difficult to be subdued." Several of
these cave-towns contained as many as 400 head. A
remarkable edict of the first or second Agrippa, fragments
of which have been found at Canatha (Kanawât), summons
the inhabitants to leave off their " animal-conditions " and
to exchange their cavern-life for civilised existence. The
non-settled Arabs live chiefly by the plundering partly of
the neighbouring peasants, partly of caravans on the march ;
the uncertainty was increased by the fact that the petty
prince Zenodorus of Abila to the north of Damascus, in the
Anti-Libanus, to whom Augustus had committed the superintendence over the Trachon, preferred to make common
cause with the robbers and secretly shared in their gains.
Just in consequence of this the emperor assigned this region
to Herod, and his remorseless energy succeeded, in some
measure, in repressing this brigandage. The king appears
to have instituted on the east frontier a line of military
posts, fortified and put under royal commanders ($\xi\pi a\rho\chi o\iota$)

He would have achieved still more if the Nabataean territory had not afforded the robbers an asylum ; this was
one of the causes of variance between him and his Arabian
colleague.[1]   His Hellenising tendency comes into prominence in this domain as strongly and less unpleasantly than
in his government at home.   As all the coins of Herod
and the Herodians are Greek, so in the land beyond the
Jordan, while the oldest monument with an inscription
that we know—the Temple of Baalsamin at Canatha—
bears an Aramaean dedication, the honorary bases erected
there, including one for Herod the Great,[2] are bilingual
or merely Greek ; under his successors Greek rules alone.

The king-
dom
of [iv. 134.
Nabat.

By the side of the Jewish kings stood the formerly-
mentioned (iv. 140) " king of Nabat," as he called himself.
The residence of this Arabian prince was the city, known
to us only by its Greek name Petra, a rock-fastness
situated midway between the Dead Sea and the north-
east extremity of the Arabian Gulf, from of old an emporium for the traffic of India and Arabia with the region
of the Mediterranean.   These rulers possessed the northern half of the Arabian peninsula ; their power extended
on the Arabian Gulf as far as Leuce Come opposite to the
Egyptian town of Berenice, in the interior at least as far
as the region of the old Thaema.[3]   To the north of the
peninsula their territory reached as far as Damascus,
which was under their protection,[4] and even beyond

---

[1] The " refugees from the tetrarchy
of Philippus," who serve in the army
of Herodes Antipas, tetrarch of Galilee, and pass over to the enemy in the
battle with Aretas the Arabian (Josephus, *Arch.* xviii. 5, 1), are beyond
doubt Arabians driven out from the
Trachonitis.

[2] Waddington, 2366 = Vogué, *In-
scr. du Haouran*, n. 3.   Bilingual is
also the oldest epitaph of this region
from Suwêda, Waddington, 2320 =
Vogué, n. 1, the only one in the Haurân, which expresses the mute *iota*.
The inscriptions are so put on both
monuments that we cannot determine
which language takes precedence.

[3] At Medain Sâlih or Hijr, south-

ward from Teimâ, the ancient Thaema,
there has recently been found by the
travellers Doughty and Huber, a
series of Nabataean inscriptions, which,
in great part dated, reach from the
time of Augustus down to the death
of Vespasian.   Latin inscriptions are
wanting, and the few Greek are of
the latest period ; to all appearance,
on the conversion of the Nabataean
kingdom into a Roman province, the
portion of the interior of Arabia that
belonged to the former was given up
by the Romans.

[4] The city of Damascus voluntarily
submitted under the last Seleucids
about the time of the dictatorship of
Sulla to the king of the Nabataeans

Damascus[1], and enclosed as with a girdle the whole of Palestinian Syria. The Romans, after taking possession of Judaea, came into hostile contact with them, and Marcus Scaurus led an expedition against them.   At that

at the time, presumably the Aretas, with whom Scaurus fought (Josephus, *Arch.* xiii. 15). The coins with the legend βασιλέως 'Αρέτου φιλέλληνος (Eckhel, iii. 330; Luynes, *Rev. de Numism.* 1858, p. 311), were perhaps struck in Damascus, when this was dependent on the Nabataeans ; the reference of the number of the year on one of them is not indeed certain, but points, it may be presumed, to the last period of the Roman republic. Probably this dependence of the city on the Nabataean kings subsisted so long as there were such kings. From the fact that the city struck coins with the heads of the Roman emperors, there follows doubtless its dependence on Rome and therewith its self-administration, but not its non-dependence on the Roman vassal-prince ; such protectorates assumed shapes so various that these arrangements might well be compatible with each other. The continuance of the Nabataean rule is attested partly by the circumstance that the ethnarch of king Aretas in Damascus wished to have the Apostle Paul arrested, as the latter writes in the 2d Epistle to the Corinthians, xi. 32, partly by the recently-established fact (see following note) that the rule of the Nabataeans to the north-east of Damascus was still continuing under Trajan.—Those who start, on the other hand, from the view that, if Aretas ruled in Damascus, the city could not be Roman, have

attempted in various ways to fix the chronology of that event in the life of Paul. They have thought of the complication between Aretas and the Roman government in the last years of Tiberius ; but from the course which this took it is not probable that it brought about a permanent change in the state of possession of Aretas. Melchior de Vogué (*Mélanges d'arch. orientale*, app. p. 33) has pointed out that between Tiberius and Nero— more precisely, between the years 33 and 62 (Saulcy, *Num. de la terre sainte*, p. 36)—there are no imperial coins of Damascus, and has placed the rule of the Nabataeans there in this interval, on the assumption that the emperor Gaius showed his favour to the Arabian as to so many others of the vassal-princes, and invested him with Damascus. But such interruptions of coinage are of frequent occurrence, and require no such profound explanation. The attempt to find a chronological basis for the history of Paul's life in the sway of the Nabataean king at Damascus, and generally to define the time of Paul's abode in this city, must probably be abandoned. If we may so far trust the representation —in any case considerably shifted— of the event in Acts ix., Paul went to Damascus before his conversion, in order to continue there the persecution of the Christians in which Stephen had perished, and then, when on his conversion he took part on the con-

---

[1] The Nabataean inscription found recently near Dmêr, to the north-east of Damascus on the road to Palmyra (Sachau, *Zeitschr. der deutschen morgenl. Gesellschaft,* xxxviii. p. 535), dates from the month Ijjar of the year 410 according to the Roman (*i. e.* Seleucid) reckoning, and the 24th year of king Dabel, the last Nabataean one, and so from May 99 A.D., has shown that this district up to the annexation of this kingdom remained under the rule of the Nabataeans. We may add that the dominions here seem to have been, geographically, a tangled mosaic ; thus the tetrarch of Galilee and the Nabataean king fought about the territory of Gamala on the lake of Gennesaret (Josephus, *Arch.* xviii. 51).

time their subjugation was not accomplished ; but it must have ensued soon afterwards.[1]   Under Augustus their king Obodas was just as subject to the empire[2] as Herod the king of the Jews, and rendered, like the latter, military service in the Roman expedition against southern Arabia. Since that time the protection of the imperial frontier in the south as in the east of Syria, as far up as to Damascus, must have lain mainly in the hands of this Arabian king. With his Jewish neighbour he was at constant feud. Augustus, indignant that the Arabian instead of seeking justice at the hand of his suzerain against Herod, had encountered the latter with arms, and that Obodas's son, Harethath, or in Greek Aretas, after the death of his father, instead of waiting for investiture, had at once entered upon the dominion, was on the point of deposing the latter and of joining his territory to the Jewish ; but the misrule of Herod in his later years withheld him from this step, and so Aretas was confirmed (about 747 U.C.). Some decades later he began again warfare at his own hand against his son-in-law, the prince of Galilee, Herod Antipas, on account of the divorce of his daughter in favour of the beautiful Herodias.   He retained the upper

7.

trary in Damascus for the Christians, the Jews there resolved to put him to death, in which case it must therefore be presupposed that the officials of Aretas, like Pilate, allowed free course to the persecution of heretics by the Jews. Moreover, it follows from the trustworthy statements of the Epistle to the Galatians, that the conversion took place at Damascus (for the ὑπέστρεψα shows this), and Paul went from thence to Arabia ; further, that he came three years after his conversion for the first time, and seventeen years after it for the second time, to Jerusalem, in accordance with which the apocryphal accounts of the Book of Acts as to his Jerusalem-journeys are to be corrected (Zeller, *Apostelgesch.* p. 216). But we cannot determine exactly either the time of the death of Stephen, much less the time intervening between this and the flight of the converted Paul from

Damascus, or the interval between his second journey to Jerusalem and the composition of the Galatian letter, or the year of that composition itself.

[1] Perhaps through Gabinius (Appian, *Syr.* 51).

[2] Strabo, xvi. 4, 21, p. 779. The coins of these kings, however, do not show the emperor's head. But that in the Nabataean kingdom dates might run by the Roman imperial years is shown by the Nabataean inscription of Hebrân (Vogué, *Syrie Centrale, insc.* n. 1), dated from the seventh year of Claudius, and so from the year 47. Hebrân, a little to the north of Bostra, appears to have been reckoned also at a later time to Arabia (Lebas-Waddington, 2287) ; and Nabataean inscriptions of a public tenor are not met with outside of the Nabataean state ; the few of the kind from Trachonitis are of a private nature.

hand, but the indignant suzerain Tiberius ordered the governor of Syria to proceed against him. The troops were already on the march, when Tiberius died (37) ; and his successor, Gaius, who did not wish well to Antipas, pardoned the Arabian. King Maliku or Malchus, the successor of Aretas, fought under Nero and Vespasian in the Jewish war as a Roman vassal, and transmitted his dominion to his son Dabel, the contemporary of Trajan, and the last of these rulers. More especially after the annexation of the state of Jerusalem and the reducing of the respectable dominion of Herod to the far from martial kingdom of Caesarea Paneas, the Arabian was the most considerable of the Syrian client-states, as indeed it furnished the strongest among the royal contingents to the Roman army besieging Jerusalem. This state even under Roman supremacy refrained from the use of the Greek language ; the coins struck under the rule of its kings bear, apart from Damascus, an Aramaic legend. But there appear the germs of an organised condition and of civilised government. The coinage itself probably only began after the state had come under Roman clientship. The Arabian-Indian traffic with the region of the Mediterranean moved in great part along the caravan-route watched over by the Romans, running from Leuce Come by way of Petra to Gaza.[1] The princes of the Nabataean kingdom made use, just like the community of Palmyra, of Greek official designations for their magistrates, *e.g.* of

[1] "Leuke Kome in the land of the Nabataeans," says Strabo under Tiberius, xvi. 4, 23, p. 780, "is a great place of trade, whither and whence the caravan - traders (καμηλέμποροι) go safely and easily from and to Petra with so large numbers of men and camels that they differ in nothing from encampments." The Egyptian merchant also, writing under Vespasian, in his description of the coasts of the Red Sea (c. 19), mentions "the port and the fortress (φρούριον) of Leuce Come, whence the route leads towards Petra to the king of the Nabataeans Malichas. It may be regarded as the emporium for the goods conveyed thither from Arabia in not very large vessels. Therefore there is sent thither (ἀποστέλλεται) a receiver of the import-dues of a fourth of the value, and for the sake of security a centurion (ἐκατοντάρχης) with men." As one belonging to the Roman empire here mentions officials and soldiers, these can only be Roman ; the centurion does not suit the army of the Nabataean king, and the form of tax is quite the Roman. The bringing of a client-state within the sphere of imperial taxation occurs elsewhere, *e.g.* in the regions of the Alps. The road from Petra to Gaza is mentioned by Plin. *H. N.* vi. 28, 144.

the titles of Eparch and of Strategos. If under Tiberius the good order of Syria brought about by the Romans and the security of the harvests occasioned by their military occupation are made prominent as matters of boasting, this is primarily to be referred to the arrangements made in the client-states of Jerusalem or subsequently of Caesarea Paneas and of Petra.

Institution of the province of Arabia. Under Trajan the direct rule of Rome took the place of these two client-states. In the beginning of his reign king Agrippa II. died, and his territory was united with the province of Syria. Not long after, in the year 106, the governor Aulus Cornelius Palma broke up the previous dominion of the kings of Nabat, and made the greater part of it into the Roman province of Arabia, while Damascus went to Syria, and what the Nabataean king had possessed in the interior of Arabia was abandoned by the Romans. The erection of Arabia is designated as subjugation, and the coins also which celebrate the taking possession of it attest that the Nabataeans offered resistance, as indeed generally the nature of their territory as well as their previous attitude lead us to assume a relative independence on the part of these princes. But the historical significance of these events may not be sought in warlike success ; the two annexations, which doubtless went together, were no more than acts of administration carried out perhaps by military power, and the tendency to acquire these domains for civilisation and specially for Hellenism was only heightened by the fact that the Roman government took upon itself the work. The Hellenism of the East, as summed up in Alexander, was a church militant, a thoroughly conquering power pushing its way in a political, religious, economic, and literary point of view. Here, on the edge of the desert, under the pressure of anti-Hellenic Judaism and in the hands of the spiritless and vacillating government of the Seleucids, it had hitherto achieved little. But now, pervading the Roman system, it develops a motive power, which stands related to the earlier, as the power of the Jewish and the Arabian vassal-princes to that of the Roman empire. In this country, where everything depended and depends on protecting the state of peace by the setting up of a superior and standing military force, the institution of a legionary camp in Bostra under a commander of senatorial rank was an epoch-making event. From this centre the requisite posts were established at suitable places and provided with garrisons. For example, the stronghold of Namara (Nemâra) deserves mention, a long day's march beyond the boundaries of the properly habitable mountainland, in the midst of the stony desert, but commanding the only spring to be found within it and the forts attached to it in the already mentioned oasis of Ruhbe and further on at Jebel Sês ; these garrisons together control the whole projection of the Haurân. Another series of forts, placed under the Syrian command and primarily under that of the legion posted at Danava (p. 95), and laid out at uniform distances of three leagues apart, secured the route from Damascus to Palmyra ; the best known of them, the second in the series, was that of Dmêr (p. 149, n. 1), a rectangle of 300 and 350 paces respectively, provided on every side with six towers and a portal fifteen paces in breadth, and surrounded by a ringwall of sixteen feet thick, once faced outwardly with beautiful blocks of hewn stone.

Never had such an aegis been extended over this land. It was not, properly speaking, denationalised. The Arabic names remained down to the latest time, although not unfrequently, just as in Syria (p. 121), a Romano-Hellenic name is appended to the local one ; thus a sheikh names himself " Adrianos or Soaidos, son of Malechos."[1] The native worship also remains unaffected ; the chief deity of the Nabataeans, Dusaris, is doubtless compared with Dionysus, but regularly continues to be worshipped under his local name, and down to a late period the Bostrenes celebrate the Dusaria in honour of him.[2] In like manner

The civilisation of east Syria under Roman rule.

---

[1] Waddington, 2196 ; Ἀδριανοῦ τοῦ καὶ Σοαίδου Μαλέχου ἐθνάρχου στρατηγοῦ νομάδων τὸ μνημεῖον.

[2] Epiphanius, *Haeres.* li. p. 483, Dind., sets forth that the 25th December, the birthday of Christ, had already been festally observed after an analogous manner at Rome in the festival of the Saturnalia, at Alexandria in the festival (mentioned also

in the province of Arabia temples continue to be consecrated, and offerings presented to Aumu or Helios, to
Vasaeathu, to Theandritos, to Ethaos. The tribes and
the tribal organisation no less continue : the inscriptions
mention lists of " Phylae " by the native name, and frequently Phylarchs or Ethnarchs. But alongside of traditional customs civilisation and Hellenising make progress.
If from the time before Trajan no Greek monument can
be shown in the sphere of the Nabataean state, on the
other hand no monument subsequent to Trajan's time in the
Arabic language has been found there ;[1] to all appearance
the imperial government suppressed at once upon the
annexation the written use of Arabic, although it certainly
remained the language proper of the country, as is attested
not only by the proper names but by the " interpreter of
the tax-receivers."

Agriculture and commerce.   As to the advance of agriculture we have no witnesses
to speak ; but if, on the whole eastern and southern slope
of the Haurân, from the summits of the mountains down to
the desert, the stones, with which this volcanic plain was
once strewed, are thrown into heaps or arranged in long
rows, and thus the most glorious fields are obtained, we
may recognise therein the hand of the only government
which has governed this land as it might and should be
governed.   In the Ledjâ, a lava-plateau thirteen leagues
long and eight to nine broad, which is now almost unin-
habited, there grew once vines and figs between the
streams of lava ; the Roman road connecting Bostra with
Damascus ran across it ; in the Ledjâ and around it are

in the decree of Canopus) of the
Kikellia, and in other heathen worships. "This takes place in Alexandria
at the so-called Virgin's shrine (Κόριον)
. . . and if we ask people what this
mystery means, they answer and say
that to-day at this hour the Virgin has
given birth to the Eternal (τὸν αἰῶνα).
This takes place in like manner at
Petra, the capital of Arabia, in the
temple there, and in the Arabic language they sing the praise of the
Virgin, whom they call in Arabic
Chaamu, that is the maiden, and Him

born of her Dusares, that is the Only-
begotten of the Lord." The name
Chaamu is perhaps akin to the Aumu
or Aumos of the Greek inscriptions of
this region, who is compared with
Ζεὺς ἀνίκητος "Ηλιος (Waddington,
2392-2395, 2441, 2445, 2456).

[1] This is said apart from the remarkable Arabo-Greek inscription (see
below) found in Harrân, not far from
Zorava, of the year 568 A.D., set up
by the phylarch Asaraelos, son of
Talemos (Waddington, 2464). This
Christian is a precursor of Mohammed.

counted the ruins of twelve larger and thirty-nine smaller
townships.   It can be shown that, at the bidding of the
same governor who erected the province of Arabia, the
mighty aqueduct was constructed which led the water
from the mountains of the Haurân to Canatha (Kerak) in
the plain, and not far from it a similar one in Arrha
(Rahâ)—buildings of Trajan, which may be named by the
side of the port of Ostia and the Forum of Rome.   The
flourishing of commercial intercourse is attested by the
very choice of the capital of the new province.   Bostra
existed under the Nabataean government, and an inscription of king Malichu has been found there; but its military and commercial importance begins with the introduction of direct Roman government.   " Bostra," says Wetz-
stein, " has the most favourable situation of all the towns
in eastern Syria; even Damascus, which owes its size to
the abundance of its water and to its situation protected
by the eastern Trachon, will excel Bostra only under a
weak government, while the latter under a strong and
wise government must elevate itself in a few decades to a
fabulous prosperity.   It is the great market for the Syrian
desert : the high mountains of Arabia and Peraea, and its
long rows of booths of stone still in their desolation,
furnish evidence of the reality of an earlier, and the possibility of a future, greatness."   The remains of the Roman
road, leading thence by way of Salchat and Ezrak to
the Persian Gulf, show that Bostra was, along with Petra
and Palmyra, a medium of traffic from the East to the
Mediterranean.   This town was probably constituted on
a Hellenic basis already by Trajan ; at least it is called
thenceforth the " new Trajanic Bostra," and the Greek
coins begin with Pius, while later the legend becomes
Latin in consequence of the bestowal of colonial rights
by Alexander.

Petra too had a Greek municipal constitution already
under Hadrian, and several other places subsequently
received municipal rights ; but in this territory of the
Arabians down to the latest period the tribe and the tribal
village preponderated.

A peculiar civilisation was developed from the mixture of national and Greek elements in these regions during the five hundred years between Trajan and Mohammed. A fuller picture of it has been preserved to us than of other forms of the ancient world, inasmuch as the structures of Petra, in great part worked out of the rock, and the buildings in the Haurân, executed entirely of stone owing to the want of wood, comparatively little injured by the sway of the Bedouins which was here again installed with Islam in its old misrule, are still to a considerable degree extant to the present day, and throw a clear light on the artistic skill and the manner of life of those centuries. The above-mentioned temple of Baalsamin at Canatha, certainly built under Herod, shows in its original portions a complete diversity from Greek architecture and in the structural plan remarkable analogies with the temple-building of the same king in Jerusalem, while the pictorial representations shunned in the latter are by no means wanting here. A similar state of things has been observed in the monuments found at Petra. Afterwards further steps were taken. If under the Jewish and the Nabataean rulers culture freed itself but slowly from the influences of the East, a new time seems to have begun here with the transfer of the legion to Bostra. "Building," says an excellent French observer, Melchior de Vogué, "obtained thereby an impetus which was not again arrested. Everywhere rose houses, palaces, baths, temples, theatres, aqueducts, triumphal arches ; towns sprang from the ground within a few years with the regular construction and the symmetrically disposed colonnades which mark towns without a past, and which are as it were the inevitable uniform for this part of Syria during the imperial period." The eastern and southern slope of the Haurân shows nearly three hundred such desolated towns and villages, while there only five new townships now exist ; several of the former, *e.g.* Bûsân, number as many as 800 houses of one to two stories, built throughout of basalt, with well-jointed walls of square blocks without cement, with doors mostly ornamented and often provided with inscriptions,

the flat roof formed of stone-rafters, which are supported
by stone arches and made rain-proof above by a layer of
cement.   The town-wall is usually formed only by the backs
of the houses joined together, and is protected by numerous
towers.   The poor attempts at re-colonising of recent
times find the houses habitable ; there is wanting only the
diligent hand of man, or rather the strong arm that pro-
tects it.   In front of the gates lie the cisterns, often subterranean, or provided with an artificial stone roof, many of
which are still at the present day, when this deserted seat
of towns has become pasturage, kept up by the Bedouins in
order to water their flocks from them in summer.   The
style of building and the practice of art have doubtless
preserved some remains of the older Oriental type, *e.g.*
the frequent form, for a tomb, of the cube crowned with a
pyramid, perhaps also the pigeon-towers often added to
the tomb, still frequent in the present day throughout
Syria ; but, taken on the whole, the style is the usual
Greek one of the imperial period.   Only the absence of
wood has here called forth a development of the stone
arch and the cupola, which technically and artistically
lends to these buildings an original character.   In contrast to the customary repetition elsewhere usual of traditional forms there prevails here an architecture independently suiting the exigencies and the conditions, moderate
in ornamentation, thoroughly sound and rational, and not
destitute even of elegance.   The burial-places, which are
cut out in the rock-walls rising to the east and west of
Petra and in their lateral valleys, with their façades of
Doric or Corinthian pillars often placed in several tiers
one above another, and their pyramids and propylaea
reminding us of the Egyptian Thebes, are not artistically
pleasing, but imposing by their size and richness.   Only
a stirring life and a high prosperity could display such
care for its dead.   In presence of these architectural
monuments it is not surprising that the inscriptions make
mention of a theatre in the " village " ($\kappa\omega\mu\eta$) Sakkaea
and a " theatre-shaped Odeon " in Canatha, and a local poet
of Namara in Batanaea celebrates himself as a " master

of the glorious art of proud Ausonian song."[1]   Thus at this eastern limit of the empire there was gained for Hellenic civilisation a frontier-domain which may be compared with the Romanised region of the Rhine; the arched and domed buildings of eastern Syria well stand comparison with the castles and tombs of the nobles and of the great merchants of Belgica.

The south-Arabian immigration before Mohammed.   But the end came.   As to the Arabian tribes who immigrated to this region from the south, the historical tradition of the Romans is silent, and what the late records of the Arabs report as to that of the Ghassanids and their precursors, can hardly be fixed, at least as to chronology.[2] But the Sabaeans, after whom the place Borechath (Brêka to the north of Kanawat) is named, appear in fact to be south-Arabian emigrants; and these were already settled here in the third century.   They and their associates may have come in peace and become settled under Roman protection, perhaps even may have carried to Syria the highly-developed and luxuriant culture of south-western Arabia.   So long as the empire kept firmly together and each of these tribes was under its own sheikh, all obeyed the Roman lord-paramount.   But in order the better to meet the Arabians or—as they were now called —Saracens of the Persian empire united under one king,

[1] Αὐσονίων μούσης ὑψινόου πρύτανις, Kaibel, *Epigr.* 440.

[2] According to the Arabian accounts the Benu Sâlih migrated from the region of Mecca (about 190 A.D., according to the conjectures of Caussin de Perceval, *Hist. des Arabes*, i. 212) to Syria, and settled there alongside of the Benu-Samaida, in whom Waddington finds anew the φυλὴ Σομαιθηνῶν of an inscription of Suwêda (n. 2308).   The Ghassanids, who (according to Caussin, about 205) migrated from Batn-Marr likewise to Syria and to the same region, were compelled by the Salihites, at the suggestion of the Romans, to pay tribute, and paid it for a time, until they (according to the same, about the year 292) overcame the Salihites, and

their leader Thalaba, son of Amos, was recognised by the Romans as phylarch.   This narrative may contain correct elements; but our standard authority remains always the account of Procopius, *de bello Pers.* i. 17, reproduced in the text.   The phylarchs of individual provinces of Arabia (*i.e.* the province Bostra; *Nov.* 102 c.) and of Palestine (*i.e.* province of Petra; Procop. *de bello Pers.* i. 19), are older, but doubtless not much. Had a sheikh-in-chief of this sort been recognised by the Romans in the times before Justinian, the Roman authors and the inscriptions would doubtless show traces of it; but there are no such traces from the period before Justinian.

Justinian, during the Persian war in the year 531, placed all the phylarchs of the Saracens subject to the Romans under Aretas son of Gabalus—Harith Abu son of Chaminos among the Arabs—and bestowed on this latter the title of king, which hitherto, it is added, had never been done. This king of all the Arabian tribes settled in Syria was still a vassal of the empire ; but, while he warded off his countrymen, he at the same time prepared the place for them. A century later, in the year 637, Arabia and Syria succumbed to Islam.

CHAPTER XI.

JUDAEA AND THE JEWS.

THE history of the Jewish land is as little the history of the Jewish people as the history of the States of the Church is that of the Catholics ; it is just as requisite to separate the two as to consider them together.

Judaea and the priestly rule under the Seleucids.

The Jews in the land of the Jordan, with whom the Romans had to do, were not the people who under their judges and kings fought with Moab and Edom, and listened to the discourses of Amos and Hosea. The small community of pious exiles, driven out by foreign rule, and brought back again by a change in the hands wielding that rule, who began their new establishment by abruptly repelling the remnants of their kinsmen left behind in the old abodes and laying the foundation for the irreconcilable feud between Jews and Samaritans— the ideal of national exclusiveness and priestly control holding the mind in chains—had long before the Roman period developed under the government of the Seleucids the so-called Mosaic theocracy, a clerical corporation with the high-priest at its head, which, acquiescing in foreign rule and renouncing the formation of a state, guarded the distinctiveness of its adherents, and dominated them under the aegis of the protecting power. This retention of the national character in religious forms, while ignoring the state, was the distinctive mark of the later Judaism. Probably every idea of God is in its formation national ; but no other God has been so from the outset the God only of his people as Jahve, and no one has so remained such without distinction of time and place. Those men returning to the Holy Land, who professed to live according to the statutes of Moses and in fact lived according to the statutes of Ezra and Nehemiah,[1] had remained just as dependent on the great-kings of the East, and subsequently on the Seleucids, as they had been by the waters of Babylon. A political element no more attached to this organisation than to the Armenian or the Greek Church under its patriarchs in the Turkish empire; no free current of political development pervades this clerical restoration; none of the grave and serious obligations of a commonwealth standing on its own basis hampered the priests of the temple of Jerusalem in the setting up of the kingdom of Jahve upon earth.

The reaction did not fail to come. That church-without-a-state could only last so long as a secular great power served it as lord-protector or as bailiff. When the kingdom of the Seleucids fell into decay, a Jewish commonwealth was created afresh by the revolt against foreign rule, which drew its best energies precisely from the enthusiastic national faith. The high priest of Salem was called from the temple to the battlefield. The family of the Hasmonaeans restored the empire of Saul and David nearly in its old limits, and not only so, but these warlike high priests renewed also in some measure the former truly political monarchy controlling the priests. But that monarchy, at once the product of, and the contrast to, that priestly rule, was not according to the heart of the pious. The Pharisees and the Sadducees separated and began to make war on one another. It was not so much doctrines and ritual differences that here confronted each other, as, on the one hand, the persistence in a priestly government which simply clung to religious ordinances and interests, and otherwise was indifferent to the independence and the self-control of the community; on the other hand, the monarchy aiming at political development

Kingdom of the Hasmonaeans.

---

[1] [This statement and several others of a kindred tenor in this chapter appear to rest on an unhesitating acceptance of views entertained by a recent school of Old Testament criticism, as to which it may at least be said : *Adhuc sub iudice lis est.*— Tr.]

and endeavouring to procure for the Jewish people, by fighting and by treaty, its place once more in the political conflict, of which the Syrian kingdom was at that time the arena. The former tendency dominated the multitude, the latter had the preponderance in intelligence and in the upper classes ; its most considerable champion was king Iannaeus Alexander, who during his whole reign was at enmity not less with the Syrian rulers than with

iv. 133. his own Pharisees (iv. 139). Although it was properly but the other, and in fact the more natural and more potent, expression of the national revival, it yet by its greater freedom of thinking and acting came into contact with the Hellenic character, and was regarded especially by its pious opponents as foreign and unbelieving.

The Jewish Diaspora. But the inhabitants of Palestine were only a portion, and not the most important portion, of the Jews ; the Jewish communities of Babylonia, Syria, Asia Minor, Egypt, were far superior to those of Palestine even after their regeneration by the Maccabees. The Jewish Diaspora in the imperial period was of more significance than the latter ; and it was an altogether peculiar phenomenon.

The settlements of the Jews beyond Palestine grew only in a subordinate degree out of the same impulse as those of the Phoenicians and the Hellenes. From the outset an agricultural people and dwelling far from the coast, their settlements abroad were a non-free and comparatively late formation, a creation of Alexander or of his marshals.[1] In those immense efforts at founding Greek towns continued throughout generations, such as never before and never afterwards occurred to a like extent, the Jews had a conspicuous share, however singular it was to invoke their aid in particular towards the Hellenising of

---

[1] Whether the legal position of the Jews in Alexandria is warrantably traced back by Josephus (*contra Ap.* ii. 4) to Alexander is so far doubtful, as, to the best of our knowledge, not he, but the first Ptolemy, settled Jews in masses there (Josephus, *Arch.* xii. 1. ; Appian, *Syr.* 50). The remarkable similarity of form assumed by the bodies of Jews in the different states of the Diadochi must, if it is not based on Alexander's ordinances, be traced to rivalry and imitation in the founding of towns. The fact that Palestine was now Egyptian, now Syrian, doubtless exercised an essential influence in the case of these settlements.

the East. This was the case above all with Egypt. The
most considerable of all the towns created by Alexander,
Alexandria on the Nile, was since the times of the first
Ptolemy, who after the occupation of Palestine transferred
thither a mass of its inhabitants, almost as much a city of
the Jews as of the Greeks, and the Jews there were to be
esteemed at least equal to those of Jerusalem in number,
wealth, intelligence, and organisation. In the first times
of the empire there was reckoned a million of Jews to
eight millions of Egyptians, and their influence, it may be
presumed, transcended this numerical proportion. We
have already observed that, on no smaller a scale, the Jews
in the Syrian capital of the empire had been similarly
organised and developed (p. 127). The diffusion and the
importance of the Jews of Asia Minor are attested among
other things by the attempt which was made under
Augustus by the Ionian Greek cities, apparently after
joint concert, to compel their Jewish fellow townsmen
either to withdrawal from their faith or to full assumption
of civic burdens. Beyond doubt there were independently
organised bodies of Jews in all the new Hellenic foundations,[1] and withal in numerous old Hellenic towns, even
in Hellas proper, *e.g.* in Corinth. The organisation was
placed throughout on the footing that the nationality of
the Jews with the far-reaching consequences drawn from
it by themselves was preserved, and only the use of the
Greek language was required of them. Thus amidst
this Graecising, into which the East was at that time
coaxed or forced by those in authority, the Jews of the
Greek towns became Greek-speaking Orientals.

That in the Jew-communities of the Macedonian
towns the Greek language not merely attained to dominion
in the natural way of intercourse, but was a compulsory

*Greek
language.*

---

[1] The community of Jews in Smyrna
is mentioned in an inscription recently
found there (Reinach, *Revue des
études juives*, 1883, p. 161) : 'Ρουφεῖνα
'Ιουδαί(α) ἀρχισυναγωγὸς κατεσκεύασεν
τὸ ἐνσόριον τοῖς ἀπελευθέροις καὶ θρέμ-
(μ)ασιν μηδένος ἄλ(λ)ου ἐξουσίαν ἔχοντος
θάψαι τινά· εἰ δέ τις τολμήσει, δώσει τῷ
ἱερωτάτῳ ταμείῳ (δηναρίους) ͵αφ, καὶ τῷ
ἔθνει τῶν 'Ιουδαίων (δηναρίους) ͵α. Ταύτης
τῆς ἐπιγραφῆς τὸ ἀντίγραφον ἀποκεῖται
εἰς τὸ ἀρχεῖον. Simple *collegia* are, in
penal threats of this sort, not readily
put on a level with the state or the
community.

ordinance imposed upon them, seems of necessity to result
from the state of the case.   In a similar way Trajan
subsequently Romanised Dacia with colonists from Asia
Minor.   Without this compulsion, the external uniformity
in the foundation of towns could not have been carried
out, and this material for Hellenising generally could not
have been employed.   The governments went in this
respect very far and achieved much.   Already under the
second Ptolemy, and at his instigation, the sacred writings
of the Jews were translated into Greek in Egypt, and at
least at the beginning of the imperial period the knowledge of Hebrew among the Jews of Alexandria was
nearly as rare as that of the original languages of Scripture is at present in the Christian world ; there was nearly
as much discussion as to the faults of translation of the
so-called Seventy Alexandrians as on the part of pious
men among us regarding the errors of Luther's translation.
The national language of the Jews had at this epoch disappeared everywhere from the intercourse of life, and
maintained itself only in ecclesiastical use somewhat like
the Latin language in the religious domain of Catholicism.
In Judaea itself its place had been taken by the Aramaic
popular language of Syria, akin no doubt to the Hebrew ;
the Jews outside of Judaea, with whom we are concerned,
had entirely laid aside the Semitic idiom, and it was not
till long after this epoch that the reaction set in, which
scholastically brought back the knowledge and the use
of it more generally among the Jews.   The literary works,
which they produced at this epoch in great number, were
in the better times of the empire all Greek.   If language
alone conditioned nationality, there would be little to tell
for this period as to the Jews.

Retention
of nation-
ality.

But with this linguistic compulsion, at first perhaps
severely felt, was combined the recognition of the distinctive nationality with all its consequences.   Everywhere in
the cities of the monarchy of Alexander the burgess-body
was formed of the Macedonians, that is, those really
Macedonian, or the Hellenes esteemed equal to them.   By
the side of these stood, in addition to foreigners, the

natives, in Alexandria the Egyptians, in Cyrene the Libyans and generally the settlers from the East, who had indeed no other home than the new city, but were not recognised as Hellenes. To this second category the Jews belonged ; but they, and they only, were allowed to form, so to speak, a community within the community, and— while the other non-burgesses were ruled by the authorities of the burgess-body—up to a certain degree to govern themselves.[1] The " Jews," says Strabo, " have in Alexandria a national head (ἐθνάρχης) of their own, who presides over the people (ἔθνος), and decides processes and disposes of contracts and arrangements as if he ruled an independent community." This was done, because the Jews indicated a specific jurisdiction of this sort as required by their nationality or—what amounts to the same thing—their religion. Further, the general political arrangements had respect in an extensive measure to the national-religious scruples of the Jews, and accommodated them as far as possible by exemptions. The privilege of dwelling together was at least frequently added ; in Alexandria, *e.g.* two of the five divisions of the city were inhabited chiefly by Jews. This seems not to have been the Ghetto system, but rather a usage resting on the basis of settlement to begin with, and thereafter retained on both sides, whereby conflicts with neighbours were in some measure obviated.

Thus the Jews came to play a prominent part in the

[1] If the Alexandrian Jews subsequently maintained that they were legally on an equal footing with the Alexandrian Macedonians (Josephus, *contra Ap.* ii. 4; *Bell. Jud.* ii. 18, 7) this was a misrepresentation of the true state of the case. They were clients in the first instance of the Phyle of the Macedonians, probably the most eminent of all, and therefore named after Dionysos (Theophilus, *ad Autolycum*, ii. 7), and, because the Jewish quarter was a part of this Phyle, Josephus in his way makes themselves Macedonians. The legal position of the population of the Greek towns of this category is most clearly apparent from the account of Strabo (in Josephus, *Arch.* xiv. 7, 2) as to the four categories of that of Cyrene : city-burgesses, husbandmen (γεωργοί), strangers, and Jews. If we lay aside the *metoeci*, who have their legal home elsewhere, there remain as Cyrenaeans having rights in their home the burgesses of full rights, that is, the Hellenes and what were allowed to pass as such, and the two categories of those excluded from active burgess-rights—the Jews, who form a community of their own, and the subjects, the Libyans, without autonomy. This might easily be so shifted, that the two privileged categories should appear as having equal rights.

Macedonian Hellenising of the East ; their pliancy and
serviceableness on the one hand, their unyielding tenacity
on the other, must have induced the very realistic statesmen
who assigned this course of action, to resolve on such
arrangements.　Nevertheless the extraordinary extent
and significance of the Jewish Diaspora, as compared with
the narrowness and poorness of their home, remains at
once a fact and a problem.　In dealing with it we may
not overlook the circumstance that the Palestinian Jews
furnished no more than the nucleus for the Jews of other
countries.　The Judaism of the older time was anything
but exclusive ; was, on the contrary, no less pervaded by
missionary zeal than were afterwards Christianity and
Islam.　The Gospel makes reference to Rabbis who
traversed sea and land to make a proselyte ; the admission
of half-proselytes, of whom circumcision was not expected
but to whom religious fellowship was yet accorded, is an
evidence of this converting zeal and at the same time one
of its most effective means.　Motives of very various kinds
came to the help of this proselytising.　The civil privileges,
which the Lagids and Seleucids conferred on the Jews,
must have induced a great number of non-Jewish Orientals and half-Hellenes to attach themselves in the new
towns to the privileged category of the non-burgesses.　In
later times the decay of the traditional faith of the country
helped the Jewish *propaganda.*　Numerous persons,
especially of the cultivated classes, whose sense of faith
and morality turned away with horror or derision from
what the Greeks, and still more from what the Egyptians
termed religion, sought refuge in the simpler and purer
Jewish doctrine renouncing polytheism and idolatry—a
doctrine which largely met the religious views resulting
from the development of philosophy among the cultured
and half-cultured circles.　There is a remarkable Greek
moral poem, probably from the later epoch of the Roman
republic, which is drawn from the Mosaic books on such
a footing that it adopts the doctrine of monotheism and
the universal moral law, but avoids everything offensive
to the non-Jew and all direct opposition to the ruling

religion, evidently intended to gain wider acceptance for this denationalised Judaism.   Women in particular addicted themselves by preference to the Jewish faith.   When the authorities of Damascus in the year 66 resolved to put to death the captive Jews, it was agreed to keep this resolution secret, in order that the female population devoted to the Jews might not prevent its execution.   Even in the West, where the cultivated circles were otherwise averse to Jewish habits, dames of rank early formed an exception ; Poppaea Sabina, Nero's wife, sprung from a noble family, was notorious for her pious Jewish faith and her zealous protectorate of the Jews, as for other things less reputable.   Cases of formal transition to Judaism were not rare ; the royal house of Adiabene for example—king Izates and his mother Helena, as well as his brother and successor—became at the time of Tiberius and of Claudius in every respect Jews.   It certainly was the case with all those Jewish bodies, as it is expressly remarked of those of Antioch, that they consisted in great part of proselytes.

This transplanting of Judaism to the Hellenic soil with the appropriation of a foreign language, however much it took place with a retention of national individuality, was not accomplished without developing in Judaism itself a tendency running counter to its nature, and up to a certain degree denationalising it.   How powerfully the bodies of Jews living amidst the Greeks were influenced by the currents of Greek intellectual life, may be traced in the literature of the last century before, and of the first after, the birth of Christ.   It is imbued with Jewish elements ; and they are withal the clearest heads and the most gifted thinkers, who seek admission either as Hellenes into the Jewish, or as Jews into the Hellenic, system. Nicolaus of Damascus, himself a Pagan and a noted representative of the Aristotelian philosophy pleaded, as a scholar and diplomatist of king Herod, the cause of his Jewish patron and of the Jews before Agrippa as before Augustus ; and not only so, but his historical authorship shows a very earnest, and for that epoch sigificant, attempt to bring the East into the circle of Occidental research,

Hellenising tendencies in the Diaspora.

while the description still preserved of the youthful years of the emperor Augustus, who came personally into close contact with him, is a remarkable evidence of the love and honour which the Roman ruler met with in the Greek world.   The dissertation on the Sublime, written in the first period of the empire by an unknown author, one of the finest aesthetic works preserved to us from antiquity, certainly proceeds, if not from a Jew, at any rate from a man who revered alike Homer and Moses.[1]   Another treatise, also anonymous, upon the Universe—likewise an attempt, respectable of its kind, to blend the doctrine of Aristotle with that of the Stoa—was perhaps written also by a Jew, and dedicated certainly to the Jew of highest repute and highest station in the Neronian age, Tiberius Alexander (p. 204), chief of the staff to Corbulo and Titus.   The wedding of the two worlds of intellect meets us most clearly in the Jewish-Alexandrian philosophy, the most acute and most palpable expression of a religious movement, not merely affecting but also attacking the essence of Judaism.   The Hellenic intellectual development conflicted with national religions of all sorts, inasmuch as it either denied their views or else filled them with other contents, drove out the previous gods from the minds of men and put into the empty places either nothing, or the stars and abstract ideas.   These attacks affected also the religion of the Jews.   There was formed a Neo-Judaism of Hellenic culture, which dealt with Jehovah not quite so badly, but yet not much otherwise, than the cultivated Greeks and Romans with Zeus and Jupiter. The universal expedient of the so-called allegorical interpretation, whereby in particular the philosophers of the Stoa everywhere in courteous fashion eliminated the heathen national religions, suited equally well and equally

---

[1] Pseudo-Longinus, περὶ ὕψους, 9: "Far better than the war of the gods in Homer is the description of the gods in their perfection and genuine greatness and purity, like that of Poseidon (*Ilias*, xiii. 18 ff.).   Just so writes the legislator of the Jews, no mean man (οὐχ ὁ τυχὼν ἀνήρ), after he has worthily apprehended and brought to expression the Divine power, at the very beginning of the Laws (*Genesis*, i. 3): 'God said'—what? 'Let there be light, and there was light; let the earth be, and the earth was.'"

ill for Genesis as for the gods of the Iliad ; if Moses had meant by Abraham in a strict sense understanding, by Sarah virtue, by Noah righteousness, if the four streams of Paradise were the four cardinal virtues, then the most enlightened Hellene might believe in the Law.   But this pseudo-Judaism was also a power, and the intellectual primacy of the Jews in Egypt was apparent above all in the fact, that this tendency found pre-eminently its supporters in Alexandria.

Notwithstanding the internal separation which had taken place among the Jews of Palestine and had but too often culminated directly in civil war, notwithstanding the dispersion of a great part of the Jewish body into foreign lands, notwithstanding the intrusion of foreign ingredients into it and even of the destructive Hellenistic element into its very core, the collective body of the Jews remained united in a way, to which in the present day only the Vatican perhaps and the Kaaba offer a certain analogy. The holy Salem remained the banner, Zion's temple the Palladium of the whole Jewish body, whether they obeyed the Romans or the Parthians, whether they spoke Aramaic or Greek, whether even they believed in the old Jahve or in the new, who was none.   The fact that the protecting ruler conceded to the spiritual chief of the Jews a certain secular power signified for the Jewish body just as much, and the small extent of this power just as little, as the so-called States of the Church in their time signified for Roman Catholics.   Every member of a Jewish community had to pay annually to Jerusalem a *didrachmon* as temple-tribute, which came in more regularly than the taxes of the state ; every one was obliged at least once in his life to sacrifice personally to Jehovah on the spot which alone in the world was well-pleasing to Him. Theological science remained common property ; the Babylonian and Alexandrian Rabbins took part in it not less than those of Jerusalem.   The feeling, cherished with unparalleled tenacity, of belonging collectively to one nation —a feeling which had established itself in the community of the returning exiles and had thereafter contributed to

Fellowship of the Jews generally.

create that distinctive position of the Jews in the Greek world
—maintained its ground in spite of dispersion and division.
Philo.   Most worthy of remark is the continued life of Judaism
itself in circles whose inward religion was detached from
it.   The most noted and, for us, the single clearly palpable
representative of this tendency in literature, Philo, one
of the foremost and richest Jews of the time of Tiberius,
stands in fact towards the religion of his country in a
position not greatly differing from that of Cicero towards
the Roman ; but he himself believed that he was not
destroying but fulfilling it.   For him as for every other
Jew, Moses is the source of all truth, his written direction
binding law, the feeling towards him reverence and devout
belief.   This sublimated Judaism is, however, not quite
identical with the so-called faith in the gods of the Stoa.
The corporeality of God vanishes for Philo, but not His
personality, and he entirely fails in—what is the essence
of Hellenic philosophy—the transferring of the deity into
the breast of man ; it remains his view that sinful man is
dependent on a perfect being standing outside of, and above,
him.   In like manner the new Judaism submits itself to
the national ritual law far more unconditionally than the
new heathenism.   The struggle between the old and the
new faith was therefore of a different nature in the Jewish
circle than in the heathen, because the stake was a greater
one ;   reformed heathenism contended only against the
old faith, reformed Judaism would in its ultimate consequence destroy the nationality, which amidst the inundation of Hellenism necessarily disappeared with the refining
away of the native faith, and therefore shrank back from
drawing this consequence.   Hence on Greek soil and in
Greek language the form, if not the substance, of the old
faith was retained and defended with unexampled ob-
stinacy, defended even by those who in substance surrendered before Hellenism.   Philo himself, as we shall have
to tell further on, contended and suffered for the cause of
the Jews.   But on that account the Hellenistic tendency
in Judaism never exercised an overpowering influence over
the latter, never was able to take its stand against the

national Judaism, and barely availed to mitigate its fanaticism and to check its perversities and crimes.   In all
essential matters, especially when confronted with oppression and persecution, the differences of Judaism disappeared;
and, unimportant as was the Rabbinical state, the religious
communion over which it presided was a considerable and
in certain circumstances formidable power.

Such was the state of things which the Romans found
confronting them when they entered on rule in the East.
Conquest forces the hand of the conqueror not less than
of the conquered.   The work of centuries, the Macedonian
urban institutions, could not be undone either by the
Arsacids or by the Caesars ; neither Seleucia on the
Euphrates nor Antioch and Alexandria could be entered
upon by the following governments under the benefit of the
inventory.   Probably in presence of the Jewish Diaspora
there the founder of the imperial government took, as in
so many other things, the policy of the first Lagids as
his guiding rule, and furthered rather than hampered the
Judaism of the East in its distinctive position ; and this
procedure thereupon became throughout the model for his
successors.   We have already mentioned that the communities of Asia Minor under Augustus made the attempt
to draw upon their Jewish fellow-citizens uniformly in the
levy, and no longer to allow them the observance of the
Sabbath ; but Agrippa decided against them and maintained the *status quo* in favour of the Jews, or rather,
perhaps, now for the first time legalised the exemption of
the Jews from military service and their Sabbath privilege,
that had been previously conceded according to circumstances only by individual governors or communities of
the Greek provinces.   Augustus further directed the governors of Asia not to apply the rigorous imperial laws respecting unions and assemblies against the Jews.   But the
Roman government did not fail to see that the exempt
position conceded to the Jews in the East was not compatible with the absolute obligation of those belonging to the
empire to fulfil the services required by the state ; that the
guaranteed distinctive position of the Jewish body carried

The Ro-
man gov-
ernment
and Juda-
ism

the hatred of race and under certain circumstances civil
war into the several towns; that the pious rule of the
authorities at Jerusalem over all the Jews of the empire
had a perilous range; and that in all this there lay a
practical injury and a danger in principle for the state.

in the   The internal dualism of the empire expresses itself in
West   nothing more sharply than in the different treatment of
the Jews in the respective domains of the Latin and Greek
languages.   In the West autonomous bodies of Jews were
never allowed.   There was toleration doubtless there for
the Jewish religious usages as for the Syrian and the
Egyptian, or rather somewhat less than for these;
Augustus showed himself favourable to the Jewish colony
in the suburb of Rome beyond the Tiber, and made supplementary allowance in his largesses for those who missed
them on account of the Sabbath.   But he personally
avoided all contact with the Jewish worship as with the
Egyptian ; and, as he himself when in Egypt had gone
out of the way of the sacred ox, so he thoroughly approved the conduct of his son Gaius, when he went to the
East, in passing by Jerusalem.   Under Tiberius in the
year 19 the Jewish worship was even prohibited along
with the Egyptian in Rome and in all Italy, and those
who did not consent openly to renounce it and to throw
the holy vessels into the fire were expelled from Italy—so
far as they could not be employed as useful for military
service in convict-companies, whereupon not a few became
liable to court-martial on account of their religious
scruples.   If, as we shall see afterwards, this same emperor in the East almost anxiously evaded every conflict
with the Rabbi, it is here plainly apparent that he, the
ablest ruler whom the empire had, just as clearly perceived the dangers of the Jewish immigration as the
unfairness and the impossibility of setting aside Judaism,
where it existed.[1]   Under the later rulers, as we shall see

[1] The Jew Philo sets down the
treatment of the Jews in Italy to the
account of Sejanus (*Leg.* 24; *in Flacc.*
1), that of the Jews in the East to
the account of the emperor himself.

But Josephus rather traces back what
happened in Italy to a scandal in the
capital, which had been occasioned
by three Jewish pious swindlers
and a lady of rank converted to

in the sequel, the attitude of disinclination towards the
Jews of the West did not in the main undergo change,
although they in other respects follow more the example
of Augustus than that of Tiberius. They did not prevent the
Jews from collecting the temple-tribute in the form of
voluntary contributions and sending it to Jerusalem. They
were not checked, if they preferred to bring a legal dispute
before a Jewish arbiter rather than before a Roman
tribunal. Of compulsory levy for service, such as Tiberius
enjoined, there is no further mention afterwards in the
West. But the Jews never obtained in heathen Rome or
generally in the Latin West a publicly recognised distinctive position and publicly recognised separate courts.
Above all in the West—apart from the capital, which in
the nature of the case represented the East also, and
already in Cicero's time included in it a numerous body
of Jews—the Jewish communities nowhere had special
extent or importance in the earlier imperial period.[1]

It was only in the East that the government yielded and in the
from the first, or rather made no attempt to change the East.
existing state of things and to obviate the dangers thence
resulting ; and accordingly, as the sacred books of the Jews
were first made known to the Latin world in the Latin
language by means of the Christians, the great Jewish
movements of the imperial period were restricted throughout to the Greek East.   Here no attempt was made
gradually to stop the spring of hatred towards the Jews
by assigning to them a separate position in law, but just
as little—apart from the caprice and perversities of individual rulers—was the hatred and persecution of the Jews
fomented on the part of the government.   In reality the
catastrophe of Judaism did not arise from the treatment
of the Jewish Diaspora in the East.   It was simply the

Judaism ; and Philo himself states
that Tiberius, after the fall of Sejanus,
allowed to the governors only certain
modifications in the procedure against
the Jews.   The policy of the emperor
and that of his ministers towards the
Jews was essentially the same.

[1] Agrippa II., who enumerates the

Jewish settlements abroad (in Philo,
Leg. ad Gaium, 36), names no country
westward of Greece, and among the
strangers sojourning in Jerusalem,
whom the Book of Acts, ii. 5 f., records,
only Romans are named from the
West.

relations, as they became fatefully developed, of the imperial government to the Jewish Rabbinical state that not merely brought about the destruction of the commonwealth of Jerusalem, but further shook and changed the position of the Jews in the empire generally. We turn to describe the events in Palestine under the Roman rule.

Judaea under the republic.

The state of things in northern Syria was organised by the generals of the republic, Pompeius and his immediate successors, on such a footing, that the larger powers that were beginning to be formed there were again reduced, and the whole land was broken up into single city-domains and petty lordships. The Jews were most severely affected by this course ; not merely were they obliged to give up all the possessions which they had hitherto gained, particularly the whole coast (iv. 142), but Gabinius had even broken up the empire formerly subsisting into five independent self-administering districts, and withdrawn from the high priest Hyrcanus his secular privileges (iv. 158). Thus, as the protecting power was restored on the one hand, so was the pure theocracy on the other.

iv. 136.

iv. 151.

Antipater the Idumaean.

This, however, was soon changed. Hyrcanus, or rather the minister governing for him, the Idumaean Antipater,[1]

---

[1] Antipater began his career as governor (στρατηγός) of Idumaea (Josephus, *Arch.* xiv. 1, 3), and is there called administrator of the Jewish kingdom (ὁ τῶν Ἰουδαίων ἐπιμελητής (Joseph. *Arch.* xiv. 8, 1), that is, nearly first minister. More is not implied in the narrative of Josephus coloured with flattery towards Rome as towards Herod (*Arch.* xiv. 8, 5 ; *Bell. Jud.* i. 10, 3), that Caesar had left to Antipater the option of himself determining his position of power (δυναστεία), and, when the latter left the decision with him, had appointed him administrator (ἐπίτροπος) of Judaea. This is not, as Marquardt, *Staatsalth.* v. 1, 408, would have it, the (at that time not yet existing) Roman procuratorship of the imperial period, but an office formally conferred by the Jewish ethnarch, an ἐπιτροπή, like that mentioned by Josephus, *Bell. Jud.* ii. 18, 6. In the official documents of Caesar's time the high priest and ethnarch Hyrcanus alone represents the Jews ; Caesar gave to Antipater what could be granted to the subjects of a dependent state, Roman burgess-rights and personal immunity (Josephus, *Arch.* xiv. 8, 3 ; *Bell. Jud.* i. 9, 5), but he did not make him an official of Rome. That Herod, driven out of Judaea, obtained from the Romans a Roman officer's post possibly in Samaria, is credible ; but the designations στρατηγὸς τῆς Κοίλης Συρίας (Josephus, *Arch.* xiv. 9, 5, c. 11, 4), or στρατηγὸς Κοίλης Συρίας καὶ Σαμαρείας (*Bell. Jud.* i. 10, 8) are at least misleading, and with as much incorrectness the same author names Herod subsequently, for the reason that he is to serve as counsellor τοῖς ἐπιτροπεύουσι

attained once more the leading position in southern Syria doubtless through Gabinius himself, to whom he knew how to make himself indispensable in his Parthian and Egyptian undertakings (iv. 345). After the pillage of the iv. 329. temple of Jerusalem by Crassus the insurrection of the Jews thereby occasioned was chiefly subdued by him (iv. 355). It was for him a fortunate dispensation that iv. 339. the Jewish government was not compelled to interfere actively in the crisis between Caesar and Pompeius, for whom it, like the whole East, had declared. Nevertheless, after the brother and rival of Hyrcanus, Aristobulus as well as his son Alexander, had on account of their taking part for Caesar lost their lives at the hands of the Pompeians, the second son, Antigonus, would doubtless after Caesar's victory have been installed by the latter as ruler in Judaea. But when Caesar, coming to Egypt after the decisive victory, found himself in a dangerous position at Alexandria, it was chiefly Antipater who delivered him from it (iv. 452), and this carried the day; Antigonus had iv. 430. to give way before the more recent, but more effective, fidelity.

Caesar's personal gratitude was not the least element in promoting the formal restoration of the Jewish state. The Jewish kingdom obtained the best position which could be granted to a client-state, complete freedom from dues to the Romans[1] and from military

Caesar's arrangements.

τῆς Συρίας (*Arch.* xv. 10, 3), even Συρίας ὅλης ἐπίτροπον (*Bell. Jud.* i. 20, 4), where Marquardt's change, *Staatsalth.* v. i. 408, Κοίλης destroys the sense.

[1] In the decree of Caesar in Josephus, *Arch.* xiv. 10, 5, 6, the reading which results from Epiphanius is the only possible one ; according to this the land is freed from the tribute (imposed by Pompeius ; Josephus, *Arch.* xiv. 4, 4) from the second year of the current lease onward, and it is further ordained that the town of Joppa, which at that time passed over from Roman into Jewish possession, should continue indeed to deliver the fourth part of field-fruits at Sidon to the Romans, but for that there should be granted to Hyrcanus, likewise at Sidon, as an equivalent annually 20,675 bushels of grain, besides which the people of Joppa paid also the tenth to Hyrcanus. The whole narrative otherwise shows that the Jewish state was thenceforth free from payment of tribute ; the circumstance that Herod pays φόροι from the districts assigned to Cleopatra which he leases from her (*Arch.* xv. 4, 2, 4, c. 5, 3) only confirms the rule. If Appian, *B. C.* v. 75, adduces among the kings on whom Antonius laid tribute Herod for Idumaea and Samaria, Judaea is not absent here without good reason ; and even for these accessory lands the

occupation and levy,[1] whereas certainly the duties and
the expenses of frontier-defence were to be undertaken
by the native government. The town of Joppa, and
thereby the connection with the sea, were given back, the
independence of internal administration as well as the
free exercise of religion was guaranteed ; the re-establishment, hitherto refused, of the fortifications of Jerusalem
47. razed by Pompeius was allowed (707). Thus under the
name of the Hasmonaean prince, a half foreigner—for
the Idumaeans stood towards the Jews proper that returned
from Babylon nearly as did the Samaritans—governed
the Jewish state under the protection and according to
the will of Rome. The Jews with national sentiments
were anything but inclined towards the new government.
The old families, who led in the council of Jerusalem,
held in their hearts to Aristobulus, and, after his death,
to his son Antigonus. In the mountains of Galilee the
fanatics fought quite as much against the Romans as
against their own government ; when Antipater's son
Herod took captive Ezekias, the leader of this wild band,
and had caused him to be put to death, the priestly
council of Jerusalem compelled the weak Hyrcanus to
banish Herod under the pretext of a violation of religious precepts. The latter thereupon entered the Roman
army, and rendered good service to the Caesarian governor
of Syria against the insurrection of the last Pompeians.
But when, after the murder of Caesar, the republicans

tribute may have been remitted to
him by Augustus. The detailed and
trustworthy account as to the census
enjoined by Quirinius shows with
entire clearness that the land was
hitherto free from Roman tribute.

[1] In the same decree it is said : καὶ
ὅπως μηδεὶς μήτε ἄρχων μήτε στρατηγὸς
ἢ πρεσβευτὴς ἐν τοῖς ὅροις τῶν Ἰουδαίων
ἀνιστᾷ ("perhaps συνιστᾷ," Wilamowitz) συμμαχίαν καὶ στρατιώτας ἐξιῇ (so
Wilamowitz, for ἐξείη) ἢ τὰ χρήματα
τούτων εἰσπράττεσθαι ἢ εἰς παραχειμασίαν ἢ ἄλλῳ τινὶ ὀνόματι, ἀλλ' εἶναι
πανταχόθεν ἀνεπηρεάστους (comp.
Arch. xiv. 10, 2 : παραχειμασίαν δὲ

καὶ χρήματα πράττεσθαι οὐ δοκιμάζω).
This corresponds in the main to the
formula of the charter, a little older,
for Termessus (*C. I. L.* i. n. 204) :
*nei quis magistratu prove magistratu
legatus ne[ive] quis alius meilites in
oppidum Thermesum . . . agrumve
. . . hiemandi caussa introducito . . .
nisei senatus nominatim utei Thermesum . . . in hibernacula meilites
deducantur decreverit.* The marching
through is accordingly allowed. In
the Privilegium for Judaea the levy
seems, moreover, to have been prohibited.

gained the upper hand in the East, Antipater was again the first who not merely submitted to the stronger but placed the new holders of power under obligation to him by a rapid levying of the contribution imposed by them.

Thus it happened that the leader of the republicans, when he withdrew from Syria, left Antipater in his position, and entrusted his son Herod even with a command in Syria. Then, when Antipater died, poisoned as it was said by one of his officers, Antigonus, who had found a refuge with his father-in-law, the prince Ptolemaeus of Chalcis, believed that the moment had come to set aside his weak uncle. But the sons of Antipater, Phasael and Herod, thoroughly defeated his band, and Hyrcanus agreed to grant to them the position of their father, nay, even to receive Herod in a certain measure into the reigning house by betrothing to him his niece Mariamne. Meanwhile the leaders of the republican party were beaten at Philippi. The opposition in Jerusalem hoped now to procure the overthrow of the hated Antipatrids at the hands of the victors ; but Antonius, to whom fell the office of arbiter, decidedly repelled their deputations first in Ephesus, then in Antioch, and last in Tyre ; caused, indeed, the last envoys to be put to death ; and confirmed Phasael and Herod formally as " tetrarchs "[1] of the Jews (713).

Herod.

41.

Soon the vicissitudes of world politics dragged the Jewish state once more into their vortex. The invasion of the Parthians in the following year (714) put an end in the first instance to the rule of the Antipatrids. The pretender Antigonus joined them, and possessed himself of Jerusalem and almost the whole territory. Hyrcanus

The Parthians in Judaea.
40.

---

[1] This title, which primarily denotes the collegiate tetrarchate, such as was usual among the Galatians, was then more generally employed for the rule of all together, nay, even for the rule of one, but always as in rank inferior to that of king. In this way, besides Galatia, it appears also in Syria, perhaps from the time of Pompeius, certainly from that of Augustus. The juxtaposition of an ethnarch and two tetrarchs, as it was arranged in the year 713 for Judaea, according to Josephus (*Arch.* xiv. 13, 1 ; *Bell. Jud.* i. 12, 5), is not again met with elsewhere ; Pherores tetrarch of Peraea under his brother Herodes (*Bell. Jud.* i. 24, 5) is analogous.

41.

went as a prisoner to the Parthians : Phasael, the eldest son of Antipater, likewise a captive, put himself to death in prison. With great difficulty Herod concealed his family in a rock-stronghold on the border of Judaea, and went himself a fugitive and in search of aid first to Egypt, and, when he no longer found Antonius there, to the two holders of power just at that time ruling in new harmony

40. (714) at Rome. Readily they allowed him—as indeed it was only in the interest of Rome—to gain back for himself the Jewish kingdom ; he returned to Syria, so far as the matter depended on the Romans, as recognised

Herod, king of Judaea. ruler, and even equipped with the royal title. But, just like a pretender, he had to wrest the land not so much from the Parthians as from the patriots. He fought his battles pre-eminently with the help of Samaritans and Idumaeans and hired soldiers, and attained at length, through the support of the Roman legions, to the possession of the long-defended capital. The Roman executioners delivered him likewise from his rival of many years, Antigonus ; his own made havoc among the noble families of the council of Jerusalem.

Herod under Antonius and Cleopatra. But the days of trouble were by no means over with his installation. The unfortunate expedition of Antonius against the Parthians remained without consequences for Herod, since the victors did not venture to advance into Syria ; but he suffered severely under the ever increasing claims of the Egyptian queen, who at that time more than Antonius ruled the East ; her womanly policy, primarily directed to the extension of her domestic power and above all of her revenues, was far indeed from obtaining at the hands of Antonius all that she desired, but she wrested at any rate from the king of the Jews a portion of his most valuable possessions on the Syrian coast and in the territory lying between Egypt and Syria, nay, even the rich balsam plantations and palm-groves of Jericho, and laid upon him severe financial burdens. In order to maintain the remnant of his rule, he was obliged either himself to lease the new Syrian possessions of the queen or to be guarantee for other lessees less able to pay. After

all these troubles, and in expectation of still worse demands as little capable of being declined, the outbreak of
the war between Antonius and Caesar was hopeful for
him, and the fact that Cleopatra in her selfish perversity
released him from active participation in the war, because
he needed his troops to collect her Syrian revenues, was
a further piece of good fortune, since this facilitated his
submission to the victor. Fortune favoured him yet further on his changing sides ; he was able to intercept a
band of faithful gladiators of Antonius, who were marching from Asia Minor through Syria towards Egypt to
lend assistance to their master. When he, before resort-
ing to Caesar at Rhodes to obtain his pardon, caused the
last male offshoot of the Maccabaean house, the eighty-
years old Hyrcanus, to whom the house of Antipater was
indebted for its position, to be at all events put to death,
he in reality exaggerated the necessary caution. Caesar
did what policy bade him do, especially as the support
of Herod was of importance for the intended Egyptian
expedition. He confirmed Herod, glad to be vanquished,
in his dominion, and extended it, partly by giving back
the possessions wrested from him by Cleopatra, partly by
further gifts ; the whole coast from Gaza to Strato's
Tower, the later Caesarea, the Samaritan region inserted
between Judaea and Galilee, and a number of towns to the
east of the Jordan thenceforth obeyed Herod. On the
consolidation of the Roman monarchy the Jewish principality was withdrawn from the reach of further external
crises.

Herod under Augustus.

From the Roman standpoint the conduct of the new
dynasty appears correct, in a way to draw tears from the
eyes of the observer. It took part at first for Pompeius,
then for Caesar the father, then for Cassius and Brutus,
then for the triumvirs, then for Antonius, lastly for Caesar
the son ; fidelity varies, as does the watchword. Nevertheless this conduct is not to be denied the merit of consistency and firmness. The factions which rent the ruling
burgess-body, whether republic or monarchy, whether
Caesar or Antonius, in reality nowise concerned the depen-

*Govern-
ment of
Herod.*

dent provinces, especially those of the Greek East. The demoralisation which is combined with all revolutionary change of government—the degrading confusion between internal fidelity and external obedience—was brought in this case most glaringly to light ; but the fulfilment of duty, such as the Roman commonwealth claimed from its subjects, had been satisfied by king Herod to an extent of which nobler and greater natures would certainly not have been capable. In presence of the Parthians he constantly, even in critical circumstances, held firmly to the protectors whom he had once chosen.

In its relation to the Jews.

From the standpoint of internal Jewish politics the government of Herod was the setting aside of the theocracy, and in so far a continuance of, and in fact an advance upon, the government of the Maccabees, as the separation of the political and the ecclesiastical government was carried out with the utmost precision in the contrast between the all-powerful king of foreign birth and the powerless high-priest often and arbitrarily changed. No doubt the royal position was sooner pardoned in the Jewish high-priest than in a man who was a foreigner and incapable of priestly consecration ; and, if the Hasmonaeans represented outwardly the independence of Judaism, the Idumaean held his royal power over the Jews in fee from the lord-paramount. The reaction of this insoluble conflict on a deeply-impassioned nature confronts us in the whole life-career of the man, who causes much suffering, but has felt perhaps not less. At all events the energy, the constancy, the yielding to the inevitable, the military and political dexterity, where there was room for it, secure for the king of the Jews a certain place in the panorama of a remarkable epoch.

Herod's character and [4. aims.

To describe in detail the government of Herod for almost forty years—he died in the year 750—as the accounts of it preserved at great length allow us to do, is not the task of the historian of Rome. There is probably no royal house of any age in which bloody feuds raged in an equal degree between parents and children, between husbands and wives, and between brothers and sisters ;

the emperor Augustus and his governors in Syria turned
away with horror from the share in the work of murder
which was suggested to them ; not the least revolting trait
in this picture of horrors is the utter want of object in
most of the executions, ordained as a rule upon groundless
suspicion, and the despairing remorse of the perpetrator,
which constantly followed.   Vigorously and intelligently
as the king took care of the interest of his country, so far
as he could and might, and energetically as, not merely
in Palestine but throughout the empire, he befriended the
Jews with his treasures and with his no small influence—
for the decision of Agrippa favourable to the Jews in the
great imperial affair of Asia Minor (p. 171) they were
substantially indebted to him—he found love and fidelity
in Idumaea perhaps and Samaria, but not among the
people of Israel ; here he was, and continued to be, not
so much the man laden with the guilt of blood in many
forms, as above all the foreigner.   As it was one of the
mainsprings of that domestic war, that his wife of the Hasmonaean family, the fair Mariamne, and their children
were regarded and dreaded by him more as Jews than as
his own, he himself gave expression to the feeling that he
was as much drawn towards the Greeks as repelled by the
Jews.   It is significant that he had the sons, for whom in
the first instance he destined the succession, brought up
in Rome.   While out of his inexhaustible riches he loaded
the Greek cities of other lands with gifts and embellished
them with temples, he built for the Jews no doubt also,
but not in the Jewish sense.   The buildings of the circus
and theatre in Jerusalem itself, as well as the temples for
the imperial worship in the Jewish towns, were regarded
by the pious Israelite as a summons to blaspheme God.
His conversion of the temple in Jerusalem into a magnificent building was done half against the will of the devout ;
much as they admired the building, his introduction into
it of a golden eagle was taken more amiss than all the
sentences of death ordained by him, and led to a popular
insurrection, to which the eagle fell a sacrifice, and thereupon doubtless the devotees as well, who tore it down.

Energy of
his rule.

Herod knew the land sufficiently not to let matters
come to extremities ; if it had been possible to Hellenise
it, the will to that effect would not have been wanting on
his part.   In energy the Idumaean was not inferior to the
best Hasmonaeans.   The construction of the great harbour
at Strato's Tower, or as the town entirely rebuilt by Herod
was thenceforth called, Caesarea, first gave to a coast poor
in harbours what it needed, and throughout the whole
period of the empire the town remained a chief emporium
of southern Syria.   What the government was able to
furnish in other respects—development of natural resources,
intervention in case of famine and other calamities, above
all things internal and external security—was furnished
by Herod.   The evil of brigandage was done away, and
the defence—so uncommonly difficult in these regions—
of the frontier against the roving tribes of the desert
was carried out with sternness and consistency.   Thereby
the Roman government was induced to place under him
still further regions, Ituraea, Trachonitis, Auranitis, Batanaea.   Thenceforth his dominion extended, as we have
already mentioned (p. 146), compactly over the region
beyond the Jordan as far as towards Damascus and to the
Hermon mountains ; so far as we can discern, after those
further assignments there was in the whole domain which
we have indicated no longer any free city or any rule
independent of Herod.   The defence of the frontier itself
fell more on the Arabian king than on the king of the
Jews ; but, so far as it devolved on him, the series of well-
provided frontier-forts brought about here a general peace,
such as had not hitherto been known in those regions.
We can understand how Agrippa, after inspecting the
maritime and military structures of Herod, should have
discerned in him an associate striving in a like spirit towards the great work of organising the empire, and should
have treated him in this sense.

The end of
Herod and
the parti-
tion of his
kingdom.

His kingdom had no lasting existence.   Herod himself apportioned it in his testament among his three sons,
and Augustus confirmed the arrangement in the main,
only placing the important port of Gaza and the Greek

towns beyond the Jordan immediately under the governor of Syria. The northern portions of the kingdom were separated from the mainland ; the territory last acquired by Herod to the south of Damascus, Batanaea with the districts belonging to it, was obtained by Philip ; Galilee and Peraea, that is, the Transjordanic domain, so far as it was not Greek, by Herod Antipas—both as tetrarchs ; these two petty principalities continued, at first as separate, then as united under Herod " the Great's" great-grandson Agrippa II., with slight interruptions to subsist down to the time of Trajan. We have already mentioned their government when describing eastern Syria and Arabia (p. 146 f.). Here it may only be added that these Herodians continued to rule, if not with the energy, at least in the sense and spirit of the founder of the dynasty. The towns established by them—Caesarea, the ancient Paneas, in the northern territory, and Tiberias in Galilee—had a Hellenic organisation quite after the manner of Herod ; characteristic is the proscription, which the Jewish Rabbis on account of a tomb found at the laying out of Tiberias decreed over the unclean city.

The main country, Judaea, along with Samaria on the north and Idumaea on the south, was destined for Archelaus by his father's will. But this succession was not accordant with the wishes of the nation. The orthodox, that is, the Pharisees, ruled with virtual exclusiveness the mass of the people ; and, if hitherto the fear of the Lord had been in some measure kept down by the fear of the unscrupulously energetic king, the mind of the great majority of the Jews was set upon re-establishing under the protectorate of Rome the pure and godly sacerdotal government, as it had once been set up by the Persian authorities. Immediately after the death of the old king the masses in Jerusalem had congregated to demand the setting aside of the high-priest nominated by Herod and the ejection of the unbelievers from the holy city, where the Passover was just to be celebrated ; Archelaus had been under the necessity of beginning his government by charging into these masses ; a number of dead were counted,

and the observance of the festival was suspended. The
Roman governor of Syria—the same Varus, whose folly
soon afterwards cost the Romans Germany—on whom it
primarily devolved to maintain order in the land during
the interregnum, had allowed these mutinous bands in
Jerusalem to send to Rome, where the occupation of the
Jewish throne was just being discussed, a deputation of
fifty persons to request the abolition of the monarchy; and,
when Augustus gave audience to it, eight thousand Jews of
the capital escorted it to the temple of Apollo.   The fanatical Jews at home meanwhile continued to help themselves ;
the Roman garrison, which was stationed in the temple, was
assailed with violence, and pious bands of brigands filled
the land ; Varus had to call out the legions and to restore
quiet with the sword.   It was a warning for the suzerain,
a supplementary justification of king Herod's violent but
effective government.   But Augustus, with all the weakness which he so often showed, particularly in later years,
while dismissing, no doubt, the representatives of those
fanatical masses and their request, yet executed in the
main the testament of Herod, and gave over the rule in
Jerusalem to Archelaus shorn of the kingly title, which
Augustus preferred for a time not to concede to the untried
young man ; shorn, moreover, of the northern territories,
and reduced also in military status by the taking away of
the defence of the frontier.   The circumstance that at the
instigation of Augustus the taxes raised to a high pitch
under Herod were lowered, could but little better the
position of the tetrarch.   The personal incapacity and
worthlessness of Archelaus were hardly needed, in addition, to make him impossible ; a few years later (6 A.D.)

Judaea a
Roman
province.

Augustus saw himself compelled to depose him.   Now he
did at length the will of those mutineers ; the monarchy
was abolished, and while on the one hand the land was
taken into direct Roman administration, on the other hand,
so far as an internal government was allowed by the side
of this, it was given over to the senate of Jerusalem.   This
procedure may certainly have been determined in part by
assurances given earlier by Augustus to Herod as regards

the succession, in part by the more and more apparent, and in general doubtless justifiable, disinclination of the imperial government to larger client-states possessing some measure of independent self-movement. What took place shortly before or soon after in Galatia, in Cappadocia, in Mauretania, explains why in Palestine also the kingdom of Herod hardly survived himself. But, as the immediate government was organised in Palestine, it was even administratively a bad retrograde step as compared with the Herodian ; and above all the circumstances here were so peculiar and so difficult, that the immediate contact between the governing Romans and the governed Jews— which certainly had been obstinately striven for by the priestly party itself and ultimately obtained—redounded to the benefit neither of the one nor of the other.

Judaea thus became in the year 6 A.D. a Roman province of the second rank,[1] and, apart from the ephemeral

Provincial organisation.

---

[1] The statement of Josephus that Judaea was attached to the province of Syria and placed under its governor (*Arch.* xvii. *fin.*: τοῦ δὲ Ἀρχελάου χώρας ὑποτελοῦς προσνεμηθείσης τῇ Σύρων; xviii. 1, 1: εἰς τὴν Ἰουδαίων προσθήκην τῆς Συρίας γενομένην ; c. 4, 6) appears to be incorrect ; on the contrary, Judaea probably formed thenceforth a procuratorial province of itself. An exact distinction between the *de iure* and *de facto* interference of the Syrian governor may not be expected in the case of Josephus. The fact that he organised the new province and conducted the first census does not decide the question what arrangement was assigned to it. Where the Jews complain of their procurator to the governor of Syria and the latter interferes against him, the procurator is certainly dependent on the legate ; but, when L. Vitellius did this (Josephus, *Arch.* xviii. 4, 2), his power extended in quite an extraordinary way over the province (Tacitus, *Ann.* vi. 32; *Staatsrecht*, ii. 822), and in the other case the words of Tacitus, *Ann.* xii. 54 : *quia Claudius ius statuendi etiam de pro-* *curatoribus dederat*, show that the governor of Syria could not have pronounced such a judgment in virtue of his general jurisdiction. Both the *ius gladii* of these procurators (Josephus, *Bell. Jud.* ii. 8, 1 : μέχρι τοῦ κτείνειν λαβὼν παρὰ τοῦ Καίσαρος ἐξουσίαν, *Arch.* xviii. 1, 1 ; ἡγησόμενος Ἰουδαίων τῇ ἐπὶ πᾶσιν ἐξουσίᾳ) and their whole demeanour show that they did not belong to those who, placed under an imperial legate, attended only to financial affairs, but rather, like the procurators of Noricum and Raetia, formed the supreme authority for the administration of law and the command of the army. Thus the legates of Syria had there only the position which those of Pannonia had in Noricum and the upper German legate in Raetia. This corresponds also to the general development of matters ; all the larger kingdoms were on their annexation not attached to the neighbouring large governorships, whose plenitude of power it was not the tendency of this epoch to enlarge, but were made into independent governorships, mostly at first equestrian.

restoration of the kingdom of Jerusalem under Claudius in the years 41-44, thenceforth remained a Roman province. Instead of the previous native princes holding office for life and, under reservation of their being confirmed by the Roman government, hereditary, came an official of the equestrian order, nominated and liable to recall by the emperor. The port of Caesarea rebuilt by Herod after a Hellenic model became, probably at once, the seat of Roman administration. The exemption of the land from Roman garrison, as a matter of course ceased, but, as throughout in provinces of the second rank, the Roman military force consisted only of a moderate number of cavalry and infantry divisions of the inferior class ; subsequently one ala and five cohorts—about 3000 men—were stationed there. These troops were perhaps taken over from the earlier government, at least in great part formed in the country itself, mostly, however, from Samaritans and Syrian Greeks.[1] The province did not obtain a legionary garrison, and even in the territories adjoining Judaea there was stationed at the most one of the four Syrian legions. To Jerusalem there came a standing Roman commandant, who took up his abode in the royal castle, with a weak standing garrison ; only during the time of the Passover, when the whole land and countless strangers flocked to the temple, a stronger division of Roman soldiers was stationed in a colonnade belonging to the temple. That on the erection of the province the obligation of tribute towards Rome set in, follows from the very circumstance that the costs of defending the land were thereby transferred to the imperial government. After the latter had suggested a reduction of the payments at the installation of Archelaus, it is far from probable that on the annexation of the country it contemplated an immediate raising of them ; but doubtless, as in every newly-

---

[1] According to Josephus (*Arch.* xx. 8, 7, more exact than *Bell. Jud.* ii. 13, 7) the greatest part of the Roman troops in Palestine consisted of Caesareans and Sebastenes. The *ala* *Sebastenorum* fought in the Jewish war under Vespasian (Josephus, *Bell. Jud.* ii. 12, 5). Comp. *Eph. epigr.* v. 194. There are no *alae* and *cohortes Iudaeorum*.

acquired territory, steps were taken for a revision of the previous land-register.[1]

For the native authorities in Judaea as everywhere the urban communities were, as far as possible, taken as a basis. Samaria, or as the town was now called, Sebaste, the newly laid out Caesarea, and the other urban communities contained in the former kingdom of Archelaus, were self-administering, under superintendence of the Roman authority. The government also of the capital with the large territory belonging to it was organised in a similar way. Already in the pre-Roman period under the Seleucids there was formed, as we saw (p. 160), in Jerusalem a council of the elders, the Synhedrion, or as Judaised, the Sanhedrin. The presidency in it was held by the high priest, whom each ruler of the land, if he was not possibly himself high priest, appointed for the time. To the college belonged the former high priests and esteemed experts in the law. This assembly, in which the aristocratic element preponderated, acted as the supreme spiritual representative of the whole body of Jews, and, so far as this was not to be separated from it, also as the secular representative in particular of the community of Jerusalem. It is only the later Rabbinism that has by a pious fiction transformed the Synhedrion of Jerusalem into a spiritual institute of Mosaic appointment. It corresponded essentially to the council of the Greek urban constitution, but certainly bore, as respected its composition as well as its sphere of working, a more spiritual character

The native authorities.

The Synhedrion of Jerusalem.

---

[1] The revenues of Herod amounted, according to Josephus, *Arch.* xvii. 11, 4, to about 1200 talents, whereof about 100 fell to Batanaea with the adjoining lands, 200 to Galilee and Peraea, the rest to the share of Archelaus; in this doubtless the older Hebrew talent (of about £390) is meant, not, as Hultsch (Metrol. ², p. 605) assumes, the denarial talent (of about £260), as the revenues of the same territory under Claudius are estimated in the same Josephus (*Arch.* xix. 8, 2), at 12,000,000 denarii (about £500,000). The chief item in it was formed by the land-tax, the amount of which we do not know; in the Syrian time it amounted at least for a time to the third part of corn and the half of wine and oil (1 Maccab. x. 30) in Caesar's time for Joppa a fourth of the fruit (p. 175, note), besides which at that time the temple-tenth still existed. To this was added a number of other taxes and customs, auction-charges, salt-tax, road and bridge moneys, and the like; it is to these that the publicans of the Gospels have reference.

than belonged to the Greek representations of the community. To this Synhedrion and its high priest, who was now nominated by the procurator as representative of the imperial suzerain, the Roman government left or committed that jurisdiction which in the Hellenic subject communities belonged to the urban authorities and the common councils. With indifferent short-sightedness it allowed to the transcendental Messianism of the Pharisees free course, and to the by no means transcendental land-consistory—acting until the Messiah should arrive—tolerably free sway in affairs of faith, of manners, and of law, where Roman interests were not directly affected thereby. This applied in particular to the administration of justice. It is true that, as far as Roman burgesses were concerned, ordinary jurisdiction in civil as in criminal affairs must have been reserved for the Roman tribunals even already before the annexation of the land. But civil jurisdiction over Jews remained even after that annexation chiefly with the local authority. Criminal justice over them was exercised by the latter probably in general concurrently with the Roman procurator ; only sentences of death could not be executed by it otherwise than after confirmation by the imperial magistrate.

The Roman provincial government.

In the main those arrangements were the inevitable consequences of the abolition of the principality, and when the Jews had obtained this request of theirs, they in fact obtained those arrangements along with it. Certainly it was the design of the government to avoid, as far as possible, harshness and abruptness in carrying them out. Publius Sulpicius Quirinius, to whom as governor of Syria the erection of the new province was entrusted, was a magistrate of repute, and quite familiar with the affairs of the East, and the several reports confirm by what they say or by their silence the fact that the difficulties of the state of things were known and taken into account. The local coining of petty moneys, as formerly practised by the kings, now took place in the name of the Roman ruler ; but on account of the Jewish abhorrence of images the head of the emperor was not even placed on the coins.

Setting foot within the interior of the temple continued to be forbidden in the case of every non-Jew under penalty of death.[1]   However averse was the attitude of Augustus personally towards the Oriental worships (p. 172), he did not disdain here any more than in Egypt to connect them in their home with the imperial government ; magnificent presents of Augustus, of Livia, and of other members of the imperial house adorned the sanctuary of the Jews, and according to an endowment by the emperor the smoke of the sacrifice of a bullock and two lambs rose daily there to the " Supreme God."   The Roman soldiers were directed, when they were on service at Jerusalem, to leave the standards with the effigies of the emperor at Caesarea, and, when a governor under Tiberius omitted to do so, the government ultimately yielded to the urgent entreaties of the pious and left matters on the old footing.   Indeed, when the Roman troops were to march through Jerusalem on an expedition against the Arabians, they obtained another route for the march in consequence of the scruples entertained by the priests against the effigies on the standards. When that same governor dedicated to the emperor at the royal castle in Jerusalem shields without imagery, and the pious took offence at it, Tiberius commanded the same to be taken away, and to be hung up in the temple of Augustus at Caesarea.   The festival dress of the high priest, which was kept in Roman custody at the castle and hence had to be purified from such profanation for seven days before

---

[1] On the marble screen (δρύφακτος), which marked off the inner court of the temple, were placed for that reason tablets of warning in the Latin and Greek language (Josephus, *Bell. Jud.* v. 5, 2 ; vi. 2, 4 ; *Arch.* xv. 11, 5). One of the latter, which has recently been found (*Revue Archéologique*, xxiii. 1872, p. 220), and is now in the public museum of Constantinople, is to this effect : μήθ' ἕνα ἀλλογενῆ εἰσπορεύεσθαι ἐντὸς τοῦ περὶ τὸ ἱερὸν τρυφάκτου καὶ περιβόλου. ὃς δ'ἂν ληφθῇ, ἑαυτῷ αἴτιος ἔσται διὰ τὸ ἐξακολουθεῖν θάνατον. The iota in the dative is present, and the writing good

and suitable for the early imperial period. These tablets were hardly set up by the Jewish kings, who would scarcely have added a Latin text, and had no cause to threaten the penalty of death with this singular anonymity. If they were set up by the Roman government, both are explained ; Titus also says (in Josephus, *Bell. Jud.* vi. 2, 4), in an appeal to the Jews: οὐχ ἡμεῖς τοὺς ὑπερβάντας ὑμῖν ἀναιρεῖν ἐπετρέψαμεν, κἂν Ῥωμαῖός τις ᾖ ;—If the tablet really bears traces of axe-cuts, these came from the soldiers of Titus.

it was put on, was delivered up to the faithful upon their complaint ; and the commandant of the castle was directed to give himself no further concern about it.   Certainly it could not be asked of the multitude that it should feel the consequences of the incorporation less heavily, because it had itself brought them about.   Nor is it to be maintained that the annexation of the land passed off without oppression for the inhabitants, and that they had no ground to complain ; such arrangements have never been carried into effect without difficulties and disturbances of the peace.   The number, moreover, of unrighteous and violent deeds perpetrated by individual governors must not have been smaller in Judaea than elsewhere.   In the very beginning of the reign of Tiberius the Jews, like the Syrians, complained of the pressure of the taxes ; especially the prolonged administration of Pontius Pilatus is charged with all the usual official crimes by a not unfair observer. But Tiberius, as the same Jew says, had during the twenty-three years of his reign maintained the time-hallowed holy customs, and in no part set them aside or violated them.   This is the more to be recognised, seeing that the same emperor in the West interfered against the Jews more emphatically than any other (p. 172), and thus the long-suffering and caution shown by him in Judaea cannot be traced back to personal favour for Judaism.

The Jewish opposition.   In spite of all this both the opposition on principle to the Roman government and the violent efforts at self-help on the part of the faithful developed themselves even in this time of peace.   The payment of tribute was assailed, not perchance merely because it was oppressive, but as being godless. " Is it allowable," asks the Rabbi in the Gospel, " to pay the census to Caesar ?"   The ironical answer which he received did not by any means suffice for all ; there were saints, though possibly not in great number, who thought themselves polluted if they touched a coin with the emperor's image.   This was something new—an advance in the theology of opposition ; the kings Seleucus and Antiochus had also not been circumcised, and had likewise received tribute in silver pieces bearing their

image. Such was the theory ; the practical application of
it was made, not certainly by the high council of Jerusalem, in which, under the influence of the imperial
government, the more pliant notables of the land directed
the vote, but by Judas the Galilean from Gamala on
the lake of Gennesaret, who, as Gamaliel subsequently
reminded this high council, " stood up in the days of the
census, and behind him the people rose in revolt." He
spoke out what all thought, that the so-called census was
bondage, and that it was a disgrace for the Jew to recognise another lord over him than the Lord of Zebaoth ;
but that He helped only those who helped themselves.
If not many followed his call to arms, and he ended his
life, after a few months, on the scaffold, the holy dead was
more dangerous to the unholy victors than the living man.
He and his followers were regarded by the later Jews
alongside of the Sadducees, Pharisees, and Essenes, as
the fourth " School ;" at that time they were called the
Zealots, afterwards they called themselves Sicarii, " men
of the knife." Their teaching was simple : God alone is
Lord, death indifferent, freedom all in all. This teaching
remained, and the children and grandchildren of Judas
became the leaders of the later insurrections.

If the Roman government had under the first two
regents, taken on the whole, skilfully and patiently sufficed
for the task of repressing, as far as possible, these ex-
plosive elements, the next change on the throne brought
matters close to the catastrophe. The change was saluted
with rejoicing, as in the whole empire, so specially by the
Jews in Jerusalem and Alexandria ; and, after the unsoci-
able and unloved old man, the new youthful ruler Gaius
was extravagantly extolled in both quarters. But speedily
out of trifling occasions there was developed a formidable
quarrel. A grandson of the first Herod and of the beautiful Mariamne, named after the protector and friend of
his grandfather Herod Agrippa, about the most worthless
and abandoned of the numerous Oriental princes' sons
living in Rome, but nevertheless or on that very account
the favourite and youthful friend of the new emperor,

*The em-
peror Gaius
and the
Jews.*

hitherto known solely by his dissoluteness and his debts, had obtained from his protector, to whom he had been the first to convey the news of the death of Tiberius, one of the vacant Jewish petty principalities as a gift, and the title of king along with it. This prince in the year 38, on the way to his new kingdom, came to the city of Alexandria, where he a few months previously had attempted as a runaway bill-debtor to borrow among the Jewish bankers. When he showed himself there in public in his regal dress with his splendidly equipped halberdiers, this naturally stirred up the non-Jewish inhabitants of the great city—fond as it was of ridicule and of scandal—who bore anything but good will to the Jews, to a corresponding parody; nor did the matter stop there. It culminated in a furious hunting-out of the Jews. The Jewish houses which lay detached were plundered and burnt; the Jewish ships lying in the harbour were pillaged; the Jews that were met with in the non-Jewish quarters were maltreated and slain. But against the purely Jewish quarters they could effect nothing by violence. Then the leaders lighted on the idea of consecrating the synagogues, which were the object of their marked attentions, so far as these still stood, collectively as temples of the new ruler, and of setting up statues of him in all of them—in the chief synagogue a statue on a *quadriga.* That the emperor Gaius deemed himself, as seriously as his confused mind could do so, a real and corporeal god, everybody knew—the Jews and the governor as well. The latter, Avillius Flaccus, an able man, and, under Tiberius, an excellent administrator, but now hampered by the disfavour in which he stood with the new emperor, and expecting every moment recall and impeachment, did not disdain to use the opportunity for his rehabilitation.[1] He not

Jew-hunt in Alexandria.

---

[1] The special hatred of Gaius against the Jews (Philo, *Leg.* 20) was not the cause, but the consequence, of the Alexandrian Jew-hunt. Since therefore the understanding of the leaders of the Jew-hunt with the governor (Philo, *in Flacc.* 4) cannot have subsisted on the footing that the Jews imagined, because the governor could not reasonably believe that he would recommend himself to the new emperor by abandoning the Jews, the question certainly arises, why the leaders of those hostile to the Jews chose this very moment for the Jew-hunt, and above all, why the governor,

merely gave orders by edict to put no hindrance in the
way of setting up the statues in the synagogues, but he
entered directly into the Jew-hunting.   He ordained the
abolition of the Sabbath.   He declared further in his
edicts that these tolerated foreigners had possessed themselves unallowably of the best part of the town ; they
were restricted to a single one of the five wards, and all
the other Jewish houses were abandoned to the rabble,
while masses of the ejected inhabitants lay without shelter
on the shore.   No remonstrance was even listened to ;
eight and thirty members of the council of the elders,
which then presided over the Jews instead of the Ethnarch,[1]
were scourged in the open circus before all the people.
Four hundred houses lay in ruins ; trade and commerce
were suspended ; the factories stood still.   There was no
help left except with the emperor.   Before him appeared
the two Alexandrian deputations, that of the Jews led
by the formerly (p. 170) mentioned Philo, a scholar of
Neojudaic leanings, and of a heart more gentle than
brave, but who withal faithfully took the part of his people
in this distress ; that of the enemies of the Jews, led by
Apion, also an Alexandrian scholar and author, the
"world's clapper" [*cymbalum mundi*], as the emperor
Tiberius called him, full of big words and still bigger lies,

whose excellence Philo so emphatically acknowledges, allowed it, and,
at least in its further course, took
personal part in it.   Probably things
occurred as they are narrated above :
hatred and envy towards the Jews
had long been fermenting in Alexandria (Josephus, *Bell. Jud.* ii. 18, 9 ;
Philo, *Leg.* 18) ; the abeyance of the
old stern government, and the evident
disfavour in which the prefect stood
with Gaius, gave room for the tumult ;
the arrival of Agrippa furnished the
occasion ; the adroit conversion of the
synagogues into temples of Gaius
stamped the Jews as enemies of the
emperor, and, after this was done,
Flaccus must certainly have seized on
the persecution to rehabilitate himself
thereby with the emperor.

the earlier Augustan period the Jews
in Alexandria were under an Ethnarch
(*Geogr.* xvii. 1, 13, p. 798, and in
Josephus, *Arch.* xiv. 7, 2).   Thereupon, when under Augustus the Eth-
narchos or Genarchos, as he was
called, died, a council of the elders
took his place (Philo, *Leg.* 10) ; yet
Augustus, as Claudius states (Josephus,
Arch. xix. 5, 2), "did not prohibit the
Jews from appointing an Ethnarch,"
which probably is meant to signify
that the choice of a single president
was only omitted for this time, not
abolished once for all.   Under Gaius
there were evidently only elders of
the Jewish body ; and also under
Vespasian these are met with (Josephus,
Bell. vii. 10, 1).   An archon of the
Jews in Antioch is named in Josephus,
Bell. vii. 3, 3.

[1] When Strabo was in Egypt in

of the most assured omniscience[1] and unlimited faith in himself, conversant, if not with men, at any rate with their worthlessness, a celebrated master of discourse as of the art of misleading, ready for action, witty, unabashed, and unconditionally loyal. The result of the discussion was settled from the outset ; the emperor received the deputies while he was inspecting the works designed in his gardens, but instead of giving a hearing to the suppliants, he put to them sarcastic questions, which the enemies of the Jews in defiance of all etiquette accompanied with loud laughter, and, as he was in good humour, he confined himself to expressing his regret that these otherwise good people should be so unhappily constituted as not to be able to understand his innate divine nature—as to which he was beyond doubt in earnest. Apion thus gained his case, and, wherever it pleased the adversaries of the Jews, the synagogues were changed into temples of Gaius.

The statue of the emperor in the temple of Jerusalem.

But the matter was not confined to these dedications introduced by the street-youth of Alexandria. In the year 39 the governor of Syria, Publius Petronius, received orders from the emperor to march with his legions into Jerusalem, and to set up in the temple the statue of the emperor. The governor, an honourable official of the school of Tiberius, was alarmed ; Jews from all the land, men and women, gray-haired and children, flocked to him, first to Ptolemais in Syria, then to Tiberias in Galilee, to entreat his mediation that the outrage might not take place ; the fields throughout the country were not tilled, and the desperate multitudes declared that they would rather suffer death by the sword or famine than be willing to look on at this abomination. In reality the governor ventured to delay the execution of the orders and to make counter-representations, although he knew that his head was at stake. At the same time the king Agrippa, lately mentioned, went in person to Rome to procure from his

---

[1] Apion spoke and wrote on all and sundry matters, upon the metals and the Roman letters, on magic and concerning the Hetaerae, on the early history of Egypt and the cookery re- ceipts of Apicius; but above all he made his fortune by his discourses upon Homer, which acquired for him honorary citizenship in numerous Greek cities. He had discovered

friend the recall of the orders.   The emperor in fact
desisted from his desire, in consequence, it is said, of his
good humour when under the influence of wine being
adroitly turned to account by the Jewish prince.   But at
the same time he restricted the concession to the single
temple of Jerusalem, and sent nevertheless to the governor
on account of his disobedience a sentence of death, which
indeed, accidentally delayed, was not carried into execution.   Gaius now resolved to break the resistance of the
Jews ; the enjoined march of the legions shows that he
had this time weighed beforehand the consequences of
his order.   Since those occurrences the Egyptians, ready
to believe in his divinity, had his full affection just as the
obstinate and simple-minded Jews had his corresponding
hatred ; secretive as he was and accustomed to grant
favours in order afterwards to revoke them, the worst
could not but appear merely postponed.   He was on the
point of departing for Alexandria in order there to receive
in person the incense of his altars ; and the statue, which
he thought of erecting to himself in Jerusalem, was—it is
said—quietly in preparation, when, in January 41, the
dagger of Chaerea delivered, among other things, the
temple of Jehovah from the monster.

The short season of suffering left behind it no outward   Jewish dis-
consequences ; with the god his altars fell.   But yet the   positions.
traces of it remained on both sides.   The history, which
is here being told, is that of an increasing hatred between
Jews and non-Jews, and in it the three years' persecution
of the Jews under Gaius marks a section and an advance.
The hatred of Jews and the Jew-hunts were as old as the
Diaspora itself ; these privileged and autonomous Oriental
communities within the Hellenic could not but develop
them as necessarily as the marsh generates the malaria.

that Homer had begun his Iliad   of the suitors ; indeed he affirmed that
with the unsuitable word μῆνις for   he had conjured up Homer himself
the reason that the first two letters,   from the nether world to question
as numerals, exhibit the number of   him about his native country, and
the books of the two epics which he   that Homer had come and had told
was to write ; he named the guest-   it to him, but had bound him not to
friend in Ithaca, with whom he had   betray it to others.
made inquiries as to the draught-board

But such a Jew-hunt as the Alexandrian of the year 38, instigated by defective Hellenism and directed at once by the supreme authority and by the low rabble, the older Greek and Roman history has not to show. The far way from the evil desire of the individual to the evil deed of the collective body was thus traversed, and it was shown what those so disposed had to will and to do, and were under circumstances also able to do. That this revelation was felt also on the Jewish side, is not to be doubted, although we are not in a position to adduce documentary evidence in support of it.[1]   But a far deeper impression than that of the Jew-hunt at Alexandria was graven on the minds of the Jews by the statue of the god Gaius in the Holy of Holies. The thing had been done once already ; a like proceeding of the king of Syria, Antiochus Epiphanes, had been followed by the rising of the Maccabees and the victorious restoration of the free

iii. 61. national state (iii. 64).   That Epiphanes—the Anti-Messiah who ushers in the Messiah, as the prophet Daniel had, certainly after the event, delineated him—was thenceforth to every Jew the prototype of abomination ; it was no matter of indifference, that the same conception came to be with equal warrant attached to a Roman emperor, or rather to the image of the Roman ruler in general. Since that fateful edict the Jews never ceased to dread that another emperor might issue a like command ; and so far certainly with reason, as according to the organisation of the Roman polity such an enactment depended solely on the momentary pleasure of the ruler for the time.

The Apocalypse of John.
This Jewish hatred of the worship of the emperor and of imperialism itself, is depicted with glowing colours in the

---

[1] The writings of Philo, which bring before us this whole catastrophe with incomparable reality, nowhere strike this chord; but, apart even from the fact that this rich and aged man had in him more of the good man than of the good hater, it is obvious of itself that these consequences of the occurrences on the Jewish side were not publicly set forth. What the Jews thought and felt may not be judged of by what they found it convenient to say, particularly in their works written in Greek. If the Book of Wisdom and the third book of Maccabees are in reality directed against the Alexandrian persecution of the Jews (Hausrath, *Neutestam. Zeitgesch.* ii. 259 ff.)—which we may add is anything but certain—they are, if possible, couched in a still tamer tone than the writings of Philo.

Apocalypse of John, for which, chiefly on that account, Rome is the harlot of Babylon and the common enemy of mankind.[1]   Still less matter of indifference was the

[1] This is perhaps the right way of apprehending the Jewish conceptions, in which the positive facts regularly run away into generalities. In the accounts of the Anti-Messias and of the Antichrist no positive elements are found to suit the emperor Gaius ; the view that would explain the name Armillus, which the Talmud assigns to the former, by the circumstance that the emperor Gaius sometimes wore women's bracelets (*armillae*, Suetonius, *Gai.* 52), cannot be seriously maintained. In the Apocalypse of John—the classical revelation of Jewish self-esteem and of hatred towards the Romans—the picture of the Anti-Messias is associated rather with Nero, who did not cause his image to be set up in the Holy of Holies. This composition belongs, as is well known, to a time and a tendency, which still viewed Christianity as essentially a Jewish sect ; those elected and marked by the angel are all Jews, 12,000 from each of the twelve tribes, and have precedence over the "great multitude of other righteous ones," *i.e.* of proselytes (ch. vii. ; comp. ch. xii. 1). It was written, demonstrably, after Nero's fall, and when his return from the East was expected. Now it is true that a pseudo-Nero appeared immediately after the death of the real one, and was executed at the beginning of the following year (Tacitus, *Hist.* ii. 8, 9) ; but it is not of this one that John is thinking, for the very exact account makes no mention, as John does, of the Parthians in the matter, and for John there is a considerable interval between the fall of Nero and his return, the latter even still lying in the future. His Nero is the person who, under Vespasian, found adherents in the region of the Euphrates, whom king Artabanus acknowledged under Titus and prepared to reinstate in Rome by military force, and whom at length the Parthians surrendered, after prolonged negotiations, about the year 88, to Domitian.   To these events the Apocalypse corresponds quite exactly.

On the other hand, in a writing of this character no inference as to the state of the siege at the time can possibly be drawn, from the circumstance that, according to xi. 1, 2, only the outer court, and not the Holy of Holies of the Temple of Jerusalem was given into the power of the heathen ; here everything in the details is imaginary, and this trait is certainly either invented at pleasure or, if the view be preferred, possibly based on orders given to the Roman soldiers, who were encamped in Jerusalem after its destruction, not to set foot in what was formerly the Holy of Holies. The foundation of the Apocalypse is indisputably the destruction of the earthly Jerusalem, and the prospect thereby for the first time opened up of its future ideal restoration ; in place of the razing of the city which had taken place there cannot possibly be put the mere expectation of its capture. If, then, it is said of the seven heads of the dragon : βασιλεῖς ἑπτά εἰσιν· οἱ πέντε ἔπεσαν, καὶ εἷς ἐστιν, ὁ ἄλλος οὔπω ἦλθεν, καὶ ὅταν ἔλθῃ ὀλίγον αὐτὸν δεῖ μεῖναι (xvii. 10), the five, presumably, are Augustus, Tiberius, Gaius, Claudius, Nero, the sixth Vespasian, the seventh undefined ; "the beast which was, and is not, and is itself the eighth, but of the seven," is, of course, Nero. The undefined seventh is incongruous, like so much in this gorgeous, but contradictory and often tangled imagery ; and it is added, not because the number seven was employed, which was easily to be got at by including Caesar, but because the writer hesitated to predicate immediately of the reigning emperor the short government of the last ruler and his overthrow by the

parallel, which naturally suggested itself, of the consequences. Mattathias of Modein had not been more than
Judas the Galilean ; the insurrection of the patriots
against the Syrian king was almost as hopeless as the

returning Nero. But one cannot possibly — as is done after others by
Renan—by including Caesar in the
reckoning, recognise in the sixth emperor, " who is," Nero, who immediately afterward is designated as he
who " was and is not," and in the
seventh, who " has not yet come and
will not rule long," even the aged
Galba, who, according to Renan's
view, was ruling at the time. It is
clear that the latter does not belong
at all to such a series, any more than
Otho and Vitellius.

It is more important, however, to
oppose the current conception, according to which the polemic is directed
against the Neronian persecution of the
Christians and the siege or the destruction of Jerusalem, whereas it is pointed
against the Roman provincial government generally, and in particular
against the worship of the emperors.
If of the seven emperors Nero alone
is named (by his numerical expression), this is so, not because he was
the worst of the seven, but because
the naming of the reigning emperor,
while prophesying a speedy end of his
reign in a published writing, had its
risk, and some consideration towards
the one " who is " beseems even a
prophet. Nero's name was given up,
and besides, the legend of his healing
and of his return was in every one's
mouth ; thereby he has become for
the Apocalypse the representative of
the Roman imperial rule, and the
Antichrist. The crime of the monster
of the sea, and of his image and in-
strument, the monster of the land, is
not the violence to the city of Jerusalem (xi. 2)—which appears not as
their misdeed, but rather as a portion
of the world-judgment (in which case
also consideration for the reigning
emperor may have been at work)—
but the divine worship, which the
heathen pay to the monster of the

sea (xiii. 8 : προσκυνήσουσιν αὐτὸν
πάντες οἱ κατοικοῦντες ἐπὶ τῆς γῆς),
and which the monster of the land—
called for that reason also the pseudo-
prophet—demands and compels for
that of the sea (xiii. 12 : ποιεῖ τὴν
γῆν καὶ τοὺς κατοικοῦντας ἐν αὐτῇ ἵνα
προσκυνήσουσιν τὸ θηρίον τὸ πρῶτον, οὗ
ἐθεραπεύθη ἡ πληγὴ τοῦ θανάτου αὐτοῦ);
above all, he is upbraided with the
desire to make an image for the former (xiii. 14 : λέγων τοῖς κατοικοῦσιν
ἐπὶ τῆς γῆς, ποιῆσαι εἰκόνα τῷ θηρίῳ ὃς
ἔχει τὴν πληγὴν τῆς μαχαίρης καὶ
ἔζησεν, comp. xiv. 9 ; xvi. 2 ; xix.
20). This, it is plain, is partly the
imperial government beyond the sea,
partly the lieutenancy on the Asiatic
continent, not of this or that province
or even of this or that person, but
generally such representation of the
emperor as the provincials of Asia and
Syria knew. If trade and commerce
appear associated with the use of the
χάραγμα of the monster of the sea
(xiii. 16, 17), there lies clearly at
bottom an abhorrence of the image
and legend of the imperial money—
certainly transformed in a fanciful
way, as in fact Satan makes the image
of the emperor speak. These very
governors appear afterwards (xvii.) as
the ten horns, which are assigned to
the monster in its copy, and are here
called, quite correctly, the "ten
kings, which have not the royal dignity, but have authority like kings ;"
the number, which is taken over from
the vision of Daniel, may not, it is
true, be taken too strictly.

In the sentences of death pronounced over the righteous, John is
thinking of the regular judicial procedure on account of the refusal to
worship the emperor's image, such as
the Letters of Pliny describe (xiii. 15 :
ποιήσῃ ἵνα ὅσοι ἐὰν μὴ προσκυνήσωσιν
τὴν εἰκόνα τοῦ θηρίου ἀποκτανθῶσιν,
comp. vi. 9 ; xx. 4). When stress is

insurrection against the monster beyond the sea. Historical parallels in practical application are dangerous elements of opposition ; only too rapidly does the structure of long years of wise government come to be shaken.

The government of Claudius turned back on both sides into the paths of Tiberius. In Italy there was repeated, not indeed precisely the ejection of the Jews, since there could not but arise a conviction that this course was impracticable, but at any rate a prohibition of the exercise of their worship[1] in common, which, it is true, amounted nearly to the same thing and probably came as little into execution. Alongside of this edict of intolerance and in an opposite sense, by an ordinance embracing the whole empire the Jews were freed from those public

Claudius and the Jews.

laid on these sentences of death being executed with special frequency in Rome (xvii. 6 ; xvii. 24), what is thereby meant is the execution of sentences wherein men were condemned to fight as gladiators or with wild beasts, which often could not take place on the spot where they were pronounced, and, as is well known, took place chiefly in Rome itself (Modestinus, *Dig.* xlviii. 19, 31). The Neronian executions on account of alleged incendiarism do not formally belong to the class of religious processes at all, and it is only prepossession that can refer the martyrs' blood shed in Rome, of which John speaks, exclusively or pre-eminently to these events. The current conceptions as to the so-called persecutions of the Christians labour under a defective apprehension of the rule of law and the practice of law subsisting in the Roman empire ; in reality the persecution of the Christians was a standing matter as was that of robbers ; only such regulations were put into practice at times more gently or even negligently, at other times more strictly, and were doubtless on occasion specially enforced from high quarters. The "war against the saints" is only a subsequent interpolation on the part of some, for whom

John's words did not suffice (xiii. 7). The Apocalypse is a remarkable evidence of the national and religious hatred of the Jews towards the Occidental government ; but to illustrate with these colours the Neronian tale of horrors, as Renan does in particular, is to shift the place of the facts and to detract from their depth of significance. The Jewish national hatred did not wait for the conquest of Jerusalem to originate it, and it made, as might be expected, no distinction between the good and the bad Caesar ; its Anti-Messias is named Nero, doubtless, but not less Vespasian or Marcus.

[1] The circumstance that Suetonius (*Claud.* 25) names a certain Chrestus as instigator of the constant troubles in Rome, that had in the first instance called forth these measures (according to him the expulsion from Rome ; in contrast to Dio, lx. 6) has been without sufficient reason conceived as a misunderstanding of the movement called forth by Christ among Jews and proselytes. The Book of Acts xviii. 2, speaks only of the expulsion of the Jews. At any rate it is not to be doubted that, with the attitude at that time of the Christians to Judaism, they too fell under the edict.

obligations which were not compatible with their religious convictions ; whereby, as respected service in war particularly, there was doubtless conceded only what hitherto it had not been possible to compel. The exhortation, expressed at the close of this edict, to the Jews to exercise now on their part also greater moderation, and to refrain from the insulting of persons of another faith, shows that there had not been wanting transgressions also on the Jewish side. In Egypt as in Palestine the religious arrangements were, at least on the whole, re-established as they had subsisted before Gaius, although in Alexandria the Jews hardly obtained back all that they had possessed ;[1] the insurrectionary movements, which had broken out, or were on the point of breaking out, in the one case as in the other, thereupon disappeared of themselves. In Palestine Claudius even went beyond the

Agrippa. system of Tiberius and committed the whole former territory of Herod to a native prince, that same Agrippa who accidentally had come to be friendly with Claudius and useful to him in the crises of his accession. It was certainly the design of Claudius to resume the system followed at the time of Herod and to obviate the dangers of the immediate contact between the Romans and Jews. But Agrippa, leading an easy life and even as a prince in constant financial embarrassment, good-humoured, moreover, and more disposed to be on good terms with his subjects than with the distant protector, gave offence in various ways to the government, for example, by the strengthening the walls of Jerusalem, which he was forbidden to carry further ; and the towns that adhered to the Romans, Caesarea and Sebaste, as well as the troops organised in the Roman fashion, were disinclined to him. When he died early and suddenly in the year 44, it appeared hazardous to entrust the position, important in

---

[1] The Jews there at least appear later to have had only the fourth of the five wards of the city in their possession (Josephus, *Bell. Jud.* ii. 18, 8). Probably, if the 400 houses that were razed had been given back again to them in so striking a manner, the Jewish authors Josephus and Philo, who lay stress on all the imperial marks of favour shown to the Jews, would not have been silent on the subject.

a political as in a military point of view, to his only son of seventeen years of age, and those who wielded power in the cabinet were reluctant to let out of their hands the lucrative procuratorships. The Claudian government had here, as elsewhere, lighted on the right course, but had not the energy to carry it out irrespective of accessory considerations. A Jewish prince with Jewish soldiers might exercise the government in Judaea for the Romans ; the Roman magistrate and the Roman soldiers offended probably still more frequently through ignorance of Jewish views than through intentional action in opposition to them, and whatever they might undertake was on their part in the eyes of believers an offence, and the most indifferent occurrence a religious outrage. The demand for mutual understanding and agreement was on both sides just as warranted of itself as it was impossible of execution. But above all a conflict between the Jewish lord of the land and his subjects was a matter of tolerable indifference for the empire ; every conflict between the Romans and the Jews in Jerusalem widened the gulf which yawned between the peoples of the West and the Hebrews living along with them ; and the danger lay, not in the quarrels of Palestine, but in the incompatibility of the members of the empire of different nationalities who were now withal coupled together by fate.

Thus the ship was driving incessantly towards the whirlpool. In this ill-fated voyage all taking part lent their help—the Roman government and its administrators, the Jewish authorities and the Jewish people. The former indeed continued to show a willingness to meet as far as possible all claims, fair and unfair, of the Jews. When in the year 44 the procurator again entered Jerusalem, the nomination of the high-priest and the administration of the temple-treasure, which were combined with the kingly office and in so far also with the procuratorship, were taken from him and transferred to a brother of the deceased king Agrippa, king Herod of Chalcis, as well as, after his death in the year 48, to his successor the younger Agrippa already mentioned. The

Preparation for the insurrection.

Roman chief magistrate, on the complaint of the Jews caused a Roman soldier, who, on occasion of orders to plunder a Jewish village, had torn in pieces a roll of the law, to be put to death. The whole weight of Roman imperial justice fell, according to circumstances, even upon the higher officials ; when two procurators acting alongside of one another had taken part for and against in the quarrel of the Samaritans and the Galileans, and their soldiers had fought against one another, the imperial governor of Syria, Ummidius Quadratus, was sent with extraordinary full powers to Syria to punish and to execute; as a result one of the guilty persons was sent into banishment, and a Roman military tribune named Celer was publicly beheaded in Jerusalem itself. But alongside of these examples of severity stood others of a weakness partaking of guilt ; in that same process the second at least as guilty procurator Antonius Felix escaped punishment, because he was the brother of the powerful menial Pallas and the husband of the sister of king Agrippa. Still more than with the official abuses of individual administrators must the government be chargeable with the fact that it did not strengthen the power of the officials and the number of the troops in a province so situated, and continued to recruit the garrison almost exclusively from the province. Insignificant as the province was, it was a wretched stupidity and an ill-applied parsimony to treat it after the traditional pattern ; the seasonable display of a crushing superiority of force and unrelenting sternness, a governor of higher rank, and a legionary camp, would have saved to the province and the empire great sacrifices of money, blood, and honour.

High-priestly rule. Ananias.
But not less at least was the fault of the Jews. The highpriestly rule, so far as it went—and the government was but too much inclined to allow it free scope in all internal affairs—was, even according to the Jewish accounts, at no time conducted with so much violence and worthlessness as in that from the death of Agrippa to the outbreak of the war. The best-known and most influential of these priest-rulers was Ananias son of Nebedaeus,

the " whitewashed wall," as Paul called him, when this
spiritual judge bade his attendants smite him on the
mouth, because he ventured to defend himself before the
judgment-seat. It was laid to his charge that he bribed
the governor, and that by a corresponding interpretation
of Scripture he alienated from the lower clergy the tithe-
sheaves.[1] As one of the chief instigators of the war
between the Samaritans and the Galileans, he had stood
before the Roman judge. Not because the reckless
fanatics preponderated in the ruling circles, but because
these instigators of popular tumults and organisers of trials
for heresy lacked the moral and religious authority whereby the moderate men in better times had guided the multitude, and because they misunderstood and misused the
indulgence of the Roman authorities in internal affairs,
they were unable to mediate in a peaceful sense between
the foreign rule and the nation. It was under their very
rule that the Roman authorities were assailed with the
wildest and most irrational demands, and popular movements arose of grim absurdity. Of such a nature was
that violent petition, which demanded and obtained the
blood of a Roman soldier on account of the tearing up
of a roll of the law. Another time there arose a popular
tumult, which cost the lives of many men, because a
Roman soldier had exhibited in the temple a part of his
body in unseemly nudity. Even the best of kings could
not have absolutely averted such lunacy ; but even the
most insignificant prince would not have confronted the
fanatical multitude with so little control of the helm as
these priests.

The actual result was the constant increase of the The
new Maccabees. It has been customary to put the out- Zealots.
break of the war in the year 66 ; with equal and perhaps
better warrant we might name for it the year 44. Since
the death of Agrippa warfare in Judaea had never ceased,
and alongside of the local feuds, which Jews fought out

---

[1] The question was, apparently, xviii. 28), to the priest generally, or to
whether the gift of the tenth sheaf the high priest (Ewald, *Jüd. Gesch.*
belonged to Aaron the priest (Numb. vi.[3] 635).

with Jews, there went on constantly the war of the Roman
troops against the seceders in the mountains, the Zealots,
as the Jews named them, or according to Roman designation, the Robbers.   Both names were appropriate ; here
too alongside of the fanatics the decayed or decaying
elements of society played their part—at any rate after
the victory one of the first steps of the Zealots was to burn
the bonds for debt that were kept in the temple.   Every
one of the abler procurators, onward from the first Cuspius Fadus, swept the land of them, and still the hydra
appeared afresh in greater strength.   The successor of
Fadus, Tiberius Julius Alexander, himself sprung from a
Jewish family, a nephew of the above-mentioned Alexandrian scholar Philo, caused two sons of Judas the Galilean,
Jacob and Simon, to be crucified ; this was the seed of
the new Mattathias.   In the streets of the towns the
patriots preached aloud the war, and not a few followed
to the desert ; these bands set on fire the houses of the
peaceful and rational people who refused to take part with
them.   If the soldiers seized bandits of this sort, they
carried off in turn respectable people as hostages to the
mountains ; and very often the authorities agreed to
release the former in order to liberate the latter.   At the
same time the " men of the knife " began in the capital
their dismal trade ; they murdered, doubtless also for
money—as their first victim the priest Jonathan is named,
as commissioning them in that case, the Roman procurator Felix—but, if possible, at the same time as
patriots, Roman soldiers or countrymen of their own
friendly to the Romans.   How, with such dispositions,
should wonders and signs have failed to appear, and persons
who, deceived or deceiving, roused thereby the fanaticism
of the masses ?   Under Cuspius Fadus the miracle-monger
Theudas led his faithful adherents to the Jordan, assuring
them that the waters would divide before them and swal-
low up the pursuing Roman horsemen, as in the times of
king Pharaoh.   Under Felix another worker of wonders,
named from his native country the Egyptian, promised
that the walls of Jerusalem would collapse like those of

Jericho at the trumpet blast of Joshua; and thereupon four thousand knife-men followed him to the Mount of Olives. In the very absurdity lay the danger. The great mass of the Jewish population were small farmers, who ploughed their fields and pressed their oil in the sweat of their brow—more villagers than townsmen, of little culture and powerful faith, closely linked to the free bands in the mountains, and full of reverence for Jehovah and his priests in Jerusalem as well as full of aversion towards the unclean strangers. The war there was not a war between one power and another for the ascendency, not even properly a war of the oppressed against the oppressors for the recovery of freedom; it was not daring statesmen,[1] but fanatical peasants that began and waged it, and paid for it with their blood. It was a further stage in the history of national hatred; on both sides continued living together seemed impossible, and they encountered each other with the thought of mutual extirpation.

The movement, through which the tumults were changed into war, proceeded from Caesarea. In this urban community—originally Greek, and then remodelled by Herod after the pattern of the colonies of Alexander—which had

Outbreak of the insurrection in Caesarea.

---

[1] It is nothing but an empty fancy, when the statesman Josephus, in his preface to his History of the war, puts it as if the Jews of Palestine had reckoned on the one hand upon a rising of the Euphrates-lands, on the other hand, upon the troubles in Gaul and the threatening attitude of the Germans and on the crises of the year of four emperors. The Jewish war had long been in full course when Vindex appeared against Nero, and the Druids really did what is here assigned to the Rabbis; and, however great was the importance of the Jewish Diaspora in the lands of the Euphrates, a Jewish expedition from that quarter against the Romans of the East was almost as inconceivable as from Egypt and Asia Minor. Doubtless some free-lances came from thence, as *e.g.* some young princes of the zealously Jewish royal house of Adiabene (Josephus, *Bell. Jud.* ii. 19, 2; vi. 6, 4), and suppliant embassies went thither from the insurgents (*ib.* vi. 6, 2); but even money hardly flowed to the Jews from this quarter in any considerable amount. This statement is characteristic of the author more than of the war. If it is easy to understand how the Jewish leader of insurgents and subsequent courtier of the Flavians was fond of comparing himself with the Parthians exiled at Rome, it is the less to be excused that modern historical authorship should walk in similar paths, and in endeavouring to apprehend these events as constituent parts of the history of the Roman court and city or even of the Romano-Parthian quarrels, should by this insipid introduction of so-called great policy obscure the fearful necessity of this tragic development.

developed into the first seaport of Palestine, Greeks and Jews dwelt, equally entitled to civic privileges, without distinction of nation and confession, the latter superior in number and property. But the Hellenes, after the model of the Alexandrians, and doubtless under the immediate impression of the occurrences of the year 38, impugned the right of citizenship of the Jewish members of the community by way of complaint to the supreme authority. The minister of Nero,[1] Burrus († 62), decided in their favour. It was bad to make citizenship in a town formed on Jewish soil and by a Jewish government a privilege of the Hellenes ; but it may not be forgotten how the Jews behaved just at that time towards the Romans, and how naturally they suggested to the Romans the conversion of the Roman capital and the Roman head-quarters of the province into a purely Hellenic urban community. The decision led, as might be conceived, to vehement street tumults, in which Hellenic scoffing and Jewish arrogance seem to have almost balanced each other, particularly in the struggle for access to the synagogue ; the Roman authorities interfered, as a matter of course, to the disadvantage of the Jews. These left the town, but were compelled by the governor to return, and then all of them were slain in a street riot (6th August 66). This the government had at any rate not commanded, and certainly had not wished ; powers were unchained which they themselves were no longer able to control.

Outbreak of
the insur-
rection in
Jerusalem.

If here the enemies of the Jews were the assailants, the Jews were so in Jerusalem. Certainly their defenders in the narrative of these occurrences assure us that the procurator of Palestine at the time, Gessius Florus, in order to avoid impeachment on account of his maladministration, wished to provoke an insurrection by the excessive measure of his torture ; and there is no doubt that the governors of that time considerably exceeded the

---

[1] Josephus (*Arch.* xx. 8, 9), makes him indeed secretary of Nero for Greek correspondence, although he, where he follows Roman sources (xx. 8, 2), designates him correctly as prefect ; but certainly the same person is meant. He is called παιδαγωγός with him as with Tacitus, *Ann.* xiii. 2 : *rector imperatoriae iuventae.*

usual measure of worthlessness and oppression. But, if
Florus in fact pursued such a plan, it miscarried. For
according to these very reports the prudent and the possessors of property among the Jews, and with them king
Agrippa II., familiar with the government of the temple,
and just at that time present in Jerusalem—he had meanwhile exchanged the rule of Chalcis for that of Batanaea
—lulled the masses so far, that the riotous assemblages
and the interference against them kept within the measure
that had been usual in the country for years. But the
advances made by Jewish theology were more dangerous
than the disorder of the streets and the robber patriots of
the mountains. The earlier Judaism had in a liberal
fashion opened the gates of its faith to foreigners ; it is
true that only those who belonged, in the strict sense, to
their religion were admitted to the interior of the Temple,
but as proselytes of the gate all were admitted without
ceremony into the outer courts, and even the non-Jew
was here allowed to pray on his part and offer sacrifices
to the Lord Jehovah. Thus, as we have already mentioned (p. 189), sacrifice was offered daily there for the
Roman emperor on the basis of an endowment of Augustus. These sacrifices of non-Jews were forbidden by the Eleazar.
master of the temple at this time, Eleazar, son of the
above-mentioned high priest Ananias, a passionate young
man of rank, personally blameless and brave and, so far,
an entire contrast to his father, but more dangerous through
his virtues than the latter was through his vices. Vainly it
was pointed out to him that this was as offensive for the
Romans as dangerous for the country, and absolutely at
variance with usage ; he resolved to abide by the im-
provement of piety and the exclusion of the sovereign
of the land from worship. Believers in Judaism had for
long been divided into those who placed their trust in the
Lord of Zebaoth alone and endured the Roman rule till
it should please Him to realise the kingdom of heaven on
earth, and the more practical men, who had resolved to
establish the kingdom of heaven with their own hand and
held themselves assured of the help of the Lord of Hosts

in the pious work, or, by their watchwords, into the Pharisees and the Zealots.   The number and the repute of the
latter were constantly on the increase.   An old saying
was discovered that about this time a man would proceed
from Judaea and gain the dominion of the world ; people
believed this the more readily because it was so very
absurd, and the oracle contributed not a little to render
the masses more fanatical.

Struggle of
parties.
Victory of
the Zealots.   The moderate party perceived the danger, and resolved
to put down the fanatics by force ; it asked for troops
from the Romans in Caesarea and from king Agrippa.
From the former no support came ; Agrippa sent a
number of horsemen.   On the other hand the patriots
and the knife-men flocked into the city, among them the
wildest Manahim, also one of the sons of the oft-named
Judas of Galilee.   They were the stronger, and soon were
masters in all the city.   The handful of Roman soldiers,
which kept garrison in the castle adjoining the temple,
was quickly overpowered and put to death.   The neighbouring king's palace, with the strong towers belonging
to it, where the adherents of the moderate party, a number
of Romans under the tribune Metilius, and the soldiers of
Agrippa were stationed, offered as little resistance.   To
the latter, on their desire to capitulate, free departure was
allowed, but was refused to the Romans ; when they at
length surrendered in return for assurance of life, they
were first disarmed, and then put to death with the single
exception of the officer, who promised to undergo circumcision and so was pardoned as a Jew.   Even the leaders
of the moderates, including the father and the brother of
Eleazar, became the victims of the popular rage, which
was still more savagely indignant at the associates of the
Romans than at the Romans themselves.   Eleazar was
himself alarmed at his victory ; between the two leaders
of the fanatics, himself and Manahim, a bloody hand-
to-hand conflict took place after the victory, perhaps
on   account   of   the   broken   capitulation :   Manahim
was   captured   and   executed.   But   the   holy   city   was
free, and the Roman detachment stationed in Jerusalem

was annihilated; the new Maccabees had conquered, like
the old.

Thus, it is alleged on the same day, the 6th August
66, the non-Jews in Caesarea had massacred the Jews,
and the Jews in Jerusalem had massacred the non-Jews ;
and thereby was given on both sides the signal to proceed
with this patriotic work acceptable to God.   In the neighbouring Greek towns the Hellenes rid themselves of the
resident Jews after the model of Caesarea.   For example,
in Damascus all the Jews were in the first instance shut
up in the gymnasium, and, on the news of a misfortune to
the Roman arms, were by way of precaution all of them
put to death.   The same or something similar took place
in Ascalon, in Scytopolis, Hippos, Gadara, wherever the
Hellenes were the stronger.   In the territory of king
Agrippa, inhabited mainly by Syrians, his energetic intervention saved the lives of the Jews of Caesarea Paneas
and elsewhere.   In Syria Ptolemais, Tyre, and more or
less the other Greek communities followed ; only the two
greatest and most civilised cities, Antioch and Apamea,
as well as Sidon, were exceptions.   To this is probably
due the fact that this movement did not spread in the
direction of Asia Minor.   In Egypt not merely did the
matter come to a popular riot, which claimed numerous
victims, but the Alexandrian legions themselves had to
charge the Jews.—In necessary reaction to these Jewish
"vespers" the insurrection victorious in Jerusalem immediately seized all Judaea and organised itself everywhere, with similar maltreatment of minorities, but in
other respects with rapidity and energy.

It was necessary to interfere as speedily as possible,
and to prevent the further extension of the conflagration ;
on the first news the Roman governor of Syria, Gaius
Cestius Gallus, marched with his troops against the insurgents.   He brought up about 20,000 Roman soldiers
and 13,000 belonging to client-states, without including
the numerous Syrian militia ; took Joppa, where the whole
body of citizens was put to death ; and already in September stood before, and in fact in, Jerusalem itself.   But

*Extension
of the Jew-
ish war.*

*Vain expe-
dition of
Cestius
Gallus.*

he could not breach the strong walls of the king's palace
and of the temple, and as little made use of the opportunity several times offered to him of getting possession
of the town through the moderate party. Whether the
task was insoluble or whether he was not equal to it,
he soon gave up the siege, and purchased even a hasty
retreat by the sacrifice of his baggage and of his rear-
guard. Thus Judaea in the first instance, including
Idumaea and Galilee, remained in, or came into, the hands
of the exasperated Jews ; the Samaritan district also was
compelled to join. The mainly Hellenic coast towns,
Anthedon and Gaza, were destroyed, Caesarea and the
other Greek towns were retained with difficulty. If the
rising did not go beyond the boundaries of Palestine, that
was not the fault of the government, but was rather due
to the national dislike of the Syro-Hellenes towards the
Jews.

The Jewish war of Vespasian.

The government in Rome took things in earnest, as
earnest they were. Instead of the procurator an imperial
legate was sent to Palestine, Titus Flavius Vespasianus,
a prudent man and an experienced soldier. He obtained
for the conduct of the war two legions of the West, which
in consequence of the Parthian war were accidentally still
in Asia, and that Syrian legion which had suffered least
in the unfortunate expedition of Cestius, while the Syrian
army under the new governor, Gaius Licinius Mucianus—
Gallus had seasonably died—by the addition of another
legion was restored to the status which it had before.[1] To

[1] It is not quite clear what were
the arrangements for the forces occupying Syria after the Parthian war was
ended in the year 63. At its close
there were seven legions stationed in
the East, the four originally Syrian,
3d Gallica, 6th Ferrata, 10th Fretensis, 12th Fulminata, and three
brought up from the West, the 4th
Scythica from Moesia (I. 213), the
5th Macedonica, probably from the
same place (I. 219 ; for which probably an upper German legion was
sent to Moesia I. 132), the 15th
Apollinaris from Pannonia (I. 219).

Since, excepting Syria, no Asiatic
province was at that time furnished
with legions, and the governor of
Syria certainly in times of peace had
never more than four legions, the
Syrian army beyond doubt had at
that time been brought back, or at
least ought to have been brought
back, to this footing. The four
legions which accordingly were to
remain in Syria were, as this was
most natural, the four old Syrian
ones ; for the 3d had in the year 70
just marched from Syria to Moesia
(Suetonius, *Vesp.* 6 ; Tacitus, *Hist.*

these burgess-troops and their auxiliaries were added the previous garrison of Palestine, and lastly the forces of the four client-kings of the Commagenians, the Hemesenes, the Jews, and the Nabataeans, together about 50,000 men, including among them 15,000 king's soldiers.[1]   In the spring of the year 67 this army was brought together at Ptolemais and advanced into Palestine.   After the

---

ii. 74), and that the 6th, 10th, 12th belonged to the army of Cestius follows from Josephus, *Bell. Jud.* ii. 18, 9, c. 19, 7 ; vii. 1, 3.   Then, when the Jewish war broke out, seven legions were again destined for Asia, and of these four for Syria (Tacitus, *Hist.* i. 10), three for Palestine ; the three legions added were just those employed for the Parthian war, the 4th, 5th, 15th, which perhaps at that time were still in course of marching back to their old quarters.   The 4th probably went at that time definitively to Syria, where it thenceforth remained ; on the other hand, the Syrian army gave off the 10th to Vespasian, presumably because this had suffered least in the campaign of Cestius.   In addition he received the 5th and the 15th.   The 5th and the 10th legions came from Alexandria (Josephus, *Bell. Jud.* iii. 1, 3, c. 4, 2) ; but that they were brought up from Egypt cannot well be conceived, not merely because the 10th was one of the Syrian, but especially because the march by land from Alexandria on the Nile to Ptolemais through the middle of the insurgent territory at the beginning of the Jewish war could not have been so narrated by Josephus. Far more probably Titus went by ship from Achaia to Alexandria on the Gulf of Issus, the modern Alexandretta, and brought the two legions thence to Ptolemais.   The orders to march may have reached the 15th somewhere in Asia Minor, since Vespasian, doubtless in order to take them over, went to Syria by land (Josephus, *Bell. Jud.* iii. 1, 3).   To these three legions, with which Vespasian began the war, there was added

under Titus a further one of the Syrian, the 12th.   Of the four legions that occupied Jerusalem the two previously Syrian remained in the East, the 10th in Judaea, the 12th in Cappadocia, while the 5th returned to Moesia, and the 15th to Pannonia (Josephus, *Bell. Jud.* vii. 1, 3 c. 5, 3).

[1] To the three legions there belonged five *alae* and eighteen cohorts, and the army of Palestine consisting of one *ala* and five cohorts.   These *auxilia* numbered accordingly 3000 alarians and (since among the twenty-three cohorts ten were 1000 strong, thirteen 720, or probably rather only 420 strong ; for instead of the startling ἑξακοσίους we expect rather τριακοσίους ἑξάκοντα) 16,240 (or, if 720 is retained, 19,360) cohortales. To these fell to be added 1000 horsemen from each of the four kings, and 5000 Arabian archers, with 2000 from each of the other three kings. This gives together—reckoning the legion at 6000 men—52,240 men, and so towards 60,000, as Josephus (*Bell. Jud.* iii. 4, 2) says. But as the divisions are thus all calculated at the utmost normal strength, the effective aggregate number can hardly be estimated at 50,000. These numbers of Josephus appear in the main trustworthy, just as the analogous ones for the army of Cestius (*Bell. Jud.* ii. 18, 9) ; whereas his figures, resting on the census, are throughout measured after the scale of the smallest village in Galilee numbering 15,000 inhabitants (*Bell. Jud.* iii. 3, 2), and are historically as useless as the figures of Falstaff.   It is but seldom, *e.g.* at the siege of Jotapata, that we recognise reported numbers.

insurgents had been emphatically repulsed by the weak garrison of the town of Ascalon, they had not further attacked the cities which took part with the Romans; the hopelessness, which pervaded the whole movement, expressed itself in the renouncing at once of all offensive. When the Romans thereupon passed over to the aggressive, the insurgents nowhere confronted them in the open field, and in fact did not even make attempts to bring relief to the several places assailed. Certainly the cautious general of the Romans did not divide his troops, but kept at least the three legions together throughout. Nevertheless, as in most of the individual townships a number —often probably but small—of the fanatics exercised terror over the citizens, the resistance was obstinate, and the Roman conduct of the war neither brilliant nor rapid.

First and second campaigns. Vespasian employed the whole first campaign (67) in bringing into his power the fortresses of the small district of Galilee and the coast as far as Ascalon; before the one little town of Jotapata the three legions lay encamped for forty-five days. During the winter of 67-8 a legion lay in Scytopolis, on the south border of Galilee, the two others in Caesarea. Meanwhile the different factions in Jerusalem fell upon one another and were in most vehement conflict; the good patriots, who were at the same time for civil order, and the still better patriots, who, partly in fanatical excitement, partly from delight in mob-riot, wished to bring about and turn to account a reign of terror, fought with each other in the streets of the city, and were only at one in accounting every attempt at reconciliation with the Romans a crime worthy of death. The Roman general, on many occasions summoned to take advantage of this disorder, adhered to the course of advancing only step by step. In the second year of the war he caused the Transjordanic territory in the first instance, particularly the important towns of Gadara and Gerasa, to be occupied, and then took up his position at Emmaus and Jericho, whence he took military possession of Idumaea in the south and Samaria

in the north, so that Jerusalem in the summer of the
year 68 was surrounded on all sides.

The siege was just beginning when the news of the Stoppage
death of Nero arrived.   Thereby *de iure* the mandate of the war,
conferred on the legate became extinct, and Vespasian,
not less cautious in a political than in a military point
of view, in fact suspended his operations until new orders
as to his attitude.   Before these arrived from Galba, the
good season of the year was at an end.   When the spring
of 69 came, Galba was overthrown, and the decision was
in suspense between the emperor of the praetorian
guard and the emperor of the army on the Rhine.   It
was only after Vitellius's victory in June 69 that Vespasian
resumed operations and occupied Hebron ; but very soon
all the armies of the East renounced their allegiance to
the former and proclaimed the previous legate of Judaea
as emperor.   The positions at Emmaus and Jericho were
indeed maintained in front of the Jews ; but, as the
German legions had denuded the Rhine to make their
general emperor, so the flower of the army went from
Palestine, partly with the legate of Syria, Mucianus, to
Italy, partly with the new emperor and his son Titus to
Syria and onward to Egypt, and it was only after the
war of the succession was ended, at the close of the
year 69, and the rule of Vespasian was acknowledged
throughout the empire, that the latter entrusted his son
with the termination of the Jewish war.

Thus the insurgents had entirely free sway in Titus
Jerusalem from the summer of 66 till the spring of 70. against
What the combination of religious and national fanaticism, Jerusalem.
the noble desire not to survive the downfall of their
fatherland, the consciousness of past crimes and of inevitable punishment, the wild promiscuous tumult of all
noblest and all basest passions in these four years of
terror brought upon the nation, had its horrors intensified
by the fact that the foreigners were only onlookers in the
matter, and all the evil was inflicted directly by Jews
upon Jews.   The moderate patriots were soon overpowered by the zealots with the help of the levy of the

rude and fanatical inhabitants of the Idumaean villages (end of 68), and their leaders were slain. The zealots thenceforth ruled, and all the bonds of civil, religious, and moral order were dissolved. Freedom was granted to the slaves, the high priests were appointed by lot, the ritual laws were trodden under foot and scoffed at by those very fanatics whose stronghold was the temple, the captives in the prisons were put to death, and it was forbidden on pain of death to bury the slain. The different leaders fought with their separate bands against one another : John of Gischala with his band brought up from Galilee ; Simon, son of Gioras from Gerasa, the leader of a band of patriots formed in the south, and at the same time of the Idumaeans in revolt against John ; Eleazar, son of Simon, one of the champions against Cestius Gallus. The first maintained himself in the porch of the temple, the second in the city, the third in the Holy of Holies ; and there were daily combats in the streets of the city between Jews and Jews. Concord came only through the common enemy ; when the attack began, Eleazar's little band placed itself under the orders of John, and although John in the temple and Simon in the city continued to play the part of masters, they, while quarrelling among themselves, fought shoulder to shoulder against the Romans.

Task of the assailants. The task of the assailants was not an easy one. It is true that the army, which had received in place of the detachments sent to Italy a considerable contingent from the Egyptian and the Syrian troops, was quite sufficient for the investment ; and, in spite of the long interval which had been granted to the Jews to prepare for the siege, their provisions were inadequate, the more especially as a part of them had been destroyed in the street conflicts, and, as the siege began about the time of the Passover, numerous strangers who had come on that account to Jerusalem were also shut in. But though the mass of the population soon suffered distress, the combatant force took what they needed where they found it, and, well provided as they were, they carried on the struggle without reference to the multitudes that were famishing and soon dying of hunger. The young general could not make up his mind to a mere blockade ; a siege with four legions, brought to an end in this way, would yield to him personally no glory, and the new government needed a brilliant feat of arms. The town, everywhere else defended by inaccessible rocky slopes, was assailable only on the north side ; here, too, it was no easy labour to reduce the threefold rampart-wall erected without regard to cost from the rich treasures of the temple, and further within the city to wrest the citadel, the temple, and the three vast towers of Herod from a strong, fanatically inspired, and desperate garrison. John and Simon not merely resolutely repelled the assaults, but often attacked with good success the troops working at the trenches, and destroyed or burnt the besieging machines.

But the superiority of numbers and the art of war decided for the Romans. The walls were stormed, and thereafter the citadel Antonia ; then, after long resistance, first the porticoes of the temple went on fire, and further on the 10th Ab (August) the temple itself, with all the treasures accumulated in it for six centuries. Lastly, after fighting in the streets which lasted for a month, on the 8th Elul (September) the last resistance in the town itself was broken, and the holy Salem was razed. The bloody work had lasted for five months. The sword and the arrow, and still more famine, had claimed countless victims ; the Jews killed every one so much as suspected of deserting, and forced women and children in the city to die of hunger ; the Romans just as pitilessly put to the sword the captives or crucified them. The combatants that remained, and particularly the two leaders, were drawn forth singly from the sewers, in which they had taken refuge. At the Dead Sea, just where once king David and the Maccabees in their utmost distress had found a refuge, the remnants of the insurgents still held out for years in the rock-castles Machaerus and Massada, till at length, as the last of the free Jews, Eleazar grandson of Judas the Galilean, and his adherents put to death first

Destruction of Jerusalem.

their wives and children, and then themselves. The work was done. That the emperor Vespasian, an able soldier, did not disdain on account of such an inevitable success over a small long-subject people to march as victor to the Capitol, and that the seven-armed candelabrum brought home from the Holy of Holies of the temple is still to be seen at the present day on the honorary arch which the imperial senate erected to Titus in the market of the capital,[1] gives no high conception of the warlike spirit of this time. It is true that the deep aversion, which the Occidentals cherished towards the Jewish people, made up in some measure for what was wanting in martial glory, and if the Jewish name was too vile for the emperors to assign it to themselves, like those of the Germans and the Parthians, they deemed it not beneath their dignity to prepare for the populace of the capital this triumph commemorative of the victor's pleasure in the misfortunes of others.

Breaking up of the Jewish central power.

The work of the sword was followed by a change of policy. The policy pursued by the earlier Hellenistic states, and taken over from them by the Romans—which reached in reality far beyond mere tolerance towards foreign ways and foreign faith, and recognised the Jews in their collective character as a national and religious community—had become impossible. In the Jewish insurrection the dangers had been too clearly brought to light, which this formation of a national-religious union —on the one hand rigidly concentrated, on the other spreading over the whole East and having ramifications even in the West—involved. The central worship was accordingly once for all set aside. This resolution of the

---

[1] This arch was erected to Titus after his death by the imperial senate. Another, dedicated to him during his short government by the same senate in the circus (*C. I. L.* vi. 944) specifies even with express words as the ground of erecting the monument, "because he, according to the precept and direction and under the superintendence of his father, subdued the people of the Jews and destroyed the town of Hierusolyma, which up to his time had either been besieged in vain by all generals, kings, and peoples, or not assailed at all." The historic knowledge of this singular document, which ignores not merely Nebuchadnezzar and Antiochus Epiphanes, but their own Pompeius, stands on the same level with its extravagance in the praise of a very ordinary feat of arms.

government stood undoubtedly fixed, and had nothing
in common with the question, which cannot be answered
with certainty, whether the destruction of the temple took
place by design or by accident ; if, on the one hand, the
suppression of the worship required only the closing of
the temple and the magnificent structure might have
been spared, on the other hand, had the temple been
accidentally destroyed, the worship might have been
continued in a temple rebuilt.   No doubt it will always
remain probable that it was not the chance of war that
here prevailed, but the flames of the temple were rather
the programme for the altered policy of the Roman
government with reference to Judaism.[1]   More clearly
even than in the events at Jerusalem the same change is
marked in the closing—which ensued at the same time
on the order of Vespasian—of the central sanctuary of
the Egyptian Jews, the temple of Onias, not far from
Memphis, in the Heliopolitan district, which for centuries
stood alongside of that of Jerusalem, somewhat as the
translation by the Alexandrian Seventy stood side by
side with the Old Testament ; it too was divested of its
votive gifts, and the worship of God in it was forbidden.

In the further carrying out of the new order of things
the high priesthood and the Synhedrion of Jerusalem
disappeared, and thereby the Jews of the empire lost their
outward supreme head and their chief authority having
jurisdiction hitherto generally in religious questions.   The
annual tribute—previously at least tolerated—on the
part of every Jew, without distinction of dwelling-place,
to the temple did not certainly fall into abeyance, but
was with bitter parody transferred to the Capitoline

---

[1] The account of Josephus, that
Titus with his council of war resolved
not to destroy the temple, excites
suspicion by the manifest intention of
it, and, as the use made of Tacitus in
the chronicle of Sulpicius Severus is
completely proved by Bernays, it may
certainly well be a question whether
his quite opposite account (*Chron.* ii.
30, 6), that the council of war had
resolved to destroy the temple, does
not proceed from Tacitus, and whether
the preference is not to be given to it,
although it bears traces of Christian
revision. This view further commends
itself through the fact that the dedication addressed to Vespasian of the
Argonautica of the poet Valerius Flaccus celebrates the victor of Solyma,
who hurls the fiery torches.

Jupiter, and his representative on earth, the Roman emperor. From the character of the Jewish institutions the suppression of the central worship involved dissolution of the community of Jerusalem. The city was not merely destroyed and burnt down, but was left lying in ruins, like Carthage and Corinth once upon a time ; its territory, public as well as private land, became imperial domain.[1] Such of the citizens of the populous town as had escaped famine or the sword came under the hammer of the slave market. Amidst the ruins of the destroyed town was pitched the camp of the legion, which, with its Spanish and Thracian auxiliaries, was thenceforth to do garrison duty in the Jewish land. The provincial troops hitherto recruited in Palestine itself were transferred elsewhere. In Emmaus, in the immediate neighbourhood of Jerusalem, a number of Roman veterans were settled, but urban rights were not conferred on this place. On the other hand, the old Sichem, the religious centre of the Samaritan community, perhaps a Greek city even from the time of Alexander the Great, was now reorganised in the forms of Hellenic polity under the name Flavia Neapolis. The capital of the land, Caesarea, hitherto a Greek urban community, obtained as "first Flavian colony" Roman organisation and Latin as the language of business. These were essays towards the Occidental municipalising of the Jewish land. Nevertheless Judaea proper, though depopulated and impoverished, remained still Jewish as before ; the light in which the government looked upon the land is shown by the thoroughly anomalous permanent military occupation, which, as Judaea was not situated on the frontier of the empire, can only have been destined to keep down the inhabitants.

The Herodians, too, did not long survive the de-

---

[1] That the emperor took this land for himself (ἰδίαν αὐτῷ τὴν χώραν φυλάττων) is stated by Josephus, *Bell. Jud.* vii. 6, 6 ; not in accord with this is his command πᾶσαν γῆν ἀποδόσθαι τῶν Ἰουδαίων (*l. c.*), in which doubtless there lurks an error or a copyist's mistake. It is in keeping with the expropriation that land was by way of grace assigned elsewhere to individual Jewish landowners (Josephus, *vit.* 16). We may add that the territory was probably employed as an endowment for the legion stationed there (*Eph. epigr.* ii. n. 696 ; Tacitus, *Ann.* xiii. 54).

struction of Jerusalem.   King Agrippa II., the ruler of The end of Caesarea Paneas and of Tiberias, had rendered faithful the Hero-
dians. service to the Romans in the war against his country-men, and had even scars, honourable at least in a military sense, to show from it ; besides, his sister Berenice, a Cleopatra on a small scale, held the heart of the conqueror of Jerusalem captive with the remnant of her much sought charms.   So he remained personally in possession of the dominion ; but after his death, some thirty years later, this last reminiscence of the Jewish state was merged in the Roman province of Syria.

No hindrances were put in the way of the Jews Further exercising their religious customs either in Palestine or treatment
of the Jews. elsewhere.   Their religious instruction itself, and the assemblies in connection with it of their law-teachers and law-experts, were at least permitted in Palestine ; and there was no hindrance to these Rabbinical unions attempting to put themselves in some measure in the room of the former Synhedrion of Jerusalem, and to fix their doctrine and their laws in the groundwork of the Talmud.   Although individual partakers in the Jewish insurrection who fled to Egypt and Cyrene produced troubles there, the bodies of Jews outside of Palestine, so far as we see, were left in their previous position.   Against the Jew-hunt, which just about the time of the destruction of Jerusalem was called forth in Antioch by the circum-stance that the Jews there had been publicly charged by one of their renegade comrades in the faith with the intention of setting the town on fire, the representative of the governor of Syria interfered with energy, and did not allow what was proposed—that they should compel the Jews to sacrifice to the gods of the land and to refrain from keeping the Sabbath.   Titus himself, when he came to Antioch, most distinctly dismissed the leaders of the movement there with their request for the ejection of the Jews, or at least the cancelling of their privileges. People shrank from declaring war on the Jewish faith as such, and from driving the far-branching Diaspora to extremities ; it was enough that Judaism was in

its political representation deleted from the commonwealth.

The conse-
quences of
the catas-
trophe.
    The alteration in the policy pursued since Alexander's
time towards Judaism amounted in the main to the
withdrawing from this religious society unity of leadership and external compactness, and to the wresting out
of the hands of its leaders a power which extended not
merely over the native land of the Jews, but over the
bodies of Jews generally within and beyond the Roman
empire, and certainly in the East was prejudicial to the
unity of imperial government. The Lagids as well as
the Seleucids, and not less the Roman emperors of the
Julio-Claudian dynasty, had put up with this ; but the
immediate rule of the Occidentals over Judaea had
sharpened the contrast between the imperial power and
this power of the priests to such a degree, that the
catastrophe set in with inevitable necessity and brought
its consequences. From a political standpoint we may
censure, doubtless, the remorselessness of the conduct of
the war—which, moreover, is pretty much common to
this war with all similar ones in Roman history—but
hardly the religious-political dissolution of the nation
ordained in consequence of it. If the axe was laid at the
root of institutions which had led, and could not but with
a certain necessity lead, to the formation of a party like
that of the zealots, there was but done what was right
and necessary, however severely and unjustly in the
special case the individual might be affected by it.
Vespasian, who gave the decision, was a judicious and
moderate ruler. The question concerned was one not
of faith but of power ; the Jewish church-state, as head
of the Diaspora, was not compatible with the absoluteness
of the secular great-state. From the general rule of
toleration the government did not even in this case
depart ; it waged war not against Judaism but against
the high priest and the Synhedrion.

The
Christians.
    Nor did the destruction of the temple wholly fail in
this its aim. There were not a few Jews and still more
proselytes, particularly in the Diaspora, who adhered

more to the Jewish moral law and to Jewish Monotheism
than to the strictly national form of faith ; the whole
important sect of the Christians had inwardly broken
off from Judaism and stood partly in open opposition to
the Jewish ritual.   For these the fall of Jerusalem was
by no means the end of things, and within these extensive
and influential circles the government obtained in some
measure what it aimed at by breaking up the central seat
of the Jewish worship.   The separation of the Christian
faith common to the Gentiles from the national Jewish,
the victory of the adherents of Paul over those of Peter,
was essentially promoted by the abolition of the Jewish
central cultus.

But among the Jews of Palestine, where the language **Palestinian**
spoken was not Hebrew indeed, but Aramaic, and **Jews.**
among the portion of the Diaspora which clung firmly
to Jerusalem, the breach between Judaism and the rest of
the world was deepened by the destruction of the temple.
The national-religious exclusiveness, which the government wished to obviate, was in this narrow circle rather
strengthened by the violent attempt to break it down,
and driven, in the first instance, to further desperate
struggles.

Not quite fifty years after the destruction of Jeru- **The Jewish**
salem, in the year 116,[1] the Jews of the eastern Medi- **rising under**
terranean rose against the imperial government.   The **Trajan.**
rising, although undertaken by the Diaspora, was of a
purely national character in its chief seats, Cyrene, Cyprus,
Egypt, directed to the expulsion of the Romans as of the
Hellenes, and, apparently, to the establishment of a separate Jewish state.   It ramified even into Asiatic territory,
and seized Mesopotamia and Palestine itself.   When the
insurgents were victorious they conducted the war with
the same exasperation as the Sicarii in Jerusalem ; they
killed those whom they seized——the historian Appian,
a native of Alexandria, narrates how he, running from

---

[1] Eusebius, *H. E.* iv. 2, puts the   the penultimate year of Trajan ; and
outbreak on the 18th, and so, accord-   therewith Dio, lxviii. 32, agrees.
ing to his reckoning (in the Chronicle),

them for his life, with great difficulty made his escape to
Pelusium—and often they put the captives to death under
excruciating torture, or compelled them—just as Titus
formerly compelled the Jews captured in Jerusalem—to
fall as gladiators in the arena in order to delight the eyes
of the victors.   In Cyrene 220,000, in Cyprus even
240,000 men are said to have been thus put to death by
them.   On the other hand, in Alexandria, which does not
appear itself to have fallen into the hands of the Jews,[1]
the besieged Hellenes slew whatever Jews were then in
the city.   The immediate cause of the rising is not clear.
The blood of the zealots, who had taken refuge at Alexandria and Cyrene, and had there sealed their loyalty to
the faith by dying under the axe of the Roman executioner, may not have flowed in vain ; the Parthian war,
during which the insurrection began, so far promoted
it, as the troops stationed in Egypt had probably been
called to the theatre of war.   To all appearance it was
an outbreak of the religious exasperation of the Jews,
which had been glowing in secret like a volcano since the
destruction of the temple and broke out after an incalculable manner into flames, of such a kind as the East
has at all times produced and produces ; if the insurgents
really proclaimed a Jew as king, this rising certainly had,
like that in their native country, its central seat in the
great mass of the common people.   That this Jewish
rising partly coincided with the formerly-mentioned (p.
68) attempt at liberation of the peoples shortly before
subdued by the emperor Trajan, while the latter was in
the far East at the mouth of the Euphrates, gave to it
even a political significance ; if the successes of this ruler
melted away under his hands at the close of his career,
the Jewish insurrection, particularly in Palestine and Mesopotamia, contributed its part to that result.   In order to
put down the insurrection the troops had everywhere to

---

[1] Eusebius himself (in Syncellus)
says only : 'Αδριανὸς 'Ιουδαίους κατὰ
'Αλεξανδρέων στασιάζοντας ἐκόλασεν.
The Armenian and Latin translations
appear to have erroneously made out
of this a restoration of Alexandria destroyed by the Jews, of which Eusebius, *H. E.* iv. 2, and Dio, lxviii. 32,
know nothing.

take the field ; against the " king " of the Cyrenaean Jews, Andreas or Lukuas, and the insurgents in Egypt, Trajan sent Quintus Marcius Turbo with an army and fleet ; against the insurgents in Mesopotamia, as was already stated, Lusius Quietus—two of his most experienced generals.   The insurgents were nowhere able to offer resistance to the regular troops, although the struggle was prolonged in Africa as in Palestine to the first times of Hadrian, and similar punishments were inflicted on this Diaspora as previously on the Jews of Palestine.   That Trajan annihilated the Jews in Alexandria, as Appian says, is hardly an incorrect, although perhaps a too blunt expression for what took place ; for Cyprus it is attested that thenceforth no Jew might even set foot upon the island, and death there awaited even the shipwrecked Israelites.   If our traditional information was as copious in regard to this catastrophe as in regard to that of Jerusalem, it would probably appear as its continuation and completion, and in some sense also as its explanation ; this rising shows the relation of the Diaspora to the home-country, and the state within a state, into which Judaism had developed.

Even with this second overthrow the revolt of Judaism against the imperial power was not at an end.   We cannot say that the latter gave further provocation to it ; ordinary acts of administration, which were accepted without opposition throughout the empire, affected the Hebrews just where the full resisting power of the national faith had its seat, and thereby called forth, probably to the surprise of the governors themselves, an insurrection which was in fact a war.   If the emperor Hadrian, when his tour through the empire brought him to Palestine, resolved in the year 130 to re-erect the destroyed holy city of the Jews as a Roman colony, he certainly did not do them the honour of fearing them, and had no thought of propagating religious-political views ; but he ordained that this legionary camp should—as shortly before or soon afterwards was the case on the Rhine, on the Danube, in Africa—be connected with an urban community recruit-

The Jewish rising under Hadrian.

ing itself primarily from the veterans, which received its name partly from its founder, partly from the god to whom at that time the Jews paid tribute instead of Jehovah. Similar was the state of the case as to the prohibition of circumcision ; it was issued, as will be observed at a later point, probably without any design of thereby making war on Judaism as such. As may be conceived, the Jews did not inquire as to the motives for that founding of the city and for this prohibition, but felt both as an attack on their faith and their nationality, and answered it by an insurrection which, neglected at first by the Romans, thereupon had not its match for intensity and duration in the history of the Roman imperial period. The whole body of the Jews at home and abroad was agitated by the movement and supported more or less openly the insurgents on the Jordan ;[1] even Jerusalem fell into their hands,[2] and the governor of Syria and indeed the emperor Hadrian appeared on the scene of conflict. The war was led, significantly enough, by the priest Eleazar[3] and the bandit-chief Simon, surnamed Bar-Kokheba, *i.e.* son of the stars, as the bringer of heavenly help, perhaps as Messiah. The financial power and the organisation of the insurgents are testified by the silver and copper coins struck through several years in the name of these two. After a sufficient number of troops was brought together, the experienced general Sextus Julius

---

[1] This is shown by the expressions of Dio, lxix. 13 : οἱ ἀπανταχοῦ γῆς Ἰουδαῖοι and πάσης ὡς εἰπεῖν κινουμένης ἐπὶ τούτῳ τῆς οἰκουμένης.

[2] If, according to the contemporary Appian (*Syr.* 50), Hadrian once more destroyed (κατέσκαψε) the town, this proves as well that it was preceded by an at least in some measure complete formation of the colony, as that it was captured by the insurgents. Only thereby is explained the great loss which the Romans suffered (Fronto, *de bello Parth.* p. 218 Nab. : *Hadriano imperium obtinente quantum militum a Iudaesis . . . caesum ;* Dio, lxix. 14) ; and it accords at least well with this, that the governor of Syria, Pub-

licius Marcellus, left his province to bring help to his colleague Tineius Rufus (Eusebius, *H. E.* iv. 6 ; Borghesi, *Opp.* iii. 64), in Palestine (*C. I. Gr.* 4033, 4034).

[3] That the coins with this name belong to the Hadrianic insurrection is now proved (v. Sallet, *Zeitschr. jür Numism.* v. 110) ; this is consequently the Rabbi Eleazar from Modein of the Jewish accounts (Ewald, *Gesch. Isr.* vii.², 418 ; Schürer, *Lehrbuch,* p. 357). That the Simon whom these coins name partly with Eleazar, partly alone, is the Bar-Kokheba of Justin Martyr and Eusebius is at least very probable.

Severus gained the upper hand, but only by a gradual and slow advance ; quite as in the war under Vespasian no pitched battle took place, but one place after another cost time and blood, till at length after a three years' warfare[1] the last castle of the insurgents, the strong Bether, not far from Jerusalem, was stormed by the Romans. The numbers handed down to us in good accounts of 50 fortresses taken, 985 villages occupied, 580,000 that fell, are not incredible, since the war was waged with inexorable cruelty, and the male population was probably everywhere put to death.

In consequence of this rising the very name of the vanquished people was set aside ; the province was thenceforth termed, not as formerly Judaea, but by the old name of Herodotus Syria of the Philistines, or Syria Palaestina. The land remained desolate ; the new city of Hadrian continued to exist, but did not prosper. The Jews were prohibited under penalty of death from even setting foot in Jerusalem ; the garrison was doubled ; the limited territory between Egypt and Syria, to which only a small strip of the Transjordanic domain on the Dead Sea belonged, and which nowhere touched the frontier of the empire, was thenceforth furnished with two legions. In spite of all these strong measures the province remained disturbed, primarily doubtless in consequence of the bandit-habits long interwoven with the national cause. Pius issued orders to march against the Jews, and even under Severus there is mention of a war against Jews and Samaritans. But no movements on a great scale among the Jews recurred after the Hadrianic war. *Judaea after Hadrian.*

It must be acknowledged that these repeated outbreaks of the animosity fermenting in the minds of the Jews against the whole of their non-Jewish fellow-citizens did not change the general policy of the government. *Position of the Jews in the second and third centuries.*

---

[1] Dio (lxix. 12) calls the war protracted (οὔτ' ὀλιγοχρόνιος) ; Eusebius in his Chronicle puts its beginning in the sixteenth, its end in the eighteenth or nineteenth year of Hadrian ; the coins of the insurgents are dated from the first or from the second year of the deliverance of Israel. We have not trustworthy dates ; the Rabbinic tradition (Schürer, *Lehrbuch*, p. 361) is not available in this respect.

Like Vespasian, the succeeding emperors maintained, as respects the Jews in the main, the general standpoint of political and religious toleration ; and not only so, but the exceptional laws issued for the Jews were, and continued to be, chiefly directed to release them from such general civil duties as were not compatible with their habits and their faith, and they are therefore designated directly as privilegia.[1]

Since the time of Claudius, whose suppression of Jewish worship in Italy (p. 199) is at least the last measure of the sort which we know of, residence and the free exercise of religion in the whole empire appear to have been in law conceded to the Jew. It would have been no wonder if those insurrections in the African and Syrian provinces had led to the expulsion generally of the Jews settled there ; but restrictions of this sort were enacted, as we saw, only locally, *e.g.* for Cyprus. The Greek provinces always remained the chief seat of the Jews ; even in the capital in some measure bilingual, whose numerous body of Jews had a series of synagogues, these formed a portion of the Greek population of Rome. Their epitaphs in Rome are exclusively Greek ; in the Christian church at Rome developed from this Jewish body the baptismal confession was uttered in Greek down to a late period, and throughout the first three centuries the literature was exclusively Greek. But restrictive measures against the Jews appear not to have been adopted even in the Latin provinces ; through and with Hellenism the Jewish system penetrated into the West, and there too communities of Jews were found, although they were still in number and importance even now, when the blows directed against the Diaspora had severely injured the Jew-communities of the East, far inferior to the latter.

Corporative unions.

Political privileges did not follow of themselves from the toleration of worship. The Jews were not hindered

---

[1] Biography of Alexander, c. 22 : *Iudaeis privilegia reservavit, Christianos esse passus est.* Clearly the privileged position of the Jews as compared with the Christians comes here to light—a position, which certainly rests in its turn on the fact that the former represent a nation the latter do not.

in the construction of their synagogues and proseuchae any more than in the appointment of a president for the same (ἀρχισυναγωγός), as well as of a college of elders (ἄρχοντες), with a chief elder (γερουσιάρχης) at its head. Magisterial functions were not meant to be connected with these positions ; but, considering the inseparableness of the Jewish church-organisation and the Jewish administration of law, the presidents probably everywhere exercised, like the bishops in the Middle Ages, a jurisdiction, although merely *de facto*. The bodies of Jews in the several towns were not recognised generally as corporations, certainly not, for example, those of Rome ; yet there subsisted at many places on the ground of local privileges such corporative unions with ethnarchs or, as they were now mostly called, patriarchs at their head. Indeed, in Palestine we find at the beginning of the third century once more a president of the whole Jewish body, who, in virtue of hereditary sacerdotal right, bears sway over his fellow-believers almost like a ruler, and has power even over life and limb, and whom the government at least tolerates.[1] Beyond question this patriarch was for the Jews the old high priest, and thus, under the eyes and under the oppression of the foreign rule, the obstinate people of God had once more reconstituted themselves, and in so far overthrown Vespasian's work.

As respects the bringing of the Jews under obligations of public service, their exemption from serving in war as incompatible with their religious principles had long since been and continued to be recognised. The special poll-

Public services.

---

[1] In order to make good that even in bondage the Jews were able to exercise a certain self-administration, Origen (about the year 226) writes to Africanus, c. 14 : "How much even now, where the Romans rule and the Jews pay to them the tribute (τὸ δίδραχμον), has the president of the people (ὁ ἐθνάρχης) among them in his power with permission of the emperor (συγχωροῦντος Καίσαρος)? Even courts are secretly held according to the law, and even on various occasions sentence of death is pronounced. This I, who have long lived in the land of this people, have myself experienced and ascertained." The patriarch of Judaea already makes his appearance in the letter forged in the name of Hadrian in the biography of the tyrant Saturninus (c. 8), in the ordinances first in the year 392 (*C. Th.* xvi. 8, 8). Patriarchs as presidents of individual Jewish communities, for which the word from its signification is better adapted, meet us already in the ordinances of Constantine I. (*C. Th.* xvi. 8, 1, 2).

tax to which they were subject, the old temple-payment, might be regarded as a compensation for this exemption, though it had not been imposed in this sense. For other services, as *e.g.* for the undertaking of wardships and municipal offices, they were at least from the time of Severus regarded in general as capable and under obligation, but those which ran counter to their "superstition" were remitted to them;[1] in connection with which we have to take into account that exclusion from municipal offices became more and more converted from a slight into a privilege. Even in the case of state offices in later times a similar course was probably pursued.

Forbidding of circumcision. The only serious interference of the state-power with Jewish customs concerned the ceremony of circumcision; the measures directed against this, however, were probably not taken from a religious-political standpoint, but were connected with the forbidding of castration, and arose doubtless in part from misunderstanding of the Jewish custom. The evil habit of mutilation, becoming more and more prevalent, was first brought by Domitian within the sphere of penal offences; when Hadrian, making the precept more stringent, placed castration under the law of murder, circumcision appears also to have been apprehended as castration,[2] which certainly could not but be felt and was felt (p. 224) by the Jews as an attack upon their existence, although this was perhaps not its intention. Soon afterwards, probably in consequence of the insurrection thereby occasioned, Pius allowed the circumcision of children of Jewish descent, while otherwise even that of the non-free Jew and of the proselyte was to involve, afterwards as before, the penalty of castration for all par-

---

[1] The jurists of the third century lay down this rule, appealing to an edict of Severus (*Dig.* xxvii. 1, 15, 6; 1. 2, 3, 3). According to the ordinance of the year 321 (*C. Th.* xvi. 8, 3) this appears even as a right, not as a duty of the Jews, so that it depended on them to undertake or decline the office.

[2] The analogous treatment of castration in the Hadrianic edict, *Dig.* xlviii. 8, 4, 2, and of circumcision in Paulus, *Sent.* v. 22, 3, 4, and Modestinus, *Dig.* xlviii. 8, 11 pr., naturally suggests this point of view. The statement that Severus *Judaeos fieri sub gravi poena vetuit* (*Vita*, 17), is doubtless nothing but the enforcement of this prohibition.

ticipating in it.   This was also of political importance, in so far as thereby the formal passing over to Judaism became a penal offence ; and probably the prohibition was, not indeed issued but, retained with this in view.[1] It must have contributed its part to the abrupt demarcation of the Jews from the non-Jews.

If we look back on the fortunes of Judaism in the epoch from Augustus to Diocletian, we recognise a thorough transformation of its character and of its position.   It enters upon this epoch as a national and religious power firmly concentrated round its narrow native land— a power which even confronts the imperial government in and beyond Judaea with arms in hand, and in the field of faith evolves a mighty propagandist energy.   We can understand that the Roman government would not tolerate the adoration of Jehovah and the faith of Moses on another footing than that on which the cultus of Mithra and the faith of Zoroaster were tolerated.   The reaction against this exclusive and self-centred Judaism came in the crushing blows directed by Vespasian and Hadrian against the Jewish land, and by Trajan against the Jews of the Diaspora, the effect of which reached far beyond the immediate destruction of the existing society and the reduction of the repute and power of the Jews as a body. In fact, the later Christianity and the later Judaism were the consequences of this reaction of the West against the East.   The great propagandist movement, which carried the deeper view of religion from the East into the West, was liberated in this way, as was already said (p. 220 f.), from the narrow limits of Jewish nationality ; if it by no means gave up the attachment to Moses and the prophets, it necessarily became released at any rate from the government of the Pharisees, which had gone to pieces.   The Christian ideals of the future became universal, since there was no longer a Jerusalem upon earth.   But as the enlarged and deepened faith, which with its nature changed

Altered position of the Jews in the imperial period.

---

[1] The remarkable account in Origen's treatise *against Celsus*, ii. 13 (written about 250), shows that the circumcision of the non-Jew involved *de iure* the penalty of death, although it is not clear how far this found application to Samaritans or Sicarii.

also its name, arose out of these disasters, so not less the
narrowed and hardened orthodoxy, which found a rallying
point, if no longer in Jerusalem, at any rate in hatred
towards those who had destroyed it, and still more in
hatred towards the more free and higher intellectual
movement which evolved Christianity out of Judaism.
The external power of the Jews was broken, and risings,
such as took place in the middle of the imperial period,
are not subsequently met with ; the Roman emperors were
done with the state within the state, and, as the properly
dangerous element—the propagandist diffusion—passed
over to Christianity, the confessors of the old faith, who
shut themselves off from the New Covenant, were set aside,
so far as the further general development was concerned.

Altered
character of
Judaism.

But if the legions could destroy Jerusalem, they could
not raze Judaism itself ; and what on the one side was
a remedy, exercised on the other the effect of a poison.
Judaism not only remained, but it became an altered
thing.　　There is a deep gulf between the Judaism of the
older time, which seeks to spread its faith, which has its
temple-court filled with the Gentiles, and which has its
priests offering daily sacrifices for the emperor Augustus,
and the rigid Rabbinism, which knew nothing and wished
to know nothing of the world beyond Abraham's bosom
and the Mosaic law.　　Strangers the Jews always were,
and had wished to be so ; but the feeling of estrangement
now culminated within them as well as against them
after a fearful fashion, and rudely were its hateful and
pernicious consequences drawn on both sides.　　From the
contemptuous sarcasm of Horace against the intruding
Jew from the Roman Ghetto there is a wide step to the
solemn enmity which Tacitus cherishes against this scum
of the human race, to which everything pure is impure
and everything impure pure ; in the interval lie those
insurrections of the despised people, and the necessity of
conquering it and of expending continuously money and
men for its repression.　　The prohibitions of maltreating
the Jew, which are constantly recurring in the imperial
ordinances, show that those words of the cultured were

translated, as might be expected, by their inferiors into
deeds. The Jews, on their part, did not mend the matter.
They turned away from Hellenic literature, which was now
regarded as polluting, and even rebelled against the use
of the Greek translation of the Bible ; the ever-increasing
purification of faith turned not merely against the Greeks
and the Romans, but quite as much against the " half-
Jews" of Samaria and against the Christian heretics ; the
reverence toward the letter of the Holy Scriptures rose to
a giddy height of absurdity, and above all an—if possible—
still holier tradition established itself, in the fetters of which
all life and thought were benumbed. The gulf between that
treatise on the Sublime which ventures to place Homer's
Poseidon shaking land and sea and Jehovah, who creates
the shining sun, side by side, and the beginnings of the
Talmud which belong to this epoch, marks the contrast between the Judaism of the first and that of the
third century. The living together of Jews and non-Jews
showed itself more and more to be just as inevitable, as
under the given conditions it was intolerable ; the contrast in faith, law, and manners became sharpened, and
mutual arrogance and mutual hatred operated on both
sides with morally disorganising effect. Not merely was
their conciliation not promoted in these centuries, but
its realisation was always thrown further into the distance,
the more its necessity was apparent. This exasperation,
this arrogance, this contempt, as they became established
at that time, were indeed only the inevitable growth of a
perhaps not less inevitable sowing ; but the heritage of
these times is still at the present day a burden on mankind.

CHAPTER XII.

EGYPT.

The annexation of Egypt.

81.

55. IV. 153.

THE two kingdoms of Egypt and Syria, which had so long striven and vied with each other in every respect, fell nearly about the same time without resistance into the power of the Romans. If these made no use of the alleged or real testament of Alexander II. († 673) and did not then annex the land, the last rulers of the Lagid house were confessedly in the position of clients of Rome ; the senate decided in disputes as to the throne, and after the Roman governor of Syria, Aulus Gabinius, had with his troops brought back the king Ptolemaeus Auletes to Egypt (699 ; comp. iv. 160), the Roman legions did not again leave the land. Like the other client-kings, the rulers of Egypt took part in the civil wars on the summons of the government recognised by them or rather imposing itself on them ; and, if it must remain undecided what part Antonius in the fanciful eastern empire of his dreams had destined for the native land of the wife whom he loved too well (p. 25), at any rate the government of Antonius in Alexandria, as well as the last struggle in the last civil war before the gates of that city, belongs as little to the special history of Egypt as the battle of Actium to that of Epirus. But doubtless this catastrophe, and the death connected with it of the last prince of the Lagid house, gave occasion for Augustus not to fill up again the vacant throne, but to take the kingdom of Egypt under his own administration. This annexation of the last portion of the coast of the Mediterranean to the sphere of direct Roman administration, and the settlement, coincident with it in point of time and of organic connection, of the new monarchy, mark—as regards the constitution and administration of the huge empire respectively— the turning-point, the end of the old and the beginning of a new epoch.

The incorporation of Egypt into the Roman empire was accomplished after an abnormal fashion, in so far as the principle—elsewhere dominating the state—of dyarchy, *i.e.* of the joint rule of the two supreme imperial powers, the princeps and the senate, found—apart from some subordinate districts—no application in Egypt alone ;[1] but, on the contrary, in this land the senate as such, as well as every individual of its members, were cut off from all participation in the government, and indeed senators and persons of senatorial rank were even prohibited from setting foot in this province.[2] We must not conceive of this position as if Egypt were connected with the rest of the empire only by a personal union ; the princeps is, according to the meaning and spirit of the Augustan organisation, an integral and permanently acting element of the Roman polity just like the senate, and his rule over Egypt is quite as much a part of the imperial rule as is the rule of the proconsul of Africa.[3] We may rather

Egypt exclusively an imperial possession.

---

[1] This exclusion of the joint rule of the senate as of the senators is indicated by Tacitus (*Hist.* i. 11) with the words that Augustus wished to have Egypt administered exclusively by his personal servants (*domi retinere ;* comp. *Staatsrecht,* ii. p. 963). In principle this abnormal form of government was applicable for all the provinces not administered by senators, the presidents of which were also at the outset called chiefly *praefecti* (*C. I. L.* v. p. 809, 902). But at the first division of the provinces between emperor and senate there was probably no other of these but just Egypt ; and subsequently the distinction here came into sharper prominence, in so far as all the other provinces of this category obtained no legions. For in the emergence of

the equestrian commandants of the legion instead of the senatorial, as was the rule in Egypt, the exclusion of the senatorial government finds its most palpable expression.

[2] This ordinance holds only for Egypt, not for the other territories administered by non-senators. How essential it appeared to the government, we see from the constitutional and religious apparatus called into requisition to secure it (*Trig. tyr.* c. 22).

[3] The current assertion that *provincia* is only by an abuse of language put for the districts not administered by senators is not well founded. Egypt was private property of the emperor just as much or just as little as Gaul and Syria—yet Augustus himself says (*Mon. Ancyr.* 5, 24) :

illustrate the exact constitutional position by saying that the British Empire would find itself in the same plight if the ministry and Parliament should be taken into account only for the mother-land, whereas the colonies should have to obey the absolute government of the Empress of India. What motives determined the new monarch at the very outset of his sole rule to adopt this deeply influential and at no time assailed arrangement, and how it affected the general political relations, are matters belonging to the general history of the empire ; here we have to set forth how the internal relations of Egypt shaped themselves under the imperial rule.

What held true in general of all Hellenic or Hellenised territories—that the Romans, when annexing them to the empire, preserved the once existing institutions, and introduced modifications only where these seemed absolutely necessary—found application in its full compass to Egypt.

Like Syria, Egypt, when it became Roman, was a land of twofold nationality ; here too alongside of, and over, the native stood the Greek—the former the slave, the latter the master. But in law and in fact the relations of the two nations in Egypt were wholly different from those of Syria.

Greek and Egyptian towns.   Syria, substantially already in the pre-Roman and entirely in the Roman epoch, came under the government of the land only after an indirect manner ; it was broken up, partly into principalities, partly into autonomous urban districts, and was administered, in the first instance, by the rulers of the land or municipal authorities. In Egypt,[1] on the other hand, there were neither native princes nor imperial cities after the Greek fashion. The two spheres of administration into which Egypt was

---

Aegyptum imperio populi Romani adieci, and assigns to the governor, since he as *eques* could not be *pro praetore*, by special law the same jurisdiction in processes as the Roman praetors had (Tacitus, *Ann.* xii. 60).

[1] As a matter of course what is here meant is the land of Egypt, not the possessions subject to the Lagids. Cyrene was similarly organised (p. 165). But the properly Egyptian government was never applied to southern Syria and to the other territories which were for a longer or a shorter time under the power of Egypt.

divided—the " land " ($\dot{\eta}$ $\chi\acute\omega\rho\alpha$) of the Egyptians, with its
originally thirty-six districts ($\nu o\mu o\iota$), and the two Greek
cities, Alexandria in lower and Ptolemais in upper
Egypt [1]—were rigidly separated and sharply opposed to
each other, and yet in a strict sense hardly different.
The rural, like the urban, district was not merely marked
off territorially, but the former as well as the latter was
a home-district ; the belonging to each was independent
of dwelling-place and hereditary. The Egyptian from
the Chemmitic nome belonged to it with his dependents,
just as much when he had his abode in Alexandria as
the Alexandrian dwelling in Chemmis belonged to the
burgess-body of Alexandria. The land-district had for
its centre always an urban settlement, the Chemmitic, for
example, the town of Panopolis, which grew up round
the temple of Chemmis or of Pan, or, as this is expressed
in the Greek mode of conception, each nome had its
metropolis ; so far each land-district may be regarded
also as a town-district. Like the cities, the nomes also
became in the Christian epoch the basis of the episcopal
dioceses. The land-districts were based on the arrangements for worship which dominated everything in Egypt ;
the centre for each one is the sanctuary of a definite
deity, and usually it bears the name of this deity or of
the animal sacred to the same ; thus the Chemmitic
district is called after the god Chemmis, or, according
to Greek equivalent, Pan ; other districts after the dog,
the lion, the crocodile. But, on the other hand, the
town-districts are not without their religious centre ;
the protecting god of Alexandria is Alexander, the
protecting god of Ptolemais the first Ptolemy, and the
priests, who are installed in the one place as in the
other for this worship and that of their successors, are
the Eponymi for both cities. The land-district is quite
destitute of autonomy : administration, taxation, justice,
are placed in the hands of the royal officials,[2] and the

[1] To these falls to be added Naucratis, the oldest Greek town already
founded in Egypt before the Ptolemies,
and further Paraetonium, which indeed in some measure lies beyond
the bounds of Egypt.

[2] There was not wanting of course
a certain joint action, similar to that

collegiate system, the Palladium of the Greek as of the
Roman commonwealth, was here in all stages absolutely
excluded.   But in the two Greek cities it was not much
otherwise.   There was doubtless a body of burgesses
divided into phylae and demes, but no common council ;[1]
the officials were doubtless different and differently
named from those of the nomes, but were also throughout officials of royal nomination and likewise without
collegiate arrangement.   Hadrian was the first to give to
an Egyptian township, Antinoopolis, laid out by him in
memory of his favourite drowned in the Nile, urban rights
according to the Greek fashion ; and subsequently Severus,
perhaps as much out of spite to the Antiochenes as for
the benefit of the Egyptians, granted to the capital of
Egypt and to the town of Ptolemais, and to several other
Egyptian communities, not urban magistrates indeed, but

which is exercised by the *regiones*
and the *vici* of self-administering
urban communities ; to this category
belongs what we meet with of ago-
ranomy and gymnasiarchy in the
nomes, as also the erection of honorary
memorials and the like, all of which,
we may add, make their appearance
only to a small extent and for the
most part but late. According to
the edict of Alexander (*C. I. Gr.*
4957, l. 34) the *strategoi* do not
seem to have been, properly speaking,
nominated by the governor, but only
to have been confirmed after an
examination ; we do not know who
had the proposing of them.

[1] The position of matters is clearly
apparent in the inscription set up at
the beginning of the reign of Pius to
the well-known orator Aristides by
the Egyptian Greeks (*C. I. Gr.*
4679) ; as dedicants are named ἡ πόλις
τῶν Ἀλεξανδρέων καὶ Ἑρμούπολις ἡ
μεγάλη καὶ ἡ βουλὴ ἡ Ἀντινοέων νέων
Ἑλλήνων καὶ οἱ ἐν τῷ Δέλτᾳ τῆς
Αἰγύπτου καὶ οἱ τὸν Θηβαϊκὸν νομὸν
οἰκοῦντες Ἕλληνες. Thus only Antinoopolis, the city of the "new
Hellenes," has a Boule ; Alexandria
appears without this, but as a Greek
city in the aggregate. Moreover

there take part in this dedication the
Greeks living in the Delta and those
living in Thebes, but of the Egyptian
towns Great-Hermopolis alone, on
which probably the immediate vicinity
of Antinoopolis has exercised an influence. To Ptolemais Strabo (xvii.
1, 42, p. 813) attributes a σύστημα
πολιτικὸν ἐν τῷ Ἑλληνικῷ τρόπῳ ;
but in this we may hardly think of
more than what belonged to the
capital according to its constitution
more exactly known to us—and so
specially of the division of the burgesses into *phylae.* That the pre-
Ptolemaic Greek city Naucratis
retained in the Ptolemaic time the
Boule, which it doubtless had, is
possible, but cannot be decisive for
the Ptolemaic arrangements.—Dio's
statement (ii. 17) that Augustus left
the other Egyptian towns with their
existing organisation, but took the
common council from the Alexandrians on account of their untrust-
worthiness, rests doubtless on misunderstanding, the more especially as,
according to it, Alexandria appears
slighted in comparison with the other
Egyptian communities, which is not
at all in keeping with probability.

at any rate an urban council.   Hitherto, doubtless, in
official language the Egyptian town calls itself Nomos, the
Greek Polis, but a Polis without Archontes and Bouleutae
is a meaningless name.   So was it also in the coinage.
The Egyptian nomes did not possess the right of coining;
but still less did Alexandria ever strike coins.   Egypt is,
among all the provinces of the Greek half of the empire,
the only one which knows no other than royal money.
Nor was this otherwise even in the Roman period.   The
emperors abolished the abuses that crept in under the last
Lagids ; Augustus set aside their unreal copper coinage,
and when Tiberius resumed the coinage of silver he gave
to the Egyptian silver money just as real value as to the
other provincial currency of the empire.[1]   But the character
of the coinage remained substantially the same.[2]   There
is a distinction between Nomos and Polis as between the
god Chemmis and the god Alexander; in an administrative
respect there is not any difference.   Egypt consisted of
a majority of Egyptian and of a minority of Greek
townships, all of which were destitute of autonomy, and
all were placed under the immediate and absolute
administration of the king and of the officials nominated
by him.

---

[1] The Egyptian coining of gold
naturally ceased with the annexation
of the land, for there was in the
Roman empire only imperial gold.
With the silver also Augustus dealt
in like manner, and as ruler of Egypt
caused simply copper to be struck,
and even this only in moderate
quantities.   At first Tiberius coined,
after 27-28 A.D., silver money for
Egyptian circulation, apparently as
token-money, as the pieces correspond
nearly in point of weight to four, in
point of silver value to one, of the
Roman denarius (Feuardent, *Numis-
matique, Égypte ancienne*, ii. p. xi.).
But as in legal currency the Alexandrian drachma was estimated as
obolus (consequently as a sixth, not
as a fourth ; comp. *Röm. Münzwesen*,
p. 43, 723) of the Roman denarius
(*Hermes*, v. p. 136), and the provincial silver always lost as compared
with the imperial silver, the Alexandrian tetradrachmon of the silver
value of a denarius has rather been
estimated at the current value of
two-thirds of a denarius.   Accordingly
down to Commodus, from whose time
the Alexandrian tetradrachmon is
essentially a copper coin, the same
has been quite as much a coin of
value as the Syrian tetradrachmon
and the Cappadocian drachma ; they
only left to the former the old name
and the old weight.
[2] That the emperor Hadrian,
among other Egyptising caprices,
gave to the nomes as well as to his
Antinoopolis for once the right of
coining, which was thereupon done
subsequently on a couple of occasions,
makes no alteration in the rule.

Absence of
a land-diet.

It was a consequence of this, that Egypt alone of all the Roman provinces had no general representation. The diet is the collective representation of the self-administering communities of the province. But in Egypt there was none such; the nomes were simply imperial or rather royal administrative districts, and Alexandria not merely stood virtually alone, but was likewise without proper municipal organisation. The priest standing at the head of the capital of the country might doubtless call himself " chief priest of Alexandria and all Egypt " (p. 248, note), and has a certain resemblance to the Asiarch and the Bithyniarch of Asia Minor, but the deep diversity of the organisations is thereby simply concealed.

The government of the Lagids.

The rule bore accordingly in Egypt a far different character than in the rest of the domain of Greek and Roman civilisation embraced under the imperial government. In the latter the community administers throughout; the ruler of the empire is, strictly taken, only the common president of the numerous more or less autonomous bodies of burgesses, and alongside of the advantages of self-administration its disadvantages and dangers everywhere appear. In Egypt the ruler is king, the inhabitant of the land is his subject, the administration that of a domain. This administration, in principle as haughtily and absolutely conducted as it was directed to the equal welfare of all subjects without distinction of rank and of estate, was the peculiarity of the Lagid government, developed probably more from the Hellenising of the old Pharaonic rule than from the urban organisation of the universal empire, as the great Macedonian had conceived it, and as it was most completely carried out in the Syrian New-Macedonia (p. 120). The system required a king not merely leading the army in his own person, but engaged in the daily labour of administration, a developed and strictly disciplined hierarchy of officials, scrupulous justice towards high and low; and as these rulers, not altogether without ground, ascribed to themselves the name of benefactor (εὐεργέτης), so the monarchy of the Lagids may be compared with that of Frederick, from which it was in its principles not far removed. Certainly Egypt had also experienced the reverse side, the inevitable collapse of the system in incapable hands. But the standard remained ; and the Augustan principate alongside of the rule of the senate was nothing but the intermarriage of the Lagid government with the old urban and federal development.

A further consequence of this form of government was the undoubted superiority, more especially from a financial point of view, of the Egyptian administration over that of the other provinces. We may designate the pre-Roman epoch as the struggle of the financially dominant power of Egypt with the Asiatic empire, filling, so far as space goes, the rest of the East ; under the Roman period this was continued in a certain sense in the fact that the imperial finances stood forth superior in contrast to those of the senate, especially through the exclusive possession of Egypt. If it is the aim of the state to work out the utmost possible amount from its territory, in the old world the Lagids were absolutely the masters of statecraft. In particular they were in this sphere the instructors and the models of the Caesars. How much the Romans drew out of Egypt we are not able to say with precision. In the Persian period Egypt had paid an annual tribute of 700 Babylonish talents of silver, about £200,000 ; the annual income of the Ptolemies from Egypt, or rather from their possessions generally, amounted in their most brilliant period to 14,800 Egyptian silver talents, or £2,850,000, and besides 1,500,000 artabae = 591,000 hectolitres of wheat ; at the end of their rule fully 6000 talents, or £1,250,000. The Romans drew from Egypt annually the third part of the corn necessary for the consumption of Rome, 20,000,000 Roman bushels[1] = 1,740,000

Egypt and the imperial administration.

---

[1] This figure is given by the so-called Epitome of Victor, c. 1, for the time of Augustus. After this payment was transferred to Constantinople there went thither under Justinian (*Ed.* xiii. c. 8) annually 8,000,000 artabae (for these are to be understood, according to c. 6, as meant), or 26⅔ millions of Roman bushels (Hultsch, *Metrol.* p. 628), to which falls further to be added the similar payment to the town of Alex-

hectolitres ; a part of it, however, was certainly derived from the domains proper, another perhaps supplied in return for compensation, while, on the other hand, the Egyptian tribute was assessed, at least for a great part, in money, so that we are not in a position even approximately to determine the Egyptian income of the Roman exchequer. But not merely by its amount was it of decisive importance for the Roman state-economy, but because it served as a pattern in the first instance for the domanial possessions of the emperors in the other provinces, and generally for the whole imperial administration, as this falls to be explained when we set it forth.

Privileged position of the Hellenes.

But if the communal self-administration had no place in Egypt, and in this respect a real diversity does not exist between the two nations of which this state, just like the Syrian, was composed, there was in another respect a barrier erected between them, to which Syria offers no parallel. According to the arrangement of the Macedonian conquerors, the belonging to an Egyptian locality disqualified for all public offices and for the better military service. Where the state made gifts to its burgesses these were restricted to those of the Greek communities ;[1] on the other hand, the Egyptians only paid the poll-tax ; and even from the municipal burdens, which fell on the settlers of the individual Egyptian district, the Alexandrians settled there were exempted.[2] Although in the case of trespass the back of the Egyptian as of the Alexandrian had to suffer, the latter might boast, and did boast, that the cane struck him, and not the lash, as in the case of the former.[3] Even the

andria, introduced by Diocletian. To the shipmasters for the freight to Constantinople 8000 solidi = £5000 were annually paid from the state-chest.

[1] At least Cleopatra on a distribution of grain in Alexandria excluded the Jews (Josephus, *contra Ap.* ii. 5), and all the more, consequently, the Egyptians.

[2] The edict of Alexander (*C. I. Gr.* 4957), l. 33 ff., exempts the ἐνγενεῖς Ἀλεξανδρεῖς dwelling ἐν τῇ χώρᾳ (not ἐν τῇ πόλει) on account of their business from the λειτουργίαι χωρικαί.

[3] "There subsist," says the Alexandrian Jew Philo (*in Flacc.* 10), "as respects corporal chastisement (τῶν μαστίγων), distinctions in our city according to the rank of those to be chastised ; the Egyptians are chastised with different scourges and by others, but the Alexandrians with canes (σπάθαις ; σπάθη is the stem of

acquiring of better burgess-rights was forbidden to the Egyptians.[1] The burgess-lists of the two large Greek towns organised by and named after the two founders of the empire in lower and upper Egypt embraced in them the ruling population, and the possession of the franchise of one of these towns was in the Egypt of the Ptolemies the same as the possession of the Roman franchise was in the Roman empire. What Aristotle recommended to Alexander—to be a ruler (ἡγεμών) to the Hellenes and a master to the barbarians, to provide for the former as friends and comrades, to use the latter like animals and plants—the Ptolemies practically carried out in all its extent. The king, greater and more free than his instructor, carried in his mind the higher idea of transforming the barbarians into Hellenes, or at least of replacing the barbarian settlements by Hellenic, and to this idea his successors almost everywhere, and particularly in Syria, allowed ample scope.[2] In Egypt this was not the case. Doubtless its rulers sought to keep touch with the natives, particularly in the religious sphere, and wished not to rule as Greeks over the Egyptians, but rather as earthly gods over their subjects in common ; but with this the inequality of rights on the part of the subjects was quite compatible, just as the preference *de iure* and *de facto* of the nobility was quite as essential a part of the government of Frederick as the equality of justice towards gentle and simple.

the palm-leaf), and by the Alexandrian cane-bearers" (σπαθηφόροι, perhaps *bacillarius*). He afterwards complains bitterly that the elders of his community, if they were to be scourged at all, should not have been provided at least with decorous burgess-lashes (ταῖς ἐλευθεριωτέραις καὶ πολιτικωτέραις μάστιξιν).

[1] Josephus, *contra Ap.* ii. 4, μόνοις Αἰγυπτίοις οἱ κύριοι νῦν 'Ρωμαῖοι τῆς οἰκουμένης μεταλαμβάνειν ἡστινοσοῦν πολιτείας ἀπειρήκασιν. 6, *Aegyptiis neque regum quisquam videtur ius civitatis fuisse largitus neque nunc quilibet imperatorum* (comp. *Eph. epigr.* v. p. 13). The same upbraids his adversary (ii. 3, 4) that he, a native Egyptian, had denied his home and given himself out as an Alexandrian.—Individual exceptions are not thereby excluded.

[2] Alexandrian science, too, protested in the sense of the king against this proposition (Plutarch, *de fort. Alex.* i. 6) ; Eratosthenes designated civilisation as not peculiar to the Hellenes alone, and not to be denied to all barbarians, *e.g.* not to the Indians, the Arians, the Romans, the Carthaginians ; men were rather to be divided into "good" and "bad" (Strabo, i. *fin.* p. 66). But of this theory no practical application was made to the Egyptian race even under the Lagids.

Personal
privileges
in the
Roman
period.

As the Romans in the East generally continued the work of the Greeks, so the exclusion of the native Egyptians from the acquiring of Greek citizenship not merely continued to subsist, but was extended to the Roman citizenship. The Egyptian Greek, on the other hand, might acquire the latter just like any other non-burgess. Entrance to the senate, it is true, was as little allowed to him as to the Roman burgess from Gaul (p. 89), and this restriction remained much longer in force for Egypt than for Gaul;[1] it was not till the beginning of the third century that it was disregarded in isolated cases, and it held good, as a rule, even in the fifth. In Egypt itself the positions of the upper officials, that is, of those acting for the whole province, and likewise the officers' posts, were reserved for Roman citizens in the form of the knight's horse being required as a qualification for them; this was given by the general organisation of the empire, and similar privileges had in fact been possessed in Egypt by the Macedonians in contrast to the other Greeks. The offices of the second rank remained under the Roman rule, as previously, closed to the Egyptian Egyptians, and were filled with Greeks, primarily with the burgesses of Alexandria and Ptolemais. If in the imperial war-service for the first class Roman citizenship was required, they, at any rate in the case of the legions stationed in Egypt itself, not seldom admitted the Egyptian Greek on the footing that Roman citizenship was conferred on him upon occasion of the levy. For the category of auxiliary troops the admission of the Greeks was subject to no limitation; but the Egyptians were little or not at all employed for this purpose, while they were employed afterwards in considerable number for the lowest class, the naval force still in the first imperial times formed of slaves. In the course of time the slighting of the native

---

[1] Admission to the equestrian positions was at least rendered difficult: *non est ex albo iudex patre Aegyptio* (*C. I. L.* iv. 1943; comp. *Staatsrecht,* ii. 919, note 2; *Eph. epigr.* v. p. 13, note 2). Yet we meet early with individual Alexandrians in equestrian offices, like Tiberius Julius Alexander (p. 246, note).

Egyptians doubtless had its rigour relaxed, and they more than once attained to Greek, and by means of it also to Roman, citizenship ; but on the whole the Roman government was simply the continuation, as of the Greek rule, so also of the Greek exclusiveness. As the Macedonian government had contented itself with Alexandria and Ptolemais, so in this province alone the Romans did not found a single colony.[1]

The linguistic arrangement in Egypt remained essentially under the Romans as the Ptolemies had settled it. Apart from the military, among whom the Latin alone prevailed, the business-language for the intercourse of the upper posts was the Greek. Of the native language, which, radically different from the Semitic as from the Arian languages, is most nearly akin perhaps to that of the Berbers in North Africa, and of the native writing, the Roman rulers and their governors never made use ; and, if already under the Ptolemies a Greek translation had to be appended to official documents written in Egyptian, at least the same held good for these their successors. Certainly the Egyptians were not prohibited from making use, so far as it seemed requisite according to ritual or otherwise appropriate, of the native language and of its time-hallowed written signs ; in this old home, moreover, of the use of writing in ordinary intercourse the native language, alone familiar to the great public, and the usual writing must necessarily have been allowed not merely in the case of private contracts, but even as regards tax-receipts and similar documents. But this was a concession, and the ruling Hellenism strove to enlarge its domain. The effort to create for the views and traditions prevailing in the land an universally valid expression also in Greek gave an extension to the system of double names in Egypt such as we see nowhere else. All Egyptian gods whose

Native language.

---

[1] If the words of Pliny (*H. N.* v. 31, 128) are accurate, that the island of Pharos before the harbour of Alexandria was a *colonia Caesaris dictatoris* (comp. iv. 574), the dictator has here too, like Alexander, gone beyond the thought of Aristotle. But there can be no doubt as to the point, that after the annexation of Egypt there never was a Roman colony there.

names were not themselves current among the Greeks,
like that of Isis, were equalised with corresponding or else
not corresponding Greek ones; perhaps the half of the
townships and a great number of persons bore as well
a native as a Greek appellation. Gradually Hellenism
in this case prevailed. The old sacred writing meets us
on the preserved monuments last under the emperor
Decius about the middle of the third, and its more
current degenerated form last about the middle of the fifth
century; both disappeared from common use considerably
earlier. The neglect and the decay of the native elements
of civilisation are expressed in these facts. The language
of the land itself maintained its ground still for long
afterwards in remote places and in the lower ranks, and
only became quite extinct in the seventeenth century,
after it—the language of the Copts—had, just like the
Syriac, experienced in the later imperial period a limited
regeneration in consequence of the introduction of
Christianity and of the efforts directed to the production
of a national-Christian literature.

Abolition of a resident court.

In the government the first thing that strikes us is
the suppression of the court and of its residency, the
necessary consequence of the annexation of the land by
Augustus. There was left doubtless as much as could
be left. On the inscriptions written in the native
language, and so merely for Egyptians, the emperors are
termed, like the Ptolemies, kings of upper and lower
Egypt, and the elect of the Egyptian native gods, and
indeed withal—which was not the case with the
Ptolemies—great-kings.[1]   Dates were reckoned in Egypt,

---

[1] The titles of Augustus run with
the Egyptian priests to the following
effect : "The beautiful boy, lovely
through worthiness to be loved, the
prince of princes, elect of Ptah and
Nun the father of the gods, king of
upper Egypt and king of lower
Egypt, lord of the two lands, Autokrator, son of the sun, lord of diadems,
Kaisar, ever living, beloved by Ptah
and Isis;" in this case the proper
names "Autokrator, Kaisar," are
retained from the Greek. The title
of Augustus occurs first in the case
of Tiberius in an Egyptian translation
(*nti χu*), and with the retention of the
Greek Σεβαστός first under Domitian.
The title of the fair, lovely boy,
which in better times was wont to be
given only to the children proclaimed
as joint - rulers, afterwards became
stereotyped, and is found employed,
as for Caesarion and Augustus, so
also for Tiberius, Claudius, Titus,

as previously, according to the current calendar of the
country and its royal year passing over to the Roman
rulers ; the golden cup which every year the king threw
into the swelling Nile was now thrown in by the Roman
viceroy. But these things did not reach far. The Roman
ruler could not carry out the part of the Egyptian king,
which was incompatible with his imperial position. The
new lord of the land had unpleasant experiences in his
representation by a subordinate on the very first occasion
of his sending a governor to Egypt ; the able officer and
talented poet, who had not been able to refrain from
inscribing his name also on the Pyramids, was deposed on
that account and thereby ruined. It was inevitable that
limits should here be set. The affairs, the transaction
of which according to the system of Alexander devolved
on the prince personally [1] not less than according to the
arrangement of the Roman principate, might be managed
by the Roman governor as by the native king ; king he
might neither be nor seem.[2] That was to a certainty
deeply and severely felt in the second city of the world.
The mere change of dynasty would not have told so very
heavily. But a court like that of the Ptolemies, regulated
according to the ceremonial of the Pharaohs, king and
queen in their dress as gods, the pomp of festal
processions, the reception of the priesthoods and of
ambassadors, the court-banquets, the great ceremonies of
the coronation, of the taking the oath, of marriage, of
burial, the court-offices of the bodyguards and the chief
of that guard ($\dot{a}\rho\chi\iota\sigma\omega\mu\alpha\tau o\phi\dot{v}\lambda\alpha\xi$), of the introducing
chamberlain ($\epsilon\dot{\iota}\sigma\alpha\gamma\gamma\epsilon\lambda\epsilon\dot{v}s$), of the chief master of the
table ($\dot{a}\rho\chi\epsilon\delta\dot{\epsilon}a\tau\rho os$), of the chief master of the huntsmen

---

Domitian. It is more important that
in deviation from the older title, as
it is found, *e.g.* in Greek on the
inscription of Rosetta (*C. I. Gr.*
4697), in the case of the Caesars
from Augustus onward the title
" prince of princes " is appended, by
which beyond doubt it was intended
to express their position of great-king,
which the earlier kings had not.

[1] If people knew, king Seleucus
was wont to say (Plutarch, *An seni,*
11), what a burden it was to write and
to read so many letters, they would
not take up the diadem if it lay at
their feet.

[2] That he wore other insignia than
the officers generally (Hirschfeld,
Verw. Gesch. p. 271), it is hardly
allowable to infer from *vita Hadr.* 4.

(ἀρχικυνηγός), the cousins and friends of the king, the wearers of decorations—all this was lost for the Alexandrians once for all with the transfer of the seat of the ruler from the Nile to the Tiber. Only the two famous Alexandrian libraries remained there, with all their belongings and staff, as a remnant of the old regal magnificence. Beyond question Egypt lost by being dispossessed of its rulers very much more than Syria ; both nations indeed were in the powerless position of having to acquiesce in what was contrived for them, and not more here than there was a rising for the lost position of a great power so much as thought of.

The officials.

The administration of the land lay, as has been already said, in the hands of the " deputy," that is, the viceroy ; for, although the new lord of the land, out of respect for his position in the empire, refrained as well for himself as for his delegates of higher station from the royal appellations in Egypt, he yet in substance conducted his rule throughout as successor of the Ptolemies, and the whole civil and military supreme power was combined in his hand and that of his representative. We have already observed that neither non-burgesses nor senators might fill this position ; it was sometimes committed to Alexandrians, if they had attained to burgess-rights, and by way of exception to equestrian rank.[1] We may add that this office stood at first before all the rest of the non-senatorial in rank and influence, and subsequently was inferior only to the commandership of the imperial guard. Besides the officers proper, in reference to whom the only departure from the general arrangement was the exclusion of the senator and the lower title, thence resulting, of the commandant of the legion (*praefectus* instead of *legatus*),

---

[1] Thus Tiberius Julius Alexander, an Alexandrian Jew, held this governorship in the last years of Nero (p. 204) ; certainly he belonged to a very rich family of rank, allied by marriage even with the imperial house, and he had distinguished himself in the Parthian war as chief of the staff of Corbulo—a position which he soon afterwards took up once more in the Jewish war of Titus. He must have been one of the ablest officers of this epoch. To him is dedicated the pseudo - Aristotelian treatise περὶ κοσμοῦ (p. 168), evidently composed by another Alexandrian Jew (Bernays, *Gesammelte Abhandl.* ii. 278).

there acted alongside of and under the governor, and likewise for all Egypt, a supreme official for justice and a supreme finance-administrator, both likewise Roman citizens of equestrian rank, and apparently not borrowed from the administrative scheme of the Ptolemies, but attached and subordinated to the governor after a fashion applied also in other imperial provinces.[1]

All other officials acted only for individual districts, and were in the main taken over from the Ptolemaic arrangement. That the presidents of the three provinces of lower, middle, and upper Egypt, provided—apart from the command—with the same sphere of business as the governor, were taken in the time of Augustus from the Egyptian Greeks, and subsequently, like the superior officials proper, from the Roman knighthood, deserves to be noted as a symptom of the increasing tendency in the course of the imperial period to repress the native element in the magistracy.

Under these superior and intermediate authorities stood the local officials, the presidents of the Egyptian as of the Greek towns, along with the very numerous subalterns employed in the collecting of the revenue and

---

[1] Unmistakably the *iuridicus Aegypti* (*C. I. L.* x. 6976; also *missus in Aegyptum ad iurisdictionem, Bull. dell' Inst.* 1856, p. 142; *iuridicus Alexandreae, C.* vi. 1564, viii. 8925, 8934; *Dig.* i. 20, 2), and the *idiologus ad Aegyptum* (*C.* x. 4862; *procurator ducenarius Alexandriae idiulogu, Eph. ep.* v. p. 30, and *C. I. Gr.* 3751; ὁ γνώμων τοῦ ἰδίου λόγου, *C. I. Gr.* 4957, v. 44, comp. v. 39), are modelled on the assistants associated with the legates of the imperial provinces för the administration of justice (*legati iuridici*) and the finances (*procuratores provinciae; Staatsrecht* 1², p. 223, note 5). That they were appointed for the whole land, and were subordinate to the *praefectus Aegypti*, is stated by Strabo expressly (xvii. 1, 12, p. 797), and this assumption is required by the frequent mention of Egypt in their style and title as well as by the turn in the edict *C. I. Gr.* 4957, v. 39. But their jurisdiction was not exclusive; "many processes," says Strabo, "are decided by the official administering justice" (that he assigned guardians, we learn from *Dig.* i. 20, 2), and according to the same it devolved on the Idiologus in particular to confiscate for the exchequer the *bona vacantia et caduca*. —This does not exclude the view that the Roman *iuridicus* came in place of the older court of thirty with the ἀρχιδικαστής at its head (Diodorus, i. 75), who was Egyptian, and may not be confounded with the Alexandrian ἀρχιδικαστής, had moreover perhaps been set aside already before the Roman period, and that the Idiologus originated out of the subsistence in Egypt of a claim of the king on heritages, such as did not occur to the same extent in the rest of the empire, which latter view Lumbroso (*Recherches*, p. 285) has made very probable.

the manifold imposts laid on business-dealings, and again in the individual district the presidents of the sub-districts and of the villages—positions, which were looked upon more as burdens than as honours, and were imposed by the higher officials upon persons belonging to, or settled in, the locality, to the exclusion, however, of the Alexandrians ; the most important among them, the presidency of the nome, was filled up every three years by the governor. The local authorities of the Greek towns were different as to number and title ; in Alexandria in particular four chief officials acted, the priest of Alexander,[1]

---

[1] The ἐξηγητής, according to Strabo, xvii. 1, 12, p. 797, the first civic official in Alexandria under the Ptolemies as under the Romans, and entitled to wear the purple, is certainly identical with the year-priest in the testament of Alexander appearing in the Alexander-romance very well instructed in such matters (iii. 33, p. 149, Müller). As the Exegetes has, along with his title, doubtless to be taken in a religious sense, the ἐπιμέλεια τῶν τῇ πόλει χρησίμων, that priest of the romance is ἐπιμελιστὴς τῆς πόλεως. The romance-writer will not have invented the payment with a talent and the hereditary character any more than the purple and the golden chaplet ; the hereditary element, in reference to which Lumbroso (*l'Egitto al tempo dei Greci e Romani*, p. 152) recalls the ἐξηγητὴς ἔναρχος of the Alexandrian inscriptions (*C. I. Gr.* 4688, 4976 c.), is presumably to be conceived to the effect that a certain circle of persons was called by hereditary right, and out of these the governor appointed the year-priest. This priest of Alexander (as well as of the following Egyptian kings, according to the stone of Canopus and that of Rosetta, *C. I. Gr.* 4697), was under the earlier Lagids the eponym for Alexandrian documents, while later as under the Romans the kings' names come in for that purpose. Not different from him probably was the "chief priest of Alexandria and all Egypt," of an inscription of the city of Rome from Hadrian's time (*C. I. Gr.* 5900 : ἀρχιερεῖ 'Αλεξανδρείας καὶ Αἰγύπτου πάσης Λευκίῳ 'Ιουλίῳ Οὐησ- τίνῳ καὶ ἐπιστάτῃ τοῦ Μουσείου καὶ ἐπὶ τῶν ἐν 'Ρώμῃ βιβλιοθηκῶν 'Ρωμαικῶν τε καὶ 'Ελληνικῶν καὶ ἐπὶ τῆς παιδείας 'Αδριανοῦ, ἐπιστολεῖ τοῦ αὐτοῦ αὐτοκρά- τορος) ; the proper title ἐξηγητής, was avoided out of Egypt, because it usually denoted the sexton. If the chief priesthood, as the tenor of the inscription suggests, is to be assumed as having been at that time permanent, the transition from the annual tenure to the at least titular, and not seldom also real, tenure for life repeats itself, as is well known, in the *sacerdotia* of the provinces, to which this Alexandrian one did not indeed belong, but the place of which it represented in Egypt (p. 238). That the priesthood and the presidency of the Museum are two distinct offices is shown by the inscription itself. We learn the same from the inscription of a royal chief physician of a good Lagid period, who is withal as well exegete as president of the Museum (Χρύσερμον 'Ηρακλείτου 'Αλεξανδρέα τὸν συγγενῆ βασιλέως Πτολεμαίου καὶ ἐξηγητὴν καὶ ἐπὶ τῶν ἰατρῶν καὶ ἐπιστάτην τοῦ Μουσείου). But the two monuments at the same time suggest that the post of first official of Alexandria and the presidency of the Museum were frequently committed to the same man, although in the Roman time the former was conferred by the prefect, the latter by the emperor.

the town-clerk (ὑπομνηματογράφος),[1] the supreme judge (ἀρχιδικαστής), and the master of the night-watch (νυκτερινὸς στρατηγός). That they were of more consequence than the *strategoi* of the nomes, is obvious of itself, and is shown clearly by the purple dress belonging to the first Alexandrian official. We may add that they originate likewise from the Ptolemaic period, and are nominated for a time by the Roman government, like the presidents of the nomes, from the persons settled therein. Roman officials of imperial nomination are not found among these urban presidents. But the priest of the Mouseion, who is at the same time president of the Alexandrian Academy of Sciences and also disposes of the considerable pecuniary means of this institute, is nominated by the emperor ; in like manner the superintendency of the tomb of Alexander and the buildings connected with it, and some other important positions in the capital of Egypt, were filled up by the government in Rome with officials of equestrian rank.[2]

As a matter of course, Alexandrians and Egyptians were drawn into those movements of pretenders which had their origin in the East, and regularly participated in them ; in this way Vespasian, Cassius, Niger, Macrianus (p. 103), Vaballathus the son of Zenobia, Probus, were here proclaimed as rulers. But the initiative in all those cases was taken neither by the burgesses of Alexandria nor by the little esteemed Egyptian troops ; and most of those revolutions, even the unsuccessful, had for Egypt no consequences specially felt. But the movement connected with the name of Zenobia (p. 107) became almost as fateful for Alexandria and for all Egypt as for Palmyra. In town and country the Palmyrene and the Roman partisans confronted each other with arms and blazing

Insurrections.

In the Palmyrene period.

---

[1] Not to be confounded with the similar office which Philo (in *Flacc.* 16) mentions and Lucian (*Apolog.* 12) held ; this was not an urban office, but a subaltern's post in the praefecture of Egypt, in Latin *a commentariis* or *ab actis.*

[2] This is the *procurator Neaspoleos et mausolei Alexandriae* (*C. I. L.*

viii. 8934 ; Henzen, 6929). Officials of a like kind and of like rank, but whose functions are not quite clear, are the *procurator ad Mercurium Alexandreae* (*C. I. L.* x. 3847), and the *procurator Alexandreae Pelusii* (*C.* vi. 1024). The Pharos also is placed under an imperial freedman (*C.* vi. 8582).

torches in their hands. On the south frontier the barbarian Blemyes advanced, apparently in agreement with
the portion of the inhabitants of Egypt favourable to
Palmyra, and possessed themselves of a great part of
upper Egypt.[1] In Alexandria the intercourse between
the two hostile quarters was cut off; it was difficult and
dangerous even to forward letters.[2] The streets were
filled with blood and with dead bodies unburied. The
diseases thereby engendered made even more havoc than
the sword ; and, in order that none of the four steeds of
destruction might be wanting, the Nile also failed, and
famine associated itself with the other scourges. The
population melted away to such an extent that, as a contemporary says, there were formerly more gray-haired
men in Alexandria than there were afterwards citizens.

When Probus, the general sent by Claudius, at length
gained the upper hand, the Palmyrene partisans, including
the majority of the members of council, threw themselves
into the strong castle of Prucheion in the immediate
neighbourhood of the city ; and, although, when Probus
promised to spare the lives of those that should come out,
the great majority submitted, yet a considerable portion
of the citizens persevered to the uttermost in the struggle
of despair. The fortress, at length reduced by hunger
(270), was razed and lay thenceforth desolate ; but the
city lost its walls. The Blemyes still maintained them-

---

[1] The alliance of the Palmyrenes
and the Blemyes is pointed to by the
notice of the *vita Firmi*, c. 3, and
by the statement, according to Zosimus, i. 71, that Ptolemais fell away to
the Blemyes (comp. Eusebius, *Hist.
Eccl.* vii. 32). Aurelian only negotiated with these (*Vita*, 34, 41) ; it
was Probus who first drove them
again out of Egypt (Zosimus, *l.c.*;
Vita, 17).

[2] We still possess letters of this
sort, addressed by the bishop of the
city, at that time Dionysius (+ 265),
to the members of the church shut
off in the hostile half of the town
(Eusebius, *Hist. Eccl.* vii. 21, 22,
comp. 32). When it is therein said :

"one gets more easily from the West
to the East than from Alexandria
to Alexandria," and ἡ μεσαιτάτη τῆς
πόλεως ὁδός, consequently the street
furnished with colonnades, running
from the Lochias point right through
the town (comp. Lumbroso, *l'Egitto
al tempo dei Greci e Romani*, 1882,
p. 137) is compared with the desert
between Egypt and the promised
land, it appears almost as if Severus
Antoninus had carried out his threat
of drawing a wall across the town
and occupying it in a military fashion
(Dio, lxxvii. 23). The razing of the
walls after the overthrow of the revolt
(Ammianus, xxii. 16, 15) would then
have to be referred to this very building.

selves for years in the land ; the emperor Probus first
wrested from them again Ptolemais and Coptos, and drove
them out of the country.

The state of distress, which these troubles prolonged Revolt
under Dio-
cletian.
through a series of years, must have produced, may pro-
bably thereupon have brought to an outbreak, the only
revolution that can be shown to have arisen in Egypt.[1]
Under the government of Diocletian, we do not know why
or wherefore, as well the native Egyptians as the burgesses
of Alexandria rose in revolt against the existing government.   Lucius Domitius Domitianus and Achilleus were
set up as opposition-emperors, unless possibly the two
names denote the same person ; the revolt lasted from
three to four years, the towns Busiris in the Delta and
Coptos not far from Thebes were destroyed by the troops
of the government, and ultimately under the leading of
Diocletian in person in the spring of 297 the capital was
reduced after an eight months' siege.   Nothing testifies
so clearly to the decline of the land, rich, but thoroughly
dependent on inward and outward peace, as the edict
issued in the year 302 by the same Diocletian, that a
portion of the Egyptian grain hitherto sent to Rome
should for the future go to the benefit of the Alexandrian
burgesses.[2]   This was certainly among the measures which
aimed at the decapitalising of Rome ; but the supply
would not have been directed towards the Alexandrians,
whom this emperor had truly no cause to favour, unless
they had urgently needed it.

Economically Egypt, as is well-known, is above all the Agricul-
ture.
land of agriculture.   It is true that the " black earth "—
that is the meaning of the native name for the country,
Chemi—is only a narrow stripe on either side of the
mighty Nile flowing from the last rapids near Syene, the

---

[1] The alleged Egyptian tyrants,
Aemilianus, Firmus, Saturninus, are
at least not attested as such.   The
so-called description of the life of the
second is nothing else than the sadly
disfigured catastrophe of Prucheion.

[2] *Chr. Pasch.* p. 514 ; Procopius,
Hist. arc. 26 ; Gothofred. on *Cod.*

Theod. xiv. 26, 2.   Stated distribu-
tions of corn had already been instituted earlier in Alexandria, but
apparently only for persons old and
decayed, and—it may be conjectured
—on account of the city, not of the
state (Eusebius, *Hist. Eccl.* vii. 21).

southern limit of Egypt proper, for 550 miles in a copious
stream, through the yellow desert extending right and
left, to the Mediterranean Sea ; only at its lower end the
"gift of the river," the Nile-delta, spreads itself out on
both sides between the manifold arms of its mouth.   The
produce of these tracts depends year by year on the Nile
and on the sixteen cubits of its flood-mark—the sixteen
children playing round their father, as the art of the
Greeks represented the river-god ; with good reason the
Arabs designate the low cubits by the name of the angels
of death, for, if the river does not reach its full height,
famine and destruction come upon the whole land of Egypt.
But in general Egypt—where the expenses of cultivation
are singularly low, wheat bears an hundred fold, and the
culture of vegetables, of the vine, of trees, particularly the
date-palm, as well as the rearing of cattle, yield good produce—is able not merely to feed a dense population, but
also to send corn in large quantity abroad.   This led to
the result that, after the installation of the foreign rule,
not much of its riches was left to the land itself.   The
Nile rose at that time nearly as in the Persian period and
as it does to-day, and the Egyptian toiled chiefly for other
lands ; and thereby in the first instance Egypt played an
important part in the history of imperial Rome.   After
the grain-cultivation in Italy itself had decayed and Rome
had become the greatest city of the world, it needed constant supplies of moderately-priced transmarine grain ;
and the principate strengthened itself above all by the
solution of the far from easy economic problem how to
make the supply of the capital financially possible and to
render it secure.   This solution depended on the possession
of Egypt, and, in as much as here the emperor bore
exclusive sway, he kept Italy with its dependencies in
check through Egypt.   When Vespasian seized the
dominion he sent his troops to Italy, but he went in
person to Egypt and possessed himself of Rome through
the corn-fleet.   Wherever a Roman ruler had, or is alleged
to have had, the idea of transferring the seat of government to the East, as is told us of Caesar, Antonius, Nero,

Geta, there the thoughts were directed, as if spontaneously, not to Antioch, although this was at that time the regular court-residence of the East, but towards the birthplace and the stronghold of the principate—to Alexandria.

For that reason, accordingly, the Roman government applied itself more zealously to the elevation of agriculture in Egypt than anywhere else. As it is dependent on the inundation of the Nile, it was possible to extend considerably the surface fitted for cultivation by systematically executed water-works, artificial canals, dykes, and reservoirs. In the good times of Egypt, the native land of the measuring-chain and of artificial building, much was done for it, but these beneficent structures fell, under the last wretched and financially oppressed governments, into sad decay. Thus the Roman occupation introduced itself worthily by Augustus subjecting the canals of the Nile to a thorough purifying and renewal by means of the troops stationed in Egypt. If at the time of the Romans taking possession a full harvest required a state of the river of fourteen cubits, and at eight cubits failure of the harvest occurred, at a later period, after the canals were put into order, twelve cubits were enough for a full harvest, and even eight cubits yielded a sufficient produce. Centuries later the emperor Probus not merely liberated Egypt from the Ethiopians but also restored the water-works on the Nile. It may be assumed, generally, that the better successors of Augustus administered in a similar sense, and that especially with the internal peace and security hardly interrupted for centuries, Egyptian agriculture stood in a permanently flourishing state under the Roman principate. What reflex effect this state of things had on the Egyptians themselves we are not able to follow out more exactly. To a great extent the revenues from Egypt rested on the possession of the imperial domains, which in Roman as in earlier times formed a considerable part of the whole area ;[1] here, especially considering the small

[1] In the town of Alexandria there appears to have been no landed property in the strict sense, but only a sort of hereditary lease (Ammianus, xxii. 11, 6 ; *Staatsrecht*, ii. 963, note 1); but otherwise private property in the soil prevailed also in Egypt, in the sense in which the pro-

cost of cultivation, only a moderate proportion of the produce must have been left to the small tenants who provided it, or a high money-rent must have been imposed. But even the numerous, and as a rule smaller, owners must have paid a high land-tax in corn or in money. The agricultural population, contented as it was, remained probably numerous in the imperial period ; but certainly the pressure of taxation, as well in itself as on account of the expenditure of the produce abroad, lay as a heavier burden on Egypt under the Roman foreign rule than under the by no means indulgent government of the Ptolemies.

Trades.   Of the economy of Egypt agriculture formed but a part ; as it in this respect stood far before Syria, so it had the advantage of a high prosperity of manufactures and commerce as compared with the essentially agricultural Africa. The linen manufacture in Egypt was at least equal in age, extent, and renown to the Syrian, and maintained its ground through the whole imperial period, although the finer sorts at this epoch were especially manufactured in Syria and Phoenicia ;[1] when Aurelian

vincial law knows such a thing at all. There is often mention of domanial possession *e.g.* Strabo, xvii. 1, 51, p. 828, says that the best Egyptian dates grow on an island on which private persons might not possess any land, but it was formerly royal, now imperial, and yielded a large income. Vespasian sold a portion of the Egyptian domains and thereby exasperated the Alexandrians (Dio, lxvi. 8)—beyond doubt the great farmers who then gave the land in sub-lease to the peasants proper. Whether landed property in mortmain, especially of the priestly colleges, was in the Roman period still as extensive as formerly, may be doubted ; as also whether otherwise large estates or small properties predominated ; petty husbandry was certainly general. We possess figures neither for that of the domanial quota nor for that of the land-tax ; that the fifth sheaf in Orosius, i. 8, 9, is copied including the *usque ad*

nunc from Genesis, is rightly observed by Lumbroso, *Recherches*, p. 94. The domanial rent cannot have amounted to less than the half ; even for the land-tax the tenth (Lumbroso, *l. c.* p. 289, 293) may have hardly sufficed. Export of grain otherwise from Egypt needed the consent of the governor (Hirschfeld, *Annona*, p. 23), doubtless because otherwise scarcity might easily set in in the thickly-peopled land. Yet this arrangement was certainly more by way of control than of prohibition ; in the Periplus of the Egyptian corn is on several occasions (c. 7, 17, 24, 28, comp. 56) adduced among the articles of export. Even the cultivation of the fields seems to have become similarly controlled ; " the Egyptians, it is said, are fonder of cultivating rape than corn, so far as they may, on account of the rape-seed oil " (Plinius, *H. N.* xix. 5, 79).

[1] In the edict of Diocletian among

extended the contributions made from Egypt to the capital of the empire to other articles than corn, linen cloth and tow were not wanting among them. In fine glass wares, both as regards colouring and moulding, the Alexandrians held decidedly the first place, in fact, as they thought, the monopoly, in as much as certain best sorts were only to be prepared with Egyptian material. Indisputably they had such a material in the papyrus. This plant, which in antiquity was cultivated in masses on the rivers and lakes of lower Egypt, and flourished nowhere else, furnished the natives as well with nourishment as with materials for ropes, baskets, and boats, and furnished writing materials at that time for the whole writing world. What produce it must have yielded, we may gather from the measures which the Roman senate took, when once in the Roman market the papyrus became scarce and threatened to fail ; and, as its laborious preparation could only take place on the spot, numberless men must have subsisted by it in Egypt. The deliveries of Alexandrian wares introduced by Aurelian in favour of the capital of the empire extended, along with linen, to glass and papyrus.[1] The intercourse with the East must have had a varied influence on Egyptian manufactures as regards supply and demand. Textures were manufactured there for export to the East, and that in the fashion required by the usage of the country ; the ordinary clothes of the inhabitants of Habesh were of Egyptian manufacture ; the gorgeous stuffs especially of the weaving in colours and in gold skilfully practised at Alexandria went to Arabia and India. In like manner the glass beads prepared in Egypt played the same part in the commerce of the African coast as at the present day. India procured partly glass cups, partly unwrought glass for its

---

the five fine sorts of linen the first four are Syrian or Cilician (of Tarsus) and the Egyptian linen appears not merely in the last place, but is also designated as Tarsian-Alexandrian, that is, prepared in Alexandria after the Tarsian model.

[1] It was related of a rich man in Egypt that he had lined his palace with glass instead of with marble, and that he possessed papyrus and lime enough to provide an army with them (*Vita Firmi*, 3).

own manufacture ; even at the Chinese court the glass
vessels, with which the Roman strangers did homage to
the emperor, are said to have excited great admiration.
Egyptian merchants brought to the king of the Axomites
(Habesh) as standing presents gold and silver vessels
prepared after the fashion of that country, to the civilised
rulers of the South-Arabian and Indian coast among
other gifts also statues, probably of bronze, and musical
instruments.　On the other hand the materials for the
manufacture of luxuries which came from the East,
especially ivory and tortoise-shell, were worked up
hardly perhaps in Egypt, chiefly, in all probability, at
Rome.　Lastly, at an epoch, which never had its match
in the West for magnificent public buildings, the costly
building materials supplied by the Egyptian quarries
came to be employed in enormous masses outside of
Egypt ; the beautiful red granite of Syene, the green
breccia from the region of Kosêr, the basalt, the alabaster,
after the time of Claudius the gray granite, and especially
the porphyry of the mountains above Myos Hormos.
The working of them was certainly effected for the most
part on imperial account by penal colonists ; but the
transport at least must have gone to benefit the whole
country and particularly the city of Alexandria.　The
extent to which Egyptian traffic and Egyptian manufactures were developed is shown by an accidentally-pre-
served notice as to the cargo of a transport ship (ἄκατος),
distinguished by its size, which under Augustus brought
to Rome the obelisk now standing at the Porta del Popolo
with its base ; it carried, besides 200 sailors, 1200 passengers, 400,000 Roman bushels (34,000 hectolitres) of
wheat, and a cargo of linen cloth, glass, paper, and pepper.
" Alexandria," says a Roman author of the third century,[1]

---

[1] That the alleged letter of Hadrian
(*Vita Saturnini*, 8) is a late fabrica-
tion, is shown *e.g.* by the fact, that
the emperor in this highly friendly
letter addressed to his father-in-law,
Servianus, complains of the injuries
which the Alexandrians at his first
departure had heaped on his son Verus,
while on the other hand it is established that this Servianus was executed
at the age of ninety in the year 136,
because he had disapproved the adoption of Verus, which had taken place
shortly before.

" is a town of plenty, of wealth, and of luxury, in which nobody goes idle ; this one is a glass-worker, that one a paper-maker, the third a linen-weaver ; the only god is money." This held true proportionally of the whole land.

Of the commercial intercourse of Egypt with the regions adjoining it on the south, as well as with Arabîa and India, we shall speak more fully in the sequel. The traffic with the countries of the Mediterranean comes less into prominence in the traditional account, partly, doubtless, because it belonged to the ordinary course of things, and there was not often occasion to make special mention of it. The Egyptian corn was conveyed to Italy by Alexandrian shipmasters, and in consequence of this there arose in Portus near Ostia a sanctuary modelled on the Alexandrian temple of Sarapis with a mariner's guild ;[1] but these transport-ships would hardly be concerned to any considerable extent in the sale of the wares going from Egypt to the West. This sale lay probably just as much, and perhaps more, in the hands of the Italian shipowners and captains than of the Egyptian ; at least there was already under the Lagids a considerable Italian settlement in Alexandria,[2] and the Egyptian merchants had not the same diffusion in the West as the Syrian.[3] The ordinances of Augustus, to be mentioned afterwards, which remodelled the commercial traffic on the Arabian and Indian Seas, found no application to the navigation of

Egyptian navigation of the Mediterranean.

---

[1] The ναύκληροι τοῦ πορευτικοῦ 'Αλεξανδρεινοῦ στόλου, who set up the stone doubtless belonging to Portus, *C. I. Gr.* 5889, were the captains of these grain-ships. From the Serapeum of Ostia we possess a series of inscriptions (*C. I. L.* xiv. 47), according to which it was in all parts a copy of that at Alexandria ; the president is at the same time ἐπιμελητὴς παντὸς τοῦ 'Αλεξανδρείνου στόλου (*C. I. Gr.* 5973). Probably these transports were employed mainly with the carriage of grain, and this consequently took place by succession, to which also the precautions adopted by the emperor Gaius in the straits of Reggio (Josephus, *Arch.* xix. 2, 5) point.

With this well comports the fact, that the first appearance of the Alexandrian fleet in the spring was a festival for Puteoli (Seneca, *Ep.* 77, 1).

[2] This is shown by the remarkable Delian inscriptions, *Eph. epigr.* i. p. 600, 602.

[3] Already in the Delian inscriptions of the last century of the republic the Syrians predominate. The Egyptian deities had doubtless a much revered shrine there, but among the numerous priests and dedicators we meet only a single Alexandrian (Hauvette-Besnault, *Bull. de corr. Hell.* vi. 316 f.). Guilds of Alexandrian merchants are known to us at Tomi (I. 310, note) and at Perinthus (*C. I. Gr.* 2024).

the Mediterranean ; the government had no interest in favouring the Egyptian merchants more than the rest in its case. The traffic there remained, presumably, as it was.

Population. Egypt was thus not merely occupied, in its portions capable of culture, with a dense agricultural population, but also as the numerous and in part very considerable hamlets and towns enable us to recognise, a manufacturing land, and hence accordingly by far the most populous province of the Roman empire. The old Egypt is alleged to have had a population of seven millions ; under Vespasian there were counted in the official lists seven and a half millions of inhabitants liable to poll tax, to which fall to be added the Alexandrians and other Greeks exempted from poll tax, so that the population, apart from the slaves, is to be estimated at least at eight millions of persons. As the area capable of cultivation may be estimated at present at 10,500 English square miles, and for the Roman period at the most at 14,700, there dwelt at that time in Egypt on the average about 520 persons to the square mile.

When we direct our glance upon the inhabitants of Egypt, the two nations inhabiting the country—the great mass of the Egyptians and the small minority of the Alexandrians—are circles thoroughly different,[1] although the contagious power of vice and the similarity of character belonging to all vice have instituted a bad fellowship of evil between the two.

Egyptian manners. The native Egyptians cannot have been far different either in position or in character from their modern descendants. They were contented, sober, capable of labour, and active, skilful artisans and mariners, and adroit merchants, adhering to old customs and to old faith. If the Romans assure us that the Egyptians were proud

---

[1] After Juvenal has described the wild drinking bouts of the native Egyptians in honour of the local gods of the several nomes, he adds that therein the natives were in no respect inferior to the Canopus, *i.e.* the Alex- andrian festival of Sarapis, notorious for its unbridled licentiousness (Strabo, xvii. 1, 17, p. 801) : *horrida sane Aegyptus, sed luxuria quantum ipse notavi, barbara famoso non cedit turba Canopo* (*Sat.* xv. 44).

of the scourge-marks received for perpetrating frauds
in taxation,[1] these are views derived from the standpoint of the tax officials.   There was no want of good
germs in the national culture ; with all the superiority of
the Greeks in the intellectual competition of the two so
utterly different races, the Egyptians in turn had the
advantage of the Hellenes in various and essential things,
and they felt this too.   It is, after all, only the plain
reflection of their own feeling, when the Egyptian priests
of the Greek conversational literature ridicule the so-called
historical research of the Hellenes and its treatment of
poetical fables as real tradition from primitive past times,
saying that in Egypt they made no verses, but their whole
ancient history was described in the temples and monuments ; although now, indeed, there were but few who
knew it, since many monuments were destroyed, and
tradition was made to perish through the ignorance and
the indifference of later generations.   But this well-war-
ranted complaint carried in itself hopelessness ; the vener-
able tree of Egyptian civilisation had long been marked
for cutting down.   Hellenism penetrated with its decom-
posing influence even to the priesthood itself.   An
Egyptian temple-scribe Chaeremon, who was called to
the court of Claudius as teacher of Greek philosophy for
the crown-prince, attributed in his *Egyptian History* the
elements of Stoical physics to the old gods of the country,
and expounded in this sense the documents written in the
native character.   In the practical life of the imperial
period the old Egyptian habits come into consideration
almost only as regards the religious sphere.   Religion was
for this people all in all.   The foreign rule in itself was
willingly borne, we might say hardly felt, so long as it did
not touch the sacred customs of the land and what was
therewith connected.   It is true that in the internal
government of the country nearly everything had such
a connection—writing and language, priestly privileges and
priestly arrogance, the manners of the court and the cus-

---

[1] Ammianus, xxii. 16, 23 : *Eru-   fitiando tributa plurimas in corpore
bescit apud (Aegyptios), si qui non in-   vibices ostendat.*

toms of the country ; the care of the government for the
sacred ox living at the moment, the provisions made for its
burial at its decease, and for the finding out of the fitting
successor, were accounted by these priests and this
people as the test of the capacity of the ruler of the
land for the time, and as the measure of the respect
and homage due to him. The first Persian king introduced himself in Egypt by giving back the sanctuary of
Neith in Sais to its destination—that is, to the priests ;
the first Ptolemy, when still a Macedonian governor,
brought back the images of the Egyptian gods, that had
been carried off to Asia, to their old abode, and restored
to the gods of Pe and Tep the land-gifts estranged from
them ; for the sacred temple-images brought home from
Persia in the great victorious expedition of Euergetes the
native priests convey their thanks to the king in the
famous decree of Canopus in the year 238 B.C.; the customary insertion of the living rulers male or female in the
circle of the native gods these foreigners acquiesced in for
themselves just as did the Egyptian Pharaohs. The
Roman rulers followed their example only to a limited
extent. As respects title they doubtless entered, as we saw
(p. 244, note) in some measure into the native cultus, but
avoided withal, even in the Egyptian setting, the customary
predicates that stood in too glaring a contrast to Occidental views. Since these ' favourites of Ptah and of Isis '
took much the same steps in Italy against the Egyptian
worship as against the Jewish, they betrayed nothing, as
may readily be understood, of such love except in hiero-
glyphic inscriptions, and even in Egypt took no part in the
service of the native gods. However obstinately the religion of the land was still retained under the foreign rule
among the Egyptians proper, the Pariah position in which
these found themselves alongside of the ruling Greeks and
Romans, necessarily told heavily on the cultus and the
priests ; and of the leading position, the influence, the
culture of the old Egyptian priestly order but scanty
remains were discernible under the Roman government.
On the other hand, the indigenous religion, from the out-

set disinclined to beauty of form and spiritual transfigura-
tion, served, in and out of Egypt, as a starting-point and
centre for all conceivable pious sorcery and sacred fraud
—it is enough to recall the thrice-greatest Hermes at
home in Egypt, with the literature attaching to his name
of tractates and marvel-books, as well as the corresponding widely diffused practice.   But in the circles of the
natives the worst abuses were connected at this epoch with
their cultus—not merely drinking-bouts continued through
many days in honour of the individual local deities, with
the unchastity thereto appertaining, but also permanent
religious feuds between the several districts for the precedence of the ibis over the cat, or of the crocodile over
the baboon.   In the year 127 A.D., on such an occasion,
the Ombites in southern Egypt were suddenly assailed by
a neighbouring community[1] at a drinking-festival, and the
victors are said to have eaten one of the slain.   Soon
afterwards the community of the Hound, in defiance of the
community of the Pike, consumed a pike, and the latter in
defiance of the other consumed a hound, and thereupon a
war broke out between these two nomes, till the Romans
interfered and chastised both parties.   Such incidents
were of ordinary occurrence in Egypt.   Nor was there a
want otherwise of troubles in the land.   The very first
viceroy of Egypt appointed by Augustus had, on account
of an increase of the taxes, to send troops to upper Egypt,
and not less, perhaps likewise in consequence of the pressure of taxation, to Heroonpolis at the upper end of the
Arabian Gulf.   Once, under the emperor Marcus, a rising   Revolt
of the native Egyptians assumed even a threatening   of the
character.   When in the marshes, difficult of access, on   "Herds-
the coast to the east of Alexandria—the so-called "cattle-   men."
pastures" (*bucolia*), which served as a place of refuge for
criminals and robbers, and formed a sort of colony of
them—some people were seized by a division of Roman
troops, the whole banditti rose to liberate them, and the

---

[1] This was according to Juvenal
Tentyra, which must be a mistake, if
the well known Tentyra is meant ;
but the list of the Ravennate chro-
nicler, iii. 2, names the two places
together.

population of the country joined the movement. The Roman legion from Alexandria went to oppose them, but it was defeated, and Alexandria itself had almost fallen into the hands of the insurgents. The governor of the East, Avidius Cassius, arrived doubtless with his troops, but did not venture on a conflict against the superiority of numbers, and preferred to provoke dissension in the league of the rebels ; after the one band ranged itself against the other the government easily mastered them all. This so-called revolt of the herdsmen probably bore, like such peasant wars for the most part, a religious character ; the leader Isidorus, the bravest man of Egypt, was by station a priest; and the circumstance that for the consecration of the league, after taking the oath, a captive Roman officer was sacrificed and eaten by those who swore, was as well in keeping with it as with the cannibalism of the Ombite war. An echo of these events is preserved in the stories of Egyptian robbers in the late-Greek minor literature. Much, moreover, as they may have given trouble to the Roman administration, they had not a political object, and interrupted but partially and temporarily the general tranquillity of the land.

Alexandria.   By the side of the Egyptians stood the Alexandrians, somewhat as the English in India stand alongside of the natives of the country. Generally, Alexandria was re-garded in the imperial period before Constantine's time as the second city of the Roman empire and the first com-mercial city of the world. It numbered at the end of the Lagid rule upwards of 300,000 free inhabitants, in the imperial period beyond doubt still more. The compari-son of the two great capitals that grew up in rivalry on the Nile and on the Orontes yields as many points of simi-larity as of contrast. Both were comparatively new cities, monarchical creations out of nothing, of symmetrical plan and regular urban arrangements. Water ran into every house in Alexandria as at Antioch. In beauty of site and magnificence of buildings the city in the valley of the Orontes was as superior to its rival as the latter excelled it in the favourableness of the locality for commerce on a large scale and in the number of the population. The great public buildings of the Egyptian capital, the royal palace, the Mouseion dedicated to the Academy, above all the temple of Sarapis, were marvellous works of an earlier epoch, whose architecture was highly developed ; but the Egyptian capital, in which few of the Caesars set foot, has nothing corresponding to set off against the great number of imperial structures in the Syrian residency.

The Antiochenes and Alexandrians stood on an equal footing in insubordination and eagerness to oppose the government ; we may add also in this, that the two cities, and Alexandria more particularly, flourished precisely under and through the Roman government, and had much more reason to thank it than to play the Fronde. The attitude of the Alexandrians to their Hellenic rulers is attested by the long series of nicknames, in part still used at the present day, for which the royal Ptolemies without exception were indebted to the public of their capital. The Emperor Vespasian received from the Alexandrians for the introducing of a tax on salt fish the title of the "sardine-dealer" (Κυβιοσάκτης) ; the Syrian Severus Alexander that of the "chief Rabbin ;" but the emperors came rarely to Egypt, and the distant and foreign rulers offered no genuine butt for this ridicule. In their absence the public bestowed at least on the viceroys the same attention with persevering zeal ; even the prospect of inevitable chastisement was not able to put to silence the often witty and always saucy tongue of these townsmen.[1] Vespasian contented himself in return for that attention shown to him with raising the poll-tax about six farthings, and got for doing so the further name of the "sixfarthing-man ;" but their sayings about Severus Antoninus, the petty ape of Alexander the Great and the favourite of Mother Jocasta, were to cost them more dearly. The spiteful ruler appeared in all friendliness, and allowed the people to keep holiday for him, but then ordered his soldiers to charge into the festal multitude, so

---

[1] Seneca, *ad Helv.* 19, 6 : *loquax et provincia . . . etiam periculosi sales in contumelias praefectorum ingeniosa placent.*

that for days the squares and streets of the great city ran with blood ; in fact, he enjoined the dissolution of the Academy and the transfer of the legion into the city itself—neither of which, it is true, was carried into effect.

Alexan-
drian
tumults.
But while in Antioch, as a rule, the matter did not go beyond sarcasm, the Alexandrian rabble took on the slightest pretext to stones and to cudgels. In street uproar, says an authority, himself Alexandrian, the Egyptians are before all others ; the smallest spark suffices here to kindle a tumult. On account of neglected visits, on account of the confiscation of spoiled provisions, on account of exclusion from a bathing establishment, on account of a dispute between the slave of an Alexandrian of rank and a Roman foot-soldier as to the value or non-value of their respective slippers, the legions were under the necessity of charging among the citizens of Alexandria. It here became apparent that the lower stratum of the Alexandrian population consisted in greater part of natives ; in these riots the Greeks no doubt acted as instigators, as indeed the rhetors, that is, in this case the inciting orators, are expressly mentioned ;[1] but in the further course of the matter the spite and the savageness of the Egyptian proper came into the conflict. The Syrians were cowardly, and as soldiers the Egyptians were so too ; but in a street tumult they were able to develop a courage worthy of a better cause.[2] The Antiochenes delighted in race-horses like the Alexandrians ; but among the latter no chariot race ended without stone-throwing and stabbing. Both cities were affected by the persecution of the Jews under

---

[1] Dio Chrysostom says in his address to the Alexandrians (*Or.* xxxii. p. 663 Reiske) : " Because now (the intelligent) keep in the background and are silent, there spring up among you endless disputes and quarrels and disorderly clamour, and bad and unbridled speeches, accusers, aspersions, trials, a rabble of orators." In the Alexandrian Jew-hunt, which Philo so drastically describes, we see these mob-orators at work.

[2] Dio Cassius, xxxix. 58 : " The Alexandrians do the utmost in all respects as to daring, and speak out everything that occurs to them. In war and its terrors their conduct is cowardly ; but in tumults, which with them are very frequent and very serious, they without scruple come to mortal blows, and for the sake of the success of the moment account their life nothing, nay, they go to their destruction as if the highest things were at stake."

the emperor Gaius ; but in Antioch an earnest word of the
authorities sufficed to put an end to it, while thousands of
human lives fell a sacrifice to the Alexandrian outbreak
instigated by some clowns with a puppet-show. The
Alexandrians, it was said, when a riot arose, gave themselves no peace till they had seen blood. The Roman
officers and soldiers had a difficult position there. " Alexandria," says a reporter of the fourth century, " is entered
by the governors with trembling and despair, for they fear
the justice of the people ; where a governor perpetrates a
wrong, there follows at once the setting of the palace on
fire and stoning." The naive trust in the rectitude of
this procedure marks the stand-point of the writer, who
belonged to this " people." The continuation of this
Lynch-system, dishonouring alike to the government and to
the nation, is furnished by what is called Church-history,
in the murder of the bishop Georgius, alike obnoxious to
the heathen and to the orthodox, and of his associates
under Julian, and that of the fair freethinker Hypatia by
the pious community of Bishop Cyril under Theodosius
II. These Alexandrian tumults were more malicious,
more incalculable, more violent than the Antiochene, but
just like these, not dangerous either for the stability of
the empire or even for the individual government. Mis-
chievous and ill-disposed lads are very inconvenient, but
not more than inconvenient, in the household as in the
commonwealth.

In religious matters also the two cities had an analogous
position. To the worship of the land, as the native population retained it in Syria as in Egypt, the Alexandrians
as well as the Antiochenes were disinclined in its original
shape. But the Lagids, as well as the Seleucids, were
careful of disturbing the foundations of the old religion of
the country; and, merely amalgamating the older national
views and sacred rites with the pliant forms of the Greek
Olympus, they Hellenised these outwardly in some measure;
they introduced, *e.g.* the Greek god of the lower world
Pluto into the native worship, under the hitherto little
mentioned name of the Egyptian god Sarapis, and then

Alexan-
drian
worship.

gradually transferred to this the old Osiris worship.[1]
Thus the genuinely Egyptian Isis and the pseudo-Egypt-
ian Sarapis played in Alexandria nearly the same part as
Belus and Elagabalus in Syria, and made their way in a
similar manner with these, although less strongly and with
more vehement opposition, by degrees into the Occidental
worship of the imperial period. As regards the immorality
developed on occasion of these religious usages and festi-
vals, and the unchastity approved and stimulated by
priestly blessing, neither city was in a position to upbraid
the other.

Down to a late time the old cultus retained its
firmest stronghold in the pious land of Egypt.[2]　The

[1] The "pious Egyptians" offered
resistance, as Macrobius, *Sat.* i. 7,
14, reports, but *tyrannide Ptolemae-
orum pressi hos quoque deos* (Sarapis
and Saturnus) *in cultum recipere Alex-
andrinorum more, apud quos potis-
simum colebantur, coacti sunt.* As
they thus had to present bloody sacrifices, which was against their ritual,
they did not admit these gods, at least
into the towns ; *nullum Aegypti oppidum intra muros suos aut Saturni
aut Sarapis fanum recepit.*

[2] The often-quoted anonymous
author of a description of the empire
from the time of Constantius, a good
heathen, praises Egypt particularly on
account of its exemplary piety : "Nowhere are the mysteries of the gods so
well celebrated as there from of old
and still at present." Indeed, he
adds, some were of opinion that the
Chaldaeans—he means the Syrian
cultus—worshipped the gods better ;
but he held to what he had seen
with his own eyes—" Here there are
shrines of all sorts and magnificently
adorned temples, and there are found
numbers of sacristans and priests and
prophets and believers and excellent
theologians, and all goes on in its
order ; you find the altars everywhere
blazing with flame and the priests
with their fillets and the incense-
vessels with deliciously fragrant
spices." Nearly from the same time

(not from Hadrian), and evidently
also from a well-informed hand, proceeds another more malicious description (*vita Saturnini*, 8) : "He
who in Egypt worships Sarapis is also
a Christian, and those who call themselves Christian bishops likewise adore
Sarapis ; every grand Rabbi of the
Jews, every Samaritan, every Christian
clergyman is there at the same time
a sorcerer, a prophet, a quack (*aliptes*).
Even when the patriarch comes to
Egypt some demand that he pray to
Sarapis, others that he pray to Christ."
This diatribe is certainly connected
with the circumstance that the Christians declared the Egyptian god to be
the Joseph of the Bible, the son of
Sara, and rightfully carrying the
bushel. The position of the Egyptian
orthodox party is apprehended in a
more earnest spirit by the author,
belonging presumably to the third
century, of the Dialogue of the Gods,
preserved in a Latin translation among
the writings attributed to Appuleius,
in which the thrice-greatest Hermes
announces things future to Asklepios :
"Thou knowest withal, Asklepios,
that Egypt is a counterpart of heaven,
or, to speak more correctly, a trans-
migration and descent of the whole
heavenly administration and activity ;
indeed, to speak still more correctly,
our fatherland is the temple of the
whole universe. And yet a time will

restoration of the old faith, as well scientifically in the philosophy annexed to it as practically in the repelling of the attacks directed by the Christians against Polytheism, and in the revival of the heathen temple-worship and the heathen divination, had its true centre in Alexandria. Then, when the new faith conquered this stronghold also, the character of the country remained nevertheless true to itself; Syria was the cradle of Christianity, Egypt was the cradle of monachism. Of the significance and the position of the Jewish body, in which the two cities likewise resembled each other, we have already spoken in another connection (p. 163). Immigrants called by the government into the land like the Hellenes, the Jews were doubtless inferior to these and were liable to poll-tax like the Egyptians, but accounted themselves, and were accounted, more than these. Their number amounted under Vespasian to a million, about the eighth part of the whole population of Egypt, and, like the Hellenes, they dwelt chiefly in the capital, of the five wards of which two were Jewish. In acknowledged independence, in repute, culture, and wealth, the body of Alexandrian Jews was even before the destruction of Jerusalem the first in the world ; and in consequence of this a good part of the last act of the Jewish tragedy, as has been already set forth, was played out on Egyptian soil.

Alexandria and Antioch were pre-eminently seats of wealthy merchants and manufacturers ; but in Antioch

The learned world of Alexandria.

set in, when it would appear as if Egypt had vainly with pious mind in diligent service cherished the divine, when all sacred worship of the gods will be without result and a failure. For the deity will betake itself back into heaven, Egypt will be forsaken, and the land, which was the seat of religious worships, will be deprived of the presence of divine power and left to its own resources. Then will this consecrated land, the abode of shrines and temples, be densely filled with graves and corpses. O Egypt, Egypt, of thy worships only rumours will be preserved, and even these will seem incredible to thy coming generations, only words will be preserved on the stones to tell of thy pious deeds, and Egypt will be inhabited by the Scythian or Indian or other such from the neighbouring barbarian land. New rights will be introduced, a new law, nothing holy, nothing religious, nothing worthy of heaven and of the celestials will be heard or in spirit believed. A painful separation of the gods from men sets in ; only the bad angels remain there, to mingle among mankind " (according to Bernays's translation, *Ges. Abh.* i. 330).

there was wanting the seaport and its belongings, and, however stirring matters were on the streets there, they bore no comparison with the life and doings of the Alexandrian artisans and sailors. On the other hand, for enjoyment of life, dramatic spectacles, dining, pleasures of love, Antioch had more to offer than the city in which " no one went idle." Literary amusements, linking themselves especially with the rhetorical exhibitions—such as we sketched in the description of Asia Minor—fell into the background in Egypt,[1] doubtless more amidst the pressure of the affairs of the day than through the influence of the numerous and well-paid *savants* living in Alexandria, and in great part natives of it. These men of the Museum, of whom we shall have to speak further on, did not prominently affect the character of the town as a whole, especially if they did their duty in diligent work. But the Alexandrian physicians were regarded as the best in the whole empire ; it is true that Egypt was no less the genuine home of quacks and of secret remedies, and of that strange civilised form of the "shepherd-medicine," in which pious simplicity and speculating deceit draped themselves in the mantle of science. Of the thrice-greatest Hermes we have already made mention (p. 261) ; the Alexandrian Sarapis, too, wrought more marvellous cures in antiquity than any one of his colleagues, and he infected even the practical emperor Vespasian, so that he too healed the blind and lame, but only in Alexandria.

Scholar-life in Alexandria.

Although the place which Alexandria occupies, or seems to occupy, in the intellectual and literary development of the later Greece and of Occidental culture generally cannot be fitly estimated in a description of the

---

[1] When the Romans ask from the famous rhetor Proaeresios (end of the third and beginning of the fourth century) one of his disciples for a professorial chair, he sends to them Eusebius from Alexandria ; "as respects rhetoric," it is said of the latter (Eunapius, *Proaer.* p. 92 Boiss.), "it is enough to say that he was an Egyptian ; for this people, no doubt, pursues versemaking passionately, but earnest oratory (ὁ σπουδαῖος Ἑρμῆς) is not at home among them." The remarkable resumption of Greek poetry in Egypt, to which, *e.g.* the epic of Nonnus belongs, lies beyond the bounds of our narrative.

local circumstances of Egypt, but only in the delineation
of this development itself, the Alexandrian scholarship
and its continuation under the Roman government are
too remarkable a phenomenon not to have its general
position touched on in this connection.   We have already
observed (p. 126) that the blending of the Oriental and
the Hellenic intellectual world was accomplished pre-
eminently in Egypt alongside of Syria ; and if the new
faith which was to conquer the West issued from Syria,
the science homogeneous with it—that philosophy which,
alongside of and beyond the human mind, acknowledges
and proclaims the supra-mundane God and the divine
revelation—came pre-eminently from Egypt : probably
already the new Pythagoreanism, certainly the philo-
sophic Neo-Judaism—of which we have formerly spoken
(p. 170)—as well as the new Platonism, whose founder,
the Egyptian Plotinus, was likewise already mentioned
(p. 126).   Upon this interpenetration of Hellenic and
Oriental elements, that was carried out especially in
Alexandria, mainly depends the fact, that—as falls to be
set forth more fully in surveying the state of things in
Italy—the Hellenism there in the earlier imperial period
bears pre-eminently an Egyptian form.   As the old-new
wisdoms associated with Pythagoras, Moses, Plato, penetrated from Alexandria into Italy, so Isis and her
belongings played the first part in the easy, fashionable
piety, which the Roman poets of the Augustan age and
the Pompeian temples from that of Claudius exhibit to
us.   Art as practised in Egypt prevails in the Campanian
frescoes of the same epoch, as in the Tiburtine villa of
Hadrian.   In keeping with this is the position which
Alexandrian erudition occupies in the intellectual life of
the imperial period.   Outwardly it is based on the care
of the state for intellectual interests, and would with
more warrant link itself to the name of Alexander than
to that of Alexandria ; it is the realisation of the thought
that in a certain stage of civilisation art and science
must be supported and promoted by the authority and
the resources of the state, the consistent sequel of the

brilliant moment in the world's history which placed
Alexander and Aristotle side by side. It is not our
intention here to inquire how in this mighty conception
truth and error, the injuring and elevating of the intellectual
life, became mingled, nor is the scanty after-bloom
of the divine singing and of the high thinking of the
free Hellenes to be once more placed side by side with
the rank and yet also noble produce of the later
collecting, investigating, and arranging. If the institutions which sprang from this thought could not, or, what
was worse, could only apparently, renew to the Greek
nation what was irrecoverably lost, they granted to it
on the still free arena of the intellectual world the only
possible compensation, and that, too, a glorious one. For
us the local circumstances are above all to be taken into
account. Artificial gardens are in some measure independent of the soil, and it is not otherwise with these
scientific institutions ; only that they from their nature
are directed towards the courts. Material support may be
imparted to them otherwise ; but more important than
this is the favour of the highest circles, which swells their
sails, and the connections, which, meeting together in the
great centres, replenish and extend these circles of science.
In the better time of the monarchies of Alexander there
were as many such centres as there were states, and that
of the Lagid court was only the most highly-esteemed
among them. The Roman republic had brought the
others one after another into its power, and had set aside
with the courts also the scientific institutes and circles
belonging to them. The fact that the future Augustus,
when he did away with the last of these courts, allowed
the learned institutes connected with it to subsist, is a
genuine, and not the worst, indication of the changed
times. The more energetic and higher Philhellenism
of the government of the Caesars was distinguished to
its advantage from that of the republic by the fact that
it not merely allowed Greek literati to earn money in
Rome, but viewed and treated the great guardianship of
Greek science as a part of the sovereignty of Alexander.

No doubt, as in this regeneration of the empire as a whole, the building-plan was grander than the building. The royally patented and pensioned Muses, whom the Lagids had called to Alexandria, did not disdain to accept the like payments also from the Romans; and the imperial munificence was not inferior to the earlier regal. The fund for the library of Alexandria and the fund for free places for philosophers, poets, physicians, and scholars of all sorts,[1] as well as the immunities granted to these, were not diminished by Augustus, and were increased by the emperor Claudius—with the injunction, indeed, that the new Claudian academicians should have the Greek historical works of the singular founder publicly read year by year in their sittings. With the first library in the world Alexandria retained at the same time, through the whole imperial period, a certain primacy of scientific work, until Islam burnt the library and killed the ancient civilisation. It was not merely the opportunity thus offered, but at the same time the old tradition and turn of mind of these Hellenes, which preserved for the city that precedence, as indeed among the scholars the native Alexandrians are prominent in number and importance. In this epoch numerous and respectable labours of erudition, particularly philological and physical, proceeded from the circle of the *savants* "of the Museum," as they entitled themselves, like the Parisians "of the Institute"; but the literary importance, which the Alexandrian and the Pergamene court-science and court-art

---

[1] A "Homeric poet" ἐκ Μουσείου is ready to sing the praise of Memnon in four Homeric verses, without adding a word of his own (*C. I. Gr.* 4748). Hadrian makes an Alexandrian poet a member in reward for a loyal epigram (Athenaeus, xv. p. 677 *e*). Examples of rhetors from Hadrian's time may be seen in Philostratus, *Vit. Soph.* i. 22, 3 c. 25, 3. A φιλόσοφος ἀπὸ Μουσείου in Halicarnassus (*Bull. de corr. Hell.* iv. 405). At a later period, when the circus was everything, we find a noted pugilist figuring (so to say) as an honorary member of the philosophical class (inscription from Rome, *C. I. Gr.* 5914 : νεωκόρος τοῦ μεγά-[λου Σαράπιδ]ος καὶ τῶν ἐν τῷ Μουσείῳ [σειτου]μένων ἀτελῶν φιλοσόφων ; comp. *ib.* 4724, and Firmicus Maternus, *de errore prof. rel.* 13, 3). Οἱ ἐν Ἐφέσῳ ἀπὸ τοῦ Μουσείου ἰατροί (Wood, *Ephesus, inscriptions from tombs*, n. 7), a society of Ephesian physicians, have relation doubtless to the Museum at Alexandria, but were hardly members of it ; they were rather trained in it.

had in the better epoch of Hellenism for the whole
Hellenic and Hellenising world, was never even remotely
attached to the Romano-Alexandrian. The cause lay
not in the want of talents or in other accidents, least of
all in the fact that places in the Museum were bestowed
by the emperor sometimes according to gifts and always
according to favour, and the government dealt with them
quite as with the horse of the knight and the posts of
officials of the household ; the case was not otherwise
at the older courts. Court-philosophers and court-poets
remained in Alexandria, but not the court ; it was here
very clearly apparent that the main matter was not
pensions and rewards, but the contact—quickening for
both sides—of great political and great scientific work.
The latter doubtless presented itself for the new monarchy
and brought its consequences with it ; but the place for
it was not Alexandria : this bloom of political development justly belonged to the Latins and to the Latin
capital. The Augustan poetry and Augustan science
attained, under similar circumstances, to a similar important and pleasing development with that attained by
the Hellenistic at the court of the Pergamenes and the
earlier Ptolemies. Even in the Greek circle, so far as the
Roman government operated upon it in the sense of the
Lagids, this development was linked more with Rome than
with Alexandria. It is true that the Greek libraries of
the capital were not equal to the Alexandrian, and there
was no institute in Rome comparable to the Alexandrian
Museum. But a position at the Roman libraries opened
up relations to the court. The professorship of Greek
rhetoric in the capital, instituted by Vespasian, filled up
and paid for by the government, gave to its holder,
although he was not an officer of the household in the
same sense as the imperial librarian, a similar position,
and was regarded, doubtless on that account, as the chief
professorial chair of the empire.[1] But, above all, the
office of imperial cabinet secretary in its Greek division
was the most esteemed and the most influential position

---

[1] 'Ο ἄνω θρόνος in Philostratus, *Vit. Soph.* ii. 10, 5.

to which a Greek man of letters could at all attain.
Transference from the Alexandrian academy to such an
office in the capital was demonstrably promotion.[1] Even
apart from all which the Greek literati otherwise found
in Rome alone, the court-positions and the court-offices
were enough to draw the most distinguished of them
thither rather than to the Egyptian "free table." The
learned Alexandria of this time became a sort of
"jointure" of Greek science, worthy of respect and useful,
but of no pervading influence on the great movement of
culture or mis-culture of the imperial period ; the places
in the Museum were, as was reasonable, not seldom
bestowed on scholars of note from abroad, and for the
institution itself the books of the library were of more
account than the burgesses of the great commercial and
manufacturing city.

The military circumstances of Egypt laid down, just
as in Syria, a double task for the troops there ; the protection of the south frontier and of the east coast, which
indeed may not be remotely compared with that required
for the line of the Euphrates, and the maintenance of
internal order in the country as in the capital. The
Roman garrison consisted, apart from the ships stationed
at Alexandria and on the Nile, which seem chiefly to
have served for the control of the customs, under Augustus
of three legions, along with the not numerous auxiliary
troops belonging to them, about 20,000 men. This was
about half as many as he destined for all the Asiatic
provinces—which was in keeping with the importance
of this province for the new monarchy. But the occupy-

The
Egyptian
army.

[1] Examples are Chaeremon, the
teacher of Nero, previously installed
in Alexandria (Suidas, Διονύσιος' Ἀλεξ-
ανδρεύς ; comp. Zeller, *Hermes*, xi.
430, and above, p. 259) ; Dionysius,
son of Glaucus, at first in Alexandria,
successor of Chaeremon, then from
Nero down to Trajan librarian in
Rome and imperial cabinet secretary
(Suidas, *l.c.*) ; L. Julius Vestinus
under Hadrian, who, even after the
presidency of the Museum, filled the
same positions as Dionysius in Rome
(p. 248 note), known also as a philological author.

ing force was probably even under Augustus himself
diminished about a third, and then under Domitian by
about a further third. At first two legions were stationed
outside of the capital ; but the main camp, and soon the
only one, lay before its gates, where Caesar the younger
had fought out the last battle with Antonius, in the
suburb called accordingly Nicopolis. The suburb had its
own amphitheatre and its own imperial popular festival,
and was quite independently organised ; so that for a
time the public amusements of Alexandria were thrown
into the shade by those of Nicopolis. The immediate
watching of the frontier fell to the auxiliaries. The same
causes therefore which relaxed discipline in Syria—the
police-character of their primary task and their immediate
contact with the great capital—came into play also for
the Egyptian troops ; to which fell to be added, that the
bad custom of allowing to the soldiers with the standards
a married life or at any rate a substitute for it, and of
filling up the troop from their camp-children, had for
long been naturalised among the Macedonian soldiers of
the Ptolemies, and soon prevailed also among the Romans,
at least up to a certain degree. Accordingly, the Egyptian corps, in which the Occidentals served still more
rarely than in the other armies of the East, and which
was recruited in great part from the citizens and the
camp of Alexandria, appears to have been among all the
sections of the army the least esteemed ; as indeed also
the officers of this legion, as was already observed, were
inferior in rank to those of the rest.

The properly military task of the Egyptian troops
was closely connected with the measures for the elevation
of Egyptian commerce. It will be convenient to take
the two together, and to set forth in connection, in the
first instance, the relations to the continental neighbours
in the south, and then those to Arabia and India.

Aethiopia.　　　Egypt reaches on the south, as was already remarked,
as far as the barrier which the last cataract, not far from
Syene (Assouan), opposes to navigation. Beyond Syene
begins the stock of the Kesch, as the Egyptians call them,

or, as the Greeks translated it, the dark-coloured, the
Aethiopians, probably akin to the Axomites to be afterwards mentioned, and, although perhaps sprung from the
same root as the Egyptians, at any rate confronting them
in historical development as a foreign people. Further
to the south follow the Nahsiu of the Egyptians, that is,
the Blacks, the Nubians of the Greek, the modern Negroes.
The kings of Egypt had in better times extended their
rule far into the interior, or at least emigrant Egyptians
had established for themselves here dominions of their
own ; the written monuments of the Pharaonic government go as far as above the third cataract to Dongola,
where Nabata (near Nûri) seems to have been the
centre of their settlements ; and considerably further up
the stream, some six days' journey to the north of Khar-
toum, near Shendy, in Sennaar, in the neighbourhood
of the long forgotten Aethiopian town Meroe, are found
groups of temples and pyramids, although destitute of
writing. When Egypt became Roman, all this development of power was long a matter of the past ; and beyond
Syene there ruled an Aethiopian stock under queens, who
regularly bore the name or the title Candace,[1] and resided
in that once Egyptian Nabata in Dongola ; a people at
a low stage of civilisation, predominantly shepherds, in a
position to bring into the field an army of 30,000, but
equipped with shields of ox-hides, armed mostly not with
swords, but with axes or lances and iron-mounted clubs,
predatory neighbours, not a match for the Romans in
combat. In the year 730 or 731 these invaded the 24, 23.
Roman territory—as they asserted, because the presidents
of the nearest nomes had injured them—as the Romans
thought, because the Egyptian troops were then to a
large extent occupied in Arabia, and they hoped to be
able to plunder with immunity. In reality they over- War with
came the three cohorts who covered the frontier, and queen
dragged away the inhabitants from the nearest Egyptian Candace.

---

[1] The eunuch of Candace, who
reads in Isaiah (Acts of the Apostles,
viii. 27) is well known ; and a
Candace reigned also in Nero's time
(Plinius, *H. N.* vi. 29, 182).

districts—Philae, Elephantine, Syene—as slaves, and the statues of the emperor, which they found there, as tokens of victory. But the governor, who just then took up the administration of the province, Gaius Petronius, speedily requited the attack ; with 10,000 infantry and 800 cavalry he not merely drove them out, but followed them along the Nile into their own land, defeated them emphatically at Pselchis (Dekkeh), and stormed their stronghold Premis (Ibrim), as well as the capital itself, which he destroyed. It is true that the queen, a brave woman, renewed the attack next year and attempted to storm Premis, where a Roman garrison had been left ; but Petronius brought seasonable relief, and so the Aethiopian queen determined to send envoys and to sue for peace. The emperor not merely granted it, but gave orders to evacuate the subject territory, and rejected the proposal of his governor to make the vanquished tributary. This event, otherwise not important, is remarkable in so far as just then the definite resolution of the Roman government became apparent, to maintain absolutely the Nile valley as far as the river was navigable, but not at all to contemplate taking possession of the wide districts on the upper Nile. Only the tract from Syene, where under Augustus the frontier-troops were stationed, as far as Hiera Sycaminos (Maharraka), the so-called Twelve-mile-land (Δωδεκάσχοινος), while never organised as a nome and never viewed as a part of Egypt, was yet regarded as belonging to the empire ; and at least under Domitian the posts were even advanced as far as Hiera Sycaminos.[1]

---

[1] That the imperial frontier reached to Hiera Sycaminos, is evident for the second century from Ptolemaeus, v. 5, 74, for the time of Diocletian from the Itineraries, which carry the imperial roads thus far. In the *Notitia dignitatum*, a century later, the posts again do not reach beyond Syene, Philae, Elephantine. In the tract from Philae to Hiera Sycaminos, the Dodecaschoinos of Herodotus (ii. 29) temple-tribute appears to have been raised already in early times for the Isis of Philae always common to the Egyptians and Aethiopians ; but Greek inscriptions from the Lagid period have not been found here, whereas numerous dated ones occur from the Roman period, the oldest from the time of Augustus (Pselchis, 2 A.D. ; *C. I. Gr.* n. 5086), and of Tiberius (*ib.* 26 A.D., n. 5104, 33 A.D., n. 5101), the most recent from that of Philippus (Kardassi, 248 A.D., n. 5010). These do not prove absolutely that the place where the inscription was found belonged to the empire ; but that of a land-measuring

On that footing substantially the matter remained. The Oriental expedition planned by Nero (p. 61) was certainly intended to embrace Aethiopia ; but it did not go beyond the preliminary reconnoitring of the country by Roman officers as far as Meroe. The relations with the neighbours on the Egyptian southern frontier down to the middle of the third century must have been on the whole of a peaceful kind, although there were not wanting minor quarrels with that Candace and with her successors, who appear to have maintained their position for a considerable time, and subsequently perhaps with other tribes, that attained to ascendency beyond the imperial bounds.

It was not till the empire was unhinged in the period of Valerian and Gallienus, that the neighbours broke over this boundary. We have already mentioned (p. 250) that the Blemyes settled in the mountains on the south-east frontier, formerly obeying the Aethiopians, a barbarous people of revolting savageness, who even centuries later had not abandoned human sacrifices, advanced at this epoch independently against Egypt, and by an understanding with the Palmyrenes occupied a good part of upper Egypt, and held it for a series of years. The vigorous emperor Probus drove them out ; but the inroads once begun did not cease,[1] and the emperor Diocletian resolved to draw

The Blemyes.

---

soldier of the year 33 (n. 5101), and that of a *praesidium* of the year 84 (Talmis, n. 5042 f.), as well as numerous others certainly presuppose it. Beyond the frontier indicated no similar stone has ever been found ; for the remarkable inscription of the *regina* (*C. I. L.* iii. 83), found at Messaurât, to the south of Shendy (16° 25′ lat., 5 leagues to the south of the ruins of Naga), the most southern of all known Latin inscriptions, now in the Berlin Museum, has been set up, not by a Roman subject, but presumably by an envoy of an African queen, who was returning from Rome, and who spoke Latin perhaps only in order to show that he had been in Rome.

[1] The *tropaea Niliaca, sub quibus*

Aethiops et Indus intremuit, in an oration probably held in the year 296 (Paneg. v. 5), apply to such a *rencontre*, not to the Egyptian insurrection ; and the oration of the year 289 speaks of attacks of the Blemyes (Paneg. iii. 17). — Procopius, *Bell. Pers.* i. 19, reports the cession of the "Twelve-mile-territory" to the Nubians. It is mentioned as standing under the dominion, not of the Nubians, but of the Blemyes by Olympiodorus, *fr.* 37, Müll. and the inscription of Silko, *C. I. Gr.* 5072. The fragment recently brought to light of a Greek heroic poem as to the victory of a late Roman emperor over the Blemyes is referred by Bücheler (*Rhein. Mus.* xxxix. 279 f.) to that of Marcianus, in the year 451 (comp. Priscus, *fr.* 27).

back the frontier. The narrow "Twelve-mile-land" demanded a strong garrison, and brought in little to the state. The Nubians, who roamed in the Libyan desert, and were constantly visiting in particular the great Oasis, agreed to give up their old abodes and to settle in this region, which was formally ceded to them; at the same time fixed annual payments were made to them as well as to their eastern neighbours the Blemyes, nominally in order to compensate them for guarding the frontier, in reality beyond doubt to buy off their plundering expeditions, which nevertheless of course did not cease. It was a retrograde step—the first, since Egypt became Roman.

Aethiopian commercial traffic.

Of the mercantile intercourse on this frontier little is reported from antiquity. As the cataracts of the upper Nile closed the direct route by water, the traffic between the interior of Africa and the Egyptians, particularly the trade in ivory, was carried on in the Roman period more by way of the Abyssinian ports than along the Nile; but it was not wanting also in this direction.[1] The Aethiopians who dwelt in numbers beside the Egyptians on the island of Philae were evidently mostly merchants, and the border-peace that here prevailed must have contributed its part to the prosperity of the frontier-towns of upper Egypt and of Egyptian trade generally.

The Egyptian east coast and general commerce.

The east coast of Egypt presented to the development of general traffic a problem difficult of solution. The thoroughly desolate and rocky shore was incapable of culture proper, and in ancient as in later times a desert.[2] On the other hand the two seas, eminently important for the development of culture in the ancient world, the Mediterranean and the Red or Indian, approach each other most closely at the two most northern extremities of the latter, the Persian and the Arabian gulfs; the former receives into it the Euphrates, which in the middle of its course comes near to the Mediterranean; the latter is only a few days' march distant from the Nile, which

[1] Juvenal (xi. 124) mentions the elephant's teeth, *quos mittit porta Syenes*.

[2] According to the mode in which Ptolemy (iv. 5, 14, 15) treats of this coast, it seems, just like the "Twelve-mile-land," to have lain outside of the division into nomes.

flows into the same sea. Hence in ancient times the commercial intercourse between the East and the West took preponderantly either the direction along the Euphrates to the Syrian and Arabian coast, or it made its way from the east coast of Egypt to the Nile. The traffic routes from the Euphrates were older than those by way of the Nile ; but the latter had the advantage of the stream being better for navigation and of the shorter land-transport ; the getting rid of the latter by preparing an artificial water-route was in the case of the Euphrates excluded, in that of Egypt found in ancient as in modern times difficult doubtless, but not impossible. Accordingly nature itself prescribed to the land of Egypt to connect the east coast with the course of the Nile and the northern coast by land or water routes ; and the beginnings of such structures go back to the time of those native rulers who first opened up Egypt to foreign countries and to traffic on a great scale. Following in the traces apparently of older structures of the great rulers of Egypt, Sethi I. and Rhamses II., king Necho, the son of Psammetichus (610-594 B.C.) began the building of a canal, which, branching off from the Nile in the neighbourhood of Cairo, was to furnish a water-communication with the bitter lakes near Ismailia, and through these with the Red Sea, without being able, however, to complete the work. That in this he had in view not merely the control of the Arabian Gulf and the commercial traffic with the Arabians, but already brought within his horizon the Persian and the Indian seas, and the more remote East, is probable, for this reason, that the same ruler suggested the only circumnavigation of Africa executed in antiquity. Beyond doubt thus thought king Darius I., the lord of Persia as well as of Egypt ; he completed the canal, but, as his memorial-stones found on the spot mention, he caused it to be filled up again, probably because his engineers feared that the water of the sea, admitted into the canal, would overflow the fields of Egypt.

The sea route to India.

The rivalry of the Lagids and the Seleucids, which dominated the policy of the post-Alexandrine period generally, was at the same time a contest between the Euphrates and the Nile. The former was in possession, the latter the pretender ; and in the better time of the Lagids the peaceful offensive was pursued with great energy. Not only was that canal undertaken by Necho and Darius, now named the "river of Ptolemaeus," opened for the first time to navigation by the second Ptolemy Philadelphus († 247 B.C.) ; but comprehensive harbour-structures were carried out at the points of the difficult east coast that were best fitted for the security of the ships and for the connection with the Nile. Above all, this was

The Egyptian eastern ports.

done at the mouth of the canal leading to the Nile, at the townships of Arsinoe, Cleopatris, Clysma, all three in the region of the present Suez. Further downward, besides several minor structures, arose the two important emporia, Myos Hormos, somewhat above the present Kosêr, and Berenice, in the land of the Trogodytes, nearly in the same latitude with Syene on the Nile as well as with the Arabian port Leuce Come, the former distant six or seven, the latter eleven days' march from the town Coptos, near which the Nile bends farthest to the eastward, and connected with this chief emporium on the Nile by roads constructed across the desert and provided with large cisterns. The goods traffic of the time of the Ptolemies probably went less through the canal than by these land routes to Coptos.

Abyssinia.

Beyond that Berenice, in the land of the Trogodytes, the Egypt proper of the Lagids did not extend. The settlements lying farther to the south, Ptolemais " for the chase" below Suâkim, and the southmost township of the Lagid kingdom, the subsequent Adulis, at that time perhaps named " Berenice the Golden" or " near Saba," Zula not far from the present Massowah, by far the best harbour on all this coast, were not more than coast-forts and had no communication by land with Egypt. These remote settlements were beyond doubt either lost or voluntarily abandoned under the later Lagids, and at the epoch when the Roman rule began, the Trogodytic Berenice was on the coast, like Syene in the interior, the limit of the empire.

In this region, never occupied or early evacuated by the
Egyptians there was formed—whether at the end of the
Lagid epoch or in the first age of the empire—an independent state of some extent and importance, that of the Axomites,[1] corresponding to the modern Habesh. It derives
its name from the town Axômis, the modern Axum, situated
in the heart of this Alpine country eight days' journey from
the sea, in the modern country of Tigre ; the already-mentioned best emporium on this coast, Adulis in the bay of
Massowah, served it as a port. The original population
of the kingdom of Axômis, of which tolerably pure remnants still maintain themselves at the present day in
individual tracts of the interior, belonged from its language,
the Agau, to the same Hamitic cycle with the modern
Bego, Sali, Dankali, Somali, Galla ; to the Egyptian
population this linguistic circle seems related in a similar
way as the Greeks to the Celts and Slaves, so that here
doubtless for research an affinity may subsist, but for
their historical existence rather nothing but contrast. But
before our knowledge of this country so much as begins,
superior Semitic immigrants belonging to the Himyaritic
stocks of southern Arabia must have crossed the narrow
gulf of the sea and rendered their language as well as
their writing at home there. The old written language of
Habesh, extinct in popular use since the seventeenth century, the Ge'ez, or as it is for the most part erroneously

---

[1] Our best information as to the
kingdom of Axomis is obtained from
a stone erected by one of its kings,
beyond doubt in the better period of
the empire, at Adulis (*C. I. Gr.*
5127 *b*), a sort of writing commemorative of the deeds of this apparent
empire-founder in the style of that of
Darius at Persepolis, or that of Augustus at Ancyra, and fixed on the
king's throne, before which down to
the sixth century criminals were executed. The skilful disquisition of
Dillmann (*Abh. der Berliner Akademie*, 1877, p. 195 f.), explains as
much of it as is explicable. From the
Roman standpoint it is to be noted
that the king does not name the
Romans, but clearly has in view their
imperial frontiers when he subdues
the Tangaites μέχρι τῶν τῆς Αἰγύπτου
ὁρίων, and constructs a road ἀπὸ τῶν
τῆς ἐμῆς βασιλείας τόπων μέχρι Αἰγύπτου, and further, names as the northern limit of his Arabian expedition
Leuce Come, the last Roman station
on the Arabian west coast. Hence
it follows further, that this inscription
is more recent than the Periplus of the
Red Sea written under Vespasian ;
for according to this (c. 5) the king of
Axomis rules ἀπὸ τῶν Μοσχοφάγων
μέχρι τῆς ἄλλης Βαρβαρίας, and this is
to be understood exclusively, since he
names in c. 2 the τύραννοι of the
Moscophages, and likewise remarks

termed, the Aethiopic,[1] is purely Semitic,[2] and the still living dialects, the Amhara and the Tigriña, are so also in the main, only disturbed by the influence of the older Agau.

Its extent and development.

As to the beginnings of this commonwealth no tradition has been preserved. At the end of Nero's time, and perhaps already long before, the king of the Axomites ruled on the African coast nearly from Suâkim to the Straits of Bab el Mandeb. Some time afterwards—the epoch cannot be more precisely defined—we find him as a frontier-neighbour of the Romans on the southern border of Egypt, and on the other coast of the Arabian Gulf in warlike activity in the territory intervening between the Roman possession and that of the Sabaeans, and so coming into immediate contact towards the north with the Roman territory also in Arabia ; commanding, moreover, the African coast outside of the Gulf perhaps as far as Cape Guardafui. How far his territory of Axômis extended inland is not clear ; Aethiopia, that is, Sennaar and Dongola, at least in the earlier imperial period, hardly belonged to it ; perhaps at this time the kingdom of Nabata may have subsisted alongside of the Axomitic. Where the Axomites meet us, we find them at a comparatively advanced stage of development. Under Augustus the Egyptian commercial traffic increased not less with these African harbours than with India. The king had the command not merely of an army, but, as his very relations to Arabia presuppose, also of a fleet. A Greek merchant, who was present in Adulis, terms king

---

in c. 14, that beyond the Straits of Bab el Mandeb there is no "king," but only "tyrants." Thus at that time the Axomitic kingdom did not reach to the Roman frontier, but only to somewhere about Ptolemais "of the chase," just as in the other direction not to Cape Guardafui, but only as far as the Straits of Bab el Mandeb. Nor does the Periplus speak of possessions of the king of Axomis on the Arabian coast, although he on several occasions mentions the dynasts there.

[1] The name of the Aethiopians was associated in the better period with the country on the Upper Nile, especially with the kingdoms of Meroe and Nabata (p. 275), and so with the region which we now call Nubia. In later antiquity, for example by Procopius, the designation is referred to the state of Axomis, and hence in more recent times is frequently employed for Abyssinia.

[2] Hence the legend that the Axomites were Syrians settled by Alexander in Africa, and still spoke Syrian (Philostorgius, *Hist. Eccl.* iii. 6).

Zoskales, who ruled in Vespasian's time in Axômis, an upright man and acquainted with Greek writing ; one of his successors has set up on the spot a memorial-writing composed in current Greek which told his deeds to the foreigners ; he even names himself in it a son of Ares —which title the kings of the Axomites retained down to the fourth century—and dedicates the throne, which bears that memorial inscription, to Zeus, to Ares, and to Poseidon. Already in Zoskales's time that foreigner names Adulis a well organised emporium ; his successors compelled the roving tribes of the Arabian coast to keep peace by land and by sea, and restored a land communication from their capital to the Roman frontier, which, considering the nature of this district primarily left dependent on communication by sea, was not to be esteemed of slight account. Under Vespasian brass pieces, which were divided according to need, served the natives instead of money, and Roman coin circulated only among the strangers settled in Adulis ; in the later imperial period the kings themselves coined. The Axomite ruler withal calls himself king of kings, and no trace points to Roman clientship ; he practises coining in gold, which the Romans did not allow, not merely in their own territory but even within the range of their power. There was hardly another land in the imperial period beyond the Romano-Hellenic bounds which had appropriated to itself Hellenic habits with equal independence and to an equal extent as the state of Habesh. That in the course of time the popular language, indigenous or rather naturalised from Arabia, gained the upper hand and dispossessed the Greek, is probably traceable partly to Arabian influence, partly to that of Christianity and the revival connected with it of the popular dialects, such as we found also in Syria and Egypt ; and it does not exclude the view that the Greek language in Axomis and Adulis in the first and second centuries of our era had a similar position to what it had in Syria and Egypt, so far as it is allowable to compare small and great.

Of political relations of the Romans to the state of

Rome and the Ax-omites.

Axomis hardly anything is mentioned from the first three centuries of our era, to which our narrative is confined. With the rest of Egypt they took possession also of the ports of the east coast down to the remote Trogodytic Berenice, which on account of that remoteness was in the Roman period placed under a commandant of its own.[1] Of extending their territory into the inhospitable and worthless mountains along the coast there was never any thought ; nor can the sparse population, standing at the lowest stage of development, in the immediately adjoining region have ever given serious trouble to the Romans. As little did the Caesars attempt, as the early Lagids had done, to possess themselves of the emporia of the Axomitic coast. There is express mention only of the fact that envoys of the Axomite kings negotiated with the emperor Aurelian. But this very silence, as well as the formerly indicated independent position of the ruler,[2] leads to the inference that here the recognised frontier was permanently respected on both sides, and that a relation of good neighbourhood subsisted, which proved advantageous to the interests of peace and especially of Egyptian commerce. That the latter, especially the important traffic in ivory, in which Adulis was the chief entrepot for the interior of Africa, was carried on predominantly from Egypt and in Egyptian vessels, cannot—considering the superior civilisation of Egypt—be subject to any doubt even as regards the Lagid period ; and in Roman times this traffic probably only increased in amount, without undergoing further change.

The west coast of Arabia.

Far more important for Egypt and the Roman empire generally than the traffic with the African south was that

---

[1] This is the *praefectus praesidiorum et montis Beronices* (*C. I. L.* ix. 3083), *praefectus montis Berenicidis* (Orelli, 3881), *praefectus Bernicidis* (*C. I. L.* x. 1129), an officer of equestrian rank, analogous to those adduced above (p. 249), as stationed in Alexandria.

[2] The letter, which the emperor Constantius in the year 356 directs to Aeizanas, the king of the Axomites at that time, is that of one ruler to another on an equal footing ; he requests his friendly and neighbourly assistance against the spread of the Athanasian heresy, and for the deposition and delivering up of an Axomitic clergyman suspected of it. The fellowship of culture comes here into the more definite prominence, as the Christian invokes against the Christian the arm of the heathen.

which subsisted with Arabia and the coasts situated farther
to the east. The Arabian peninsula remained aloof from
the sphere of Hellenic culture. It would possibly have
been otherwise had king Alexander lived a year longer ;
death swept him away amidst the preparations for sailing
round and occupying the already-explored south coast of
Arabia, setting out from the Persian Gulf. But the voyage
which the great king had not been able to enter on was
never undertaken by any Greek after him. From the
most remote times, on the other hand, a lively intercourse
had taken place between the two coasts of the Arabian
Gulf over its moderately broad waters. In the Egyptian
accounts from the time of the Pharaohs the voyages to
the land of Punt, and the spoils thence brought home in
frankincense, ebony, emeralds, leopards' skins, play an
important part. It has been already (p. 148) mentioned
that subsequently the northern portion of the Arabian
west coast belonged to the territory of the Nabataeans,
and with this came into the power of the Romans. This
was a desolate beach ;[1] only the emporium Leuce Come,
the last town of the Nabataeans and so far also of the
Roman empire, was not merely in maritime intercourse

---

[1] Inland lay the primeval Teimâ, the son of Ishmael of Genesis, enumerated by the Assyrian king Tiglath-Pilesar in the eighth century before Christ among his conquests, named by the prophet Jeremiah together with Sidon, around which gather in a remarkable way Assyrian, Egyptian, Arabian relations, the further unfolding of which, after bold travellers have opened up the place, we may await from Oriental research. In Teimâ itself Euting recently found Aramaic inscriptions of the oldest epoch (Nöldeke, *Sitzungsberichte der Berliner Akademie*, 1884, p. 813 f.) From the not far distant place Medâin-Sâlih (Hijr) proceed certain coins modelled after the Attic, which in part replace the owl of Pallas by that image of a god which the Egyptians designate as Besa the lord of Punt, *i.e.* of Arabia (Erman, *Zeitschrift für Numismatik*, ix. 296 f.) We have already mentioned the Nabataean inscriptions just found there (p. 148, note 3). Not far from thence, near 'Ola (el-Ally) inscriptions have been found, which correspond in the writing and in the names of gods and kings to those of the South-Arabian Minaeans, and show that these had a considerable station here, sixty days' journey from their home, but on the frankincense - route mentioned by Eratosthenes, from Minaea to Aelana ; and alongside of these others of a cognate but not identical south. Arabian stock (D. H. Müller in the *Berichte der Wiener Akademie* of 17th December 1884). The Minaean inscriptions belong beyond doubt to the pre-Roman period. As on the annexation of the Nabataean kingdom by Trajan these districts were abandoned (p. 152), from that time another south-Arabian tribe may have ruled there.

with Berenice lying opposite, but was also the starting-point of the caravan-route leading to Petra and thence to the ports of southern Syria, and in so far, one of the centres of the traffic between the East and the West (p. 151). The adjoining regions on the south, northward and southward of the modern Mecca, corresponded in their natural character to the opposite Trogodyte country, and were, like this, neither politically nor commercially of importance, nor yet apparently united under one sceptre, but occupied by roving tribes. But at the south end of this gulf was the home of the only Arabic stock, which attained to greater importance in the pre-Islamic period. The Greeks and the Romans name these Arabs in the earlier period after the people most prominent at that time Sabaeans, in later times after another tribe usually Homerites, as, according to the new Arabic form of the latter name, now for the most part Himjarites.

The state of the Homerites.

The development of this remarkable people had reached a considerable stage long before the beginning of the Roman rule over Egypt.[1] Its native seat, the Arabia Felix of the ancients, the region of Mocha and Aden, is surrounded by a narrow plain along the shore intensely hot and desolate, but the healthy and temperate interior of Yemen and Hadramaut produces on the mountain-slopes and in the valleys a luxuriant vegetation, and the numerous mountain-waters permit in many respects with careful management a garden-like cultivation. We have even at the present day an expressive testimony to the rich and peculiar civilisation of this region in the remains

---

[1] The accounts connected with the trade in frankincense in Theophrastus († 287 B.C.; *Hist. plant.* ix. 4) and more fully in Eratosthenes († 194 B.C.); in Strabo (xvi. 4, 2, p. 768) of the four great tribes of the Minaeans (Mamali Theophr.?) with the capital Carna; the Sabaeans (Saba Theophr.) with the capital Mariaba; the Catta-banes (Kitibaena Theophr.) with the capital Tamna; the Chatramotitae (Hadramyta Theophr.) with the capital Sabata, describe the very circle out of which the Homerite kingdom developed itself, and indicate its beginnings. The much sought for Minaei are now pointed out with certainty in Ma'in in the interior above Marib and Hadramaut, where hundreds of inscriptions have been found, and have yielded already no fewer than twenty-six kings' names. Mariaba is even now named Marib. The region Chatramotitis or Chatramitis is Hadramaut.

of city-walls and towers, of useful buildings, particularly
aqueducts, and temples covered with inscriptions, which
completely confirm the description of ancient authors as
to the magnificence and luxury of this region ; the
Arabian geographers have written books concerning the
strongholds and castles of the numerous petty princes of
Yemen. Famous are the ruins of the mighty embankment which once in the valley of Mariaba dammed up
the river Dana and rendered it possible to water the fields
upwards,[1] and from the bursting of which, and the migration alleged to have been thereby occasioned of the inhabitants of Yemen to the north the Arabs for long counted
their years. But above all this district was one of the
original seats of wholesale traffic by land and by sea, not
merely because its productions, frankincense, precious
stones, gum, cassia, aloes, senna, myrrh, and numerous
other drugs called for export, but also because this Semitic
stock was, just like that of the Phoenicians, formed by its
whole character for commerce ; Strabo says, just like the
more recent travellers, that the Arabs are all traders and
merchants. The coining of silver is here old and peculiar ;
the coins were at first modelled after Athenian dies, and

---

[1] The remarkable remains of this
structure, executed with the greatest
precision and skill, are described by
Arnaud (*Journal Asiatique*, 7 série,
tome 3, for the year 1874, p. 3 f.
with plans ; comp. Ritter, *Erdkunde*,
xii. 861). On the two sides of the
embankment, which has now almost
wholly disappeared, stand respectively
two stone structures built of square
blocks, of conical almost cylindrical
form, between which a narrow opening is found for the water flowing out
of the basin ; at least on the one
side a canal lined with pebbles leads
it to this outlet. It was once closed
with planks placed one above another,
which could be individually removed,
to carry the water away as might be
needed. The one of those stone
cylinders bears the following inscription (according to the translation, not
indeed quite certain in all its details,

of D. H. Müller, *Wiener Sitzungsberichte*, vol. xcvii. 1880, p. 965):
"Jata'amar the glorious, son of Sa-
mah'alî the sublime, prince of Saba,
caused the Balap (mountain) to be
pierced (and erected) the sluice-struc-
ture named Rahab for easier irrigation." We have no secure basis for
fixing the chronological place of this
and numerous other royal names of
the Sabaean inscriptions. The Assyrian king Sargon says in the Khor-
sabad inscription, after he has narrated
the vanquishing of the king of Gaza,
Hanno, in the year 716 B.C.: "I
received the tribute of Pharaoh the
king of Egypt, of Shamsiya the queen
of Arabia, and of Ithamara the Sabaean ; gold, herbs of the eastern land,
slaves, horses, and camels" (Müller,
l. c. p. 988 ; Duncker, *Gesch. des
Alterthums*, ii.⁵ p. 327).

later after Roman coins of Augustus, but on an independent, probably Babylonian basis.[1]   From the land of these
Arabians the original frankincense-routes led across the
desert to the marts on the Arabian gulf, Aelana and the
already-mentioned Leuce Come, and the emporia of Syria,
Petra and Gaza ;[2] these routes of the land-traffic, which
along with those of the Euphrates and the Nile, furnish
the means of intercourse between East and West from the
earliest times, may be conjectured to be the proper basis
of the prosperity of Yemen.   But the sea-traffic likewise
soon became associated with them ; the great mart for
this was Adane, the modern Aden.   From this the goods
went by water, certainly in the main in Arabian ships,
either to those same marts on the Arabian gulf and so to
the Syrian ports, or to Berenice and Myos Hormos, and
from thence to Coptos and Alexandria.   We have already
stated that the same Arabs likewise at a very early time
possessed themselves of the opposite coast, and transplanted their language, their writing and their civilisation to Habesh.   If Coptos, the Nile-emporium for the
eastern traffic, had just as many Arab as Egyptian
inhabitants, if even the emerald-mines above Berenice
(near Jebel Zebâra) were worked by the Arabs, this shows
that in the Lagid state itself they had the trade up to
a certain degree in their hands ; and its passive attitude
in respect to the traffic on the Arabian Sea, whither at
most an expedition against the pirates was once undertaken,[3] is the more readily intelligible, if a state well

---

[1] Sallet in the *Berliner Zeitschrift
für Numismatik*, viii. 243 ; J. H.
Mordtmann in the *Wiener Numism.
Zeitschrift*, xii. 289.

[2] Pliny, *H. N.* xii. 14, 65,
reckons the cost of a camel's load of
frankincense by the land-route from
the Arabian coast to Gaza at 688
denarii (= £30).   " Along the whole
tract fodder and water and shelter
and various custom-dues have to be
paid for ; then the priests demand
certain shares and the scribes of the
kings ; moreover the guards and the
halberdiers and the body-guards and

servants have their exactions ; to
which our imperial dues fall to be
added." In the case of the water-trans-
port these intervening expenses were
not incurred.

[3] The chastising of the pirates is
reported by Agatharchides in Diodorus, iii. 43, and Strabo, xvi. 4, 18,
p. 777.   But Ezion-Geber in Palestine, on the Elanitic gulf, ἡ νῦν Βερε-
νίκη καλεῖται (Josephus, *Arch.* viii. 6,
4), was so called certainly not from
an Egyptian princess (Droysen, *Hellenismus*, iii. 2, 349), but from the
Jewess of Titus.

organised and powerful at sea ruled these waters. We meet the Arabs of Yemen even beyond their own sea. Adane remained down to the Roman imperial times a mart of traffic on the one hand with India, on the other with Egypt, and, in spite of its own unfavourable position on the treeless shore, rose to such prosperity that the name of "Arabia Felix" had primary reference to this town. The dominion, which in our days the Imam of Muscat in the south-east of the peninsula has exercised over the islands of Socotra and Zanzibar and the African east coast from Cape Guardafui southward, pertained in Vespasian's time " from of old " to the princes of Arabia ; the island of Dioscorides, that same Socotra, belonged then to the king of Hadramaut, Azania, that is, the coast of Somal and further southward, to one of the viceroys of his western neighbour, the king of the Homerites. The southernmost station on the east African coast which the Egyptian merchants knew of, Rhapta in the region of Zanzibar, was leased from this sheikh by the merchants of Muza, that is nearly the modern Mocha, " and they send thither their trading-ships, mostly manned by Arabian captains and sailors, who are accustomed to deal and are often connected by marriage with the natives, and are acquainted with the localities and the languages of the country." The cultivation of the soil and industry went hand in hand with commerce ; in the houses of rank in India, Arabian wine was drunk alongside of the Falernian from Italy and the Laodicene from Syria ; and the lances and shoemakers' awls, which the natives of the coast of Malabar purchased from the foreign traders were manu-factured at Muza. Thus this region, which moreover sold much and bought little, became one of the richest in the world.

How far its political development kept pace with the economic, cannot be determined for the pre-Roman and earlier imperial period ; only this much seems to result both from the accounts of the Occidentals and from the native inscriptions, that this south-west point of Arabia was divided among several independent rulers with territories of moderate size. There subsisted in that quarter, alongside of the more prominent Sabaeans and Homerites, the already-mentioned Chatramotitae in the Hadramaut, and northward in the interior the Minaeans, all under princes of their own.

With reference to the Arabians of Yemen the Romans pursued the very opposite policy to that adopted towards the Axomites. Augustus, for whom the non-enlargement of the empire was the starting-point of the imperial government, and who allowed almost all the plans of conquest of his father and master to drop, made an exception of the south-west coast of Arabia, and here took aggressive measures of his own free will. This was done on account of the position which this group of peoples occupied at that time in Indo-Egyptian commercial intercourse. In order to bring the province of his dominions, which was politically and financially the most important, up, in an economic aspect, to the level which his predecessors in rule had neglected to establish or had allowed to decline, he needed above all to obtain inter-communication between Arabia and India on the one hand and Europe on the other. The Nile-route for long competed successfully with the Arabian and the Euphrates routes; but Egypt played in this respect, as we saw, a subordinate part at least under the later Lagids. A trading rivalry subsisted not with the Axomites, but doubtless with the Arabians; if the Egyptian traffic was to be converted from a passive into an active, from indirect into direct, the Arabs had to be overthrown; and this it was that Augustus desired and the Roman government in some measure achieved.

25.
Expedi-
tion of
Gallus.

In the sixth year of his reign in Egypt (end of 729) Augustus despatched a fleet, fitted out expressly for this expedition, of 80 warships and 130 transports, and the half of the Egyptian army, a corps of 10,000 men, without reckoning the contingents of the two nearest client kings, the Nabataean Obodas and the Jew Herod, against the states of Yemen, in order either to subjugate or at least to ruin them,[1] while at the same time the treasures there accumulated were certainly taken into account. But the enterprise completely miscarried, and that from the incapacity of the leader, the governor of Egypt at the time, Gaius Aelius Gallus.[2] Since the occupation and the possession of the desolate coast from Leuce Come downwards to the frontier of the enemy's territory was of no consequence at all, it was necessary that the expedition should be directed immediately against the latter, and that the army should be conducted from the most southern Egyptian port at once into Arabia Felix.[3] Instead of this

---

[1] This (προσοικειοῦσθαι τούτους — τοὺς Ἄραβας — ἢ καταστρέφεσθαι : Strabo, xvi. 4, 22 p. 780; εἰ μὴ ὁ Συλλαῖος αὐτὸν—τὸν Γάλλον—προὐδίδου, κἂν κατεστρέψατο τὴν Εὐδαίμονα πᾶσαν : ib. xvii. 1, 53, p. 819) was the proper aim of the expedition, although also the hope of spoil, just at that time very welcome for the treasury, is expressly mentioned.

[2] The account of Strabo (xvi. 4, 22 f., p. 780) as to the Arabian expedition of his "friend" Gallus (φίλος ἡμῖν καὶ ἑταῖρος, Strabo, ii. 5, 12, p. 118), in whose train he travelled in Egypt, is indeed trustworthy and honest, like all his accounts, but evidently accepted from this friend without any criticism. The battle in which 10,000 of the enemy and two Romans fell, and the total number of the fallen in this campaign, which is seven, are self-condemned ; but not better is the attempt to devolve the want of success on the Nabataean vizier Syllaeos by means of a "treachery," such as is familiar with defeated generals. Certainly the latter was so far fitted for a scapegoat, as he some years afterwards was on the instigation of Herod brought to trial before Augustus, condemned and executed (Josephus, *Arch.* xvi. 10) ; but although we possess the report of the agent who managed this matter for Herod in Rome, there is not a word to be found in it of this betrayal. That Syllaeos should have had the design of first destroying the Arabians by means of the Romans, and then of

destroying the latter themselves, as Strabo "thinks," is, looking to the position of the client-states of Rome, quite irrational. It might rather be thought that Syllaeos was averse to the expedition, because the commercial traffic through the Nabataean land might be injured by it. But to accuse the Arabian minister of treachery because the Roman transports were not fitted for navigating the Arabian coast, or because the Roman army was compelled to carry water with it on camels, to eat durra and dates instead of bread and flesh, and butter instead of oil ; to bring forward the deceitfulness of the guidance as an excuse for the fact that 180 days were employed for the forward march over a distance overtaken on the return march in 60 days ; and lastly, to criticise the quite correct remark of Syllaeos that a march by land from Arsinoe to Leuce Come was impracticable, by saying that a caravan route went thence to Petra, only shows what a Roman of rank was able to make a Greek man of letters believe.

[3] The sharpest criticism of the campaign is furnished by the detailed account of the Egyptian merchant as to the state of the Arabian coast from Leuce Come (el-Haura to the north of Janbô, the port of Medina) to the Catacecaumene island (Jebel Taik near Lôhaia). "Different peoples inhabit it, who speak languages partly somewhat different, partly wholly so. The inhabitants of the coast live in

the fleet was got ready at the most northerly, that of Arsinoe (Suez), and the army was landed at Leuce Come, just as if it were the object to prolong as much as possible the voyage of the fleet and the march of the troops. Besides, the war-vessels were superfluous, since the Arabians possessed no war-fleet, the Roman sailors were unacquainted with the navigation on the Arabian coast, and the transports, although specially built for this expedition, were unsuited for their purpose. The pilots had difficulty in finding their way between the shallows and the rocks, and even the voyage in Roman waters from Arsinoe to Leuce Come cost many vessels and men. Here the winter was passed ; in the spring of 730 the campaign in the enemy's country began. The Arabians offered no hindrance, but Arabia undoubtedly did so. Wherever the double axes and the slings and bows came into collision with the pilum and the sword, the natives dispersed like chaff before the wind ; but the diseases, which are endemic in the country, scurvy, leprosy, palsy, decimated the soldiers worse than the most bloody battle, and all the more as the general did not know how to move rapidly forward the unwieldy mass of his army. Nevertheless the Roman army arrived in front of the walls of Mariaba, the capital of the Sabaeans first affected by the attack. But, as the inhabitants closed the gates of their powerful walls still standing,[1] and offered

pens like the ' fish-eaters' on the opposite coast " (these pens he describes, c. 2, as isolated and built into the clefts of the rocks), " those of the interior in villages and pastoral companies ; they are ill-disposed men speaking two languages, who plunder the seafarers that drift out of their course and drag the shipwrecked into slavery. For that reason they are constantly hunted by the viceroys and chief kings of Arabia ; they are called Kanraites (or Kassanites). In general navigation on all this coast is dangerous, the shore is without harbours and inaccessible, with a troublesome surf, rocky and in general very bad. Therefore, when we sail into these waters, we keep to the middle and hasten to get to the Arabian territory at the island

Catacecaumene ; from thence onward the inhabitants are hospitable, and we meet with numerous flocks of sheep and camels." The same region between the Roman and the Homeritic frontiers, and the same state of things are in the view of the Axomite king, when he writes : πέραν δὲ τῆς ἐρυθρᾶς θαλάσσης οἰκοῦντας 'Αρραβίτας καὶ Κιναιδοκολπίτας (comp. Ptolemaeus vi. 7, 20), στράτευμα ναυτικὸν καὶ πεζικὸν διαπεμψάμενος καὶ ὑποτάξας αὐτῶν τοὺς βασιλέας, φόρους τῆς γῆς τελεῖν ἐκέλευσα καὶ ὁδεύεσθαι μετ᾽ εἰρήνης καὶ πλέεσθαι, ἀπό τε Λευκῆς κώμης ἕως τῶν Σαβαίων χώρας ἐπολέμησα.

[1] These walls, built of rubble, form a circle of a mile in diameter. They are described by Arnaud (*l.c.*, comp. p. 287, note 1).

energetic resistance, the Roman general despaired of solving
the problem proposed to him ; and, after he had lain six
days in front of the town, he entered on his retreat, which
the Arabians hardly disturbed in earnest, and which was
accomplished with comparative rapidity under the pressure
of need, although with a severe loss in men.

It was a bad miscarriage ; but Augustus did not abandon
the conquest of Arabia.   It has already been related
(p. 39) that the journey to the East, which the crown-
prince Gaius entered upon in the year 753, was to
terminate at Arabia ; it was this time contemplated after
the subjugation of Armenia to reach, in concert with the
Parthian government or in case of need after the overthrow of their armies, the mouth of the Euphrates, and
from thence to take the sea-route which the admiral
Nearchus had once explored for Alexander, towards
Arabia Felix.[1]   These hopes ended in another but not
less unfortunate way, through the Parthian arrow which
struck the crown-prince before the walls of Artageira.
With him was buried the plan of Arabian conquest for
all the future.   The great peninsula remained through the
whole imperial period—apart from the stripes of coast on
the north and north-west—in possession of that freedom
from which Islam, the executioner of Hellenism, was in
its own time to issue.

But the Arabian commerce was at all events broken
down partly by the measures, to be explained further on,
of the Roman government for protecting the Egyptian
navigation, partly by a blow struck by the Romans against
the chief mart of Indo-Arabian traffic.   Whether under
Augustus himself, possibly among the preparations for the
invasion to be carried out by Gaius, or under one of his
immediate successors, a Roman fleet appeared before
Adane and destroyed the place ; in Vespasian's time it

Marginal notes: Further enterprises
against the
Arabs.
1.

Injury to
Arabian
commerce.

---

[1] That the Oriental expedition of
Gaius had Arabia as its goal, is stated
expressly by Pliny (particularly *H. N.*
xii. 14, 55, 56 ; comp. ii. 67, 168 ;
vi. 27, 141, c. 28, 160 ; xxxii. 1,
10).   That it was to set out from the
mouth of the Euphrates, follows from
the fact that the expedition to Armenia
and the negotiations with the Parthians
preceded it.   For that reason the
Collectanea of Juba as to the impending expedition were based upon the
reports of the generals of Alexander
as to their exploring of Arabia.

was a village, and its prosperity was gone. We know only the naked fact,[1] but it speaks for itself. A counterpart to the destruction of Corinth and of Carthage by the republic, it, like these, attained its end, and secured for the Romano-Egyptian trade the supremacy in the Arabian gulf and in the Indian Sea.

Later fortunes of the Homerites.

The prosperity, however, of the blessed land of Yemen was too firmly founded to succumb to this blow ; politically it was even perhaps in this epoch only that it more

---

[1] Our only information as to this remarkable expedition has been preserved to us by the Egyptian captain, who about the year 75 has described his voyage on the coasts of the Red Sea. He knows (c. 26) the Adane of later writers, the modern Aden, as a village on the coast (κώμη παραθαλάσσιος), which belongs to the realm of Charibael, king of the Homerites, but was earlier a flourishing town, and was so termed (εὐδαίμων δ᾽ ἐπεκλήθη πρότερον οὖσα πόλις) because before the institution of the direct Indo-Egyptian traffic this place served as a mart : νῦν δὲ οὐ πρὸ πολλοῦ τῶν ἡμετέρων χρόνων Καῖσαρ αὐτὴν κατεστρέψατο. The last word can here only mean "destroy," not, as more frequently, "subdue," because the conversion of the town into a village is to be accounted for. For Καῖσαρ Schwanbeck (Rhein. Mus. neue Folge, vii. 353) has proposed Χαριβαήλ, C. Müller Ἰλασάρ (on account of Strabo, xvi. 4, 21, p. 782) : neither is possible —not the latter, because this Arabian dynast ruled in a far remote district and could not possibly be presumed as well known ; not the former, because Charibael was a contemporary of the writer, and there is here reported an incident which occurred before his time. We shall not take offence at the tradition, if we reflect what interest the Romans must have had in setting aside the Arabian mart between India and Egypt, and in bringing about direct intercourse. That the Roman accounts are silent as to this occurrence is in keeping with their habit ; the expedition, which beyond doubt was exe-

cuted by an Egyptian fleet and simply consisted in the destruction of a presumably defenceless place on the coast, would not be from a military point of view of any importance ; about great commercial dealings the annalists gave themselves no concern, and generally the incidents in Egypt came still less than those in the other imperial provinces to the knowledge of the senate and therewith of the annalists. The naked designation Καῖσαρ, in which from the nature of the case the ruler then reigning is excluded, is probably to be explained from the circumstance that the reporting captain, while knowing doubtless the fact of the destruction by the Romans, knew not its date or author.—It is possible that to this the notice in Pliny (H. N. ii. 67, 168) is to be referred : maiorem (oceani) partem et orientis victoriae magni Alexandri lustravere usque in Arabicum sinum, in quo res gerente C. Caesare Aug. f. signa navium ex Hispaniensibus naufragiis feruntur agnita. Gaius did not reach Arabia (Plin. H. N. vi. 28, 160) ; but during the Armenian expedition a Roman squadron may very well have been conducted by one of his sub-commanders to this coast, in order to pave the way for the main expedition. That silence reigns elsewhere respecting it cannot surprise us. The Arabian expedition of Gaius had been so solemnly announced and then abandoned in so wretched a way, that loyal reporters had every reason to obliterate a fact which could not well be mentioned without also reporting the failure of the greater plan.

energetically rallied its resources.   Mariaba, at the time
when the arms of Gallus failed before its walls, was
perhaps no more than the capital of the Sabaeans ; but
already at that time the tribe of the Homerites, whose
capital Sapphar lay somewhat to the south of Mariaba,
also in the interior, was the strongest in Arabia Felix.
A century later we find the two united under a king of
the Homerites and of the Sabaeans reigning in Sapphar,
whose rule extends as far as Mocha and Aden, and, as was
already said, over the island of Socotra and the coast of
Somal and Zanzibar ; and at least from this time we may
speak of a kingdom of the Homerites.   The desert northwards from Mariaba as far as the Roman frontier did not
at that time belong to it, and was under no regular
authority at all ;[1] the principalities of the Minaei and
of the Chatramotitae continued also to be under sovereigns
of their own.   The eastern half of Arabia formed constantly a part of the Persian empire (p. 13), and never was
under the sceptre of the rulers of Arabia Felix.   Even
now therefore the bounds were narrow and probably
remained so ; little is known as to the further development of affairs.[2]   In the middle of the fourth century the
kingdom of the Homerites was united with that of the
Axomites, and was governed from Axomis[3]—a subjection,
however, which was subsequently broken off again.   The

---

[1] The Egyptian merchant distinguishes the ἔνθεσμος βασιλεύς of
the Homerites (c. 23) sharply from
the τύραννοι, the tribal chiefs sometimes subordinate to him, sometimes
independent (c. 14), and as sharply
distinguishes these organised conditions from the lawlessness of the
inhabitants of the desert (c. 2).   If
Strabo and Tacitus had had eyes as
open for these things as that practical
man had, we should have known somewhat more of antiquity.

[2] The war of Macrinus against the
Arabes eudaemones (*vita*, 12) and their
envoys sent to Aurelian (*vita*, 33),
who are named along with those of
the Axomites, would prove their continued independence at that time, if

these statements could be depended
on.

[3] The king names himself, about
the year 356 (p. 284, note 2), in a
document (*C. I. Gr.* 5128) βασιλεὺς
'Αξωμιτῶν καὶ Ὁμηριτῶν καὶ τοῦ 'Ραειδὰν
(castle in Sapphar, the capital of the
Homerites ; Dillmann, *Abh. der Berl.
Akad.* 1878, p. 207) . . . καὶ Σαβα
ειτῶν καὶ τοῦ Σιλεῆ (castle in Mariaba,
the capital of the Sabaeans ; Dillmann, *l.c.*).   With this agrees the
contemporary mission of envoys *ad
gentem Axumitarum et Homerita[rum]*
(*C. Th.* xii. 12, 2).   As to the later
state of things comp. especially Non-
nosus (*fr. hist. Gr.* iv. p. 179, Müll.)
and Procopius, *Hist. Pers.* i. 20.

kingdom of the Homerites, as well as the united Axomitico-Homeritic, stood as independent states in intercourse and treaty with Rome during the later imperial period.

In commerce and navigation the Arabians of the south-west of the peninsula occupied, if no longer the place of supremacy, at any rate a prominent position throughout the whole imperial period. After the destruction of Adane, Muza became the commercial metropolis of this region. The representation formerly given is still in the main appropriate for the time of Vespasian. The place is described to us at this time as exclusively Arabian, inhabited by shipowners and sailors, and full of stirring mercantile life ; the Muzaites with their own ships navigate the whole east coast of Africa and the west coast of India, and not merely carry the goods of their own country, but bring also the purple stuffs and gold embroideries prepared according to Oriental taste in the workshops of the West, and the fine wines of Syria and Italy, to the Orientals, and in turn to the western lands the precious wares of the East. In frankincense and other aromatics Muza and the emporium of the neighbouring kingdom of Hadramaut, Cane to the east of Aden, must always have retained a sort of practical monopoly ; these wares, used in antiquity very much more than at present, were produced not only on the southern coast of Arabia, but also on the African coast from Adulis as far as the "promontory of spices," Cape Guardafui, and from thence the merchants of Muza fetched them and brought them into general commerce. On the already mentioned island of Dioscorides there was a joint trading settlement of the three great seafaring nations of these seas, the Hellenes, that is, the Egyptians, the Arabians, and the Indians. But of relations to Hellenism, such as we found on the opposite coast among the Axomites (p. 283), we meet no trace in the land of Yemen ; if the coinage is determined by Occidental types (p. 287 f.), these were current throughout the East. Otherwise writing and language and the exercise of art, so far as we are able to judge, developed themselves here just as independently as commerce and navigation ; and certainly this co-operated in producing the result that the Axomites, while they subjected to themselves the Homerites in a political point of view, subsequently reverted from the Hellenic path into the Arabic (p. 283).

In the same spirit as for the relations to southern Africa and to the Arabian states, and in a more pleasing way, provision was made in Egypt itself for the routes of commercial intercourse, in the first instance by Augustus, and beyond doubt by all its intelligent rulers. The system of roads and harbours established by the earlier Ptolemies in the footsteps of the Pharaohs had, like the whole administration, fallen into sad decay amidst the troubles of the last Lagid period. It is not expressly mentioned that Augustus put again into order the land and water routes and the ports of Egypt ; but that it was done, is none the less certain. Coptos remained through the whole imperial period the rendezvous of this traffic.[1] From a recently found document we gather that in the first imperial period the two routes leading thence to the ports of Myos Hormos and of Berenice were repaired by the Roman soldiers and provided at the fitting places with the requisite cisterns.[2] The canal which connected the Red Sea with the Nile, and so with the Mediterranean Sea, was in the Roman period only of secondary rank, employed chiefly perhaps for the conveyance of blocks of marble and porphyry from the Egyptian east coast to the Mediterranean ; but it remained navigable throughout the imperial period. The emperor Trajan renewed and probably also enlarged it—perhaps it was he who placed it in communication with the still undivided Nile near

Land-routes and harbours in Egypt.

---

[1] Aristides (*Or.* xlviii. p. 485, Dind.) names Coptos the Indian and Arabian entrepôt. In the romance of Xenophon the Ephesian (iv. 1), the Syrian robbers resort to Coptos, "for there a number of merchants pass through, who are travelling to Aethiopia and India."

[2] Hadrian later constructed "the new Hadrian's road" which led from his town Antinoopolis near Hermopolis, probably through the desert to Myos Hormos, and from Myos Hormos along the sea to Berenice, and provided it with cisterns, stations ($\sigma\tau\alpha\theta\mu\omega\iota$), and forts (inscription in *Revue Archéol.* N. S. xxi. year 1870, p. 314). However there is no mention of this road subsequently, and it is a question whether it continued to subsist.

Babylon (not far from Cairo), and thereby increased its water-supply—and assigned to it the name of Trajan's or the emperor's river (*Augustus amnis*), from which in later times this part of Egypt was named (*Augustamnica*).

Piracy.

Augustus exerted himself also in earnest for the suppression of piracy on the Red and Indian Seas; the Egyptians long even after his death thanked him, that through his efforts piratical sails disappeared from the sea and gave way to trading vessels. No doubt what was done in that respect was far from enough. The facts that, while the government doubtless from time to time set naval squadrons to work in these waters, it did not station there a standing war-fleet; and that the Roman merchantmen regularly took archers on board in the Indian Sea to repel the attacks of the pirates, would be surprising, if a comparative indifference to the insecurity of the sea had not everywhere—here, as well as on the Belgian coast, and on those of the Black Sea—clung like a hereditary sin to the Roman imperial government or rather to the Roman government in general. It is true that the governments of Axomis and of Sapphar were called by their geographical position still more than the Romans at Berenice and Leuce Come to check piracy, and it may be partly due to this consideration that the Romans remained, upon the whole, on a good understanding with these weaker but indispensable neighbours.

Growth of the Egyptian active traffic to the East.

We have formerly shown that the maritime intercourse of Egypt, if not with Adulis (p. 284), at any rate with Arabia and India at the epoch which immediately preceded the Roman rule, was not carried on in the main through the medium of Egyptians. It was only through the Romans that Egypt obtained the great maritime traffic to the East. "Not twenty Egyptian ships in the year," says a contemporary of Augustus, "ventured forth under the Ptolemies from the Arabian gulf; now 120 merchantmen annually sail to India from the port of Myos Hormos alone." The commercial gain, which the Roman merchant had been obliged hitherto to share with the Persian or Arabian intermediary, flowed to him in all

its extent after the opening up of direct communication
with the more remote East.   This result was probably
brought about in the first instance by the circumstance
that the Egyptian ports were, if not directly barred, at
any rate practically closed, by differential custom-dues
against Arabian and Indian transports ;[1] only by the
hypothesis of such a navigation-act in favour of their
own shipping could this sudden revolution of commercial
relations be explained.   But the traffic was not merely
violently transformed from a passive into an active one ; it
was also absolutely increased, partly in consequence of the
increased inquiry in the West for the wares of the East,
partly at the expense of the other routes of traffic through
Arabia and Syria.   For the Arabian and Indian commerce
with the West the route by way of Egypt more and more
proved itself the shortest and the cheapest.   The frankincense, which in the olden time went in great part by the
land-route through the interior of Arabia to Gaza (p. 288,
note 2), came afterwards for the most part by water through
Egypt.   The Indian traffic received a new impulse about
the time of Nero, when a skilled and courageous Egyptian
captain, Hippalus, ventured, instead of making his way
along the long stretch of coast, to steer from the mouth of
the Arabian Gulf directly through the open sea for India ;
he knew the monsoon, which thenceforth the mariners, who
traversed this route after him, named the Hippalus.   Thenceforth the voyage was not merely materially shortened, but
was less exposed to the land and sea pirates.   To what
extent the secure state of peace and the increasing luxury

[1] This is nowhere expressly said,
but it is clearly evident from the
Periplus of the Egyptian.   He
speaks at numerous places of the intercourse of the non-Roman Africa
with Arabia (c. 7, 8), and conversely
of the Arabians with the non-Roman
Africa (c. 17, 21, 31 ; and after him
Ptolemaeus, i. 17, 6), and with Persia
(c. 27, 33), and India (c. 21, 27,
49) ; as also of that of the Persians
with India (c. 36), as well as of the
Indian merchantmen with the non-
Roman Africa (c. 14, 31, 32), and
with Persia (c. 36) and Arabia (c. 32).
But there is not a word indicating
that these foreign merchants came to
Berenice, Myos Hormos, or Leuce
Come ; indeed, when he remarks with
reference to the most important mart
of all this circle of traffic, Muza, that
these merchants sail with their own
ships to the African coast outside of
the Straits of Bab El Mandeb (for
that is for him τὸ πέραν), and to India,
Egypt cannot possibly be absent by
accident.

raised the consumption of Oriental wares in the West, may
be discerned in some measure from the complaints, which
were in the time of Vespasian loudly expressed, regarding
the enormous sums which went out of the empire for that
purpose.   The whole amount of the purchase-money
annually paid to the Arabians and the Indians is estimated
by Pliny at 100,000,000 sesterces ($=£1,100,000$), for
Arabia alone at 55,000,000 sesterces ($=£600,000$), of
which, it is true, a part was covered by the export of goods.
The Arabians and the Indians bought doubtless the metals
of the West, iron, copper, lead, tin, arsenic, the Egyptian
articles mentioned formerly (p. 254), wine, purple, gold and
silver plate, also precious stones, corals, saffron, balm ; but
they had always far more to offer to foreign luxury than
to receive for their own.   Hence the Roman gold and
silver money went in considerable quantities to the great
Arabian and Indian emporia.   In India it had already
under Vespasian so naturalised itself that the people there
preferred to use it.   Of this Oriental traffic the greatest
part went to Egypt ; and if the increase of the traffic
benefited the government-chest by the increased receipts
from customs, the need for building ships and making
mercantile voyages of their own elevated the prosperity of
private individuals.

While thus the Roman government limited its rule in
Egypt to the narrow space which is marked off by the
navigableness of the Nile, and, whether in pusillanimity or
in wisdom, at any rate never attempted with consistent
energy to conquer either Nubia or Arabia, it strove as
energetically after the possession of the Arabian and the
Indian wholesale traffic, and attained at least an important
limitation of the competitors.   As the unscrupulous pursuit
of commercial interests characterised the policy of the
republic, so not less did it mark that of the principate,
especially in Egypt.

Romano-
Indian
commercial
intercourse.
We can only determine approximately how far the
direct Roman maritime traffic went towards the East.
In the first instance it took the direction of Barygaza
(Barôtch on the Gulf of Cambay above Bombay), which

great mart must have remained through the whole imperial period the centre of the Egyptio-Indian traffic ;
several places in the peninsula of Gujerat bear among the
Greeks Greek designations, such as Naustathmos and
Theophila.   In the Flavian period, in which the monsoon-
voyages had already become regular, the whole west coast
of India was opened up to the Roman merchants as far
down as the coast of Malabar, the home of the highly-
esteemed and dear-priced pepper, for the sake of which
they visited the ports of Muziris (probably Mangaluru)
and Nelcynda (in Indian doubtless Nilakantha from one
of the surnames of the god Shiva, probably the modern
Nîlêswara); somewhat farther to the south at Kananor
numerous Roman gold coins of the Julio-Claudian epoch
have been found, formerly exchanged against the spices
destined for the Roman kitchens.   On the island Sa-
lice, the Taprobane of the older Greek navigators, the
modern Ceylon, in the time of Claudius a Roman official,
who had been driven thither from the Arabian coast by
storms, had met with a friendly reception from the ruler
of the country, and the latter, astonished, as the report
says, at the uniform weight of the Roman pieces of money
in spite of the diversity of the emperor's heads, had sent
along with the shipwrecked man envoys to his Roman
colleague.   Thereby in the first instance it was only the
sphere of geographical knowledge that was enlarged ; it
was not till later apparently that navigation was extended
as far as that large and productive island, in which on
several occasions Roman coins have come to light.   But
coins are found only by way of exception beyond Cape
Comorin and Ceylon,[1] and hardly has even the coast of
Coromandel and the mouth of the Ganges, to say nothing
of the Further Indian peninsula and China, maintained
regular commercial intercourse with the Occidentals.

[1] In Bâmanghati (district Singh-
bhum) westward from Calcutta, a
great treasure of gold coins of Roman
emperors (Gordian and Constantine
are named), is said to have come to
light (Beglar, in Cunningham's *Archae-*
ological Survey of India, vol. xiii. p.
72); but such an isolated find does
not prove that regular intercourse
extended so far.   In Further India
and China Roman coins have very
seldom been found.

Chinese silk was certainly already at an early period sold regularly to the West, but, as it would appear, exclusively by the land-route, and through the medium partly of the Indians of Barygaza, partly and chiefly of the Parthians ; the Silk-people or the Seres (from the Chinese name of silk Sr) of the Occidentals were the inhabitants of the Tarim-basin to the north-west of Thibet, whither the Chinese brought their silk, and the Parthian intermediaries jealously guarded the traffic thither.   By sea, certainly, individual mariners reached accidentally or by way of exploration at least to the east coast of Further India and perhaps still farther ; the port of Cattigara known to the Romans at the beginning of the second century A.D. was one of the Chinese coast-towns, perhaps Hang-chow-foo at the mouth of the Yang-tse-kiang.   The report of the Chinese annals that in 166 A.D. an embassy of the emperor Antun of Ta-(that is Great) Tsin (Rome) landed in Ji-nan (Tonkin), and thence by the land-route arrived at the capital Lo-yang (or Ho-nan-foo on the middle Hoang-ho) to the emperor Hwan-ti, may warrantably be referred to Rome and to Marcus Antoninus.   This event, however, and what the Chinese authorities mention as to a similar appearance of the Romans in their country in the course of the third century, can hardly be understood of public missions, since as to these Roman statements would hardly have been wanting ; but possibly individual captains may have passed with the Chinese court as messengers of their government.   These connections had perceptible consequences only in so far as the earlier tales regarding the procuring of silk gradually gave way to better knowledge.

CHAPTER XIII.

THE AFRICAN PROVINCES.

NORTH AFRICA, in a physical and ethnographic point of North Africa and the Berber stock. view, stands by itself like an island. Nature has isolated it on all sides, partly by the Atlantic and the Mediterranean Sea, partly by the widely-extended shore, incapable of cultivation, of the Great Syrtis below the modern Fezzan, and, in connection therewith, by the desert, likewise closed against cultivation, which shuts off the steppe-land and the oases of the Sahara to the south. Ethnographically the population of this wide region forms a great family of peoples, distinguished most sharply from the Blacks of the south, but likewise strictly separated from the Egyptians, although perhaps with these there may once have subsisted a primeval fellowship. They call themselves in the Riff near Tangier Amâzigh, in the Sahara Imôshagh, and the same name meets us, referred to particular tribes, on several occasions among the Greeks and Romans, thus as Maxyes at the founding of Carthage (ii. 8), as Mazices in the Roman period at different ii. 7. places of the Mauretanian north coast ; the similar designation that has remained with the scattered remnants proves that this great people has once had a consciousness, and has permanently retained the impression, of the relationship of its members. To the peoples who came into contact with them this relationship was far from clear ; the diversities which prevail among their several parts are not merely at the present day glaring, after in the past thousands of years the mixture with the neighbouring peoples, particularly the Negroes in the south and the

Arabs in the north, has had its effect upon them, but
certainly were as considerable even before these foreign
influences as their extension in space demands. A universally valid expression for the nation as such is wanting
in all other idioms ; even where the name goes beyond
the designation of stock,[1] it yet does not describe the
circle as a whole. That of Libyans, which the Egyptians,
and after their precedent the Greeks use, belongs originally to the most easterly tribes coming into contact with
Egypt, and has always remained specially pertaining to
those of the eastern half. That of Nomades, of Greek
origin, expresses in the first instance only the absence
of settlement, and then in its Roman transformation as
Numidians, has become associated with that territory
which king Massinissa united under his sway. That of
Mauri, of native origin, and current among the later Greeks
as well as the Romans, is restricted to the western parts
of the land, and continues in use for the kingdoms here
formed and the Roman provinces that have proceeded
from them. The tribes of the south are comprehended
under the name of the Gaetulians, which, however, the
stricter use of language limits to the region on the
Atlantic Ocean to the south of Mauretania. We are
accustomed to designate the nation by the name of
Berbers, which the Arabs apply to the northern tribes.

Type.

As to their type they stand far nearer to the Indo-
Germanic than to the Semitic, and form even at the
present day, when since the invasion of Islam North Africa
has fallen to the Semitic race, the sharpest contrast to the
Arabs. It is not without warrant that various geographers
of antiquity have refused to let Africa pass at all as a
third continent, but have attached Egypt to Asia and the

---

[1] The designation *Afer* does not
belong to this series. So far as we can
follow it back in linguistic usage, it
is never given to the Berber in contrast to other African stocks, but
to every inhabitant of the Continent
lying over against Sicily, and particularly also to the Phoenician ; if it has
designated a definite people at all,
this can only have been that, with
which the Romans here first and
chiefly came into contact (comp.
Suetonius, *vita Terent.*). Reasons
philological and real oppose themselves to our attempt in i. 162 to trace
back the word to the name of the
Hebrews ; a satisfactory etymology
has not yet been found for it.
i. 154.

Berber territory to Europe. As the plants and animals of northern Africa correspond in the main to those of the opposite south-European coast, so the type of man, where it has been preserved unmixed, points altogether to the north :—the fair hair and the blue eyes of a considerable portion, the tall stature, the slender but powerfully knit form, the prevailing monogamy and respect for the position of woman, the lively and emotional temperament, the inclination to settled life, the community founded on the full equality in rights among the grown-up men, which in the usual confederation of several communities affords also the basis for the formation of a state.[1] To strictly political development and to full civilisation this nation, hemmed round by Negroes, Egyptians, Phoenicians, Romans, Arabs, at no time attained ; it must have approximated to it under the government of Massinissa. The alphabet, derived independently from the Phoenician, of which the Berbers made use under Roman rule, and which those of the Sahara still use at the present day, as well as the feeling which, as we have observed, they once had of common national relationship, may probably be referred to the great Numidian king and his descendants, whom the later generations worshipped as gods.[2] In spite of all

---

[1] A good observer, Charles Tissot, (*Géogr. de la province romaine de l'Afrique*, i. p. 403) testifies that upwards of a third of the inhabitants of Morocco have fair or brown hair, and in the colony of the inhabitants of the Riff in Tangier two-thirds. The women made the impression on him of those of Berry and of Auvergne. *Sur les hauts sommets de la chaîne atlantique, d'après les renseignements qui m'ont été fournis, la population tout entière serait remarquablement blonde. Elle aurait les yeux bleus, gris ou " verts," comme ceux des chats," pour reproduire l'expression même dont s'est servi le cheikh qui me renseignait.* The same phenomenon meets us in the mountain masses of Grand Kabylia and of the Aures, as well as on the Tunisian island Jerba and the Canary Islands. The Egyptian representations also

show to us the Libu not red, like the Egyptians, but white, and with fair or brown hair.

[2] Cyprian, *Quod idola dii non sint*, c. 2 : *Mauri manifeste reges suos colunt nec ullo velamento hoc nomen obtexunt.* Tertullian, *Apolog.* 24 : *Mauretaniae (dei sunt) reguli sui. C. I. L.* viii., 8834 : *Iemsali L. Percenius L. f. Stel. Rogatus v. (s. l. a.),* found at Thubusuptu in the region of Sitifis, which place may well have belonged to the Numidian kingdom of Hiempsal. Thus the inscription also of Thubursicum (*C. I. L.* viii. n. 7* (comp. *Eph. epigr.* v. p. 651, n. 1478) must have rather been badly copied than falsified. Still, in the year 70, it was alleged that in Mauretania a pretender to the throne had ascribed to himself the name of Juba (Tacitus, *Hist.* ii. 58).

invasions they have maintained their original territory to a considerable extent ; in Morocco now about two-thirds, in Algiers about half of the inhabitants are reckoned of Berber descent.

Phoenician immigration.

The immigration, to which all the coasts of the Mediterranean were subjected in the earliest times, made North Africa Phoenician. To the Phoenicians the natives had to give up the largest and best part of the north coast ; the Phoenicians withdrew all North Africa from Greek civilisation. The Great Syrtis again forms the linguistic as well as the political line of separation ; as on the east the Pentapolis of Cyrene belongs to the Greek circle, so on the west the Tripolis (Tripoli) of Great-Leptis became and remained Phoenician. We have formerly narrated how the Phoenicians after several hundred years of struggle succumbed to the Romans. Here we have to give account of the fortunes of Africa, after the Romans had occupied the Carthaginian territory and had made the neighbouring regions dependent on them.

The government of the Roman republic.

The short-sightedness and narrow-mindedness—we may here say, the perversity and brutality—of the foreign government of the Roman republic had nowhere so full sway as in Africa. In southern Gaul, and still more in Spain, the Roman government pursued at least a consolidated extension of territory, and, half involuntarily, the rudiments of Latinising ; in the Greek East the foreign rule was mitigated and often almost compensated by the power of Hellenism forcing the hand even of hard policy. But as to this third continent the old national hatred towards the Poeni seemed still to reach beyond the grave of Hannibal's native city. The Romans held fast the territory which Carthage had possessed at its fall, but less in order to develop it for their own benefit than to prevent its benefiting others, not to awaken new life there, but to watch the dead body ; it was fear and envy, rather than ambition and covetousness, that created the province of Africa. Under the republic it had not a history ; the war with Jugurtha was for Africa nothing but a lion-hunt, and its historical significance lay in its connection with the republican party struggles. The land was, as a matter of course, turned to full account by Roman speculation ; but neither might the destroyed great city rise up afresh, nor might a neighbouring town develop into a similar prosperity ; there were here no standing camps as in Spain and Gaul ; the Roman province, with its narrow bounds, was on all sides surrounded by relatively civilised territory of the dependent king of Numidia, who had helped in the work of the destruction of Carthage, and now, as a reward for it, received not so much the spoil as the task of protecting it from the inroads of the wild hordes of the interior. That thereby a political and military importance was given to this state, such as no other client-state of Rome ever possessed, and that even on this side the Roman policy, in order merely to banish the phantom of Carthage, conjured up serious dangers, was shown by the share of Numidia in the civil wars of Rome ; never during all the internal crises of the empire before or after did a client-prince play such a part as the last king of Numidia in the war of the republicans against Caesar.

All the more necessarily the state of things in Africa became transformed by this decision of arms. In the other provinces, as a consequence of the civil wars, there was a change of rule ; in Africa there was a change of system. The African possession of the Phoenicians itself was not a proper dominion over Africa ; it may be in some measure compared with the dominion in Asia Minor of the Hellenes before Alexander. Of this dominion the Romans had then taken over but a small part, and of that part they had nipped the bud. Now Carthage arose afresh, and, as if the soil had only been waiting for the seed, soon flourished anew. The whole country lying behind—the great kingdom of Numidia—became a Roman province, and the protection of the frontier against the barbarians was undertaken by the Roman legionaries. The kingdom of Mauretania became, in the

Caesar's African policy.

first instance, a Roman dependency, and soon also a part
of the Roman empire. With the dictator Caesar the
civilising and Latinising of Africa took their place among
the tasks of the Roman government. Here we have to
set forth how the task was carried out, first as to the
outward organisation, and then as to the arrangements
made and results achieved for the several districts.

Extent of
the Roman
rule.
Territorial sovereignty over the whole of North Africa
had doubtless already been claimed on the part of the
Roman republic, perhaps as a portion of the Carthaginian
inheritance, perhaps because "our sea" early became one
of the fundamental ideas of the Roman commonwealth ;
and, in so far, all its coasts were regarded by the Romans
even of the developed republic as their true property.
Nor had this claim of Rome ever been properly contested
by the larger states of North Africa after the destruction
of Carthage ; if in many places the neighbours did not
submit to the dominion, they were just as little obedient
to their local rulers. That the silver moneys of king
Juba I. of Numidia and of king Bogud of Mauretania
were coined after the Roman standard, and the Latin
legend—little as it was suited to the relations of language
and of intercourse then subsisting in North Africa—was
never absent from them, was the direct recognition of the
Roman supremacy, a consequence, it may be presumed,
of the new organisation of North Africa that in the
80. year 674 U.C. was accomplished by Pompeius. The
generally insignificant resistance which the Africans, apart
from Carthage, opposed to the Romans, came from the
descendants of Massinissa ; after king Jugurtha, and later
king Juba, were vanquished, the princes of the western
country submitted without more ado to the dependence
required of them. The arrangements which the emperors
made were carried out quite after the same way in the
territory of the dependent princes as in the immediate
territory of Rome ; it was the Roman government that
regulated the boundaries in all North Africa, and constituted Roman communities at its discretion in the
kingdom of Mauretania no less than in the province of

Numidia.   We cannot therefore speak, in the strict sense,
of a Roman subjugation of North Africa.   The Romans
did not conquer it like the Phoenicians or the French ;
but they ruled over Numidia as over Mauretania, first as
suźerains, then as successors of the native governments.
It is so much the more a question, whether the notion of
frontier admits of application to Africa in the usual sense.
The states of Massinissa, of Bocchus, of Bogud, as also
the Carthaginian, proceeded from the northern verge, and
all the civilisation of North Africa is based pre-eminently
on this coast ; but, so far as we can discern, they all
regarded the tribes settled or roving in the south as
subjects, and, if they withdrew themselves from subjection,
as insurgents, so far as the distance and the desert did
not by doing away with contact do away with control.
Neighbouring states, with which relations of right or of
treaty might have subsisted, can hardly be pointed out
in the south of northern Africa, or where such a one
appears, such as, in particular, the kingdom of the Garamantes, its position is not to be strictly distinguished from
that of the hereditary principalities within the civilised
territory.   This was the case also as regards Roman
Africa ; as for the previous rulers, so also doubtless for
Roman civilisation there was to be found a limit to the
south, but hardly so for the Roman territorial supremacy.
There is never mention of any formal extension or taking
back of the frontier in Africa ; the insurrections in the
Roman territory, and the inroads of the neighbouring
peoples, look here all the more similar to each other, as
even in the regions undoubtedly in Roman possession,
still more than in Syria or Spain, many a remote and
impassable district knew nothing of Roman taxation and
of Roman recruiting.   For that reason it seems appropriate
to connect with the view of the several provinces at the
same time the slight information which has been left
to us in historical tradition, or by means of preserved
monuments, respecting the friendly or hostile relations
of the Romans with their southern neighbours.

    The former territory of Carthage and the larger part

Province of Africa and Numidia. of the earlier kingdom of Numidia, united with it by the dictator Caesar, or, as they also called it, the old and the new Africa, formed until the end of the reign of Tiberius the province of that name, which extended from the boundary of Cyrene to the river Ampsaga, embracing the modern state of Tripoli as well as Tunis and the French iv, 447. province of Constantine (iv. 470 f.). The government, however, for this territory, which was considerable, and required an extended frontier-defence, reverted under the emperor Gaius in the main to the twofold division of the republican times, and committed the portion of the province that did not stand in need of special border-defence to the civil government, and the rest of the territory furnished with garrisons to a military commandant not further amenable to its authority. The cause of this was, that Africa in the partition of the provinces between emperor and senate was given to the latter, and, as from the state of things there a command on a larger scale could not be dispensed with, the co-ordination of the governor delegated by the senate and of the military commandant nominated by the emperor—which latter according to the subsisting hierarchy was placed under the orders of the former—could not but provoke and did provoke collisions between these officials and even between emperor and senate. To this an end was put in the year 37 by an arrangement that the coast-land from Hippo (Bonah), as far as the borders of Cyrene, should retain the old name of Africa and should remain with the proconsul, whereas the western part of the province with the capital Cirta (Constantine), as well as the interior with the great military camps to the north of the Aures, and generally all territory furnished with garrisons, should be placed under the commandant of the African legion. This commandant had senatorial rank, but belonged not to the consular, but to the praetorial class.

The two Mauretan-[iv. 438. ian king-doms. The western half of North Africa was divided at the time of the dictator Caesar (iv. 461) into the two kingdoms of Tingi (Tangier), at that time under king Bo ud and of Iol, the later Caesarea (Zershell), at that time under king Bocchus. As both kings had as decidedly taken the side of Caesar in the struggle against the republicans as king Juba of Numidia had taken the side of the opposite party, and as they had rendered most essential services to him during the African and the Spanish wars, not merely were both left in possession of their rule, but the domain of Bocchus, and probably also that of Bogud, was enlarged by the victor.[1] Then, when the rivalries between Antonius and Caesar the younger began, king Bogud alone in the west placed himself on the side of Antonius, and on the instigation of his brother and of his wife invaded Spain during the Perusine war (714); but his neighbour Bocchus and his own capital Tingis took part for Caesar and against him. At the conclusion of peace Antonius allowed Bogud to fall, and Caesar gave the rest of his territory to king Bocchus, but gave Roman municipal rights to the town of Tingis. When, some years later, a rupture took place between the two rulers, the ex-king took part energetically in the struggle in the hope of regaining his kingdom on this occasion, but at the capture of the Messenian town Methone he was taken prisoner by Agrippa and executed.

Already some years before (721) king Bocchus had died ; his kingdom, the whole of western Africa, was soon

40.

33.

49.

47.

[1] This is attested for the year 705 as regards both by Dio, xli. 42 (comp. Suetonius, *Caes.* 54). In the year 707 Bogud lends assistance to the Caesarian governor of Spain (*Bell. Alex.* 59, 60), and repels an incursion of the younger Gnaeus Pompeius (*Bell. Afric.* 23). Bocchus, in combination with P. Sittius, in the African war makes a successful diversion against Juba and conquers even the important Cirta (*Bell. Afr.* 23 ; Appian, ii. 96 ; Dio, xliii. 3). The two obtained in return from Caesar the territory of the prince Massinissa (Appian, iv. 54). In the second Spanish war Bogud appears in the army of Caesar (Dio, xliii. 36, 38) ; the statement that the son of Bocchus had served in the Pompeian army (Dio, *l.c.*) must be a confusion, probably with Arabio the son of Massinissa, who certainly went to the sons of Pompeius (Appian, *l.c.*). After Caesar's death Arabio possessed himself afresh of his dominion (Appian, *l.c.*), but after his death in the year 714 (Dio, xlviii. 22) the Caesarian arrangement must have again taken effect in its full extent. The bestowal on Bocchus and Sittius is probably to be understood to the effect that, in the western part of the former Numidian kingdom otherwise left to Bocchus, the colony of Cirta to be founded by Sittius was to be regarded as an independent Roman town, like Tingi subsequently in the kingdom of Mauretania.

40.

25.   afterwards (729) obtained by the son of the last Numidian
king, Juba II., the husband of Cleopatra, the daughter
Juba II.   of Antonius by the Egyptian queen.[1]   Both had been
exhibited to the Roman public in early youth as captive
kings' children, Juba in the triumphal procession of
Caesar the father, Cleopatra in that of the son ; it was a
wonderful juncture that they now were sent away from
Rome as king and queen of the most esteemed vassal-
state of the empire, but it was in keeping with the
circumstances.   Both were brought up in the imperial
family ; Cleopatra was treated by the legitimate wife of
her father with motherly kindness like her own children ;
Juba had served in Caesar's army.   The youth of the
dependent princely houses, which was numerously represented at the imperial court and played a considerable
part in the circle around the imperial princes, was generally
employed in the early imperial period for the filling up of
the vassal principalities, after a similar manner, according
to free selection, as the first class in rank of the senate
was employed for the filling up of the governorships
of Syria and Germany.   For almost fifty years (729—
775 U.C., B.C. 25—A.D. 23) he, and after him his son
Ptolemaeus, bore rule over western Africa ; it is true that,
like the town Tingis from his predecessor, a considerable
number of the most important townships, particularly on
the coast, was withdrawn from him by the bestowal of

---

[1] If, according to Dio, xl. 43,
33.   Caesar in the year 721, after the
death of Bocchus, nominates no
successor, but makes Mauretania a
province, and then (li. 15) in the
30.   year 724, on occasion of the end of
the queen of Egypt, there is mention
of the marriage of her daughter with
Juba and his investiture with his
father's kingdom, and, lastly (liii.
25.   26), under the year 729 there is
reported Juba's investiture with a
portion of Gaetulia instead of his
hereditary kingdom, as well as with
the kingdoms of Bocchus and Bogud ;
only the last account confirmed by
Strabo, xvii. 3, 7, p. 828, is correct.
The first is at least incorrect in its

way of apprehending the matter, as
Mauretania evidently was not made a
province in 721, but only the investi-   33.
ture was held in abeyance for the
time being ; and the second partly
anticipates, since Cleopatra, born before the triumph about 719 (*Eph.
epigr.* i., p. 276), could not possibly
be married in 724, and is partly mis-
taken, because Juba certainly never
got back his paternal kingdom as
such.   If he had been king of Numidia before 729, and if it had been
merely the extent of his kingdom that
then underwent a change, he would
have counted his years from the first
installation and not merely from 729.

Roman municipal rights, and, apart from the capital, these kings of Mauretania were almost nothing but princes of the Berber tribes.

This government lasted up to the year 40, when it appeared fitting to the emperor Gaius, chiefly on account of the rich treasure, to call his cousin to Rome, to deliver him there to the executioner, and to take the territory into imperial administration. Both rulers were unwarlike, the father a Greek man of letters after the fashion of this period, compiling so-called memorabilia of a historical or geographical kind, or relative to the history of art, in endless books, noteworthy by his—we might say—international literary activity, well read in Phoenician and Syrian literature, but exerting himself above all to diffuse the knowledge of Roman habits and of so-called Roman history among the Hellenes, moreover, a zealous friend of art and frequenter of the theatre ; the son a prince of the common type, passing his time in court-life and princely luxury. Among their subjects they were held of little account, whether as regards their personality or as vassals of the Romans ; against the Gaetulians in the south king Juba had on several occasions to invoke the help of the Roman governor, and, when in Roman Africa the prince of the Numidians, Tacfarinas, revolted against the Romans, the Moors flocked in troops to his banner. Nevertheless the end of the dynasty and the introduction of Roman provincial government into the land made a deep impression. The Moors were faithfully devoted to their royal house ; altars were still erected under the Roman rule in Africa to the kings of the race of Massinissa (p. 305). Ptolemaeus, whatever he might be otherwise, was Massinissa's genuine descendant in the sixth generation, and the last of the old royal house. A faithful servant of his, Aedemon, after the catastrophe called the mountain-tribes of the Atlas to arms, and it was only after a hard struggle that the governor Suetonius Paullinus—the same who afterwards fought with the Britons (I. 179)—was able to master the revolt (in the year 42). In the organisation of the new territory the Romans reverted to the earlier division into

Erection of the provinces of Caesarea and Tingi.

an eastern and a western half, or, as they were thenceforth
called from the capitals, into the provinces of Caesarea and
of Tingi ; or rather they retained that division, for it was, as
will be afterwards shown, necessarily suggested by the
physical and political relations of the territory, and must
have continued to subsist even under the same sceptre in
one or the other form.   Each of these provinces was
furnished with imperial troops of the second class, and
placed under an imperial governor not belonging to the
senate.

The state and the destinies of this great and peculiar
new seat of Latin civilisation were conditioned by the
physical constitution of North Africa.   It is formed by
two great mountain-masses, of which the northern falls
steeply towards the Mediterranean, while the southern, the
Atlas, slopes off slowly in the Sahara-steppe dotted with
numerous oases towards the desert proper.   A smaller
steppe, similar on the whole to the Sahara and dotted with
numerous salt-lakes, serves in the middle portion, the modern
Algeria, to separate the mountains on the north coast and
those on the southern frontier.   There are in North Africa
no extensive plains capable of culture ; the coast of the
Mediterranean Sea has a level foreland only in a few districts ;
the land capable of cultivation, according to the modern
expression the Tell, consists essentially of the numerous
valleys and slopes within those two broad mountain-masses,
and so extends to its greatest width where, as in the
modern Morocco and in Tunis, no steppe intervenes between
the northern and the southern border.

Tripolis.   The region of Tripolis, politically a part of the province
of Africa, stands as respects its natural relations outside of
the territory described, and is annexed to it in peninsular
fashion.   The frontier-range sloping down towards the
Mediterranean Sea touches at the bay of Tacapae (Gabes),
with its foreland of steppe and salt-lake, immediately on
the shore.   To the south of Tacapae as far as the Great
Syrtis there extends along the coast the narrow Tripolitan
island of cultivation, bounded inland towards the steppe
by a chain of moderate height.   Beyond it begins the

steppe-country with numerous oases. The protection of
the coast against the inhabitants of the desert is here of
special difficulty, because the high margin of mountains is
wanting ; and traces of this are apparent in the accounts
that have come to us of the military expeditions and the
military positions in this region.

It was the arena of the wars with the Garamantes.
Lucius Cornelius Balbus, who in his younger years had
fought and administered under Caesar with the most
adventurous boldness as well as with the most cruel reck-
lessness, was selected by Augustus to reduce these inconvenient neighbours to quiet, and in his proconsulate (735)
he subdued the interior as far as Cidamus (Ghadames),
twelve days' journey inland from Tripolis, and Garama
(Germa) in Fezzan;[1] at his triumph—he was the last com-
moner who celebrated such an one—a long series of towns
and tribes, hitherto unknown even by name, were displayed
as vanquished. This expedition is named a conquest ;
and so doubtless the foreland must have been thereby
brought in some measure under the Roman power. There
was fighting subsequently on many occasions in this region.
Soon afterwards, still under Augustus, Publius Sulpicius
Quirinius made an expedition against the tribes of Mar-
marica, that is, of the Libyan desert above Cyrene, and
at the same time against the Garamantes. That the war
against Tacfarinas under Tiberius extended also over this
region will be mentioned further on. After its termination
the king of the Garamantes sent envoys to Rome, to procure pardon for his having taken part in it. In the year 70
an irruption of the Garamantes into the pacified territory
was brought about by the circumstance that the town

---

[1] That Balbus carried on this
campaign as proconsul of Africa, is
shown in particular by the triumphal
Fasti ; but the consul L. Cornelius of
the year 732 must have been another
person, since Balbus, according to
Velleius ii. 51, obtained that consular
governorship, *ex privato consularis*,
i.e. without having filled a curule
office. The nomination, therefore, cannot have taken place according to the
usual arrangement by lot. To all
appearance he fell into disgrace with
Augustus for good reasons on account
of his Spanish quaestorship (Drumann
ii. 609), and was then, after the lapse
of more than twenty years, sent, as an
extraordinary measure, to Africa, on
account of his undoubted aptitude for
this specially difficult task.

Oea (Tripoli) called the barbarians to help the Tripolis in a quarrel, which had grown into war, with the neighbouring town Great-Leptis (Lebda), whereupon they were beaten back by the governor of Africa and pursued to their own settlements. Under Domitian on the coast of the Great Syrtis, which had been from of old held by the Nasamones, a revolt of the natives provoked by the exorbitant taxes had to be repressed with arms by the governor of Numidia; the territory already poor in men was utterly depopulated by this cruelly conducted war. The emperor Severus took conspicuous care of this his native province—he was from Great-Leptis—and gave to it stronger military protection against the neighbouring barbarians. With this we may bring into connection the fact, that in the time from Severus to Alexander the nearest oases, Cidamus (Ghadames), Gharia el Gharbia, Bonjem, were provided with detachments of the African legion, which, it is true, owing to the distance from the headquarters, could not be much more than a nucleus for the probably considerable contingents of the subject tribes here rendering services to the Romans. In fact the possession of these oases was of importance not merely for the protection of the coast, but also for the traffic, which at all times passed by way of these oases from the interior of Africa to the harbours of Tripolis. It was not till the time of decay that the possession of these advanced posts was abandoned; in the description of the African wars under Valentinian and Justinian we find the towns of the coast directly harassed by the natives.

The Africano-Numidian territory and army.

The basis and core of Roman Africa was the province of that name, including the Numidian, which was a branch from it. Roman civilisation entered upon the heritage partly of the city of Carthage, partly of the kings of Numidia, and if it here attained considerable results, it may never be forgotten that it, properly speaking, merely wrote its name and inscribed its language on what was already there. Besides the towns, which were demonstrably founded by the former or by the latter, and to which we shall still return, the former as well as the latter led the Berber tribes, inclined at any rate to agriculture, towards

fixed settlements.   Even in the time of Herodotus the
Libyans westward of the bay of Gabes were no longer
nomads, but peacefully cultivated the soil ; and the Numidian
rulers carried civilisation and agriculture still farther into
the interior.   Nature, too, was here more favourable for
husbandry than in the western part of North Africa ; the
middle depression between the northern and the southern
range is indeed here not quite absent, but the salt lakes
and the steppe proper are less extensive than in the two
Mauretanias.   The military arrangements were chiefly
designed to plant the troops in front of the mighty Aurasian mountain-block, the Saint Gotthard of the southern
frontier-range, and to check the irruption of the non-
subject tribes from the latter into the pacified territory of
Africa and Numidia.   For that reason Augustus placed
the stationary quarters of the legion at Theveste (Tebessa),
on the high plateau between the Aures and the old
province ; even to the north of it, between Ammaedara and
Althiburus, Roman forts existed in the first imperial period.
Of the details of the warfare we learn little ; it must have
been permanent, and must have consisted in the constant
repelling of the border-tribes, as well as in not less constant
pillaging raids into their territory.

Only as to a single occurrence of this sort has information in some measure accurate come to us ; namely, as
to the conflicts which derive their name from the chief
leader of the Berbers, Tacfarinas.   They assumed unusual
proportions ; they lasted eight years (17-24), and the
garrison of the province otherwise consisting of a legion
was on that account reinforced during the years 20-22 by
a second despatched thither from Pannonia.   The war had
its origin from the great tribe of the Musulamii on the south
slope of the Aures, against whom already under Augustus
Lentulus had conducted an expedition, and who now under
his successor chose that Tacfarinas as their leader.   He
was an African Arminius, a native Numidian, who had
served in the Roman army, but had then deserted and
made himself a name at the head of a band of robbers.
The insurrection extended eastwards as far as the Cinithii

War against Tacfarinas.

on the Little Syrtis and the Garamantes in Fezzan, westwards over a great part of Mauretania, and became dangerous through the fact that Tacfarinas equipped a portion of his men after the Roman fashion on foot and on horseback, and gave them Roman training ; these gave steadiness to the light bands of the insurgents, and rendered possible regular combats and sieges. After long exertions, and after the senate had been on several occasions induced to disregard the legally prescribed ballot in filling up this important post of command, and to select fitting men instead of the usual generals of the type of Cicero, Quintus Iunius Blaesus in the first instance made an end of the insurrection by a combined operation, inasmuch as he sent the left flank column against the Garamantes, and with the right covered the outlets from the Aures towards Cirta, while he advanced in person with the main army into the territory of the Musulamii and permanently occupied it (year 22). But the bold partisan soon afterwards renewed the struggle, and it was only some years later that the proconsul Publius Cornelius Dolabella, after he had nipped in the bud the threatened revolt of the just chastised Musulamii by the execution of all the leaders, was able with the aid of the troops of the king of Mauretania to force a battle in his territory near Auzia (Aumale), in which Tacfarinas lost his life. With the fall of the leader, as is usual in national wars of insurrection, this movement had an end.[1]

Later conflicts.

From later times detailed accounts of a like kind are lacking ; we can only follow out in some measure the general course of the Roman work of pacification. The tribes to the south of Aures were, if not extirpated, at any rate ejected and transplanted into the northern districts ; so in particular the Musulamii themselves,[2] against whom

---

[1] The tribes whom Tacitus names in his account of the war, far from clear, as always, in a geographical point of view, may be in some measure determined ; and the position between the Leptitanian and the Cirtensian columns (*Ann.* iii. 74) points for the middle column to Theveste. The town of Thala (*Ann.* iii. 20) cannot possibly be sought above Ammaedara, but is probably the Thala of the Jugurthan war in the vicinity of Capsa. The last section of the war has its arena in western Mauretania about Auzia (iv. 25), and accordingly in Thubuscum (iv. 24) there lurks possibly Thubusuptu or Thubusuctu. The river Pagyda (*Ann.* iii. 20) is quite indefinable.

[2] Ptolemaeus, iv. 3, 23, puts the

an expedition was once more conducted under Claudius. The demand made by Tacfarinas to have settlements assigned to him and his people within the civilised territory, to which Tiberius, as was reasonable, only replied by redoubling his exertions to annihilate the daring claimant, was supplementarily after a certain measure fulfilled in this way, and probably contributed materially to the consolidation of the Roman government. The camps more and more enclosed the Aurasian mountain-block. The garrisons were pushed farther forward into the interior ; the headquarters themselves moved under Trajan away from Theveste farther to the west ; the three considerable Roman settlements on the northern slope of the Aures, Mascula (Khenschela), at the egress of the valley of the Arab and thereby the key to the Aures mountains, a colony at least already under Marcus and Verus ; Thamugadi, a foundation of Trajan's ; and Lambaesis, after Hadrian's day the headquarters of the African army, formed together a settlement comparable to the great military camps on the Rhine and on the Danube, which, laid out on the lines of communication from the Aures to the great towns of the north and the coast Cirta (Constantine), Calama (Gelma), and Hippo regius (Bonah), secured the peace of the latter. The intervening steppe-land was, so far as it could not be gained for cultivation, at least intersected by secure routes of communication. On the west side of the Aures a strongly occupied chain of posts which followed the slope of the mountains from Lambaesis over the oases Calceus Herculis (el Kantara) and Bescera (Beskra), cut off the connection with Mauretania. Even the interior of the mountains subsequently became Roman ; the war,

---

Musulamii southward from the Aures, and it is only in accord therewith that they are called in Tacitus ii. 52, dwellers beside the steppe and neighbours of the Mauri ; later they are settled to the north and west of Theveste (*C. I. L.* viii. 270, 10667). The Nattabutes dwelt according to Ptolemaeus *l.c.* southward of the Musulamii ; subsequently we find them to the south of Calama (*C. I. L.* viii. 484). In like manner the *Chellenses Numidae,* between Lares and Althiburus (*Eph. epigr.* V. n. 639), and the *conventus* (*civium Romanorum et*) *Numidarum qui Mascululae habitant* (*ib.* n. 597), are probably Berber tribes transplanted from Numidia to the proconsular province.

which was waged under the emperor Pius in Africa, and concerning which we have not accurate information, must have brought the Aurasian mountains into the power of the Romans. At that time a military road was carried through these mountains by a legion doing garrison duty in Syria and sent beyond doubt on account of this war to Africa, and in later times we meet at that very spot traces of Roman garrisons and even of Roman towns, which reach down to Christian times; the Aurasian range had thus at that time been occupied, and continued to be permanently occupied. The oasis Negrin, situated on its southern slope, was even already under or before Trajan furnished by the Romans with troops, and still somewhat farther southward on the extreme verge of the steppe at Bir Mohammed ben Jûnis are found the ruins of a Roman fort; a Roman road also ran along the southern base of this range. Of the mighty slope which falls from the tableland of Theveste, the watershed between the Mediterranean and the desert, in successive stages of two to three hundred mètres down to the latter, this oasis is the last terrace; at its base begins, in sharp contrast towards the jagged mountains piled up behind, the sand desert of Suf, with its yellow rows of dunes similar to waves, and the sandy soil moved about by the wind, a huge wilderness, without elevation of the ground, without trees, fading away without limit into the horizon. Negrin was certainly of old, as it still is in our time, the standing rendezvous and the last place of refuge of the robber chiefs as well as of the natives defying foreign rule—a position commanding far and wide the desert and its trading routes. Even to this extreme limit reached Roman occupation and even Roman settlement in Numidia.

Roman civilisation in Mauretania. Mauretania was not a heritage like Africa and Numidia. Of its earlier condition we learn nothing; there cannot have been considerable towns even on the coast here in earlier times, and neither Phoenician stimulus nor sovereigns after the type of Massinissa effectively promoted civilisation in this quarter. When his last descendants exchanged the Numidian crown for the Mauretanian, the capital, which

changed its name Iol into Caesarea, became the residence
of a cultivated and luxurious court, and a seat of seafaring
and of traffic. But how much less this possession was
esteemed by the government than that of the neighbouring
province, is shown by the difference of the provincial
organisation ; the two Mauretanian armies were together
not inferior in number to the Africano-Numidian,[1] but here
governors of equestrian rank and imperial soldiers of the
class of *peregrini* sufficed. Caesarea remained a considerable commercial town ; but in the province the fixed
settlement was restricted to the northern mountain-range,
and it was only in the eastern portion that larger [inland
towns were to be found. Even the fertile valley of the
most considerable river of this province, the Shelif, shows
weak urban development ; further to the west in the
valleys of the Tafna and the Malua it almost wholly disappears, and the names of the divisions of cavalry here
stationed serve partly in place of local designations. The
province of Tingi (Tangier) even now embraced nothing
but this town with its immediate territory and the stripe
of the coast along the Atlantic Ocean as far as Sala, the
modern Rebât, while in the interior Roman settlement did
not even reach to Fez. No land-route connects this
province with that of Caesarea ; the 220 miles from Tingi
to Rusaddir (Melilla) they traversed by water, along the
desolate and insubordinate coast of the Riff. Consequently for this province the communication with Baetica
was nearer than that with Mauretania; and if subsequently,
when the empire was divided into larger administrative
districts, the province of Tingi fell to Spain, that measure
was only the outward carrying out of what in reality had
long subsisted. It was for Baetica what Germany was
for Gaul ; and, far from lucrative as it must have been,
it was perhaps instituted and retained for the reason that
its abandonment would even then have brought about an

---

[1] In the year 70 the troops of the
two Mauretanias amounted together,
in addition to militia levied in large
numbers, to 5 alae and 19 cohortes
(Tacitus, *Hist.* ii. 58), and so, if we
reckon on the average every fourth as
a double troop, to about 15,000 men.
The regular army of Numidia was
weaker rather than stronger.

invasion of Spain similar to that which Islam accomplished
after the collapse of the Roman rule.

The Gae-
tulian wars.
Beyond the limit of fixed settlement herewith indicated,
—the line of frontier tolls and of frontier posts—and in various non-civilised districts enclosed by it, the land in the two
Mauretanias during the Roman times remained doubtless
with the natives, but they came under Roman supremacy;
there would be claimed from them, as far as possible,
taxes and war-services, but the regular forms of taxation
and of levy would not be applied in their case. For
example, the tribe of Zimizes, which was settled on the
rocky coast to the west of Igilgili (Jijeli) in eastern
Mauretania, and so in the heart of the domain of the
Roman power, had assigned to it a fortress designed to
cover the town of Igilgili, to be occupied on such a footing
that the troops were not allowed to pass beyond the radius
of 500 paces round the fort.[1] They thus employed these
subject Berbers in the Roman interest, but did not organise
them in the Roman fashion, and hence did not treat them
as soldiers of the imperial army. Even beyond their own
province the irregulars from Mauretania were employed in
great numbers, particularly as horsemen in the later period,[2]
while the same did not hold of the Numidians.

How far the field of the Roman power went beyond the
Roman towns and garrisons and the end of the imperial
roads, we are not able to say. The broad steppe-land round
the salt-lakes to the west of Lambaesis, the mountain-region

[1] Inscription *C. I. L.* viii. 8369
of the year 129: *Termini positi inter
Igilgilitanos, in quorum finibus kastel-
lum Victoriae positum est, et Zimiz(es),
ut sciant Zimizes non plus in usum se
habere ex auctoritate M. Vetti Latronis
pro(curatoris) Aug(usti) qua(m) in
circuitu a muro kast(elli) p(edes)* D.
The *Zimises* are placed by the Peu-
tingerian map alongside of Igilgili to
the westward.

[2] If the praefect of a cohort doing
garrison duty in Numidia held the
command at the same time over six
Gaetulian tribes (*nationes, C. I. L.* v.
5267), men that were natives of
Mauretania were employed as irregulars in the neighbouring province.
Irregular Mauretanian horsemen frequently occur, especially in the later
imperial period. Lusius Quietus under
Trajan, a Moor and leader of a Moorish
troop (Dio lxviii. 32), no Λίβυς ἐκ
τῆς ὑπηκόου Λιβύης, ἀλλ' ἐξ ἀδόξου καὶ
ἀπῳκισμένης ἐσχατιᾶς (Themistius, *Or.*
xvi. p. 250 Dind.), was without doubt
a Gaetulian sheikh, who served with
his followers in the Roman army.
That his home was formally independent of the empire, is not affirmed in
the words of Themistius; the "subject-
territory" is that with Roman organisation, the ἐσχατιά its border inhabited
by dependent tribes.

from Tlemsen till towards Fez, including the coast of the
Riff, the fine corn-country on the Atlantic Ocean southward from Sala as far as the high Atlas, the civilisation of
which in the flourishing time of the Arabs vied with the
Andalusian, lastly, the Atlas range in the south of Algeria
and Morocco and its southern slopes, which afforded for
pastoral people abundant provision in the alternation of
mountain and steppe pastures, and developed the most
luxuriant fertility in the numerous oases—all these regions
remained essentially untouched by the Roman civilisation;
but from this it does not follow that they were in the
Roman time independent, and still less that they were not
at least reckoned as belonging to the imperial domain.
Tradition gives us but slight information in this respect.
We have already mentioned (p. 313) that the proconsuls of
Africa helped to make the Gaetulians—that is, the tribes in
southern Algeria—subject to king Juba; and the latter constructed purple dyeworks at Madeira (p. 338, note). After
the end of the Mauretanian dynasty and the introduction
of the immediate Roman administration, Suetonius Paullinus crossed, as the first Roman general, the Atlas (p. 313),
and carried his arms as far as the desert-river Ger, which
still bears the same name, in the south-east of Morocco.
His successor, Gnaeus Hosidius Geta, continued this enterprise, and emphatically defeated the leader of the Mauri
Salabus.   Subsequently several enterprising governors of
the Mauretanian provinces traversed these remote regions,
and the same holds true of the Numidian, under whose
command, not under the Mauretanian, was placed the
frontier-range stretching southward behind the province of
Caesarea;[1] yet nothing is mentioned from later times of
war-expeditions proper in the south of Mauretania or
Numidia.   The Romans can scarcely have taken over the
empire of the Mauretanian kings in quite the same extent
as these had possessed it; but yet the expeditions that
were undertaken after the annexation of the country were

[1] To the inscriptions, which prove
this (*C. I.L.* viii. p. xviii. 747), falls
now to be added the remarkable dedication of the leader of an expedi-
tionary column from the year 174,
found in the neighbourhood of Géry-
ville (*Eph. epigr.* v. n. 1043).

probably not without lasting consequences.　At least a portion of the Gaetulians submitted, as the auxiliary troops levied there prove, even to the regular conscription during the imperial period ; and, if the native tribes in the south of the Roman provinces had given serious trouble to the Romans, the traces of it would not have been wholly wanting.[1]　Probably the whole south as far as the great desert passed as imperial land,[2] and even the effective dependence extended far beyond the domain of Roman civilisation, which, it is true, does not exclude frequent levying of contributions and pillaging raids on the one side or the other.

Incursions of the Moors into Spain.
　　The pacified territory experienced attack, properly so called, chiefly from the inhabitants of the shore settled around and along the Riff, the Mazices, and the Baquates ; and this indeed took place, as a rule, by sea, and was directed chiefly against the Spanish coast (I. 67). Accounts of inroads of the Moors into Baetica run through the whole imperial period,[3] and show that the Romans, in consequence of the absence of energetic

[1] The *tumultus Gaetulicus* (*C. I. L.* viii. 6958) was rather an insurrection than an invasion.

[2] Ptolemy certainly takes as boundary of the province of Caesarea the line above the Shott, and does not reckon Gaetulia as belonging to it ; on the other hand he extends that of Tingis as far as the Great Atlas. Pliny v. 4, 30, numbers among the subject peoples of Africa "all Gaetulia as far as the Niger and the Ethiopian frontier," which points nearly to Timbuctoo.　The latter statement will accord with the official conception of the matter.

[3] Already in Nero's time Calpurnius (*Egl.* iv. 40) terms the shore of Baetica *trucibus obnoxia Mauris*. —If under Pius the Moors were beaten off and driven back as far as and over the Atlas (*vita Pii*, 5 ; Pausanias viii. 43). The sending of troops at that time from Spain to the Tingitana (*C. I. L.* iii. 5212-5215) makes it probable that this attack of the Moors

affected Baetica, and the troops of the Tarraconensis marching against these followed them over the straits.　The probably contemporary activity of the Syrian legion at the Aures (p. 320) suggests moreover that this war extended also to Numidia.—The war with the Moors under Marcus (*vita Marci*, 21, 22 ; *vita Severi*, 2), had its scene essentially in Baetica and Lusitania.—A governor of Hither Spain under Severus had to fight with the "rebels" by water and by land (*C. I. L.* ii. 4114).—Under Alexander (*vita*, 58) there was fighting in the province of Tingi, but without mention of Spain in the case.—From the time of Aurelian (*vita Saturnini*, 9) there is mention of Mauro-Spanish conflicts.　We cannot exactly determine the time of a sending of troops from Numidia to Spain and against the Mazices (*C. I. L.* viii. 2786), where presumably not the Mazices of the Caesariensis but those of the Tingitana on the Riff (Ptolem. iv. 1, 10), are meant ; per-

offensive, found themselves here permanently on a defensive, which indeed did not involve a vital danger for the empire, but yet brought constant insecurity and often sore harm over rich and peaceful regions.   The civilised territories of Africa appear to have suffered less under the Moorish attacks, probably because the headquarters of Numidia, immediately on the Mauretanian frontier, and the strong garrisons on the west side of the Aures, did their duty.   But on the collapse of the imperial power in the third century the invasion here also began ; the feud of Five Peoples, as it was called, which broke out about the time of Gallienus, and on account of which twenty years later the emperor Maximianus went personally to Africa, arose from the tribes beyond the Shott on the Numido-Mauretanian frontier, and affected particularly the towns of Eastern Mauretania and of Western Numidia, such as Auzia and Mileu.[1]

Quinquegentiani.

We come to the internal organisation of the country. In respect of language, that which belonged properly to the people was treated like the Celtic in Gaul and the Iberian in Spain ; here in Africa all the more, as the earlier foreign rule had already set the example in that respect, and certainly no Roman understood this popular

Continuance of the Berber language.

haps with this is connected the fact that Gaius Vallius Maximianus, as governor of Tingitana, achieved in the province Baetica (according to Hirschfeld, *Wiener Stud.* vi. 123, under Marcus and Commodus) a victory over the Moors and relieved towns besieged by them (*C. I. L.* ii. 1120, 2015) ; these events prove at least that the conflicts with the Moors on the Riff and the associates that flocked to them from the country lying behind did not cease.   When the Baquates on the same coast besieged the pretty remote Cartenna (Tenes) in the Caesariensis (*C. I. L.* viii. 9663), they perhaps came by sea.   Where the wars with the Moors under Hadrian (*vita*, 5, 12) and Commodus (*vita*, 13) took place is not known.

[1] More information than in the scanty accounts of Victor and Eu-

tropius is supplied as to this war by the inscribed stones, *C. I. L.* viii. 2615, 8836, 9045, 9047.   According to these the *Quinquegentiani* may be followed out from Gallienus to Diocletian. The beginning is made by the Baquates who, designated as *Transtagnenses*, must have dwelt beyond the Shott.   Four "kings" combine for an expedition.   The most dreaded opponent is Faraxen with his *gentiles Fraxinenses.*   Towns like Mileu in Numidia not far from Cirta and Auzia in the Caesariensis are attacked, and the citizens must in good part defend themselves against the enemy.   After the end of the war Maximian constructs great magazines in Thubusuctu not far from Saldae.   These fragmentary accounts give in some measure an insight into the relations of the time.

idiom.   The Berber tribes had not merely a national language, but also a national writing (p. 305) ; but never, so far as we see, was use made of it in official intercourse, at least it was never put upon the coins.   Even the native Berber dynasties formed no exception to this, whether because in their kingdoms the more considerable towns were more Phoenician than Libyan, or because the Phoenician civilisation prevailed so far generally.   The language was written indeed also under Roman rule, in fact most of the Berber votive or sepulchral inscriptions proceed certainly from the imperial period ; but their rarity proves that it attained only to limited written use in the sphere of the Roman rule.   It maintained itself as a popular language above all naturally in the districts, to which the Romans came little or not at all, as in the Sahara, in the mountains of the Riff of Morocco, in the two Kabylias ; but even the fertile and early cultivated island of the Tripolis, Girba (Jerba), the seat of the Carthaginian purple manufacture, still at the present day speaks Libyan.   Taken on the whole, the old popular idiom in Africa defended itself better than among the Celts and the Iberians.

Continuance of the Phoenician language.
The language which prevailed in North Africa, when it became Roman, was that of the foreign rule which preceded the Roman.   Leptis, probably not the Tripolitan, but that near Hadrumetum, was the only African town which marked its coins with a Greek legend, and thus conceded to this language an at least secondary position in public intercourse.   The Phoenician language prevailed at that time so far as there was a civilisation in North Africa, from Great Leptis to Tingi, most thoroughly in and around Carthage, but not less in Numidia and Mauretania.[1]   To this language of a highly developed

[1] Apart from the coins this is proved also by the inscriptions. According to the comparison, for which I am indebted to Herr Euting, the great mass of the old Punic inscriptions, that is, those written probably before the destruction of Carthage, falls to Carthage itself (about 2500), the rest to Hadrumetum (9), Thugga (the famous Phoenico-Berber one), Cirta (5), Iol-Caesarea (1). The new Punic occur most numerously in and around Carthage (30), and generally they are found not unfrequently in the proconsular province, also in Great Leptis (5) and on the islands of Girba

although foreign culture certain concessions were made
on the change in the system of administration.   Perhaps
already under Caesar, certainly under Augustus and
Tiberius, as well the towns of the Roman province,
such as Great Leptis and Oea, as those of the Mauretanian
kingdom, like Tingi and Lix, employed in official use the
Phoenician language, even those which like Tingi had
become Roman burgess-communities.   Nevertheless they
did not go so far in Africa as in the Greek half of the
empire.   In the Greek provinces of the empire the Greek
language prevailed, as in business intercourse generally,
so particularly in direct intercourse with the imperial
government and its officials ; the coin of the city organised after the Greek fashion names also the emperor in
Greek.   But in the African the coin, even if it speaks in
another language, names the emperor or the imperial
official always in Latin.   Even on the coins of the kings
of Mauretania the name of the Greek queen stands
possibly in Greek, but that of the king—also an imperial
official—uniformly in Latin, even where the queen is
named beside him.   That is to say, even the government
did not admit the Phoenician in its intercourse with the
communities and individuals in Africa, but it allowed
it for internal intercourse ; it was not a third imperial
language, but a language of culture recognised in its own
sphere.

But this limited recognition of the Phoenician language
did not long subsist.   There is no document for the public
use of Phoenician from the time after Tiberius, and it
hardly survived the time of the first dynasty.[1]   How and
when the change set in we do not know ; probably the

(1) and Cossura (1) ; in Numidia, in
and near Calama (23), and in Cirta
(15) ; in Mauretania hitherto only in
Portus Magnus (2).

[1] The coining in Africa ceases in
the main after Tiberius, and thereafter, since African inscriptions from
the first century after Christ are before us only in very small numbers,
for a considerable period documents
fail us.   The coins of Babba in the
Tingitana, going from Claudius down
to Galba, have exclusively Latin
legends ; but the town was a colony.
The Latin-Punic inscriptions of Great
Leptis, *C. I. L.* viii. 7, and of Na-
raggara, *C. I. L.* viii. 4636, may
doubtless belong to the time after Tiberius, but as bi-lingual tell rather for
the view that, when they were set up,
the Phoenician language was already
degraded.

government, perhaps Tiberius or Claudius, spoke the decisive word and accomplished the linguistic and national
annexation of the African Phoenicians as far as it could
be done by state authority.   In private intercourse the
Phoenician held its ground still for a long time in Africa,
longer apparently than in the motherland ; at the beginning of the third century ladies of genteel houses in Great
Leptis spoke so little Latin or Greek, that there was no
place for them in Roman society ; even at the end of the
fourth there was a reluctance to appoint clergymen in the
environs of Hippo Regius (Bona), who could not make
themselves intelligible in Punic to their countrymen ; these
termed themselves at that time still Canaanites, and Punic
names and Punic phrases were still current.   But the
language was banished from the school[1] and even from
written use, and had become a popular dialect ; and even
this probably only in the region of the old Phoenician
civilisation, particularly the old Phoenician places on
the coast that stood aloof from intercourse on a large
scale.[2]   When the Arabs came to Africa they found
as language of the country doubtless that of the Berbers,
but no longer that of the Poeni ;[3] with the Carthagino-
Roman civilisation the two foreign languages disappeared,
while the old native one still lives in the present day.
The civilised foreign dominions changed ; the Berbers remained like the palm of the oasis and the sand of the desert.
The heritage of the Phoenician language fell not to

[1] From the expression in the epitome of Victor, that the emperor
Severus was *Latinis litteris suf-
ficienter instructus, Graecis sermoni-
bus eruditus, Punica eloquentia promp-
tior, quippe genitus apud Leptim*, we
may not infer a Punic course of rhetoric in the Tripolis of that time ; the
late and inferior author has possibly
given a scholastic version of the well-
known notice.

[2] On the statement of the younger
Arnobius, writing about 460 (*ad
Psalm.* 104, p. 481 Migne : *Cham
vero secundus filius Noe a Rhinocoruris
usque Gadira habens linguas sermone
Punico a parte Garamantum, Latino
a parte boreae, barbarico a parte meri-
diani, Aethiopum et Aegyptiorum ac
barbaris interioribus vario sermone
numero viginti duabus linguis in
patriis trecentis nonaginta et quattuor*),
no reliance is to be placed, still less
upon the nonsense of Procopius, *de
bello Vand.* ii. 10, as to the Phoenician
inscription and language in Tigisis.
Authorities of this sort were hardly
able to distinguish Berber and Punic.

[3] In a single place on the Little
Syrtis the Phoenician may still have
been spoken in the eleventh century
(Movers, *Phön.* ii. 2, 478).

Greek, but to Latin. This was not involved in the natural development. In Caesar's time the Latin and the Greek were alike in North Africa foreign languages, but as the coins of Leptis already show, the latter by far more diffused than the former ; Latin was spoken then only by the officials, the soldiers, and the Italian merchants. It would have at that time been probably easier to introduce the Hellenising of Africa than the Latinising of it. But it was the converse that took place. Here the same will prevailed, which did not allow the Hellenic germs to spring up in Gaul, and which incorporated Greek Sicily into the domain of Latin speech ; the same will, which drew the boundaries between the Latin West and the Greek East, assigned Africa to the former.

In a similar sense the internal organisation of the country was regulated. It was based, as in Italy on the Latin and in the East on the Hellenic urban community, so here on the Phoenician. When the Roman rule in Africa began, the Carthaginian territory at that time consisted predominantly of urban communities, for the most part small, of which there were counted three hundred, each administered by its sufetes ;[1] and the republic had made no change in this respect. Even in the kingdoms the towns formerly Phoenician had retained their organisation under the native rulers, and at least Calama—an inland town of Numidia hardly of Phoenician foundation—had demonstrably the same Phoenician municipal constitution ; the civilisation which Massinissa gave to his kingdom must have consisted essentially in his transforming the villages

[1] More clearly than by the Latin inscriptions found in Africa, which begin too late to illustrate the state of things before the second century A.D., this is shown by the four contracts of *patronatus* from the time of Tiberius, quoted in next note, concluded by two small places of the proconsular province Apisa maius and Siagu, and two others nowhere else mentioned, probably adjacent, Themetra and Thimiligi ; according to which the statement of Strabo (xvii. 3, 15, p. 833) that at the beginning of the last war the Carthaginian territory numbered 300 towns, appears not at all incredible. In each of those four smaller places there were sufetes ; even where the old and new Punic inscriptions name magistrates, there are regularly two sufetes. That these are comparatively frequent in the proconsular province, and else where can only be pointed out in Calama, serves to show how much more strongly the Phoenician urban organisation was developed in the former.

of the agricultural Berbers into towns after the Phoenician model. The same will hold good of the few older urban communities which existed in Mauretania before Augustus. So far as we see, the two annually changing sufetes of the African communities coincide in the main with the analogous presidents of the community in the Italian municipal constitution ; and that in other respects, *e.g.* in the common councils among the Carthaginians formed after a fashion altogether divergent from the Italian (ii. 16), the Phoenician urban constitution of Roman Africa has preserved national peculiarities, does not at least admit of proof.[1] But the fact itself that the contrast, if even but formal, of the Phoenician town to the Italian was retained was, like the permission of the language, a recognition of the Phoenician nationality and a certain security for its continuance even under Roman rule. That it was recognised in the first instance as the regular form of administration of the African territory, is proved by the establishment of Carthage by Caesar primarily as a Phoenician city as well under the old sufetes[2] as in a certain measure with the old inhabitants, seeing that a great, perhaps the greatest part of the new burgesses was taken from the surrounding townships, again also under the protection of the great goddess of the Punic Carthage, the queen of heaven

ii. 15.

---

[1] The contracts of *patronatus* from the time of Caesar (*C. I. L.* viii. 10525), of Augustus (*ib.* 68 comp. 69), and Tiberius (*C. I. L.* v. 4919-4922), concluded by the *senatus populusque* of African communities (*civitates*) of peregrine rights with Romans of rank, appear to have been entered into quite after the Roman fashion by the common council, which represents and binds the community.

[2] On the coin undoubtedly struck under Caesar (Müller *Num. de l'Afr.* ii. 149) with *Kar*(*thago*) *Veneris* and *Aristo Mutumbal Ricoce suf*(*etes*), the first two names are probably to be taken together as a Graeco-Phoenician double name, such as elsewhere is not rare (comp. *C. I. L.* v. 4922 : *agente Celere Imilchonis Gulalsae filio*

sufete). Since on the one hand sufetes cannot be assigned to a Roman colony, and on the other hand the conducting of such a colony to Carthage itself is well attested, Caesar himself must either have subsequently changed the form of founding the city, or the founding of the colony must have been carried into effect by the triumvirate as a posthumous ordinance of the dictator (as is hinted by Appian, *Pun.* 136). We may compare the fact that Curubis stands in the earlier time of Caesar under sufetes (*C. I. L.* viii. 10525), in the year 709 U.C. as a Caesarian colony under duoviri (*ib.* 977); yet the case is different, since this town did not, like Carthage, owe its existence to Caesar.

Astarte, who at that time marched in with her votaries anew into her old abode. It is true that in Carthage itself this organisation soon gave place to the Italian colonial constitution, and the protecting patroness Astarte became the—at least in name—Latin Caelestis. But in the rest of Africa and in Numidia the Phoenician urban organisation probably remained throughout the first century the predominant one, in so far as it pertained to all communities of recognised municipal rights and lacking Roman or Latin organisation. Abolished in the proper sense it doubtless was not, as in fact sufetes still occur under Pius ; but by degrees they everywhere make way for the duoviri, and the changed principle of government entails in this sphere also its ultimate consequences.

The transformation of Phoenician urban rights into Italian began under Caesar. The old Phoenician town of Utica, predecessor and heiress of Carthage—as some compensation for the severe injury to its interests by the restoration of the old capital of the country—obtained, as the first Italian organisation in Africa, perhaps from the dictator Caesar, Latin rights, certainly from his successor Augustus the position of a Roman *municipium*. The town of Tingi received the same rights, in gratitude for the fidelity which it had maintained during the Perusine war (p. 311). Several others soon followed ; yet the number of communities with Roman rights in Africa down to Trajan and Hadrian remained limited.[1] Thenceforth there were assigned on a great scale—although, so far as we see, throughout by individual bestowal—to communities hitherto Phoenician municipal or else colonial rights ;

Transformation of the Phoenician towns into Italian.

---

[1] For Africa and Numidia Pliny (*H. N.*, v. 4, 29 f.) numbers in all 516 communities, among which are 6 colonies, 15 communities of Roman burgesses, 2 Latin towns (for the *oppidum stipendiarium* must, according to the position which is given to it, have been also of Italian rights), the rest either Phoenician towns (*oppida*), among which were 30 free, or else Libyan tribes (*non civitates tantum,* *sed pleraeque etiam nationes iure dici possunt*). Whether these figures are to be referred to Vespasian's time or to an earlier, is not ascertained ; in any case they are not free from errors, for, besides the six colonies specially adduced, six are wanting (Assuras, Carpi, Clupea, Curubi, Hippo Diarrhytos, Neapolis), which are referable, partly with certainty partly with probability, to Caesar or Augustus.

for the latter too were subsequently as a rule conferred merely in a titular way without settlement of colonists. If the dedications and memorials of all sorts, that formerly appeared but sparingly in Africa, present themselves in abundance from the beginning of the second century, this was doubtless chiefly the consequence of the adoption of numerous townships into the imperial union of the towns with best rights.

Settlement of Italian colonists in Africa.

Besides the conversion of Phoenician towns into Italian *municipia* or colonies, not a few towns of Italian rights arose in Africa by means of the settlement of Italian colonists. For this too the dictator Caesar laid the foundation—as indeed for no province perhaps so much as for Africa were the paths prescribed by him—and the emperors of the first dynasty followed his example. We have already spoken of the founding of Carthage ; the town obtained not at once, but very soon, Italian settlers and therewith Italian organisation and full rights of Roman citizenship. Beyond doubt from the outset destined once more to be the capital of the province and laid out as a great city, it rapidly in point of fact became so. Carthage and Lugudunum were the only cities of the West which, besides the capital of the empire, had a standing garrison of imperial troops. Moreover in Africa—in part certainly already by the dictator, in part only by the first emperor—a series of small country-towns in the districts nearest to Sicily, Hippo Diarrhytus, Clupea, Curubi, Neapolis, Carpi, Maxula, Uthina, Great-Thuburbo, Assuras, were furnished with colonies, probably not merely to provide for veterans, but to promote the Latinising of this region. The two colonies which arose at that time in the former kingdom of Numidia, Cirta with its dependencies, and New-Cirta or Sicca, were the result of special obligations of Caesar towards the leader of free bands Publius Sittius from Nuceria and his Italiano-African bands (iv. 470, 574). The former, inasmuch as the territory on which it was laid out belonged at that time to a client-state (p. 311, note), obtained a peculiar and very independent organisation, and retained it in

iv. 447, 544.

part even later, although it soon became an imperial city. Both rose rapidly and became considerable centres of Roman civilisation in Africa.

The colonisation, which Augustus undertook in the kingdom of Juba and Claudius carried forward, bore another character. In Mauretania, still at that time very primitive, there was a want both of towns and of the elements for creating them ; the settlement of soldiers of the Roman army, who had served out their time, brought civilisation here into a barbarous land. Thus in the later province of Caesarea along the coast Igilgili, Saldae, Rusazu, Rusguniae, Gunugi, Cartenna (Tenes), and farther away from the sea Thubusuptu and Zuccabar, were settled with Augustan, and Oppidum Novum with Claudian, veterans ; as also in the province of Tingi under Augustus Zilis, Babba, Banasa, under Claudius Lix   These communities with Roman burgess-rights were not, as was already observed, under the kings of Mauretania, so long as there were such, but were attached administratively to the adjoining Roman province ; consequently there was involved in these settlements, as it were, a beginning towards the annexation of Mauretania.[1] The pushing forward of civilisation, such as Augustus and Claudius aimed at, was not subsequently continued, or at any rate continued only to a very limited extent, although there was room enough for it in the western half of the province of Caesarea and in that of Tingi ; that the later colonies regularly proceeded from titular bestowal without settlement, has already been remarked (p. 332).

Alongside of this urban organisation we have specially to mention that of the large landed estates in this province. According to Roman arrangement it fitted itself regularly into the communal constitution ; even the extension of

And in Maure-tania.

Large landed estates.

---

[1] Pliny, v. 1, 2, says indeed only of Zulil or rather Zili *regum dicioni exempta et iura in Baeticam petere iussa*, and this might be connected with the transfer of this community to Baetica as *Iulia Traducta* (Strabo, iii. 1, 8, p. 140). But probably Pliny gives this notice in the case of Zili alone, just because this is the first colony laid out beyond the imperial frontier which he names. The burgess of a Roman colony cannot possibly have had his forum of justice before the king of Mauretania.

the *latifundia* affected this relationship less injuriously than we should think, since these, as a rule, were not locally compact and were often distributed among several urban territories. But in Africa the large estates were not merely more numerous and more extensive than elsewhere, but these assumed also the compactness of urban territories ; around the landlord's house there was formed a settlement, which was not inferior to the small agricultural towns of the province, and, if its president and common councillors often did not venture and still oftener were not able to subject such a fellow-burgess to the full payment of the communal burdens falling upon him, the *de facto* release of these estates from the communal bond of union became still further marked, when such a possession passed over into the hands of the emperor.[1] But this early occurred in Africa to a great extent ; Nero in particular, lighted with his confiscations on the landowners, as is said, of half Africa, and what was once imperial was wont to remain so. The small lessees, to whom the domanial estate was farmed out, appear for the most part to have been brought from abroad, and these imperial *coloni* may be reckoned in a certain measure as belonging to the Italian immigration.

Organisation of the Berber communities.

We have formerly remarked (p. 306) that the Berbers formed a considerable portion of the population of Numidia and Mauretania through the whole time of the Roman rule. But as to their internal organisation hardly more can be ascertained than the emergence of the clan (*gens*)[2]

---

[1] Frontinus in the well-known passage, p. 53 Lachm., respecting processes between the urban communities and private persons, or, as it may be, the emperor, appears not to presuppose state-districts *de iure* independent and of a similar nature with urban territories—such as are incompatible with Roman law—but a *de facto* refractory attitude of the great landowner towards the community which makes him liable, *e.g.* for the furnishing of recruits or compulsory services, basing itself on the allegation that the piece of land made liable is not within the bounds of the community requiring the service.

[2] The technical designation *gens* comes into prominence particularly in the fixed title of the *praefectus gentis Musulamiorum, etc. ;* but, as this is the lowest category of the independent commonwealth, the word is usually avoided in dedications (comp. *C. I. L.* viii. p. 1100) and *civitas* put instead, a designation, which, like the *oppidum* of Pliny foreign to the technical language (p. 331, note), includes in it all communities of non-Italian or Greek organisation. The nature of the *gens*

instead of the urban organisation under duoviri or sufetes. The societies of the natives were not, like those of North Italy, assigned as subjects to individual urban communities, but were placed like the towns immediately under the governors, doubtless also, where it seemed necessary, under a Roman officer specially placed over them (*praefectus gentis*), and further under authorities of their own[1]—the "headman" (*princeps*), who in later times bore possibly the title of king, and the "eleven first." Presumably this arrangement was monarchical in contrast to the collegiate one of the Phoenician as of the Latin community, and there stood alongside of the tribal chief a limited number of elders instead of the numerous senate of de-

is described by the paraphrase (*C. I. L.* viii. 68) alternating with *civitas Gurzensis* (*ib.* 69) : *senatus populusque civitatium stipendiariorum pago Gurzenses*, that is, the "elders and community of the clans of tributary people in the village of Gurza."

[1] When the designation *princeps* (*C. I. L.* viii. p. 1102) is not merely enunciative but an official title, it appears throughout in communities which are neither themselves urban communities nor parts of such, and with special frequency in the case of the *gentes*. We may compare the "eleven first" (comp, *Eph. epigr.* v. n. 302, 521, 533) with the *seniores* to be met with here and there. An evidence in support of both positions is given in the inscription *C. I. L.* viii. 7041 : *Florus Labaeonis f. princeps et undecimprimus gentis Saboidum*. Recently at Bu Jelîda, a little westward of the great road between Carthage and Theveste, in a valley of the Jebel Rihan, and so in a quite civilised region, there have been found the remains of a Berber village, which calls itself on a monument of the time of Pius (still unprinted) *gens Bacchuiana*, and is under "eleven elders" ; the names of gods (*Saturno Achaiaei* [?] *Aug[uslo]*, like the names of men (*Candidus Braisamonis fil.*), are half local, half Latin. In Calama the dating after the two sufetes and the *prin-*

ceps (*C. I. L.* viii. 5306, comp. 5369) is remarkable ; it appears that this probably Libyan community was first under a chief, and then obtained sufetes without the chief being dropped. It may readily be understood that our monuments do not give much information upon the *gentes* and their organisation ; in this field doubtless little was written on stone. Even the Libyan inscriptions belong, at least as regards the majority, to towns in part or wholly inhabited by Berbers ; the bilingual inscriptions found at Tenelium (*C. I. L.* viii. p. 514), in Numidia westward from Bona in the Sheffia plain, the same place that has furnished till now most of the Berber stone inscriptions, show indeed in their Latin part Libyan names, *e.g. Chinidial Misicir* f. and *Naddhsen Cotuzanis* f., both from the clan (*tribu*) of the *Misiciri* or *Misictri ;* but one of these people, who has served in the Roman army and has acquired the Roman franchise, names himself in the Latin text *in civitate sua Tenelio flamen perpetuus*, according to which this place seems to have been organised like a town. If, therefore, success should ever attend the attempt to read and decipher the Berber inscriptions with certainty, they would hardly give us sufficient information as to the internal organisation of the Berber tribes.

curiones of the towns. The communities of natives in Roman Africa seem to have attained afterwards to Italian organisation only by way of exception ; the African towns with Italian rights, which did not originate from immigration, had doubtless for the most part Phoenician civic rights previously. Exceptions occur chiefly in the case of transplanted tribes, as indeed the considerable town Thubursicum originated from such a forced settlement of Numidians. The Berber communities possessed especially the mountains and the steppes ; they obeyed the foreigners, without either the masters or the subjects feeling any desire to come to terms with one another ; and, when other foreigners invaded the land, their position in presence of the Vandals, the Byzantines, the Arabs, the French, remained almost on the old footing.

Husbandry.

In the economy of the soil the eastern half of Africa vies with Egypt. Certainly the soil is unequal, and rocks and steppes occupy not only the greater portion of the western half, but also considerable tracts in the eastern ; here too there were various inaccessible mountain-regions, which yielded but slowly or not at all to civilisation ; particularly on the rocky ridges along the coast the Roman rule left few or no traces. Even the Byzacene, the south-eastmost part of the proconsular province, is only designated as a specially productive region by an erroneous generalisation of what holds good as to individual coast districts and oases ; from Sufetula (Sbitla) westward the land is waterless and rocky ; in the fifth century A.D. Byzacene was reckoned to have about a half less per cent of land capable of culture than the other African provinces. But the northern and northwestern portion of the proconsular province, above all the valley of the largest river in north Africa, the Bagradas (Mejerda), and not less a considerable part of Numidia, yield abundant grain crops, almost like the valley of the Nile. In the favoured districts the country towns, very frequent, as their ruins show, lay so near to each other that the population here cannot have been much less dense than in the land of the Nile, and according to all traces it prosecuted especially husbandry. The mighty armed masses, with which after the defeat at Pharsalus the republicans in Africa took up the struggle against Caesar, were formed of these peasants, so that in the year of war the fields lay untilled. Since Italy used more corn than it produced, it was primarily dependent, in addition to the Italian islands, on the almost equally near Africa ; and after it became subject to the Romans, its corn went thither not merely by way of commerce, but above all as tribute. Already in Cicero's time the capital of the empire doubtless subsisted for the most part on African corn ; through the admission of Numidia under Caesar's dictatorship the corn thenceforth coming in as tribute increased according to the estimate about 1,200,000 Roman bushels (525,000 hectolitres) annually. After the Egyptian corn supplies were instituted under Augustus, for the third part of the corn used in Rome North Africa was reckoned upon, and Egypt for a like amount ; while the desolated Sicily, Sardinia, and Baetica, along with Italy's own production, covered the rest of the need. In what measure the Italy of the imperial period was dependent for its subsistence on Africa is shown by the measures taken during the wars between Vitellius and Vespasian and between Severus and Pescennius ; Vespasian thought that he had conquered Italy when he occupied Egypt and Africa ; Severus sent a strong army to Africa to hinder Pescennius from occupying it.

Oil, too, and wine had already held a prominent place in the old Carthaginian husbandry, and on Little-Leptis (near Susa), for example, an annual payment of 3,000,000 pounds of oil (nearly 10,000 hectolitres) could be imposed by Caesar for the Roman baths, as indeed Susa still at the present day exports 40,000 hectolitres of oil. Accordingly the historian of the Jugurthan war terms Africa rich in corn, poor in oil and wine, and even in Vespasian's time the province gave in this respect only a moderate yield. It was only when the peace with the empire became permanent—a peace which the fruit-tree

Oil and wine.

needed even far more than the fruits of the field—that the culture of olives extended ; in the fourth century no province supplied such quantities of oil as Africa, and the African oil was predominantly employed for the baths in Rome. In quality, doubtless, it was always inferior to that of Italy and Spain, not because nature there was less favourable, but because the preparation lacked skill and care. The cultivation of the vine acquired no prominent importance in Africa for export. On the other hand the breeding of horses and of cattle flourished, especially in Numidia and Mauretania.

Manufactures and commerce.

Manufactures and trade never had the same importance in the African provinces as in the East and in Egypt. The Phoenicians had transplanted the preparation of purple from their native country to these coasts, where the island of Gerba (Jerba) became the African Tyre, and was inferior only to the latter itself in quality. This manufacture flourished through the whole imperial period. Among the few deeds which king Juba II. has to show, is the arrangement for obtaining purple on the coast of the Atlantic Ocean and on the adjacent islands.[1] Woollen stuffs of inferior quality and leather goods were manufactured in Mauretania, apparently by the natives, also for export.[2] The trade in slaves was very considerable. The products of the interior of the country naturally passed by way of North Africa into general commerce, but not to such an extent as by way of Egypt. The elephant,

---

[1] That the Gaetulian purple is to be referred to Juba is stated by Pliny, *H. N.* vi. 31, 201 : *paucas (Mauretaniae insulas) constat esse ex adverso Autololum a Iuba repertas, in quibus Gaetulicam purpuram tinguere instituerat ;* by these *insulae purpurariae* (*ib.* 203) can only be meant Madeira. In fact the oldest mention of this purple is that in Horace, *Ep.* ii. 2, 181. Proofs are wanting as to the later duration of this manufacture, and, as the Roman rule did not extend to these islands, it is not probable, although from the *sagum purpurium* of the tariff of Zarai (*C. I. L.*

viii. 4508) we may infer Mauretanian manufactures of purple.

[2] The tariff of Zarai set up at the Numidian customs - frontier towards Mauretania (*C. I. L.* viii. 4508) from the year 202 gives a clear picture of the Mauretanian exports. Wine, figs, dates, sponges, are not wanting ; but slaves, cattle of all sorts, woollen stuffs (*vestis Afra*), and leather wares play the chief part. The Description of the earth also from the time of Constantius says, c. 60, that Mauretania *vestem et mancipia negotiatur.*

it is true, was the device of Mauretania in particular, and there, where it has now for long disappeared, it was still hunted down to the imperial period ; but probably only small quantities came thence into commerce.

The prosperity which subsisted in the part of Africa at all cultivated is clearly attested by the ruins of its numerous towns, which, in spite of the narrow bounds of their domains, everywhere exhibit baths, theatres, triumphal arches, gorgeous tombs, and generally buildings of luxury of all kinds, mostly mediocre in art, often excessive in magnificence.   Not quite in the villas of the superior nobility, as in the Gallic land, but in the middle class of the farming burgesses must the economic strength of these regions have lain.[1] *Prosperity.*

The frequency of intercourse, so far as we may judge of it from our knowledge of the network of roads, must within the civilised territory have corresponded to the density of the population.   During the first century the imperial roads originated, which connected the head-quarters of that time, Theveste, partly with the coast of the Lesser Syrtis—a step, having close relation to the formerly narrated pacification of the district between the Aures and the sea—partly with the great cities of the north coast, Hippo regius (Bona) and Carthage.   From the second century onward we find all the larger towns and several smaller active in providing the necessary communications within their territory ; this, however, doubtless holds true of most of the imperial lands, and only comes into clearer prominence in Africa, because this opportunity was made use of more diligently here than elsewhere to do homage to the reigning emperor. *Roads.*

---

[1] According to an epitaph found in Mactaris in the Byzacene (*Eph. epigr.* v. n. 279), a man of free birth there, after having been actively engaged in bringing in the harvests far around in Africa, first throughout twelve years as an ordinary reaper and then for other eleven as a foreman, purchased for himself with the savings of his pay a town and a country house, and became in his turn a member of council and burgomaster. His poetical epitaph shows, if not culture, at least pretensions to it.   A development of life of this sort was in the Roman imperial period doubtless not so rare as it at first may seem, but probably occurred in Africa more frequently than elsewhere.

As to the road-system of the districts, which though Roman were yet not Romanised, and as to the routes which were the medium of the important traffic through the desert, we have no general information.

Introduc-
tion of
camels.
But probably a momentous revolution occurred in the desert-traffic during that time by the introduction of the camel. In older times it meets us, as is well known, only in Asia as far as Arabia, while Egypt and all Africa knew simply the horse. During the first three centuries of our era the countries effected an exchange, and, like the Arabian horse, the Libyan camel, we may say, made its appearance in history. Mention of the latter first occurs in the history of the war waged by the dictator Caesar in Africa; when here among the booty by the side of captive officers twenty-two camels of king Juba are adduced, such a possession must at that time have been of an extraordinary nature in Africa. In the fourth century the Roman generals demand from the towns of Tripolis thousands of camels for the transport of water and of provisions before they enter upon the march into the desert. This gives a glimpse of the revolution that had taken place during the interval in the circumstances of the intercourse between the north and the south of Africa; whether it originated from Egypt or from Cyrene and Tripolis we cannot tell, but it redounded to the advantage of the whole north of this continent.

Character
and culture
of the
people.
Thus North Africa was a valuable possession for the finances of the empire. Whether the Roman nation generally gained or lost more by the assimilation of North Africa, is less ascertained. The dislike which the Italian felt from of old towards the African did not change after Carthage had become a Roman great city, and all Africa spoke Latin; if Severus Antoninus combined in himself the vices of three nations, his savage cruelty was traced to his African father, and the ship captain of the fourth century, who thought that "Africa was a fine country but the Africans were not worthy of it, for they were cunning and faithless, and there might be some good people among them, but not many," was at

least not thinking of the bad Hannibal, but was speaking
out the feeling of the great public at the time.   So far
as the influence of African elements may be recognised
in the Roman literature of the imperial period, we meet
with specially unpleasant leaves in a book generally far
from pleasant.   The new life, which bloomed for the
Romans out of the ruins of the nations extirpated by
them, was nowhere full and fresh and beautiful ; even the
two creations of Caesar, the Celtic land and North Africa
—for Latin Africa was not much less his work than
Latin Gaul—remained structures of ruins.   But the
toga suited, at any rate, the new-Roman of the Rhone
and the Garonne better than the " Seminumidians and
Semigaetulians."   Doubtless Carthage remained in the
numbers of its population and in wealth not far behind
Alexandria, and was indisputably the second city of the
Latin half of the empire, next to Rome the most lively,
perhaps also the most corrupt, city of the West, and the
most important centre of Latin culture and literature.
Augustine depicts with lively colours how many an
honest youth from the province went to wreck there
amid the dissolute doings of the circus, and how powerful
was the impression produced on him—when, a student of
seventeen years of age, he came from Madaura to Carthage
—by the theatre with its love-pieces and with its tragedy.
There was no lack in the African of diligence and talent ;
on the contrary, perhaps more value was set upon the
Latin and along with it the Greek instruction, and on its
aim of general culture, in Africa than anywhere else in the
empire, and the school-system was highly developed.   The
philosopher Appuleius under Pius, the celebrated Christian
author Augustine, both descended from good burgess-
families—the former from Madaura, the latter from the
neighbouring smaller place Thagaste—received their first
training in the schools of their native towns ; then
Appuleius studied in Carthage, and finished his training
in Athens and Rome ; Augustine went from Thagaste
first to Madaura, then likewise to Carthage ; in this way
the training of youth was completed in the better houses

throughout. Juvenal advises the professor of rhetoric who would earn money to go to Gaul or, still better, to Africa, "the nurse of advocates." At a nobleman's seat in the territory of Cirta there has recently been brought to light a private bath of the later imperial period equipped with princely magnificence, the mosaic pavement of which depicts how matters went on once at the castle ; the palaces, the extensive hunting-park with the hounds and stags, the stables with the noble race-horses, occupy no doubt most of the space, but there is not wanting also the " scholar's corner " (*filosofi locus*), and beside it the noble lady sitting under the palms.

Scholas-
ticism.
But the black spot of the African literary character is just its scholasticism. It does not begin till late ; before the time of Hadrian and of Pius the Latin literary world exhibits no African name of repute, and subsequently the Africans of note were throughout, in the first instance, schoolmasters, and came as such to be authors. Under those emperors the most celebrated teachers and scholars of the capital were native Africans, the rhetor Marcus Cornelius Fronto from Cirta, instructor of the princes at the court of Pius, and the philologue Gaius Sulpicius Apollinaris from Carthage. For that reason there prevailed in these circles sometimes the foolish purism that forced back the Latin into the old-fashioned paths of Ennius and of Cato, whereby Fronto and Apollinaris made their repute, sometimes an utter oblivion of the earnest austerity innate in Latin, and a frivolity producing a worse imitation of bad Greek models, such as reaches its culmination in the—in its time much admired—" Ass-romance " of that philosopher of Madaura. The language swarmed partly with scholastic reminiscences, partly with unclassical or newly coined words and phrases. Just as in the emperor Severus, an African of good family and himself a scholar and author, his tone of speech always betrayed the African, so the style of these Africans, even those who were clever and from the first trained in Latin, like the Carthaginian Tertullian, has regularly something strange and incongruous, with its diffuseness of petty detail, its

minced sentences, its witty and fantastic conceits.   There
is a lack of both the graceful charm of the Greek and of
the dignity of the Roman.   Significantly we do not meet
in the whole field of Africano-Latin authorship a single
poet who deserves to be so much as named.

It was not till the Christian period that it became   Christian
otherwise.   In the development of Christianity Africa   literature
in Africa.
plays the very first part ; if it arose in Syria, it was in
and through Africa that it became the religion for the
world.   As the translation of the sacred books from the
Hebrew language into the Greek, and that into the popular
language of the most considerable Jewish community out
of Judaea, gave to Judaism its position in the world, so
in a similar way for the transference of Christianity from
the serving East to the ruling West the translation of its
confessional writings into the language of the West
became of decisive importance ; and this all the more,
inasmuch as these books were translated, not into the
language of the cultivated circles of the West, which early
disappeared from common life and in the imperial age
was everywhere a matter of scholastic attainment, but
into the decomposed Latin already preparing the way
for the structure of the Romance languages—the Latin
of common intercourse at that time familiar to the great
masses.   If Christianity was by the destruction of the
Jewish church-state released from its Jewish basis (p. 229),
it became the religion of the world by the fact, that in
the great world-empire it began to speak the universally
current imperial language ; and those nameless men, who
since the second century Latinised the Christian writings,
performed for this epoch just such a service, as at the
present day, in the heightened measure required by the
enlarged horizon of the nations, is carried out in the
footsteps of Luther by the Bible Societies.   And these
men were in part Italians, but above all Africans.[1]   In

[1] How far our Latin texts of the   from one and the same translation as
Bible are to be referred to several   a basis by means of manifold revision
translations originally different, or   with the aid of the originals, are
whether, as Lachmann assumed, the   questions which can scarcely be
different recensions have proceeded   definitely decided—for the present at

Africa to all appearance the knowledge of Greek, which is able to dispense with translations, was far more seldom to be met with than at least in Rome ; and, on the other hand, the Oriental element, that preponderated particularly in the early stages of Christianity, here found a readier reception than in the other Latin-speaking lands of the West. Even as regards the polemic literature called especially into existence by the new faith, since the

least—in favour of either one or the other view. But that both Italians and Africans took part in this work —whether of translation or of correction—is proved by the famous words of Augustine, *de doctr. Christ.* ii. 15, 22, *in ipsis autem interpretationibus Itala ceteris praeferatur, nam est verborum tenacior cum perspicuitate sententiae,* over which great authorities have been perplexed, but certainly without reason. Bentley's proposal, approved afresh of late (by Corssen, *Jahrb. für protestant. Theol.* vii. p. 507 f.), to change *Itala* into *illa* and *nam* into *quae,* is inadmissible alike philologically and in substance. For the twofold change is destitute of all external probability, and besides *nam* is protected by the copyist Isidorus, *Etym.* vi. 4, 2. The further objection that linguistic usage would require *Italica,* is not borne out (*e.g.* Sidonius and Iordanes as well as the inscriptions of later times, *C. I. L.* x. p. 1146, write *Italus* by turns with *Italicus*), and the designation of a single translation as the most trustworthy on the whole is quite consistent with the advice to consult as many as possible ; whereas by the change proposed an intelligent remark is converted into a meaningless commonplace. It is true that the Christian Church in Rome in the first three centuries made use throughout of the Greek language, and that we may not seek *there* for the *Itali* who took part in the Latin Bible. But that in Italy outside of Rome, especially in Upper Italy, the knowledge of Greek was not much more diffused than in Africa, is most clearly shown by the names of freedmen ; and it is just to

the non-Roman Italy that the designation used by Augustine points ; while we may perhaps also call to mind the fact that Augustine was gained for Christianity by Ambrosius in Milan. The attempt to identify the traces of the recension called by Augustine *Itala* in such remains as have survived of Bible translations before Jerome's, will at all events hardly ever be successful ; but still less will it admit of being proved that Africans only worked at the pre-Hieronymian Latin Bible texts. That they originated largely, perhaps for the most part, in Africa has certainly great probability. The contrast to the one *Itala* can only in reason have been several *Afrae;* and the vulgar Latin, in which these texts are all of them written, is in full agreement with the vulgar Latin, as it was demonstrably spoken in Africa. At the same time we must doubtless not overlook the fact that we know the vulgar Latin in general principally from African sources, and that the proof of the restriction of any individual linguistic phenomenon to Africa is as necessary as it is for the most part unadduced. There existed side by side as well vulgarisms in general use as African provincialisms (comp. *Eph. epigr.* iv. p. 520, as to the cognomina in *-osus*) ; but that forms like *glorificare, nudificare, justificare,* belong to the second category, is by no means proved from the fact that we first meet with them in Africa, since analogous documents to those which we possess, *e.g.* for Carthage in the case of Tertullian, are wanting to us as regards Capua and Milan.

Roman church at this epoch belonged to the Greek circle (p. 226), Africa took the lead in the Latin tongue. The whole Christian authorship down to the end of this period is, so far as it is Latin, African; Tertullian and Cyprian were from Carthage, Arnobius from Sicca, Lactantius, and probably in like manner Minucius Felix, were, in spite of their classic Latin, Africans, and not less the already mentioned somewhat later Augustine. In Africa the growing church found its most zealous confessors and its most gifted defenders. For the literary conflict of the faith Africa furnished by far the most and the ablest combatants, whose special characteristics, now in eloquent discussion, now in witty ridicule of fables, now in vehement indignation, found a true and mighty field for their display in the onslaught on the old gods. A mind—intoxicated first by the whirl of a dissolute life, and then by the fiery enthusiasm of faith—such as utters itself in the Confessions of Augustine, has no parallel elsewhere in antiquity.

APPENDIX: ROMAN BRITAIN

(Chapter V. Vol. I. pp. 170-194)

MOMMSEN'S sketch of Roman Britain has often been called deficient and inaccurate. As a general judgment, this is wholly unjust. The sketch has real and distinct merits. When first issued in 1885, it marked a great advance towards a right conception of its subject. It differed conspicuously, and all for the better, from the other sketches of Roman Britain which were then current and accepted, Hübner's papers since collected in his *Römische Herrschaft in Westeuropa*, Wright's *Celt, Roman, and Saxon*, Scarth's *Roman Britain*. To-day it is perhaps the best existing account of the conquest and military administration of the province, and it contains much which no one—least of all, our English archaeologists—can afford to neglect. On the other hand, it is undeniably not one of the best sections in the volume to which it belongs, and it treats some parts of its theme, notably the civil life and civilisation, very shortly. One may be pardoned for taking the occasion of its republication in English dress, to make a few additions and corrections which may interest English readers, while they fill some gaps and take note of some recent discoveries.

The accounts of the Claudian invasion and the early years of the conquest (pp. 172-9) are, in their broad outlines, beyond reasonable doubt. But details can perhaps be added or altered. The army which started in A.D. 43 in three corps ($\tau\rho\iota\chi\hat{\eta}$ $\nu\epsilon\mu\eta\theta\acute{\epsilon}\nu\tau\epsilon\varsigma$, Dio, 60, 20) may well have landed in the three harbours afterwards used by the Romans in Kent, Lymne, Dover, and Richborough—the last named being the principal port for passengers to and from Britain throughout the Roman period. The difficult river crossed shortly afterwards by Plautius may be the Medway near Rochester, where in after years the Roman road from the Kentish ports to London had its bridge. The subsequent course of the invading armies is not easy to trace. But it would seem that, when they had won London and Colchester, they advanced from this base-line in three separate corps to the conquest of the South and Midlands. The left wing, the Second Legion Augusta under Vespasian, overran the south as far (probably) as South Wales and Exeter (Suet. *Vesp.* 4; Tac. *Agric.* 13; *Hist.* iii. 44; tile of Legio ii. Aug. at Seaton, *Archæological Journal,* xlix. 180). The centre, the Fourteenth and Twentieth Legions, crossed the Midlands to Wroxeter and Chester (tile of Legio xx. at Whittlebury, *Vict. Hist. of Northants,* i. 215; inscriptions at Wroxeter and Chester). The right wing, the Ninth, moved up the east side of Britain to Lincoln (tile of Legio ix. at Hilly Wood, on the road towards Lincoln, *Vict. Hist. of Northants,* i. 214; inscriptions at Lincoln). These three lines of advance led direct to the positions of the fortresses where we find the legions presently posted. They agree also with the three main groups of Roman roads which radiate from London : (1) the south-west route to Silchester, and thence by branches to Winchester, Exeter, Bath, South Wales; (2) the Midland "Watling Street," by St. Albans to Wroxeter and Chester; (3) the eastern route to Colchester, Cambridge, and Castor near Peterborough, to Lincoln.[1]

In any case there can be little doubt that by A.D. 47 or 48— within four or five years of the first landing — the Roman troops had reached the basins of the Humber and the Severn, as Mommsen observes (p. 176). Thus much is plain from the fact that Ostorius, who came out in 47, had at once to deal with the Iceni of Norfolk, the Decangi of Flintshire, the Brigantes of Yorkshire, the Silures of Monmouthshire (Tac. *Ann.* xii. 31). But the difficult corruption of Tacitus (*ibid.*), *cuncta castris antonam et Sabrinam fluvios cohibere parat,* is probably to be emended (with Dr. H. Bradley, *Academy,* April and May 1883) *cuncta cis Trisantonam, i.e.* the Roman frontier at the moment was, roughly, Severn and Trent. This is preferable both to Mommsen's suggestion (given above, p. 176 note) and to mine (*Journ. Phil.* xvii. 268). The older and more violent remedy, *Avonam inter et Sabrinam,* though revived in the text of the second edition of Furneaux's *Tacitus* (1907), is pretty certainly wrong; indeed, it is not Latin.

It would seem then that, by 47 or 48, practically the whole lowlands were in the hands of the Romans. Whether Chester had already been occupied or (as seems likelier) was first garrisoned when Ostorius attacked the Decangi, must remain uncertain; it must in any case have been occupied soon (*Eph. Epigr.* vii. 903; Domaszewski, *Rhein. Mus.* xlviii. 344). Caerleon, connected by Mommsen with Tac. *Ann.* xii. 32,

---

[1] The arguments of Mr. B. W. Henderson (*English Hist. Review,* 1903, 1-23) for a different advance seem to me to be based on a misconception of some of the evidence. Thus, there is no tile of Leg. ix. at Leicester, nor any trace yet noted of Leg. ii. Aug. at Cirencester or Gloucester.

presents more difficulty, since it has yielded hardly any datable remains earlier than about A.D. 70-80 ; however, no other site can be suggested on our present evidence for the *hiberna* of the Second Legion Augusta before 70. Wroxeter rests its claim to a fortress on two early inscriptions of Legio xiv. (*Vict. Hist. Shropshire*, i. 243, 244), and this may be adequate, though Domaszewski doubts it. The course of Watling Street seems to show that Wroxeter was occupied before the troops pushed on to Chester.

Mommsen's account of the Boadicean revolt (pp. 179-181) is famous for his denunciation of Tacitus as "the most unmilitary of all authors." It must be conceded that Tacitus is unmilitary—not so much because he is condensed or discontinuous or ignorant of geography (E. G. Hardy, *Journ. Phil.* xxxi. 123), as because he has a literary horror of all technical detail, and desires to give the general effect of each situation without distracting the reader by vexatious precision and difficult *minutiae.* But in this case his narrative (*Ann.* xii. 32 foll.) is better than Mommsen (or indeed Domaszewski) allows. Paullinus doubtless marched to London, as Horsley long ago observed, because it lay on the road (Watling Street) from Chester to Colchester ; that he hurried on in front of his main forces is implied in the *iam* at the beginning of c. 34.

The conquest of Wales (p. 182) was completed, as Mommsen says, in the decade A.D. 70-80. But his statements require some re-wording. Roman remains are not "completely absent" in the interior ; the continuance of native resistance to Rome is very doubtful ; the existence of Celtic speech and nationality in Wales to-day is—in large part, at least—due to a Celtic revival in the late fourth or the fifth century, and to immigration of new Celtic elements at that time, and cannot therefore be cited as here. So far as present evidence goes, the district as a whole seems during the first, second, and third centuries to have closely resembled the similar mountainous districts of northern England, save only that the Welsh tribes never revolted after A.D. 80, while the Brigantes gave trouble throughout the second century. The same system of small auxiliary *castella* was established in Wales as in northern England. These forts are at present almost wholly unexplored. But we can detect unquestionable examples at Caerhun (Canovium, *Eph.* vii. 1099) and Carnarvon, in the north ; at Tommen-y-mur, Llanio-i-sa, and Caio, in the west ; at Caergai (*Eph.* vii. 863), Castle Collen near Llandrindod (*ibid.* 862), Caersws in the upper valley of the Severn, and the Gaer near Brecon, in the interior ; at Gelligaer (*Trans. Cardiff Nat. Soc.* xxxv. 1903), Merthyr Tydfil, Cardiff, Abergavenny, Usk, in the south, besides others not yet satisfactorily identified as military sites. Several of these have yielded remains suggestive of the first century, and indeed of the Flavian period. The only one as yet properly excavated, Gelligaer, seems to have been occupied under the Flavians, and dismantled after no very long occupation, probably early in the second century. Such dismantlement suggests that the land was then growing less unquiet. But Wales never reached any higher degree of Roman civilisation than the north of England. Towns and country houses were always rare, and its population lived mostly, it would seem, in primitive villages (*Arch. Cambrensis*, 1907). Later on, in the fourth century, Celts began to come in from Ireland, much as other barbarians entered other parts of the Empire, but their dates and numbers are very little known; see my *Romanisation of Roman Britain*, pp. 27 foll. and reff. there given.

The invasion of Caledonia (p. 183) by Agricola has been illustrated by recent discoveries. As I have pointed out elsewhere, we have traces of Agricola's line of forts (Tac. *Agr.* 23) at Camelon (*Proc. Soc. Antiq. Scotland*, xxxv. fig. 10) and Bar Hill (G. Macdonald, *Roman Forts on the Bar Hill*, Glasgow, 1906). Farther north, near the junction of the Tay and Isla, at Inchtuthill, in the policies of Delvine, a large encampment of Roman type has yielded a few objects datable to the Agricolan age (*Proc. Soc. Antiq. Scot.* xxxvi. pp. 237, 242), and may give a clue to the site of Mons Graupius. Farther south, the large fort lately excavated by Mr. James Curle, at Newstead, near Melrose (*C. I. L.* vii. 1080, 1081 ; *Scottish Hist. Review*, 1908), was certainly occupied in the Agricolan age. To this date, too, may perhaps be assigned the siege works round the native fortress on Birrenswark in Dumfriesshire, with their leaden sling-bullets (*Proc. Soc. Antiq. Scot.* xxxiii. 198 foll.). Evidence that the Legio ii. Adiutrix was then posted at Chester, probably forming a double-legion fortress with Legio xx., was obtained in the excavations of 1890 (*Catal. of the Grosvenor Museum, Chester* (1900), pp. 7 foll. and Nos. 23-35). An inscription from Camelon with the letters MILITES L·II·Λ·DIE may have been intended to refer to this legion, but is a forgery (*Class. Review*, xix. 57). No trace of Agricolan or of Flavian remains has yet been found on the line of Hadrian's Wall, except at two points, which, strictly speaking, are near but not on the wall, Carlisle (Luguvallium), and Corbridge (Corstopitum), where the two great north roads pass on towards Caledonia. For the influence of continental frontier troubles on the British operations of Agricola see also Ritterling, *Jahreshefte des österr. arch. Instituts*, vii. 26.

The years between the recall of Agricola and the building of Hadrian's Wall (roughly A.D. 85-120) are a historical blank. Even the position of the northern frontier during these years is unknown. The Romans seem to have soon withdrawn from the line of the Clyde and Forth (Macdonald, *Bar Hill*, pp. 14, 15). Whether they also withdrew south of Cheviot is not quite clear, in the present state of the Newstead excavations.

Hadrian's Wall from Tyne to Solway (p. 186) has assumed a very different historical appearance since Mommsen wrote his paragraphs on it in 1885. Then, the theory of Hodgson and Bruce held the field—that the stone wall which is still visible, and the double rampart and ditch to the south of it (called by English antiquaries the "Vallum"), were both Hadrian's work, the wall for defence against Caledonia and the "Vallum" for defence against stray foes from the south. This view was accepted by Mommsen. But later excavation and observation have shown that the "Vallum" cannot be regarded as a military work—though it is certainly Roman and connected with the wall. Excavations have also shown that the wall itself falls into two periods. At Birdoswald (Amboglanna) there was first a wall of turf (*murus caespiticius*); later, almost but not quite on the same line, came the wall of stone and the fort of Amboglanna in its present form. Similarly at Chesters (Cilurnum) two building periods are discernible; the character of the first is obscure, but the stone wall and the fort of Cilurnum belong unquestionably to the second (*Cumberland Arch. Soc.* xiv. 187, 415, xv. 180, 347, xvi. 84; *Arch. Aeliana*, xxiii. 9). As our ancient authorities persistently mention two wall-builders, Hadrian and Severus, and as the earlier wall of turf can be assigned to no one but Hadrian, it would seem that we may assume a first fortification of the Tyne and Solway line in turf about A.D. 120, and a rebuilding in stone, on almost exactly the same *tracé*, about A.D. 208 by Severus. The "Vallum" seems to have been built in relation to one or the other—more probably the earlier—of these stone walls, and may represent a civil frontier contemporaneous with it (Mommsen, *Gesammelte Schriften*, v. 461; Pelham, *Trans. Cumberland Arch. Soc.* xiv. 175). The attempt of Dr. E. Krueger (*Bonner Jahrbücher*, cx. 1-38) to show that the "Vallum" is an earlier independent work, built by Hadrian, while the turf and stone walls are post-Hadrianic, seems to me both unproven and contradicted by recent excavations.

Mommsen's account of the Wall of Pius between Forth and Clyde and of the Roman occupation of Scotland also needs modification. Statistics of coins found in Scotland (printed in *Antonine Wall Report*, 1899, pp. 158 foll., confirmed by all later finds) show that the Romans had retired south of Cheviot by about A.D. 180, and never reoccupied the positions thus lost. The mass of inscriptions, to which Mommsen alludes, also contains nothing later than the reign of Marcus. It becomes, therefore, impossible to connect the Wall of Pius with the literary evidence relating to wall-building by Severus. That evidence must belong to the Tyne and Solway. The length which it assigns to the wall, cxxxii. miles, suits the southern line best. The numeral in any case needs emendation, but it is as easy to read lxxxii. as xxxii., and 82 Roman miles fit closer to the length of the southern line ($73\frac{1}{2}$ English miles) than do 32 Roman miles to the $36\frac{1}{2}$ English miles of the northern wall. Our knowledge of the northern wall itself and of forts either north of it, like Ardoch, or south, like Lyne and Newstead, has been much widened by excavation, but the gain has been rather to the archaeologist than to the pure historian.

In the later history of north Britain the chief recent addition has been evidence of a serious rising about A.D. 158, which perhaps covered all the land of the Brigantes from Derbyshire to Dumfriesshire. Inscriptions found at Birrens, at Netherby between Birrens and Carlisle, at Newcastle-on-Tyne, and at Brough in north Derbyshire, mention a governor Iulius Verus as then specially active, and special reinforcements as then arriving from Germany (*Proc. Soc. Antiq. Scot.* xxxviii. 454). It is natural to connect these with the words of Pausanias (cited on p. 188, note 2), and the connection had the approval of Mommsen. For the division of the province into two by Severus see Domaszewski, *Rangordnung*, p. 173. The boundary between the two provinces is unknown ; perhaps a line from the Humber to the Mersey is not altogether improbable. Nor is there evidence to show how long the division lasted.

Of the civil life and Romanisation of Britain (pp. 191-4) I have written somewhat fully in a paper on *The Romanisation of Roman Britain*. Here I may indicate some points. Mommsen's view that the cantonal system adopted in Gaul was dropped in Britain is opposed by an inscription found at Caerwent in 1903, which records the erection of a monument by the canton of the Silures after a decree of the local senate—*ex decreto ordinis respublica civitatis Silurum* (*Athenaeum*, Sept. 26, 1903 ; *Archaeologia*, lix. 290) ; other inscriptions, if less decisive, suggest that the case of the Silures was not unique in the province. Indeed, a list of the cantonal capitals, and therefore of the cantons, seems to survive mutilated in the *Ravennas* (ed. Parthey and Pinder, pp. 425 foll.). There we meet, besides three municipalities carefully so labelled, nine or ten towns with tribal affixes—Isca Dumnoniorum, Exeter ; Venta Belgarum, Winchester ; Venta Silurum, Caerwent ; Corinium Dobunorum, Cirencester ; Calleva Atrebatum, Silchester ; Durovernum Cantiacorum, Canterbury ; Viroconium Cornoviorum, Wroxeter ; Ratae Coritanorum, Leicester ; Venta Icenorum, Caistor-by-Norwich—and perhaps Noviomagus Regentium, Chichester. Add to these Isurium Brigantum, known otherwise by this title, and Dorchester in Dorset, and there emerges a fairly complete list of just those towns which are declared by their remains to have been the chief "country towns" of Roman Britain. The reasons why so little is heard of the cantons are, I think, plain. They were smaller, poorer, and less important than those of Gaul—as, indeed, a comparison of the town-remains shows; there was, further, no British literature to mention them; and, lastly, they quickly fell before the barbarians in the fifth century.

The town-life of Roman Britain (p. 192) was somewhat more extensive than Mommsen allows. There were four *coloniae*— Colchester or *Camulodunum*, founded about A.D. 48 (Tac. *Ann.* xii. 32); Lincoln, *Lindum*, established after the transference of the Ninth Legion to York, probably in the late first century; Gloucester or *Glevum*, founded A.D. 96-98 (*C. I. L.* vi. 3346); York or *Eburacum*, planted at an unknown date, on the opposite bank of the Ouse to the legionary fortress; and one *municipium*, Verulamium, outside St. Albans, founded before A.D. 60. There were also about a dozen "country towns," already enumerated in the last paragraph. These were for the most part not large villages, but actual towns, furnished with temples, *fora*, houses, and street plans of Roman fashion, and inhabited, so far as our scanty evidence goes, by populations of which both upper and lower classes spoke and wrote Latin. At Bath, *Aquae Sulis*, were well-built baths, and a stately temple of the goddess of the waters. At London, *Londinium* (later *Augusta*), was a prosperous and wealthy trading-centre. But London was the only town of real size or splendour. The rest, like the cantons mentioned above, were small and unimportant as compared with similar towns elsewhere, and though it is not strictly true that Gloucester and Verulam have produced no inscriptions (p. 193; *Eph. Epigr.* iv. p. 195), the epigraphic yield has been scanty in every town except perhaps York.

The roads of the province (p. 192) are numerous, though fewer than our English antiquaries sometimes suppose. Those in the south, as Mommsen rightly saw, radiate from London: see p. 192 above. The northern military district is traversed by three main routes. One runs up the west coast to the Solway and Carlisle. A second runs through the east of the island, from York to Corbridge and to various points on the eastern part of Hadrian's Wall. The third, diverging from the second, crossed the Yorkshire and Westmorland hills and thus reached Carlisle. From Corbridge and Carlisle roads ran on northwards, and the eastern, if not the western, of these gave access to the Wall of Pius. The Roman roads of Wales are still imperfectly known, but there was a road from Chester to Carnarvon, another from Caerleon past Neath to Carmarthen, and a third joined the western parts of these two, while others connected the forts in the interior.

More doubt surrounds the Romanisation of the province. Vinogradoff (*Growth of the Manor*, p. 83) thinks that the Roman civilisation spread like a river with many channels which traverse a wide area, but only affect the immediate neighbourhood of their banks. I agree rather with Mommsen's conclusion (pp. 193, 194)—though the real difference between the two writers is not so very great. The towns, both municipalities and "country towns," seem to have been thoroughly Romanised. The numerous farms and country-houses (often styled "villas") are also in nearly every respect Roman, and the very scanty evidence which we possess as to the language used in them favours the idea that it was Latin. Even the villages, such as Pitt-Rivers excavated (*Excavations in Cranborne Chase*, etc., 1887-98), show little survival of native culture. It is to be noted, too, that Celtic inscriptions of Roman date, such as occur occasionally in Gaul (Rhys, *Proc. British Acad.* ii. 275 foll.), are wholly wanting in Britain. Probably, therefore, Roman civilisation came to predominate throughout the lowlands, though not in its more elaborate and splendid forms. There were, however, thinly populated areas where we can trace hardly any population of any sort, Romanised or other, as, for example, the Weald of Kent and Sussex, and a large part of the Midlands (*Vict. Hist. of Warwickshire*, i. 228), while the Cornish, Welsh, and northern hills seem never to have admitted very much Romanisation outside the forts which garrisoned parts of them. The analogies of other western provinces, of Gaul (above, vol. i. p. 101) and Africa (ii. 328), suggest that Celtic speech may have lingered on in such districts for centuries, though not as an element hostile to the Roman; it is also quite probable that Celtic private law and custom survived beside the Roman (L. Mitteis, *Reichsrecht und Volksrecht*, p. 8). But we have no distinct evidence of either fact.

The spellings Ordovici (p. 182 and map) and Cartimandus (pp. 182, 183) are Mommsen's own choice.

INDEX

THE END.

Printed by R. & R. Clark, Limited, *Edinburgh.*

By Dr. MOMMSEN

THE HISTORY OF ROME

FROM THE EARLIEST TIMES
TO THE PERIOD OF ITS DECLINE

BY

PROFESSOR THEODOR MOMMSEN

TRANSLATED BY

WILLIAM PURDIE DICKSON, D.D., LL.D.

A Newer and Cheaper Edition, Revised, and embodying all the most recent alterations and additions made by Dr. MOMMSEN.

In Five vols. Crown 8vo. 7s. 6d. each.

Abridged Edition for the use of Schools and Colleges. By C. BRYANS and F. J. R. HENDY. One vol. Crown 8vo. 7s. 6d.

TIMES.—"A work of the very highest merit; its learning is exact and profound; its narrative full of genius and skill; its descriptions of men are admirably vivid. We wish to place on record our opinion that Dr. Mommsen's is by far the best history of the decline and fall of the Roman Commonwealth."

PALL MALL GAZETTE.—"Dr. Mommsen is the latest scholar who has acquired European distinction by writing on Roman History. But he is much more than a scholar. He is a man of genius, of great original force, and daring to the extreme in his use of it; a philosopher in his power of dealing with facts; a painter in his power of reproducing men; witty, with a dash of poetic fancy; and humorous after a dry, sarcastic fashion, which, combined with his erudition, recalls Scott's Oldbucks and Bradwardines. His elaborate portrait of Caesar is, we venture to say, one of the best pieces of biographical delineation that this century has produced. Dr. Mommsen's style of character-drawing is his own. He neither reveals a face by lightning flashes, like Mr. Carlyle, nor sets it in a framework of epigrammatic oil lamps, like Mr. Lamartine, nor dashes it off with bold crayon-strokes, like Lord Macaulay. But his keen and rather naturally satirical genius softens in the presence of what he admires. He analyses skilfully, describes with fine pencil-lines, and colours with a touch that is not too warm, and yet quite warm enough to give the hues of life."

DR. SCHMITZ.—"Since the days of Niebuhr, no work on Roman history has appeared that combines so much to attract, instruct, and charm the reader. Its style—a rare quality in a German author—is vigorous, spirited, and animated. Professor Mommsen's work can stand a comparison with the noblest productions of modern history."

WESTMINSTER REVIEW.—"An original work from the pen of a master. The style is nervous and lively, and its vigour fully sustained. This English translation fills up a gap in our literature. It will serve as a sample of historical inquiry for all ages and all lands."

EDINBURGH REVIEW.—"The best history of the Roman republic, taking the work on the whole—the author's complete mastery of his subject, the variety of his gifts and acquirements, his graphic power in the delineation of natural and individual character, and the vivid interest which he inspires in every portion of his book. He is without an equal in his own sphere."

GEORGE ELIOT.—"Mommsen's *History of Rome* is so fine that I count all minds graceless who read it without the deepest stirrings."

MACMILLAN AND CO., LTD., LONDON.

WORKS ON
GREEK AND ROMAN HISTORY

A HISTORY OF THE LATER ROMAN EMPIRE FROM ARCADIUS TO IRENE. (395 A.D. to 800 A.D.). By J. B. BURY, Litt.D., LL.D. Two vols. 8vo. 32s.

ROMAN SOCIETY DURING THE LAST CENTURY OF THE EMPIRE OF THE WEST. By SAMUEL DILL, M.A. New Edition. Revised. Extra Crown 8vo. 8s. 6d. net.

ROMAN SOCIETY FROM NERO TO MARCUS AURELIUS. By SAMUEL DILL, M.A. Second Edition. 8vo. 15s. net.

SOCIAL LIFE AT ROME IN THE AGE OF CICERO. By W. WARDE FOWLER, M.A. 8vo. 10s. net.

HISTORY OF ANTIQUITY. From the German of the late Professor MAX DUNCKER. By EVELYN ABBOTT, M.A., LL.D., of Balliol College, Oxford. Six vols. 8vo. 21s. each.

A HISTORY OF GREECE TO THE DEATH OF ALEXANDER THE GREAT. By J. B. BURY, Litt.D., L.L.D. Illustrated. Crown 8vo. 8s. 6d. *Library Edition.* Two vols. 8vo. 25s. net.

THE ANCIENT GREEK HISTORIANS (HARVARD LECTURES). By J. B. BURY, Litt.D., LL.D. 8vo. 7s. 6d. net.

HISTORY OF GREECE FROM ITS COMMENCEMENT TO THE CLOSE OF THE INDEPENDENCE OF THE GREEK NATION. By ADOLF HOLM. Authorised Translation from the German. Revised by F. CLARKE, M.A. In Four vols. Crown 8vo. Vol. I. up to the end of the Sixth Century B.C. Vol. II. The Fifth Century B.C. Vol. III. The Fourth Century B.C. up to the death of Alexander. 6s. net each. Vol. IV. 7s. 6d. net.

MACMILLAN AND CO., LTD., LONDON.